Where Fate Beckons

LIVES OF GREAT EXPLORERS SERIES

The Lives of Great Explorers series publishes
authoritative works on pivotal figures in the
history of exploration of the circumpolar North
and Pacific Rim.

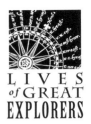

No. 1   *Storms and Dreams: The Life of Louis de Bougainville*
by John Dunmore

No. 2   *Where Fate Beckons: The Life of Jean-François
de la Pérouse*
by John Dunmore

Where Fate Beckons

THE LIFE OF JEAN-FRANÇOIS DE LA PÉROUSE

JOHN DUNMORE

University of Alaska Press
Fairbanks

First North American edition published by
University of Alaska Press, 2007
P.O. Box 756240
Fairbanks, AK 99775-6240

No. 2 in the Lives of Great Explorers series

ISBN 13: 978-1-60223-003-3 (paperback)
ISBN 10: 1-60223-003-X

The Library of Congress has cataloged the hardcover edition as follows:
Dunmore, John, 1923–
  Where fate beckons : the life of Jean-François de la Pérouse / John
Dunmore.
     p. cm. — (Lives of great explorers series)
  Originally published: Titirangi, Auckland : Exisle Publishing, 2006.
  Includes bibliographical references and index.
  ISBN 978-1-60223-002-6 (hardcover : alk. paper)
  1. La Pérouse, Jean-François de Galaup, comte de, 1741–1788. 2. Explorers—
France—Biography. 3. Pacific Area—Discovery and exploration—French.
I. Title.
  G256.L3D87 2007
  910.92—dc22
  [B]   2007003293

This publication was printed on paper that meets the minimum
requirements for ANSI/NISO Z39.48–1992 (R2002) (Permanence of Paper).

Cover design: Dixon J. Jones, Rasmuson Library Graphics

Originally published 2006 as *Where Fate Beckons: The Life of Jean-François
de la Pérouse* by Exisle Publishing Ltd.

CONTENTS

PROLOGUE

IT WAS THE kind of oppressively hot November day that settles on India when the dry monsoon begins, but Peter Dillon felt light and nimble as he arrived at the British administrative buildings. A short, stocky, well-built man in his late thirties, he had a weatherbeaten complexion, the result of years spent sailing in tropical waters. He was a familiar figure in Calcutta, which had been his home base for years, but mostly as a mere merchant sailor and trader, something of an eccentric, and seldom welcomed by senior administrators. Now times had changed. He was being much talked about among the leaders of Calcutta society – and the Chief Secretary had once again asked him to call.

A young official was waiting to usher him through the corridors, a smooth-mannered, impeccably courteous young man, the product of the best English public schools.

'The Secretary will see you at once,' he assured Dillon, as they walked past the usual clusters of supplicants gathered outside various offices. 'Mr Lushington has a final proposition to lay before you.'

The Chief Secretary wasted no time. He gestured to the parcel Dillon was carrying in both arms, like an offering. 'Good. You did not forget to bring the famous relic with you,' he said.

Dillon carefully unwrapped his treasure and presented it with a proud flourish. This was a dramatic moment that could immortalise his name.

'A French silver sword guard, sir. French and ancient, found on an island in the Santa Cruz group. I have no doubt whatever that this is evidence that the great expedition of the Frenchman La Pérouse was lost on that island.'

Charles Lushington looked at it briefly, then handed it to the secretary. 'Right, Mr Dillon,' he said. 'It will be sent to Paris for examination by specialists. They should tell us the exact date of manufacture. And possibly which officer it belonged to. Now, we have given a great deal of thought to an expedition to that now famous island, and the French authorities concur with our suggestion. But first, please summarise the story from the beginning.'

The Irishman began, relishing his role.

'I have, sir, as you know, been sailing through the Pacific islands ever since I moved to these parts in 1806. After I had served in the Royal Navy at the great Battle of Trafalgar, as no doubt you know, sir.'

He paused briefly for Lushington to assimilate this information. The Chief Secretary remained patiently impassive.

'Then in 1813, while I was serving as third officer on the *Hunter* on a sandalwood buying expedition, we were attacked by some Fijians. It was a fierce fight indeed, sir, but I – I must say, we – drove them back. The place where we fought is now called Dillon's Rock.'

Again Dillon paused, then went on. 'We set down on a small island in the Santa Cruz, called Tikopia, one of our people, Martin Bushart or Buchert, who had married a Fijian woman and wanted to try his luck ashore. As well as that couple, we left behind a lascar. Years went by. I became my own captain, owner of the ship *St Patrick*, and then, just a few months ago, while on my way back to India from Chile, I decided to put into Tikopia. And there they were, fine all three of them. That was when the lascar fellow brought out this silver sword guard, with all these markings, which he wanted to sell.

'I bought it, no trouble, but I asked him where he had got it and what else there might be. He told me that it came from a nearby island called Manicollo or Wanicollo or some such name. The natives told him that – this was apparently quite a long time ago – two ships rather like the *Hunter,* but even larger, had been wrecked, and that quite a few items still remained there following that wreck. The lascar told me that he then went to Manicollo and conversed with two old men who had survived the wreck. I immediately came to the conclusion that this wreck must have been that of the far-famed and much-lamented Count de la Pérouse, as no other European ships have been lost or posted as missing at so remote a period. I then sailed for the island myself, but the weather was so bad that I decided instead to make at once for Calcutta and seek your worship's assistance.'

He made a slight bow towards Lushington to indicate he had finished.

'As we have already mentioned to you, Mr Dillon,' said the Chief Secretary, 'England will indeed be honoured to help find traces of the La Pérouse expedition. We know that your own ship needs a full refit and is not suitable, so we have decided to provide you with one of our own survey vessels. The *Research* has been selected and my secretary will see to the details.'

'I am ready to sail at a day's notice, sir.'

Charles Lushington saw him to the door and shook his hand. 'Mr Dillon,' he said, 'it seems that you may have solved the greatest mystery of the Pacific Ocean. It has been a long time since the expedition vanished.'

'It has, sir. It vanished in the very year that I was born, 1788.'

'A lengthy period, indeed. You will be honoured for your discovery, Captain, and I wish you Godspeed.'

Part 1
A TEENAGER AT WAR

1. ALBI

25 August 1741

IT WAS HIGH summer. All the windows of the family country house at Le Gô were opened and the scents of the ripening countryside wafted in. A summertime birth was always reassuring in days when child mortality was high. Even so, Victor-Joseph and Marguerite de Galaup were not taking any chances. The baby, Jean-François, looked so frail, so dangerously weak when he was born that they decided, as many did in those days, to go ahead with an informal baptism. This *ondoiement*, as it was called, ensured that, if he should die in infancy, the baby would not enter into the uncertain afterworld of limbo, but would be welcomed, free from any stain of original sin, into the full joys of paradise.

The official christening would take place nearly two months later, in October, when the family moved back into the town of Albi after their period of summer residence at Le Gô. Though set among meadows and small forest glades, Le Gô looked rather forbidding. It still does, even today. There are few windows along its frontage, and the small inner courtyard is enclosed by a high wall with a double door that makes one think more of a prison than of a country home. Its appearance reflects the turbulent history of the region. Albi is a charming country town, nestling in the curve of the River Tarn, but its cathedral and the bishop's palace still look like ancient fortresses, for this is a settlement that has been threatened time and again over the centuries.

Settled by Gauls in early days, it was taken over by the Romans, then by ruthless Germanic Visigoth invaders. It managed to survive all those upheavals, and grow into a prosperous trading city, but then it was almost destroyed during the brutal repression of a religious sect, the Albigenses. Then came the murderous Hundred Years War, when time and again Albi was under threat, and saved only thanks to a great wall of ramparts which the desperate residents maintained with fierce determination. Their character forged in adversity, the townspeople rebuilt their lives and prospered, their wealth based on the vineyards the Romans had planted so many years ago and on the surrounding expanses of fertile fields, as well as the river that was navigable enough for some profitable trade.

The heart of old Albi has been preserved, saved from the modern high-rise buildings of glass and concrete that disfigure so many ancient towns. The twisting narrow streets in the inner city, with its houses clustering close together, still give one the impression of a population that had been forced to huddle to keep the outside world at bay and to survive, whatever the odds. They enable us to visualise Jean-François de Galaup in his youth, a lively young schoolboy racing along with his friends, or leaning on the bridge parapet, dreamily watching the river making its sluggish journey down to a distant sea. Boats of all sizes brought produce from the country and on fair days or market days, shouts and the heavy clutter of carts and barrows filled the streets, with all the combined smells and stench of fresh fruit and decaying vegetables.

The fortunes of the Galaup family had risen with those of the town. Merchants at first, they moved towards the law, occasionally venturing into medicine. As typical burghers, they kept their eye on every area of profit, be it land, trade or the professions.

The first Galaup to appear in existing town records was one Huc Galaup who, back in 1478 and again in 1487, served as a member of the town council. The Romans had left a Latin term for such officials: he was a *consul*. His sons Jehan and Pierre both became *consuls* between 1503 and 1527. A family tradition had been established.

In 1558, we find firm evidence of the Galaups' progress. One Jean de Galaup signed a contract for the purchase of an estate at Orban from the Cardinal de Clermont. He became Lord and Baron of Brens and Saint-Felix, entitled to enter the rank of the minor nobility, a status recognised by a document dated 18 August 1558.[1] At this point, therefore, the Galaups acquired the yearned-for nobiliary particle, the *de*. His descendants, including Jean-François, would be known as de Galaup. This stamped them as belonging to the aristocracy, even though by then so many people had acquired a piece of land in order to add something that sounded like a title to their name that the practice was becoming a little absurd.

Jean's son Claude consolidated the family fortunes by marrying Catherine de Giron, the daughter of a magistrate, and bought the Gô property. Then his sister married a member of the landed nobility, Clément de la Jonquière. The Galaups continued to strengthen their social position by making what were known as good marriages. Pierre de Galaup, a doctor and lawyer, married Catherine-Isabeau de Carrière, the daughter of an army captain, thereby coming closer to the *noblesse d'épée* (the aristocracy of the sword), which was more highly regarded than the legal or administrative *noblesse de robe* (the aristocracy of the gown). Doing even better, Jean-Antoine de Galaup in 1704 married Catherine de Metge, the daughter of a captain in the cavalry. When she died, he moved over to the church, taking holy orders and becoming canon of St Salvy, a thirteenth-century church with quiet, elegant cloisters, close to the powerful cathedral of Albi.

It was Father Jean-Antoine who stood as godfather when the formal baptism of his grandson took place at the Church of St Julien, in Albi, on 6 October. The baby now looked stronger, wailing loudly when the officiating priest poured the holy water over his small forehead. 'A good sign,' nodded the old man. 'He will become a man with a powerful will, not to be trifled with. A true Galaup.'

The Galaup family had now moved away from direct involvement in trade, something that was always regarded as socially inferior. They had money, property and a growing network of connections in the army and the church. Jean-François' maternal grandfather was a colonel who had commanded the famous *Régiment de Condé*. The christening, therefore, was a special occasion in the town, attended by a large gathering of local notabilities.

The earlier *ondoiement* proved to have been a wise precaution. Child mortality rates in the eighteenth century, even in well-to-do families, were appalling. The Galaup parents had ten children in all, but six of them (including three boys) died in infancy or early childhood. Jean-François would be the only surviving son.[2] He spent his early boyhood at Le Gô, and later went to school in Albi. At the age of nine, he entered the local Jesuit college, now the large state-run Lycée Lapérouse, and stayed there for six years. Then, in December 1756, having just turned fifteen, he left Albi to join the navy.

It is somewhat puzzling to find a youth who had never even seen the sea wanting to make his career in the navy. Jean-François de Galaup's birthplace is in Languedoc, south-west France. The Mediterranean Sea lies some 150 kilometres to the east, the Atlantic Ocean 300 kilometres to the west. In those days, when tourism was almost unknown and holidays were rarely spent away from home, it would have taken two to three days of uncomfortable travel to reach either sea.

His obvious future seemed to be the law, some senior position in local administration, or the army where several of his family had distinguished themselves. Unlike his paternal grandfather, he had no real desire to enter the church. He lacked a vocation, and later evidence shows that he was a lukewarm Christian, more interested in the arguments of the modern philosophers than in the finer points of theology. Furthermore, he had to bear in mind that he was his father's only surviving son. If Jean-François were to enter the church, he would have been forced into celibacy and the proud name of Galaup would have died with him. So his father had no objection when he spoke with enthusiasm about joining the navy. Jean-François may have been fascinated by the tales of his older cousin, Clément Taffanel de la Jonquière.

Then in his forties, La Jonquière had had a brilliant career. He had commanded several frigates, including the *Émeraude*, which had played a major part in a sea fight off Cape Ortegal in 1747. During his rare periods of home leave, he brought back tales of life on board ship, of exotic places visited, of the magic of nights at sea and fierce gun battles against enemy vessels. La Jonquière was home in 1749, when Jean-François was eight. It is easy to imagine the scene, with the boy, wide-eyed, listening to the great captain's stories.

La Jonquière was back four years later, and this time he had with him another naval personality, the Chevalier d'Arsac de Ternay, who had just completed three years with the Knights of Malta. They both stayed at Le Gô, regaling their audience with more exciting tales, bringing an unaccustomed glamour to the humdrum life of the provincial town. More significantly, they provided precise information for the boy and his father on what a naval career implied, and what the prospects would be. This was important for Victor-Joseph, who was a down-to-earth man, determined that his family's progress and prosperity should not be hampered by a teenager's dreams. According to a story handed down in the La Jonquière family, he tackled the sailor in 1756, by which time young Jean-François had decided that he wanted to join the navy:

'You tell me you have received some good news, cousin.'

'Yes, indeed. My share of prize money this year has reached forty thousand *livres*.'

'Truly? And what share would a *garde de la marine* have received?'

'At a guess, three or four thousand *livres*.'

'In that case, you are welcome to take Jean-François with you.'[3]

Both La Jonquière and D'Arsac de Ternay eventually became the young boy's protectors. La Jonquière, in particular, helped him adapt to his new life and acted as his banker. Victor-Joseph agreed to give his son a good allowance but, with proper bourgeois caution, he was anxious that the boy, far from home and exposed to unmentionable temptations, should not squander it, so he sent it through La Jonquière. The older man's careful account of his expenditure has survived and provides us with a valuable insight into the life of young Jean-François.

The boy's enthusiasm for the sea was shared by a couple of his friends at the Jesuit college. One was Henri Pascal de Rochegude, the scion of an old Albi family, prominent in local affairs since the mid-seventeenth century. He would join the navy at roughly the same time as Jean-François, and would one day become Albi's

Albi

second famous captain, rising to the rank of admiral. The boys became inseparable playmates, talking of the Austrian War that had recently ended, re-enacting distant victories and defeats, daydreaming of the future battles they would join in, far away in the West Indies or the East.[4] Another who joined them was Charles Mengaud de la Hage, a little younger but equally keen on a naval career, which his older brother Jean had already taken up.

One anecdote from his schooldays tells us something of young Jean-François' character. Discipline at the college was maintained by one Musson, whose energetic floggings had earned him the nickname *Bras-de-Fer* – arm of iron. When a teacher threatened to send him to Musson, Jean-François is reputed to have replied, 'I will meet his arm of iron with a backside of brass.'[5] The other boys in the classroom gave him a great cheer.

Once Jean-François had decided on a naval career, his father gave him his full support. He had agreed to grant him an adequate allowance, but to ensure his success, he went a step further. The boy's social status needed to be assured. There was constant tension in the navy between aristocratic officers – known as the Reds from the predominant colour of their uniform – and others coming from the merchant service, usually with a temporary commission, and known as the Blues. La Jonquière had probably warned Victor-Joseph that a Galaup, with his family background in the *noblesse de robe*, might be subjected to petty innuendoes from his more snobbish fellow cadets. A good way to avoid this was to add another landed title to Jean-François' name, to place him on an even footing with the Taffanel de la Jonquière and the d'Arsac de Ternay.

The Galaups owned a tenanted farm property on the Chemin de Fauch, near Albi, known as the Domaine de la Peyrouse, or La Pérouse – the two spellings were common and recur in various documents; it means 'the stony one'. Victor-Joseph did not actually transfer the title to his son until 1782, but the boy was allowed to adopt the name and became known as Jean-François de Galaup de la Pérouse, a suitably resounding name to take with him into the navy. It enabled him to join up as a *garde de la marine*, or royal cadet, which was the jealously guarded preserve of the nobility. Before long, he would become known simply as La Pérouse, and in time as the Comte de la Pérouse.[6]

He was now ready to face the world. Equipped with new clothes and money, he set out to begin his career on a sea he had only ever seen in his dreams. It was December 1756. He had to travel from his native Albi down in faraway Languedoc to Brest, the great naval port at the western tip of Brittany. It took him a week.

13

2. Brest

December 1756–March 1757

As JEAN-FRANÇOIS made his way to Brest, the mild Languedoc winter gradually gave way to damp and sleet, with occasional flurries of snow, and finally to the grey mists of Brittany.

He was entering another world. The sky loomed threateningly overhead, with none of the sunshine and lazy white clouds of his native town. The houses had a solid appearance, grey granite combining defensiveness with a touch of surliness, the roofs made of dark slate instead of the wavy red tiles of the south. The streets were filled with some indefinable odour, which he realised was a compound of ocean and fish smells, with none of the sweet warm scents of the Languedoc countryside. It seemed threatening, yet somehow exhilarating. Here, indeed, his new life was beginning.

He had travelled by coach along muddy, often rutted, roads, stopping at wayside inns built around cluttered courtyards with stables that reeked of horse dung and hay. He experienced the mind-boggling complexity of life under the Old Regime, with toll gates at the entrance to towns, fees to be paid at river crossings, local customs guards searching under the driver's seat and among the luggage for smuggled goods. They were looking particularly for salt, which was taxed, an imposition that was as hated by the people as it was valued by the treasury.

Accustomed to the lilting speech patterns of the Albigeois, Jean-François now discovered the burr of Poitou, the strange patois of country districts, and Breton villages where only the innkeeper spoke any French. There were new sights to wonder at, new food to be sampled, the hurly burly of country fairs, the distant view of an elegant château standing by the banks of a river. He saw for the first time seagoing ships, preludes to the forests of swaying masts he would find in the great ports. He had his first glimpse of the sea, a long grey line softly drawn across the distant horizon. Then, as he drew nearer, he came upon thundering white waves foaming around the rocks, a foretaste of the storms he would soon encounter and a warning of the death that eventually awaited him.

As the coach tossed and struggled its way along the country roads, he saw the poverty-stricken peasants sheltering in the doorway of their hovels. In the towns thronged their counterparts – beggars clamouring for alms around the coach, the women further back with their dead, staring eyes and each, almost inevitably, with a child in her arms. But the merchants he met at mealtimes, the laden drays creaking their way to the market place, the roadworks and the new buildings, reminded him that France was a prosperous country, whatever the evidence of social inequality that met his eyes.

The country had been at peace for eight years, since the end of the complex and costly War of the Austrian Succession. That struggle had cost France and Spain together some 3500 ships of various sizes; their enemy Britain had lost 3000. All three countries had been busy restoring their navies, knowing that the peace treaty of 1748 was little more than a truce signed by war-weary powers, and that hostilities would soon resume.

France's main naval base on the Atlantic, Brest reflected the government's determination. It was, as one visitor reported, a hive of activity:

> The channel is crowded with ships of every description, crowds of workmen are busy in every workshop along the harbour. Four great vessels and two frigates are being built on the slipways, two warships and a frigate are ready and at anchor, a ship of 84 guns is in the repairs dock, six hundred convicts are breaking stones to widen the quays. Great solidly built stores and two immense rope factories are laid out in the shape of an amphitheatre, near the convict settlement and the hospital. All these great undertakings give one an impressive sense of power.[1]

Successive Ministers of Marine had pursued a policy of development, not just in Brest, but also in Rochefort and Toulon. Brest, however, was the navy's showpiece.

The town, with some 20,000 inhabitants, was almost entirely dominated by its function as a naval base and its location was ideal for its purpose. It was protected by a long narrow entrance – the Goulet, literally the Bottleneck – defended by fearsome granite rocks and islets. The town itself had grown on both banks of the steep-sided Penfeld, defended by the château, a near-impregnable structure of ramparts and barracks that has survived centuries of assaults, even the devastating attacks of 1944.

Past the château, one could see the masting-yards, built in 1681; the Toulan repair shops; the new general stores; the prison built in 1750 and large enough to house up to 3000 convicts carrying out their sentences of hard labour. Nearby were the rope works, the sheds where sulphur, hemp and tar were

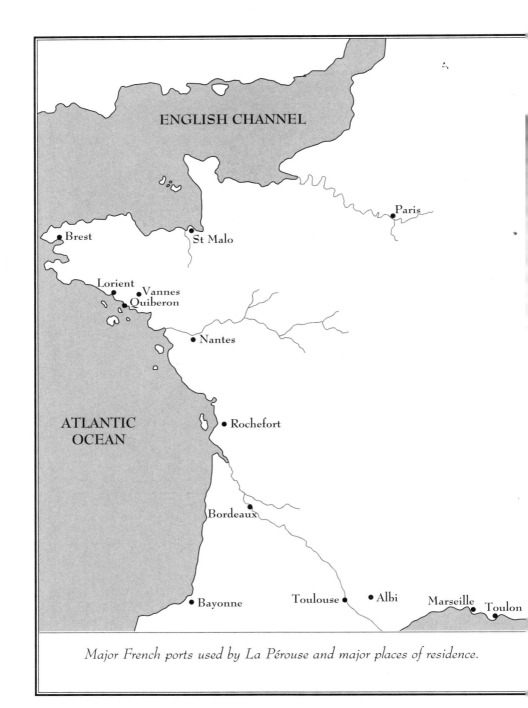

ENGLISH CHANNEL

Paris

Brest

St Malo

Lorient
Vannes
Quiberon

Nantes

ATLANTIC
OCEAN

Rochefort

Bordeaux

Bayonne

Toulouse • • Albi

Marseille
Toulon

Major French ports used by La Pérouse and major places of residence.

stored and, on the north bank, a line of food stores, carpenters' workshops and no fewer than six repair docks.

This was the town that would be Jean-François' home base for the rest of his life. Only the island of the Isle de France, in the Indian Ocean, would rival Brest in his affections. He would spend time in Paris later in his career and occasionally go back to Albi, but only when periods of extended leave allowed him to make the long and tiring journey to the south. To all intents and purposes, Brest was his home.

He now made his way to the Hôtel Saint Pierre, in the Rue de Siam, close by the arsenal and the navy's administration building. The term 'hotel' does not imply that this was a boarding establishment, but simply a large town house. Bought four years earlier from the heirs of the late Marquis de Crèvecoeur, as a much-needed replacement for the *gardes'* old ramshackle premises, it was a substantial building with an elegant façade, a ground floor boasting extensive reception rooms, two upper storeys and an attic with mansard windows. The property included the usual outbuildings, kitchens, stables, storerooms, implement sheds, as well as an attractive terraced garden and a large vegetable garden adequate for the needs of a noble establishment.

Jean-François reported to the commanding officer, Captain Paul Bidé de Chézac, who showed him around and outlined to him the establishment's routine. Roll call was at 7 a.m. in summer and 8 a.m. in winter. The morning was taken up with a Mass, breakfast and classwork, consisting mostly of mathematics, astronomy, hydrography and the theory of navigation. There was a weekly test on Saturdays, and it was pointed out to Jean-François that promotion was conditional on the young men learning by heart the standard text, *Cours de Mathématiques* by Etienne Bézout.

After a fairly lengthy lunch break, the young cadets were taken to various ships and workshops, to observe the working of ships and the manufacture of sails and ropes. When a ship was about to undertake a short period of manoeuvres, some of the *gardes* were taken on board, to follow a carefully pre-ordained routine:

At midday the *gardes* were brought together on the quarterdeck to learn the use of the instruments. At 3 p.m. the master taught them the various manoeuvres and the manner of dealing with accidents, and gave them a correct idea of the ship's layout. Twice a week, the gunner took them for gun practice. Once a week, the master carpenter taught them how to carry out repairs, and the master caulker showed them how to use the pumps.[2]

Jean-François had little opportunity during his four months in Brest to join a ship on manoeuvres. It was winter, and increasing talk of war meant that all the vessels in port were kept on war alert. All he did was to accompany his fellows on their brief afternoon tours and at least set foot on some of the impressive new ships of the line that were anchored in the port.

The *gardes* had been created to train the sons of the nobility, and the upper class clung to the privilege of exclusive admission with a determination akin to desperation. Jean-François' fellows at the Hôtel Saint Pierre would have questioned him with consummate tact, but with determination, to satisfy themselves that he met the central criterion – in their eyes almost the only one – of true noble birth. Whenever Chézac welcomed a newcomer to the school, he would say loudly and firmly:

'*Monsieur, vous êtes maintenant un Garde de la Marine royale. Ne l'oubliez jamais.* You are now a guard in the king's navy. Never forget it.' And indeed, they formed a group pledged to work together and to help each other throughout their career.

The pressure to accept middle-class recruits, now that war was threatening, was a matter of concern for the port commandant at Brest, Hilarion Josselin Du Guay, who wanted to defend the practice of only appointing officers and cadets drawn from the ranks of the nobility. In June, the new Minister for War sent him a clear rebuke – shouldn't the country's need override what the nobility considered to be its birthright?

> I have read with some surprise your letter of the 20th … Should your desire to see naval officers recruited on every occasion from the nobility of the kingdom … take precedence over the needs of the service? … I cannot conceal from you my intention – while carefully keeping to the established rule under which the *gardes* are drawn only from the nobility of the kingdom – to take every opportunity of associating with the service those members of another Estate who deserve it because of their acts of valour or of recognised talents.[3]

Jean-François certainly looked the part of a *Garde de la Marine* in his brand-new uniform – breeches and silk stockings, blue coat cut away to reveal the scarlet waistcoat that as a young noble, a 'red', he was privileged to wear, gold-braid epaulettes, cocked hat and black shoes with gold buckles.

Brest offered just a few opportunities to display this finery: the drawing rooms of the senior officers, whose wives were happy to welcome the young men; the public garden, where well-to-do bourgeois strolled on fine days; the nearby theatre, although frowned upon somewhat as too much of a distraction from serious studies and not entirely respectable. Even churchgoing presented a chance to show oneself and to bow to demure young ladies one had earlier met at a reception.

Jean-François soon realised that it was not compulsory for him to stay at the Hôtel Saint Pierre, and that a number of the cadets were lodging in town. His father might have been a little worried by the thought of a fifteen-year-old boarding in some side street or even in the Grande Rue, which in spite of its name was a mere thoroughfare of small shops, inns and taverns, soon making way for low-grade grog shops and brothels as it neared the quayside. Fortunately, the boy had a patron and supervisor in La Jonquière, who took his task seriously. He sent meticulous accounts to Victor-Joseph, detailing how the sums entrusted to him were spent.

> On 15 December I gave him 48 *livres* to pay a month's board at the inn; on the 24th 75 *livres* 5 *sols* 5 *deniers* to remake his two suits and make a waistcoat and breeches. On 1 January 6 *livres* for light. On 15 January for a month at the inn 42 *livres* plus 9 *livres* for the second room and for firewood. On the 19th paid postage on two letters 1 *livre* 8 *sols*. On the 20th to Oudart, tailor, to repair two suits and make a waistcoat 7 *l* 4 *s*. On 25 January paid 8 *livres* 8 *s* plus 1 *livre* 4 *s* to the innkeeper, money lent for a broken glass, and 12 *sols* for the sword, total 1 *l* 16 *s*. To Mr de Lapérouse for his entertainment 6 *livres*. On 16 February 16 *livres* to the prison inn. On 15 February, to repair his sword 3 *livres*. Total 239 *livres* 15 *sols* 5 *deniers*, leaving 19 *s*. which I gave to Mr de Lapérouse. Account as at 16 February 1757.[4]

What these sums represent is not too easy to assess in modern terms. The *livre* fluctuated as France's finances rose and fell, but an article on feasts in François Marie Arouet de Voltaire's *Dictionnaire philosophique* of 1764 records that a silk weaver in Lyons supported his wife and eight children on 45 *sous* a working day, or 639 *livres* a year. Jean-François' basic board at the rate of 576 *livres* a year suggests modest, but quite comfortable, lodgings.

The report also tells us that the young man spent some time in jail, probably a little over a fortnight. Jail and a broken sword suggest a duel. Did one of his fellow *gardes* make a disparaging remark about his family background? Alternatively, a fight may have broken out when a group of *gardes* visited a tavern, behaviour more frowned upon by their superiors than a duel in defence of one's honour.

All too often, historic figures are depicted in exclusively heroic stances, never telling a lie or losing their temper, assiduous about their studies, concerned only with the career that will ensure their place in history. From La Jonquière's notes emerges a more human personality, a hot-blooded young man from the region that gave birth to the dashing musketeer D'Artagnan, getting into serious scrapes, facing the reprimands of the stern Captain de Chézac, and serving a short sentence, which involved no dishonour but some temporary discomfort. And, in any case, the jail was probably not the city prison, dark and filthy, filled with common criminals, thieves and prostitutes, but a fairly run-down section of the Hôtel Saint Pierre, close to the tool sheds, where troublemakers could be confined to meditate upon their misdeeds.

His time at the *École des Gardes* was coming to an end. War had broken out and most of the cadets were being assigned to warships. Jean-François was appointed to La Jonquière's own *Célèbre*, an imposing ship of 64 guns due to sail for French Canada. The classrooms and the lectures were left behind in favour of more practical work, although the stern admonition to continue memorising Bézout's *Cours de Mathématiques* still sounded in his ears as he walked down to the quayside.

3. A Teenager at War

April 1757–November 1759

writes in a way to set the scene for readers.

IN 1757 FRANCE was home to some 21 million, but it is doubtful whether more than a small fraction of that number understood the complexities of the international situation that underlay what became known as the Seven Years' War.

The peasants, labourers and artisans who made up the bulk of the population knew that the enemy was, as it had been over the centuries, England. They also knew that Spain, with a member of the Bourbon family on the throne, was France's ally – an alliance popularly known as 'the family pact'. Beyond France's eastern frontier, there were other traditional enemies, such as Austria and Prussia, and potential allies in Russia and Sweden, although these continental powers changed sides from time to time, creating new alliances among themselves or with France. But all these were complicated matters that not many understood or cared about.

There were a few newspapers, to be sure, the *Mercure de France* and a few gazettes as they were called, but so few people among the great lower and lower middle classes could read, or afford to buy these news sheets – or would want to – that gossip down at the local tavern was all they had to go by. There were more important matters to talk about, such as the state of the crops, the price of bread or, more simply, the weather and goings-on in the neighbouring village.

One event that did echo through much of France, especially in the ports and in areas close to the sea, was a series of attacks on French shipping that took place from mid-1755. The British government had sent Admiral Edward Boscawen to Canada with secret instructions to capture or destroy 'any French ships or other vessels having on board troops or warlike stores' that he came across on his way there. As it turned out, on that occasion he had managed to capture only two ships, the *Lys* and the *Alcide*. So new instructions were issued to all British commanders to capture merchantmen as well as naval ships. In October and November 1755, Admirals Boscawen and Edward Hawke seized some 300 French commercial vessels in the Channel and the Atlantic. More than 6000 French sailors, almost all of them from ports and inland villages along the Breton and Normandy coasts, were taken prisoner, and some of them were pressed into service on British ships. And all this occurred during peacetime. When their wives and families realised why the men had not come back, there was an understandable outbreak of fury.

News from French Canada made things worse. Canada may well have been a distant colony, about which most French citizens knew very little, but a number of country people, especially in the west, had relatives who had migrated there many years earlier, and others lived in villages where stories were still handed down of ancestors who had gone to settle in the great country across the Atlantic. There was shock and indignation when news came that thousands of these 'Acadians' had been roughly deported from their homes and farms in New Brunswick and Nova Scotia.

Both these former French possessions had passed under British rule in 1713 following the Treaty of Utrecht. France had accepted those losses fairly philosophically, as long as her former citizens were not ill-treated. But Britain had never felt comfortable about the large French population that still lived in these territories, and in 1755 Charles Lawrence, the Governor of Nova Scotia, issued orders to round up the French-speaking population and hold their boats to prevent them from fleeing to French Canada – now mostly consisting of Quebec province. In this way, when war came, as seemed inevitable, they would present no danger to the British authorities.

In all, between 6000 and 7000 men, women and children were arrested in the period between September and December 1755 and scattered among various American colonies along the Atlantic seaboard, where it was hoped they would be absorbed and eventually disappear among the English-speaking population. Deportations continued for some years, a number making their way down to Louisiana, until the Acadians were reduced to less than 30 per cent of their original number.[1]

This *Grand Dérangement*, as it became known, had repercussions through much of France, especially among the peasant and labouring classes, and added to the general feeling of dislike for all things English. The ruling classes were less affected – the victims, after all, were mostly rural lower classes – but the political implications were serious, and the continuing series of incidents insulting to the French crown.

When La Pérouse joined the *Célèbre*, La Jonquière was getting ready to sail as part of a squadron escorting troop transports to French Canada. It sailed from Brest on 3 May 1757. In addition to the *Célèbre*, there were two great ships of 80 guns, the *Formidable* and the *Duc de Bourgogne*, and four ships of 74 guns, three of 64 and two frigates of 32. They made an impressive sight, with sailors feverishly working in the rigging, their petty officers shouting orders from below, the officers on deck resplendent in their red and gold uniforms, and the Goulet opening out before them with a colourful vista of islands and open sea.

The overall commander, Emmanuel-Auguste de Cadiheuc du Bois de la Motte, was as famous as his name was resounding. Now in his sixties, he was making his final crossing of the Atlantic before retirement. He had sailed, back in 1711, to Rio de Janeiro on an expedition that had captured that Portuguese-held city. He then served on a number of ships during the various wars that plagued the eighteenth century, but more recently had enjoyed a quieter period ashore as Governor of the Leeward Islands. All the Marquis de la Motte had to do now was to complete the crossing as quickly and as safely as possible. He knew there were fast British frigates roaming off the coast and likely to pounce without warning, but the Breton fog and drizzle enabled him to avoid them. He took a fast, if circuitous, route to Canada, aware as he approached the coast that the naval nets of Boscawen, Hawke and others were stretched out to catch him. Luck favoured him: unnoticed until the last moment, the La Motte squadron put into the French Canadian port of Louisbourg on 19 June.

For Jean-François, not yet sixteen years old, this was a great experience, allowing him to put into practice all the theory that had been dinned into him in the classroom at Brest. He had lookout duties to carry out, but he could also watch the officers taking the midday readings of the sun's altitude that helped to fix the ship's position; he could assist with marking the route on the charts; and above all he could observe life on board a naval ship in what was, in effect, wartime. He was fortunate, too, in having his protector Taffanel de la Jonquière as his captain. His 'naval godfather', as some have called him, made sure that he was given every opportunity to learn, and he was an assiduous pupil. In faraway Albi he had dreamt of a naval career. His vocation was the sea. Now he could follow it under the very best of conditions.

Landing at Louisbourg, Jean-François received a warm personal welcome from the governor, Augustin de Drucourt, who had once been in charge of the Brest *École des Gardes* and who was always pleased to welcome any of the young *gardes* who chanced to land in Louisbourg. Although busy with his duties, he saw that La Pérouse was shown around and well looked after during his brief stay. The youth had little chance to see much of Canada or even the surroundings of Louisbourg, tucked away defensively on the north-west coast of Cape Breton Island. The *Célèbre* and another vessel, the *Bizarre*, soon sailed for the mainland with the troops they had brought, and then left for France the moment all the soldiers had landed. They were back in Brest by 4 November.

That was just as well, because, when the rest of La Motte's squadron arrived just a month later, they brought back with them an estimated 4000 sick sailors and soldiers from the Louisbourg garrison. Most of them were suffering from typhus, also variously known at the time as the putrid fever, prison fever, hospital fever, famine fever, camp fever and ship fever. It was a virulent disease for which the doctors had no remedy. All they could do was resort to the usual purges and bleedings to clear the blood of 'evil humours'. In reality, they were so overwhelmed by the numbers that they simply set up makeshift hospitals and tried to keep as many as possible isolated from the people of Brest. Barracks, churches, even the Hôtel Saint Pierre were taken over. The government in Paris sent 150,000 *livres* to pay off the healthy men before they too became affected. It was all in vain. The epidemic raced through the town, affecting even the convicts on whom Brest depended for many of its services, from refuse collection to gravedigging. The stench of death and corruption rose over the plague-stricken port, hanging over it like a pall of gloom until the epidemic burnt itself out.

Jean-François had been given a few days' leave before all this happened, and was then transferred to the frigate *Pomone*. This was a fortunate assignment for two reasons. First, it kept him away from the city when the epidemic broke out, and second it was commanded by a man he had once met in Albi who would become his protector and mentor for many years to come, Charles de Ternay, or to give him his full name, Charles Henri Louis d'Arsac de Ternay.

Ternay, like La Pérouse, had entered the *gardes* at the age of fifteen, and then seen service in the Mediterranean, Canada, Louisiana and the West Indies. An earnest, serious man, aged only thirty-five, he took at once to the young man from Albi and guided him in his career for a number of years. After a couple of months, he was appointed to command the frigate *Zéphire*, due to sail to Canada as part of Louis Charles du Chaffault's squadron. He took Jean-François with him.

They could no longer land at Louisbourg: the French ports were now completely blockaded by the British. Du Chaffault was forced to sail cautiously towards a point along the coast near Port Dauphin. He was carrying reinforcements, and he was forced to sneak them ashore in small boats, to make their way overland as best they could to the beleaguered French fortress. The operation was successful, in spite of heavy seas and morning fog, but the unfortunate soldiers reached Louisbourg just as an extra 8000 British troops were being landed further along the coast. Totally besieged by sea and land, it fell a few weeks later.

Du Chaffault's instructions required him to continue to Quebec, as he had further reinforcements for the French forces on the mainland, so he decided to send back the *Zéphire*, which had landed all her men, so that Ternay could report to the French government on the Nova Scotia situation. Since Ternay's route home was now effectively barred by British ships, he decided to sail north towards Newfoundland. Even then, hugging the Newfoundland coast and attempting to make straight for the Atlantic Ocean and the port of Brest was too risky. Instead, he crossed Cabot Strait and sailed into the Gulf of Saint Lawrence, then followed the western coast of Newfoundland to pass through the Strait of Belle Isle and round the northern tip of the island. This enabled him to sail east, away from the route frequented by most ships, including British warships, and to reach Brest without any problems in mid-July.

However dangerous the *Zéphire's* mission had been, it provided Jean-François with some invaluable lessons in coastal navigation. Sailing between the Canadian and Newfoundland coasts involved a cautious navigation in little-known waters, past black cliffs lapped by angry waves, struggling through swift tidal currents, finding a way through sudden swirling blankets of fog, and along a lonely seascape occupied only briefly by an occasional fisherman's boat that fled from the threatening stranger into the safety of a hidden cove. Precision, vigilance and attention to detail were essential to survival. They had some charts on board to guide their route, but they contained a number of inaccuracies that proved more dangerous than helpful. It was not until 1763 that a talented British mariner, James Cook, would set out to chart these waters, with a determination and an accuracy that decided his superiors, a few years later, to appoint him to command a major voyage of exploration into the Pacific.

Jean-François left the *Zéphire* on 21 July. He had three weeks' leave – time to relax, to write to his family and friends in Albi, and to reassure them that, though the war in Canada was going badly for France, he had come through his first campaigns without a scratch.

The war and the typhus epidemic had caused a great deal of uncertainty and confusion in Brest. Ships were being prepared for expeditions that had to be cancelled at the last minute, largely because of the British vessels, warships and privateers that were roaming the coast, ready to pounce on anyone who ventured out. A sixteen-year-old could cope with the situation: life could still be fun. Jean-François went out with his fellow *gardes*, visiting the taverns and comparing notes on their brief campaigns, boasting a little no doubt, exaggerating the dangers they had experienced. They joked with each other, and flirted a little – in the drawing rooms, where wives of naval officers invited them, much less in the taverns where girls offered rather more than mere flirting, but often carried the seeds of diseases against which the tutors at the *École des Gardes* had taken great pains to warn them.

His next appointment, in mid-August, was a fairly safe one. His ship, the *Cerf*, was relatively new, but not about to sail on any dangerous mission. There was still indecision in the Ministry of Marine about what should be done next, and there was no point in sending ill-prepared expeditions into seas infested with a marauding enemy. So there were no risky manoeuvres, not even around the island of Ushant just off the coast, so often used for educational manoeuvres and exercises. There was only a little more shiplife and some opportunities to catch up with his studies. He also celebrated his seventeenth birthday with friends, toasting it with quality southern wine sent from Albi – he never lost his fondness for the rich red wines of his home district.

When he left the *Cerf* in November 1758, he could take pride in having gained more experience than many young cadets in recent years. He had spent a total of nineteen months on board ship, as against little more than three months at the school, had sailed twice to Canada and had taken part in some dangerous operations. He had lived the life of a naval officer in wartime, met army officers and watched with amusement the constant exchange of jokes and insults between the sailors and the soldiers they were transporting across the Atlantic. Now it was winter, when the authorities avoided sending ships out to sea unless they were forced to, so Jean-François went back to his studies – to the ponderous mathematics manual, now made a little more readable through the practical work he had done on board ship; to the standard treatise on masting and rigging; and to Duhamel du Monceau's *Eléments de l'architecture navale*, published in Paris that year and now required reading for all the *gardes*.

In May 1759, he was posted to the *Formidable*. It was well named: a fine ship of 80 guns, with a total complement of 971 officers, men and servants, commanded by the Chevalier de Saint-André du Verger. This time, the aim was not to sail to Canada, but to invade Britain, and this required a large force. Some 18,000 men were being gathered under the Duc d'Aiguillon, Governor of Brittany, together with a great flotilla of ships, large and small. The plan was, first, to establish a beachhead; once that was done, more men would follow, the beachhead would turn into a large base and the British would be threatened at the very heart of their growing empire. If nothing else, it would cut off all help to their forces in Canada, who were now threatening the city of Quebec.

Keeping such preparations a secret was impossible. British informers had been able to pass on details to their masters in London about the movements of the French troops, but not the likely date of the attack or the chosen location of the landings. Secrecy, however, was not essential. The project was in part a bluff. It was enough for the British government to be kept on tenterhooks by the presence of thousands of men in Brest, and to learn through its spies that preparations were being made for a major naval undertaking rumoured to be directed at England. If the government in London was sufficiently worried about these reports, they would not send any more men or supplies to North America. Gradually, however, Versailles firmed up its plans: a diversionary raid on the British Isles won broad acceptance.

When Jean-François went on board on 1 June, ten of his fellow *gardes* went with him. They watched as 200 fusiliers struggled up the gangways with their impedimenta, followed by a further 146 men from the coastguard defence force. The officers were now told that there would be a double-pronged attack, with one force landing in Scotland and another at the mouth of the Thames. There had been a great deal of talk about the likely strategy. Some among the officers had thought that the ships might simply make for the coast of Cornwall or Devon, landing troops that would march on to Plymouth or Bristol; others had plumped for the south coast of Ireland. Now they were faced with a far more complex and ambitious plan.

Planning a campaign on a map was easy enough. Getting the expedition away from Brest and the smaller ports along the north-west coast of Brittany was another matter, because the British navy was patrolling nearby. Jean-François argued the pros and cons of the campaign with his friends. Each had his own favourite strategy, but they were all carried by a sense of excitement and tension. This was to be their first real experience of war, a long step away from their previous quick crossings to Canada.

Some still believed that the entire operation was little more than an elaborate game meant to worry the British. However, it became increasingly obvious that it was more serious than they had first thought. An invasion was truly in the making, and they might yet land on British soil – as long as they could get around the British navy's increasingly frequent patrols. Two main forces were lying in wait for them. Admiral Hawke's ships were patrolling off Brest and in the western approaches of the Channel, while Commodore Robert Duff's fleet lay to the south near Quiberon Bay. Summer was not a good time to elude them. Visibility was simply too good, favouring the light frigates that could harass any large fleet that included slow troop transport vessels, and give time for the heavier British warships to come up. Weeks went by, marked by more uncertainty and increasing restlessness.

Finally, around the middle of November, the French commander, 69-year-old Maréchal Hubert de Conflans, found the opportunity he had been waiting for. A storm had raged for days along the coast of Brittany, driving Hawke's ships out to sea. When the weather cleared, coast watchers reported that they could see no sign of the English vessels. A convoy recently arrived from Canada had met none on the way across, and informers from England reported rumours that Hawke had put into his home base for repairs. Conflans gave orders for an immediate departure. The only problem was that the main bulk of the transport vessels were gathered on the south coast of Brittany, close to where Commodore Duff still waited, watching for any movement. It was therefore necessary to sail south to Quiberon and destroy his fleet before Hawke could come to his help.

The weather, which always played a major role in the days of sailing ships, was favourable. It kindly helped the fleet to sail out of the Goulet and make for the open sea. Then, unkindly, the breeze died down, leaving Conflans' ships floundering. When it revived, it was blowing, fairly gently, from the south-south-east, so that, to go down towards Quiberon Bay, the French had to tack endlessly about, wasting more time. The delay enabled Duff to get advance warning from his informers – and it gave time for Hawke to get his ships together and speed to his aid. A serious naval engagement was now inevitable.

The Battle of Quiberon Bay began on the morning of 20 November 1759, when the French got their first glimpse of Duff's fleet: eight ships of the line and three supporting vessels. The British were outnumbered – this was France's opportunity. Conflans set off in pursuit, crowding on all sails, but less than three hours later, another fleet appeared to the west. The French counted twenty-one ships advancing towards them. They were Admiral Hawke's, coming to Duff's aid. Conflans was now trapped between two lines of enemy ships – and this time he was the one who was outnumbered.

The wind joined in on the British side. A westerly gale blew up, helping Hawke to make full speed towards his enemy, while Conflans was being driven towards the shore. He decided to seek the shelter of Quiberon Bay, an oblong-shaped gulf defended by rocks and islets. Keen though his officers might be to stand and fight, his orders were to organise an attack on the British mainland, not risk France's Atlantic fleet in an unequal engagement. It was too late. A full naval battle was on. And, in seeking to evade his enemies, Conflans had become trapped in a narrow bay, with no chance of escape and little room for manoeuvring. He had allowed himself to be 'driven into a mousetrap'.[2]

The *Formidable* found herself facing fifteen British ships, which poured the fire of their guns into her as they filed past one after the other. At one time, she was being raked by the cannon of no fewer than four enemy warships. Jean-François found himself in the middle of a scene of carnage, with dead and wounded officers and men all around him, masts splintering and crashing down, torn sails hanging everywhere, the rudder shot away, acrid smoke in his nostrils, the deafening roar of guns and the cries of the wounded and the dying in his ears. The ship's guns continued to fire until the late afternoon, although by now the *Formidable* was merely drifting around helplessly. At dusk, the English captain of the *Resolution* sent his men to take over. What he saw appalled him. A hardened naval man, he had never before seen such carnage.

The chief surgeon of the *Formidable* later drew up his official report: over 300 men had been killed, there were 150 wounded. The captain, Saint-André du Verger, was dead, his head smashed by a cannon ball; so was his older brother and first officer, cut in half by a ball.

> Lieutenant d'Arcouges, struck by a cannon ball in the chest; Monsieur Colline, a Danish officer, totally cut in half; Sub-lieutenant De Grammont, back broken; De Chaunes, a young *garde*, cut in two; another *garde*, D'Herneville, head blown off. From the Saintonge Regiment, Lieutenant de la Picotière, riddled with bullets, a cannon ball in the stomach; Mr de Montluc, leg shot away; Mr Durienne, assistant surgeon, leg blown away and dead; Sub-lieutenant du Cluzel, head blown off.'[3]

Jean-François was one of six *gardes* who were wounded, but not seriously: he suffered minor wounds to the stomach, to the shoulder and to one arm. Although the battle continued into the next day, for him the fighting was over. He was now, like the other survivors, a prisoner of the English.

Their future was the subject of negotiations between the British and the French. The options were prison in England, possibly on a ship's hulk in some port, possibly on parole ashore, or if luck came their way some compromise that allowed them to stay on French soil. Hawke had neutralised the Atlantic fleet. All he now had to do was to clean up the aftermath. He decided to have the *Formidable* repaired so that she could be taken to Plymouth. She turned out to be more a war trophy than a prize of any value, because she was in such a bad way that the Admiralty eventually decided to have her broken up. Some of the captured officers were transferred to the *Resolution*, to be sent to England. However, she had been damaged in the battle and sank shortly after; two of the young *gardes* went down with her. Admiral Hawke had decided that there was room on board for only a few of the French and he had no wish to see his own ship cluttered up with prisoners, some of them badly wounded, so La Pérouse, looking fairly harmless, but limping along in bloodstained bandages, was sent ashore, at first as a prisoner under guard. However, in mid-December, his status was changed to that of a prisoner on parole. He was to remain on French soil 'on condition that he gave his word that he would not serve again until such time as a British prisoner of equal status could be exchanged for him and returned to England'.[4]

He probably spent some time hospitalised in the neighbouring town of Vannes. When he was fit enough to travel, he went to Brest. From there, he was no doubt given long leave to visit his anxious parents in Albi. He had not seen his family for three years, since he left as a fifteen-year-old setting out for distant Brittany. Now he came back to them, however briefly, as a mature, bloodied young man with tales of places and adventures they could scarcely imagine.

4. The Slow End of a Disastrous War

January 1760–January 1763

BEING A PRISONER on parole meant living in a strange state of limbo. La Pérouse was free in every respect except one. He could travel freely around France or even abroad should he wish to; he could live where he liked, meet whom he wished. The only thing he could not do was to take any part in what modern generations would call 'the war effort'. He was not suspended from the navy; he simply could not work for it. He was not under any supervision. He had no probation officer to report to, as a released criminal might have. The British had let him go, and he was totally out of their hands. They might never find out if he did work for the French Navy. He was simply a prisoner of his honour and of his good name. Had he broken his parole, his fellow officers would not have smiled or praised him for fooling the enemy: they would have been shocked. Going back on his word would sully his reputation, ruin his career.

Continuing with his studies, however, was not a breach of his parole. He could work on his books, studying mathematics, astronomy and navigation. He could read accounts of voyages to distant countries, study maps and sea charts, and discuss with retired officers their travels, what they had seen and what they believed remained to be discovered. He could in fact return to school, and become a more highly trained naval officer. So, after his return from Albi, he re-entered the *École des Gardes*, under the guidance of Monsieur de Chézac, who sympathised with the young cadet who had lost a number of his friends in the sea battle off Quiberon and was now prevented from living an active life.

The atmosphere in Brest was one of increasing gloom. The port was firmly blockaded by the waiting British squadrons outside and the town was isolated from the rest of France by bad roads, most of them rendered impassable by winter conditions. Supplies of food were irregular, trade had slowed down, bringing many families to the brink of ruin, while the growing shortages were causing prices to rise day by day.

The news was mostly bad. Quebec had fallen, Montreal soon followed, then

Detroit. French Canada ceased to exist. The collapse spread further south, as the French outposts along the Mississippi River began to fall, one by one. The war in Europe was not easy to follow. There were some victories to celebrate, but they seldom seemed to be followed up by any real advances, and within weeks new reverses cancelled out any gain.

Brest had not come to a total standstill, however. There were still dinner parties, gambling evenings, a mediocre theatre, the occasional ball, but little feeling of purpose and even less of optimism. There was, inevitably, a great deal of gossiping, including comments on Conflans' moves at Quiberon. These were widely criticised, with some pointing out that he was luckier than the English Admiral John Byng, who had been shot after a disastrous defeat off Minorca. The worst that had happened to Conflans was banishment to his country estate. 'We have no wish to see him,' was Louis XV's judgement. Families in Brest and the surrounding area that had lost sons and husbands at Quiberon felt a stronger expression of disapproval would have been warranted.

Individual initiatives replaced what the paralysed navy could not attempt to do. Corsairs set off from Saint-Malo and other ports to harry English ships, and often brought back a prize or some rich booty. It was dangerous work, and sometimes they never returned, but it could be rewarding, and it broke the crippling monotony of the blockaded ports. For the sailors who had previously manned merchant ships or the fishermen who had sailed to the rich cod-fishing grounds off Newfoundland, it was their only alternative to starvation.

Finally, in December 1760, Jean-François was released from his parole – he had been exchanged for an English prisoner of equal status – but the war was far from over and the port was still blockaded. Being freed from his parole did not mean the navy had anything for him to do. He offered his services to a shipowner in Bordeaux who was planning to undertake a little cautious trading along the Atlantic coast and down to Spain. 'No one in the world is more determined than I,' wrote the keen and bored twenty-year-old.[1] It is not certain whether he received a reply, but a better opportunity, more in keeping with his status as a *garde de la marine*, eventually presented itself.

Towards the end of the Battle of Quiberon, several ships had taken refuge in the nearby Vilaine River, where they had remained. A couple finally managed to sneak out in January 1761, towed by longboats during a spell of heavy winter fog. But getting the others out became more difficult when the British captured the island of Belle Isle, which lay like a formidable barrier across Quiberon Bay. A growing body of opinion in Versailles was beginning to feel that keeping men and ships bottled up in a rivermouth, unable to do anything, was a total waste of money. All they could do was keep the ships clean and stroll down to the nearest tavern. It seemed more sensible to pay off the crews, and send the officers to other duties in Brest or Rochefort, or better still send them home on half-pay.

Even the Minister of Marine, the Duc d'Aiguillon, was heard to grumble about sailors who lived on board ship, went to visit friends on land when they felt like it, and 'always found excuses for inaction in the winds, the tides and the moon'.[2] Arguments breaking out between officers from the nobility and officers from the merchant service, the reds and the blues, did not help. The blues were keen to undertake a little privateering, raiding enemy shipping in smallish, fast vessels. It was something to do, it could be profitable and it certainly was a way of keeping the enemy on their toes. The reds, however, considered these profit-motivated activities beneath their dignity. Gentlemen did not take on work that suggested trade, let alone some form of waterborne highway robbery. Mutterings that they seemed to think it was more honourable to sit around playing cards led to an exchange of insults – challenging a blue to a duel was considered by some to be beneath a nobleman's dignity.

The authorities decided on one more attempt to get some of the ships out. In May 1761, they sent the Chevalier de Ternay down from Brest, travelling, of necessity, by land. He took with him his young protégé, Jean-François de la Pérouse. They joined the *Robuste*, a ship of 74 guns, but summer was not a good time for them to try escaping. The weather was too clear, the British were landing more troops at Belle Isle, capturing the citadel in June, and enemy shipping seemed to be everywhere.

Eventually, on 28 November, they managed to get the *Robuste* out of the estuary, taking with them another vessel, the *Éveillé*. To fool the waiting British, they sailed south, intending to veer north later. Then, realising what poor condition his ships were in, Ternay continued on to the port of La Coruña on the northern coast of Spain. After a few hasty repairs, they sailed north in a wide arc to avoid the enemy ships patrolling along the French coast, and reached Brest without incident in early December.

The Duc d'Aiguillon had by now left the Ministry of Marine. Etienne François, Duc de Choiseul, who had held the Foreign Affairs portfolio since 1758, had taken over the navy as well. With his cousin, César Gabriel de Choiseul-Praslin, he was to dominate French politics for over a decade, backed by the influential Marquise de Pompadour. Knowing that the war was lost, he was in the process of negotiating a peace treaty that would not be too disastrous for France. He was also thinking of the future. If France was to play a major role in European politics, the navy would have to be rebuilt.

Encouraging and rewarding promising officers was an essential part of that process. When De Ternay brought the *Robuste* and the *Éveillé* safely into Brest, he rewarded him with an annuity of 3000 *livres*, to be added to his captain's salary. The young *gardes* who had taken part in the operation each received a grant of 300 *livres*. This included La Pérouse. He was also given a period of shore leave – not that he needed it, after over a year of inaction. More important was the confirmation of his appointment to the *Robuste*. As soon as she had been properly repaired – a job that was given top priority – she was to sail for Newfoundland.

Part of Choiseul's strategy was to reassert France's presence in the north-west Atlantic. He held little hope of regaining much of French Canada. In 1761, William Pitt had stated his intention to hold on to all of Canada, including the valuable fishing grounds, which he regarded as 'a great nursery for sailors' and formerly the best source of skilled sailors for the French Navy. The war, to all intents and purposes, would put an end to close on two centuries of French activities in North America. Choiseul, however, believed that, even if France could not retain a territorial foothold on the North American continent, it could at least keep some fishing rights in the Gulf of Saint Lawrence. This would have a symbolic value, saving French influence in North America from total eradication. It would also be of considerable economic importance to the people of Brittany, many of whom drew their livelihood from the cod-fishing industry.

Being seen to stand up for the rights of the provinces was a great way for Choiseul to shore up his position. He took up similar stances in other regions of France, creating a responsive mood when he asked the people for their co-operation to rebuild the navy. The treasury was empty: all he had to work on was their goodwill. He asked the local parliaments, the States, to make voluntary gifts to the government. He suggested in particular that they donate ships of the line, as tangible evidence of their patriotism. And they would get something for their money: impressive ships they could take pride in. The States of Languedoc were the first to come forward, followed soon by other provinces, and even by some of the cities. Paris and Marseilles followed the example of Burgundy, Flanders, Artois and Guyenne. Even the clergy was moved to contribute a million *livres*. In this way, 15 large warships, carrying from 54 to 90 guns, were built, a number of backpay claims were settled, which was a great relief to sailors and dock workers who had received no wages for months, and the depleted naval stores were restocked. By the end of the war, in 1763, the navy was in a better condition than it had been since 1760.

Sending Ternay to Newfoundland was therefore a move that fitted into Choiseul's overall plan. He had no illusions, however, that he would recapture any lost possessions. Louisbourg was gone for ever, Quebec city could not be retaken, Montreal would never again be 'Mont Réal', the Royal Mount. But the imposing *Robuste* could show that France was still a force to be reckoned with.

There was some talk of a landing, of capturing and holding a beachhead somewhere until peace finally came, but Ternay was told firmly that he was not off to reconquer Canada. His main instructions were limited to raiding fishing settlements along the coast of Newfoundland, clearing away British influence and thereby giving the impression to British strategists that some new offensive in Canadian waters was being prepared. It was showing the flag with a vengeance, although it was still part of a massive piece of bluff.

The *Robuste*, with Jean-François on board, sailed from Brest on 8 May 1762. With her went the *Éveillé*, the frigate *Licorne* and the storeship *Garonne*. They took with them an infantry force of 570 men and 31 officers under the orders of Colonel Louis Bernard d'Haussonville.

They had no difficulty in getting away, and began to scour the horizon for enemy ships. Informers had told them that two convoys had recently left Cork, one with supplies for Canada, the other making for Lisbon. Confident that they had cleared the seas of potential French raiders, the British authorities were said to have provided only one warship, two at the most, to escort these convoys. Furthermore, May was the month when English fishing vessels set off for the cod fisheries off Newfoundland, and they too were said to be confident that there were no French enemies to worry about. So Ternay and his captains, hopeful that the English would not be expecting them, looked forward to real successes, with rich prizes to take home, as well as prisoners, and some much-needed supplies that they could reroute to Brest.

Unhappily, the seas remained empty. There was not a sail to be seen, whether a fishing smack from Truro or Falmouth, or an escorting warship from Cork with a half-dozen transports around it. In a way, this simplified Ternay's task: he could sail to Newfoundland without worrying about detaching one of his ships to take any captured ships or supplies back to Brest, and it meant that the English were less likely to discover his whereabouts.

La Pérouse, less experienced and more eager for a spectacular revenge on the English, could not hide his disappointment. This looked like a simple, uneventful and consequently inglorious crossing of the Atlantic. However, there were eventually a few minor engagements. By the time the division reached the Newfoundland coast, they had captured and burnt three small merchantmen. On the debit side, a fourth had managed to escape, reach a British settlement and raise the alarm. The hoped-for element of surprise had vanished.

'We do need a base of sorts,' Ternay had said. He decided to try for Saint John's, the main settlement and today the capital of Newfoundland. It was a quiet place, inhabited mostly by fishermen and their families, but it had a garrison that would be sure to resist any attempt to land. Worse still, the chances were that they had now been forewarned of Ternay's approach and were well prepared for it.

Ternay decided to land most of D'Haussonville's troops in Bull Bay, some 25 kilometres further south. He gave them time to get organised and march overland towards Saint John's; then he sailed up to the port. As expected, the British had trained their guns towards the sea and their troops were lining up to repel any landing. As Ternay's ships appeared, the alarm sounded through the small town and everyone rushed down to the shore. At this point, D'Haussonville's troops marched up from the rear and attacked. Caught between two fires, Saint John's surrendered.

It was not a large garrison – a mere 82 officers and men were taken prisoner – but there was a single frigate at anchor in the harbour, the *Grammont*, and her 125 men were also taken prisoner. There was certainly no chance of sending them as prisoners to France or anywhere else. They were merely disarmed and kept under guard – as far as this was practicable – while the French carried out their instructions: destroying the port facilities, burning the equipment and stores, and breaking up forty or so fishing boats.

What was missing was the English cod-fishing fleet. It should have been making for Saint John's, where it usually obtained fresh supplies, dried out some of the catch on the racks available along the shore and repaired the ships in readiness for the voyage back home, but there was no sign of it anywhere.

Ternay reviewed his option with his officers. He could leave a small detachment of D'Haussonville's men to guard the prisoners and keep order among the locals, while he sailed further up the coast to look for other settlements to raid, but this meant a dangerous splitting up of his forces. The British might counter-attack at any moment. Should he hold Saint John's, keeping a French foothold for further raids in the spring? This was not impossible. He could fortify the port, using his own men and local volunteers, mostly Irish, and remain there throughout the winter, a time when a British counter-attack was unlikely. Choiseul could then send reinforcements in the spring, allowing Ternay to attempt a landing on the Quebec coast or on the Ile Royale, where the local French-Canadian population might rise up in support.

Cold reason soon prevailed. He did not have enough supplies to last through the winter. Newfoundland, in spite of a small number of disaffected Irish, was firmly pro-British. He told himself that, if he were a British administrator, he would try to recapture Saint John's before the real winter set in.

He called a full meeting of his officers on 8 September and they decided on some sort of compromise. They realised that Choiseul would not send any reinforcements in the early spring unless he knew exactly what the situation was, so it was decided that Ternay would hurry back to France and tell him, returning at the earliest opportunity with whatever ships and men he could persuade the minister to give him. Meanwhile, D'Haussonville would hold the port, and for this he would keep back about 300 men. Work began at once on strengthening the defences and arranging winter quarters, while the *Robuste* and the *Éveillé* prepared to sail.

On 12 September, however, while the French waited for a favourable wind, the British appeared – four warships, two frigates and 1500 men in nine transports. Totally outgunned and outnumbered, Ternay had to make a quick decision. He prepared to get under sail just as the British soldiers were landing nearby. He had not worked and plotted so hard to get his ships out of the Vilaine rivermouth merely to lose them off the coast of Newfoundland. On the 15th, thanks to an early autumn fog, he slipped away. D'Haussonville politely surrendered three days later. The capture and recapture of Saint John's had, at least, been a fairly bloodless episode.

Ternay meanwhile was sailing back to France. He had almost reached Brest when he sighted an enemy squadron off the island of Ushant. He decided to avoid the area altogether, veered south in a narrow arc and made for Port-Louis, near Lorient. It was no safer there – British warships were still lurking about. He continued south, going on to La Coruña, where he dropped anchor on 4 October. He did find one consolation on the way. As he neared the coast, he came upon a British privateer of 26 guns with a crew of 80. The corsair, well outnumbered by the French, had the good sense not to try anything on and promptly gave himself up. It was a prize of sorts.

The preliminary peace documents were signed while the *Robuste* was still in Spain.[3] Ternay decided he could now go home. The British blockading fleet was getting ready to leave; privateers were turning back into peaceful merchants. Life was beginning to return to something like normality. He sailed from La Coruña on 9 January 1763. Ten days later, he was in Brest. The crew were paid off, and the officers sent on leave.

La Pérouse had been delighted to go on the expedition, to escape from the boredom of port life, exhilarated at the thought of taking part in some action. Capturing Saint John's, with almost no casualties on either side, was equally exciting. France had managed to secure a beachhead, if a temporary one, on Canadian soil. And it was not a part of the old French Canada, where they might have found sympathisers and helpers: Newfoundland was solid British territory, which made the achievement an even greater challenge to English power. The *Robuste* squadron had shown what might yet be achieved. La Pérouse could go around the drawing rooms of Brest and boast a little. Just a little: it had not been too glamorous an affair, and sneaking down to Coruña and back was not showing the flag with a flourish great enough to cow the British. Nevertheless, some aspects of the voyage could be put forward to impress his audience, and Ternay's foray had certainly irritated the enemy.

The war was now winding down to its close. Peace was just around the corner, and when it came, it would undoubtedly damp his prospects for the future. Like his fellow *gardes*, Jean-François was given a period of long leave. His superiors told him that he needed to recuperate after a hard and costly war. They were more discreet about his future and kindly did not tell him that they had no posting to offer him. He was not the only one: there would be few opportunities for officers to further their careers in the post-war period, let alone for *gardes*. La Pérouse made a few calls on friends and settled a few personal matters in Brest, then set off for Albi.

Part 2
INTERLUDE

5. MARKING TIME

February 1763–December 1771

ALBI HAD NOT been much affected by the war. News had trickled down from Versailles and other centres occasionally, worrying the few families who had a son or a husband in the army or the navy, but for most people the daily routine had gone on unchanged, and at a slow pace that had now become unfamiliar to La Pérouse. There had been the usual seesawing of local fortunes – a merchant having problems with buying or selling his goods, a slow slide into decay here, a rise towards a wealthier status there, but that was all. Politics meant the ongoing rivalry between Albi and neighbouring town of Castres, a more frequent topic of conversation than the clash of the great powers in central Europe or the struggles between rival factions at court.

In spite of the letters his parents or his sisters had written to him at regular intervals, La Pérouse found that Albi had receded into a remote background. It was all so different from the cold grey mists and the strong summer skies of Brittany. The smells and the streets were both familiar and strange; the people's accent and intonations especially now sounded odd. He recaptured memories of his youth, but when people stopped to greet him in the street, he had to make an effort to remember who they were. They gossiped about engagements and marriages, births and deaths, but it all merely served to underline that he was drifting away from those with whom he had grown up.

Victor-Joseph did raise the question of Jean-François' own marriage: he was the only son left alive, and the survival of the family name depended on him. Those were days when a father plotted out the family's future, and usually arranged his children's marriages. He made sure that his son had no serious attachment back in Brest that might require him to check on the girl's suitability and to contact her father to discuss such questions as a dowry and an eventual wedding date. He may have mentioned a few worthwhile prospects in Albi itself, families with whom an alliance might be worth considering, but La Pérouse was still young – only twenty-one. His career lay ahead of him, and there was plenty of time left to plan a suitable match. Before long, if all went well, he would qualify for full officer status, become someone of status in the naval establishment. Then the family could look forward to a sound and useful marriage, better possibly and more appropriate than what might be on offer in Albi.

After a few weeks, the young *garde* set out on the long journey back to Brest. He had had quite a pleasant time, and taken the period of rest his superiors had told him he needed, but he was now keen to move on. The future was full of uncertainties. Sailors were being paid off, to look for work on merchantmen or to go back to their villages and hope for the best. Older officers were put on the retired list; some were put on half-pay; most had to wait for what the navy might be able to spare for them. A few, with large landed estates they could retire to, had simply handed in their resignations and gone home.

La Pérouse's career was safe, at least for a time. He was still a *garde de la marine*, welcomed back by Chézac as one of his most promising and experienced senior students. In British terminology, he had risen from the rank of cadet to that of midshipman, even though he still wore the same uniform and bore the same title. Compared with the handful of young recruits who were still arriving at the Hôtel Saint Pierre, he had a record worth boasting about. He had sailed on several expeditions, including the Battle of Quiberon, been taken prisoner, released from his parole and taken part in the capture of Saint John's. He still needed to finish his formal studies, pass a few final tests and graduate. None of his tutors expected him to have any problems in doing so. Not only had he been a serious student, but he also had a great deal of practical experience to back his theoretical knowledge.

He was a well-known figure about town. Shortish in stature, with a tendency towards plumpness, he was frequently invited to dinners or receptions. Life had returned to something approaching normality after the difficult last few years of the war, and social activities were in full swing. Over the dinner table or across the drawing room, mothers with daughters of marriageable age looked at him carefully, evaluating his prospects, looking for some hint of a coming attachment with a demure young lady, but nothing serious eventuated. He was pleasant, attentive, often charming, and a few hearts did flutter when he entered a room, but nothing more. Mothers and aunts consoled themselves with the thought that his family could not be classed among the 'real aristocracy' and that there were younger sons of noble families about who would make a better catch.

La Pérouse became more animated when he discussed the international situation. Under the terms of the peace treaty, France effectively lost its Indian territories and all of Canada. It did, however, retain a few footholds – five ports on the Indian continent and two small islands in the Gulf of Saint Lawrence, Saint-Pierre and Miquelon. This, he could claim, was a consequence of Ternay's determined last-minute capture of Saint John's. It had made Britain realise that keeping French fishermen away from the Newfoundland fishing grounds was not worth the trouble. They could do little harm, and neither of the two islands, covering an area not much greater than half the Isle of Wight, with a couple of thousand settlers at most, could be used as a naval base. To the ordinary folk of Brittany, however, it was a worthwhile consolation.

After the initial period of despondency, the officers' spirits began to rise. They realised that the war had proved even more ruinous for Britain than for France. The French treasury was seriously depleted – empty might be a truer word – but Choiseul had succeeded in raising funds for the navy and for other aspects of reconstruction. The voluntary donations made by the local parliaments and various merchant guilds were proof of a general goodwill. They aroused pride in the regions, and were much better than the standard forms of taxation, with their compulsory and permanent features, which inevitably raised hackles.

The gifts of ships to the navy gave La Pérouse his one opportunity to go to sea in 1763. The Paris merchants had paid for a large warship to be built at Lorient. Named in their honour the *Six Corps* (the six guilds), it now needed to be taken to Brest. This task fell to Chézac, who went down to Lorient with a number of officers and several *gardes*, including La Pérouse.

It was September, a pleasant month, with the tail end of the summer tempered by the first cool breeze of autumn. They completed the short voyage to Brest without problems and were discharged at the end of the month. Their arrival in a brand-new ship, all colours flying, was a major event. They were cheered all the way into the harbour, where the leading local merchants were waiting to see what their Paris counterparts had given the navy. The crowds that had gathered along the quays waved and sang, and later there was a lavish dinner with speeches and endless toasts. There had been so little to feel cheerful about in the last few years. The *Six Corps* raised everyone's spirits and made the town fathers glad that they had voted in favour of the Breton parliament making a similar gift. The *Bretagne*, as their ship was to be called, would give rise to even greater rejoicing.

Then winter came and with it began a period of inaction. A few vessels sailed in and out, bringing supplies for the shipyards, and the occasional frigate went out on a patrolling mission, but there was nothing for La Pérouse to do, apart from finishing his studies, sitting his final examinations and at last graduating out of the *gardes*.

On 1 October 1764 he was finally promoted, to the rank of *enseigne de vaisseau*, a grade roughly equivalent to that of English sub-lieutenant. He sent a letter to '*Mon cher père*', telling him the good news; the whole family were delighted. Now, they were sure, he was well on his way to a successful career, and they could feel more at ease with the choice he had made when he left Albi.

But promotion did not ensure him a posting. There were too many officers waiting for one, and still too few ships to satisfy them. All he could do was to mark time, carry out a few minor duties ashore when a need arose for his services, and continue his studies. He had completed the demands of the curriculum, so he could now follow his fancy. He heard – through the grapevine, as the matter was being kept confidential – that Louis de Bougainville had set up a French colony on the Falkland Islands. He knew of Bougainville, as most people did, because of the role he had played in Canada during the war, fighting down in the lakes area of New York State and Vermont, and being present at the fall of Quebec. With the Duc de Choiseul, Bougainville looked forward to the future and felt that Britain should not be allowed to dominate the seas.

The North Atlantic, as were the Channel and the North Sea, was effectively under British control. The same could be said of the route to India and the Far East. Only the Dutch still controlled the East Indies, their 'Spice Islands', jealously guarding them against all intruders, but the French India Company, its trade drastically curtailed, was facing total bankruptcy.

The only other sea power of any importance was Spain, which held most of Central and South America, as well as the Philippines, but she had been struggling to maintain her position in world affairs since the beginning of the century. France at times shored up her position, but Madrid often viewed such offers of help with a fair amount of suspicion. Britain was the rising power. All that was needed to complete her domination of all the sea routes was the conquest of the Pacific, which had for so long been viewed as a 'Spanish Lake' or, as some have called it, 'The Castilian Lake'.[1] The Pacific Ocean was still imperfectly known, and who knew what rich islands – or better still, whether a continent – lay hidden in the north, or more probably in the south, where Spanish navigators had not ventured.

Bougainville had realised that the Falklands, in the South Atlantic, could hold the key to the Pacific route. The islands were uninhabited, although loosely claimed by Spain on the grounds that they formed part of Argentina. The French, however, had sailed there over the years, making a brief call or simply using them as a checkpoint on their way south. They knew them as the Islands of Saint-Malo or the Malouines, because most of those who had called there came from that port. It was a name even the Spanish recognised, calling them – then, as now – the Malvinas.

Bougainville had taken with him as settlers a number of Acadian refugees, hardy characters who could cope with the fairly harsh climate of the islands. He had set out in September 1763 and founded a small settlement he had called Port Saint-Louis.

The few who knew of this expedition realised that it was only the first step in sailing into the Pacific. France and Spain were allies. While certainly uneasy about a possible French intrusion into the Spanish Lake, Madrid was unlikely to do much more than register a protest. Skilful politicians like the Duc de Choiseul could handle diplomatic recriminations without difficulty.

So La Pérouse turned his attention to the Pacific world. He read an important work that had been published in 1756 by a French historian: Charles de Brosses' *Histoire des Navigations aux Terres Australes*. It was a meticulous reconstruction of all the voyages that had been made to the South Seas – as well as a passionate plea for France to explore them and to find there the bases for settlements that would enable France to stake its claim to the Pacific world. La Pérouse discovered from this work and several others a wealth of theories and legends about the vast Pacific Ocean.

There were the Solomon Islands, discovered by the Spanish, then 'lost' because no one knew exactly where they were, and now surrounded by a host of legends about their wealth, in potential trade as well as gold and silver. There was David Land or Davis Land, discovered by some British buccaneers, then similarly mislaid and now believed by most people to have been a mirage or a garbled report by men who were better corsairs than navigators. Above all, there was the great Southern Continent that no one had yet found, but which most people, De Brosses included, believed existed. Some thought it had to exist in order to balance the weight of the continents in the northern hemisphere. Land and rocks were heavier than water, it was argued with some logic, and if it was all concentrated on the north, with only ocean in the south, the globe would topple over. Supporters of the theory could prove it to you by placing a ball on a table, heaping up a little soil mixed with pebbles on the top of it, and watching it roll over …

However, the earliest navigators to venture into the Pacific had found very little land there. The first European to cross it, Ferdinand Magellan, had cut a swathe from the south of America to the Philippines, and found almost none. The Spaniards Alvaro Mendaña and Pedro de Quiros, and the Dutchmen Willem Schouten, Jacob Le Maire and Jacob Roggeveen, had sailed roughly east to west below the equator, and none of them had found anything like a continental mass. The hoped-for southern land had gradually shrunk into the south-west corner of the Pacific, about which little was known. Some cynics suggested the impossible: maybe the globe had already toppled over, and the north was in the south!

De Brosses belonged to the school that thought there was a land mass of sorts, much smaller in size than had been believed, but still substantial, and that the larger number of small islands known to fill the South Pacific was enough to keep the balance. There had been too many reports over the centuries, vague though they might have been. He did not labour the point, but stressed at every stage that a great deal of the ocean still needed to be explored, and that France should take part in the search. He was a highly respected *savant*, associated with the *philosophes*, quick to answer questions and write letters. La Pérouse looked at the maps and realised how much needed to be done. De Brosses, a systematic man, had divided the southern world into three regions, and given them names: there was the south-east Atlantic, which he named Magellanica, the South Pacific, which he called Polynesia, or the place of the many islands, and the southern Indian Ocean, for which he coined the name Australasia, or southern Asia.

La Pérouse realised how right De Brosses was in urging his compatriots to explore the Pacific and not leave it all to the British. Spanish power was waning, no one could doubt that. The voyage of George Anson in 1741 had proved it: he had sailed with several ships to the Pacific coast of South America, sacking the town of Paita in Peru in November and looting and destroying other Spanish settlements as far north as Acapulco. He had then crossed the Pacific to China, and sailed back again to capture the richly laden *Nuestra Señora de Cobagonda*. He had gone home and joined the Admiralty Board, a wealthy and much-admired man.

More recently, in 1764, Commodore John Byron had sailed in the *Dolphin* on a voyage of exploration to look for the famous Davis Land and to rediscover the long-lost Islands of Solomon. The Falklands, now settled by the French, though claimed by Britain, lay in his path, so it was expected that he would overpower Bougainville's fledgling Port Saint-Louis. He actually achieved none of these tasks, but Britain's intentions were clear. Now that the war was over, France's rival was turning her attention to the Pacific. If anyone still harboured doubts about it, they were soon convinced by the departure in 1766 of the expeditions of Samuel Wallis and Philip Carteret.

Choiseul's policies were directed at preventing this dangerous situation from developing. There was not a great deal he could do at the time, apart from building up the navy and quietly encouraging Bougainville with his Falklands scheme and, following this, with his planned circumnavigation, right across the Pacific and back via the Indian Ocean. Tact and caution were needed with these plans, because France had little money to spare for new ventures, and Louis XV was dead set against anything that might lead to another war. Choiseul, however, was skilled in the art of juggling several balls at the same time – and looking quite innocent while doing it.

None of all this, unfortunately, translated into opportunities for junior officers like La Pérouse. Dreaming about faraway places was all very well, but there were no calls for his services. He was not alone. His friends discussed what they might do to gain experience at sea, instead of marking time in Brest. What future did an *enseigne de vaisseau* have before him, if all he could claim was time spent behind a desk in some faraway town?

In the absence of a naval appointment, they could offer their services to private shipowners. For young men of aristocratic background, this option remained unacceptable: it smelt too much of trade, something that was quite beneath them. As Captain La Rochefoucault de Cousage had put it back in December 1761 in a letter to the minister, who had suggested that some of the youths might serve on privateers or supply vessels:

> You will have no difficulty in appreciating, My Lord, that the young *gardes*, who have the honour of being born people of quality, possess feelings that are in keeping with their rank, and that they would soon realise that they were not born to serve under the orders of merchant captains or corsairs … and one might fear that those captains, ill-brought up as most of them are, since they have risen from the ranks of the sailors, among whom one learns little about politeness and manners, least of all how one should speak to persons of quality, might feel some bloated pride at having *gardes* under them, which could lead them to behave improperly towards these *gardes*.

He added a warning:

> Furthermore, My Lord, we have to face the likelihood that, once this is made public, a considerable number [he used the words '*une infinité*'] of *gardes* will ask to leave the service, either of their own volition, or following the instructions of their father and mother who will not be willing to expose their children to any misfortune that might befall them as a consequence of having to serve under the orders of people who are, in no respect, qualified to hold authority over them.[2]

The minister had not insisted. Even to a reform-minded man like him, the possibility of a young nobleman being bawled out by an irate merchant captain risen from the ranks was unthinkable. But Cousage had hinted that a solution might be to allocate certain transport vessels and storeships for particular tasks, survey work or other, along the coast or even further, and handpick the captains, who would be men with particular talents and tact. Not every *garde* by any means would agree to serve in such vessels, but others might. The 'others' in question would no doubt be those whose family background was less elevated – those whose ancestors had not led their vassals to the Crusades, as some put it – for whom serving outside the royal navy or on behalf of it was better than nothing.

La Pérouse was one of those. His family background made him less of a snob, and times were changing. The *philosophes* were questioning the entire social structure of France and of other European countries, and there was a rising current of democratic feeling flowing around the country. La Pérouse was by no means unaffected. In fact, he sympathised with their analysis of the modern world and was gradually moving over to their point of view.

He had once before offered his services to a shipowner. The opportunity that came his way in August 1765 was a little above this. He was offered an appointment on a small transport vessel, the 80-tonne *Adour*. Her purpose was to fetch timber from Bayonne, near the Spanish frontier, and deliver it to the naval yards at Rochefort and Brest. This was working indirectly for the navy and not trade in the true sense. Furthermore, her captain was a nobleman, Nicolas de Clugny.

Clugny was an *enseigne* like La Pérouse, but more senior to him, and the pair got on well. Neither was worried about whether their duties were *infra dig*. Their ship was small, not very fast, but sound enough for coastal navigation. Clugny enjoyed the work, the life and bustle of Bayonne, a busy commercial port that exported not just timber, but hemp, sails, tar, anchors, guns and a host of supplies. Sailing back with a heavy load was a struggle, but a good challenge for their talents. He was happy with this first undertaking and he wrote to his superiors, expressing the hope that he might get a further command of the same nature. And he praised La Pérouse for his 'vigilance and energy'.[3]

Clugny got a new appointment, but Jean-François' posting came to an end on 31 January 1766. He looked around for some other opportunity, but even Ternay could not help him. He, too, was largely marking time. He had been given command of a small ship, and even sent on long leave, which enabled him to travel and carry out some hydrographic work on a personal basis.

La Pérouse's willingness to serve and the good reports he had received from Clugny brought their reward, although he had to wait three months for it. He was appointed to the *Dorade*, another transport vessel engaged in ferrying timber from Bayonne to Brest. Again, it was nothing particularly glorious, but it kept him active and taught him a great deal about close offshore navigation. The navy was quite happy for a young *enseigne* like La Pérouse to do this work and gain experience. It ensured that the Breton shipyards were well supplied at a time when they were becoming increasingly busy – and it cost the navy nothing. A letter from the commodore in charge, Charles de Roquefeuil, to Choiseul, the Minister of Marine, confirms this:

> Mr de Kergariou, the *enseigne* in charge of this vessel, has requested permission to take on an additional officer at his own expense, and I have given him Mr de la Pérouse, an *enseigne* younger than he ... As an officer in charge of these vessels works on contract, and consequently the King does not have to meet extra costs in this operation, while getting his young officers to sail and improve their knowledge of the coasts, I believe, My Lord, that I acted in accordance with your wishes ...[4]

Kergariou was getting 15 *livres* a day for his command, a modest enough sum, out of which he had to provide for any officers and servants he employed, which now included La Pérouse. It was not all altruism on his part. We may assume that there was a little quiet bargaining on the side with the various suppliers, and that possibly some additional trading was also going on. There was always room in the hold or even in the cabin for a few extra items – a few cases of quality wine and brandy or even the ham for which Bayonne was becoming renowned. However, young officers like Kergariou had to be careful to leave no evidence behind, as private deals, although common among merchant service officers, were frowned upon in the navy.

The *Dorade* was back at Brest in late July. Kergariou and La Pérouse received thanks and praise for their work, the usual report being filed by the port authorities in the naval records. In it, we find La Pérouse being referred to for the first time as a *chevalier*, a knight: 'The *chevaliers* de Kergariou and La Pérouse, *enseignes*, carried out their duties with all the skill their diligence has developed in them'.[5] This does not mean that he had been knighted, merely that he was being recognised as a worthy and mature member of the nobility. A young *garde* might be thought of as an *écuyer*, a squire. La Pérouse had now achieved a higher status in the eyes of his superiors. One day, he would commonly be referred to as a *comte*. Again, this does not imply any formal promotion: he was regarded as what the British might call a count because of his rank and status. There was no actual conferment of the title through any honours list or ceremony.

He wasted no time in finding another transport vessel he could serve on. The *Gave*, with a friend of his, Saige de la Mettrie, in charge, was about to sail, not just for Bayonne, but this time for Toulon. He had never been to the Mediterranean and relished the experience. It was a new world, full of light and noise, with a distinct local accent that made him think of his youth in Albi, and a bustling naval base that promised much for the future. It also meant going through the Strait of Gibraltar, past a large naval base built some 50 years earlier on what had once been Spanish territory. From there, the victors of the Seven Years War kept watch on all the ships that sailed past. La Pérouse could only feel bitterness when he saw the British flag flying over the town, and at the thought that the watchers knew quite well that, for all the braid and colour of their uniforms, the French officers were merely doing a merchant's work.

The *Gave* was back at Brest on 1 May 1767. Jean-François spent a few months ashore, then received his first command. Back in Albi, Victor-Joseph might be able to boast, 'My son now has his own ship', but it was only a slow and unglamorous storeship, the *Adour*, and La Pérouse was still only required to ferry goods between Bayonne and Brest. He had yet another command ahead of him, the *Dorothée*, which he took over on 15 November 1767. He continued to sail down to Bayonne and back with timber and other material. This particular command – a truer term would be 'contract' – came to an end in May 1768.

Now, at last, things began to change. He met Ternay who had been carrying out hydrographic and survey work around Brittany for some years, and was now working on improving the charts of the Brest roadstead. It was Choiseul's plan to make Brest impregnable by fortifying the island of Ushant, and having such precise charts available to all his captains that they could beat any future blockade by sailing blind at night. This involved a great deal of painstaking work, and Ternay was happy that La Pérouse was available to help him. The young man worked with him from mid-July to mid-September, gaining more invaluable experience of inshore navigation, depth soundings and the precise recording of even the smallest landmarks.

The problem with fortifying Ushant was that the island was privately owned. Given by Henry IV to the Comte de Rieux in 1594, it was still held by the family, which was by no means keen to lose control of it. But such private property, ill-defended, could all too easily fall into English hands. Choiseul reminded the Rieux of their property's precarious situation, and then negotiated a sale by making an offer the Rieux could not refuse: a cash payment of 30,000 *livres* and an annuity of 3000 *livres* extinguishable only on the death of the countess and of her son. Considering that the storm-wracked island produced on average a return of some 700 *livres* a year, the offer was irresistible.[6] With Ushant now fortified and Ternay's meticulous charts available, Choiseul felt confident that France's leading naval base was fully protected.

For the moment, however, there was no new work in sight for La Pérouse, who spent the winter months ashore, increasingly bored. If all he was doing was reading in his lodgings and visiting friends in theirs, he might as well go home. In the spring of 1769 he asked for long leave and was given it without difficulty. He remained on the navy's books, admittedly without pay, but also without losing the seniority he had gained. He made his way in a fairly leisurely manner down to Albi. He did a little sightseeing on the way, staying for a day or two if the fancy took him, the nearest thing to a tourist one could find in the eighteenth century. He saw castles, churches and abbeys, sampling the local food and wines and reaching his hometown probably towards the end of June.

Six years had gone by since his last visit. The city had not changed, but time had affected his father, who was now turning 60 and whose eyesight was failing. His manner was more dignified than ever, however, his back quite straight, his head high, and when he walked through the old twisting streets – on someone's arm, admittedly – people greeted him respectfully or effusively, according to their own rank. He was in every respect the patriarch, the city father brooking no challenge to his authority.

La Pérouse celebrated his twenty-eighth birthday on a warm summer day at Le Gô. He was now at an age when marriage had to be seriously discussed. The names of young ladies of a suitable rank and fortune were mentioned, one after the other, with comments from his mother and sisters. Garden parties and dinners were arranged so that he could meet them, admire their charms – and be evaluated by their parents. But nothing came out of it. The suggested matches were pleasant young women, well educated, well connected, but none stood out sufficiently for him to give up his freedom.

The older man was pleased with his son's progress in the navy, his maturity and his self-confidence. Even his tendency to put on a little too much weight, something La Pérouse struggled against all his life (difficult for someone who was something of a gourmet and wine buff) helped to build up the picture of a serious young man on his way up in the world. His father pressed him over the need to marry. A union with a young lady of means and of good standing would help to shore up his promising future, and ensure that the name of Galaup de la Pérouse did not die out.

La Pérouse returned to Brest at the end of September. Not a great deal had happened during his absence, but there were political and naval matters to discuss. The Choiseuls' hold on the political reins was being increasingly threatened by the enmity of Louis XV's new favourite, Madame du Barry. The ministers believed that France was now in a position to challenge British supremacy. There were increasing rumours about George III's mental instability and there was growing unrest in Britain's American colonies. Even India had its problems, with an acrimonious dispute between the City financiers and the

Crown over the renewal of the East India Company's charter. However, Louis XV was still set against any action that might lead to hostilities between France and England. The Choiseuls' policies seemed set in that direction, and they would soon pay the price by being dismissed from positions they had held for years.

Meanwhile, those who feared that Britain would soon gain the upper hand in the Pacific Ocean were being proved right. Wallis and Carteret had each completed a voyage of exploration, and the first voyage of James Cook had soon followed. Islands of importance such as Tahiti had been discovered. New Zealand, briefly visited by the Dutchman Abel Tasman back in 1642, had been carefully surveyed, and the east coast of Australia had been claimed 'in the Name of his Majesty King George III' and given the name of New South Wales. An ocean sprinkled with Spanish names – Santa Catalina, Santa Cruz, La Solitaria, San Bernardo – was now being filled with English ones: Duke of York's Island, Queen Charlotte's Island, Prince William Henry Island, Sir Charles Hardy's Island. All these seemed to proclaim that Britain was the coming power in the Pacific Ocean.

Louis de Bougainville's Malouines colony was no more; not taken over by England, but given over to Spain. During the voyage of exploration that followed this handing over, he had flown the French flag right across the Pacific and made a number of discoveries, but even the island of Tahiti, where he landed, a stay that made a great impression in France, had already been named, grandly if clumsily, King George the Third's Island.

The growth of the French Navy under Choiseul's governance and France's growing confidence in a changing Europe now provided La Pérouse with real opportunities. His days of ferrying timber in dreary little storeships or carrying out coastal surveys were no more. He put in his claim for a posting and, within a few months, was appointed to serve on a frigate of twenty-six guns, the *Belle-Poule*, a fine new ship launched only a couple of years earlier and now commanded by Thomas d'Orves.

The situation in Europe was growing more tense by the day. Fishing vessels from Saint-Malo and from Dunkirk were coming back to port, afraid that they might be caught up in a pre-war raid by British ships, as had happened before the outbreak of the previous war. The *Belle-Poule*, together with several other warships, was holding herself in readiness to join a squadron that might be despatched at any moment.

But nothing happened. A few more weeks went by, while they waited for instructions. Meanwhile, the Brest port captain had received reports of a couple of English frigates roaming around the outer approaches. He decided to send a small vessel to investigate, and asked La Pérouse to command her. He was glad to accept, though the vessel in question was only a lighter used to carry ammunition and supplies to ships inside the bay. It had a small crew of no more than seven men, and it did not even have a name, but at least it offered a break from the monotony of life on board a warship that stayed at anchor day after day.

He sailed close to the shore along the Goulet and out into what was known as the Sea of Iroise, a somewhat pompous name for the outer approaches. However, part of it was called the Élorn which, according to local tradition, meant the Waters of Dread. There was no sign of any British ships, so La Pérouse installed on a number of small islets a succession of flagpoles that could be used to send signals of any enemy activity. This took him three months, from late September to the end of December, a bleak time of the year to be sailing in those waters. François de Rosilis, now in charge of the Brest naval establishment, expressed gratitude for this meticulous work and assured him that his services were appreciated and would soon result in his being given a command. The corvette, *Lunette*, recently completed, was mentioned. Getting a refund for his expenses, however, was not mentioned. La Pérouse found himself well out of pocket, because he had had to pay for his own food and that of his small crew. All that happened was that Rosilis sent a flattering report to the ministry, thus keeping his promise to recommend him for promotion.

The ministry, however, was in a state of upheaval, following the dismissal, just before Christmas, of both the Choiseuls, and the temporary appointment of the Abbé Terray as Minister. Rosilis' report was either mislaid or ignored, and the *Lunette* went to an *enseigne* named Bernard de Tromelin.

La Pérouse was furious. He took his pen and wrote a long letter of protest to the minister. Even though it was couched in the courteous and at times flowery terms that were normal in the eighteenth century, it expressed his views in no uncertain terms. He pointed out that he had been asked to undertake a mission 'in the smallest and worst vessel available in the port', which he had completed to such satisfaction that he had been recommended for a command. He had carried out his task 'without payment, in spite of the meagreness of my fortune'.

Having served in the navy for more than fifteen years, I have been on twelve campaigns, I was wounded in the most murderous battle of the last war; but in spite of that, Mr de Tromelin, a port officer of six months' standing, is reaping what I have sown, and obtains the command Mr de Rosilis had requested for me. I look in vain, My Lord, in my past life for what could have justified so harsh a treatment.

He went on to assure the minister that his zeal and his noble sense of ambition remained undulled, and placed his hopes in justice and fairness. Then he dropped in, as a reference, the name of his protector: 'Close to you, My Lord, is the Chevalier de Ternay, with whom I have sailed on four campaigns. His friendship for me and the interest he shows in me are the clearest proofs of my good behaviour.'[7]

This was something of a mistake. Ternay was at Versailles to assure the new minister of his loyalty, manoeuvring his way, like many others, through the political upheaval that followed the fall of the Choiseuls and their supporters. Ternay was just one of a group seeking the minister's good graces and looking for a new appointment for himself. Being thus linked to a complaining young officer from Brest who was angry at the way the navy was treating him was not something he welcomed.

The minister sent off a prompt reply – not to La Pérouse direct, but to Rosilis: 'Please tell Mr de la Pérouse that this is not an appropriate time to take him away from the *Belle-Poule* that may be sailing in the near future and where his services will be of greater use. And let this officer be told that Mr de Tromelin had joined the service before him.'[8] It was, not unexpectedly, a sharp reply. La Pérouse had to swallow his pride, and sell the supplies and equipment he had earlier bought in anticipation of his appointment to the *Lunette*. Once more he had to settle down to the daily routine of a warship in port, and cope with a few tart comments from his colleagues about counting one's chickens before they were hatched. Two famous writers had created the French equivalent of that English proverb: La Fontaine in one of his *Fables* had warned against selling a bearskin before the bear had been killed, and Molière had one of his characters saying that one should wait until a feast day had arrived before celebrating it.

Things brightened up in the spring. In early May 1771, the *Belle-Poule* finally had orders to sail, for the West Indies. With La Pérouse went another *enseigne*, Paul-Antoine Fleuriot de Langle, who would one day join him on his great voyage through the Pacific. The second-in-command was Cillard de Suville, who had been on the *Robuste* with him and Ternay on the 1763 expedition to Newfoundland.

The French West Indies were going through a period of great prosperity, their trade figures eclipsing the British and Spanish totals. A thousand ships a year traded through the ports of Santo Domingo and the islands of Guadeloupe, Martinique and Saint Lucia. Exports of sugar and its byproducts such as rum, plus coffee, indigo and other goods, produced an annual surplus of some 130 million *livres*. The French had opened two free ports, Mole Saint Nicolas in Santo Domingo and Le Carénage in Saint Lucia. Traders came down from New England, selling grain, fish and barrels in exchange for sugar, molasses and rum – which the French settlers, being wine drinkers, did not have much need for locally. Local sugar, being cheaper than its Jamaican counterpart, was in fact often re-exported and sent to Britain, labelled as English colonial sugar.

It was all based on slavery. The original Carib Indians Christopher Columbus had met back in 1493 had almost all died off, killed or absorbed into the waves of immigrants, so that labour had to be imported. This meant slaves from Africa, largely supplied by British traders. There were fewer of them, proportionally speaking, in French Guadeloupe and Martinique, but in Santo Domingo one could gain the impression of being in Africa.

The centre of administration was Port-au-Prince, now the capital of Haiti, but the first port of call and by far the larger town was Cap Français, with a population of 12,000, which included 2500 whites. It was not an unattractive place, with streets laid out in straight lines, intersecting at right angles and covered with sandy gravel. They were pleasant to walk along in summer and reasonably free of mud in winter. La Pérouse joined his fellow officers for a stroll along its main street, the Cours Villeverd. It was warm, but by no means oppressively hot, even though this was summertime. The street was lined with stone houses, mostly single-storeyed, many of them built with material imported from France, including tiles from Normandy and slates from Anjou. They dropped into some of the larger taverns – the town boasted over twenty of them, some admittedly not too salubrious. The hospital, with 100 beds, was well filled whenever a ship came in with its usual load of scurvy cases, or when there was a local outbreak of fever or dysentery.

They went on to Port-au-Prince, then a smaller settlement, much less impressive, with wider streets but mostly rutted and dirty. As one visitor wrote at the time, 'if it rained overnight you could not walk in the streets that are like great muddy tracks lined by ditches from which frogs croak out at you'.[9] Things had been made worse by a recent earthquake that had destroyed a number of buildings: the authorities had issued instructions that all new structures had to be built of timber or timbered masonry.

The *Belle-Poule's* mission was to keep watch on British and Spanish activities around the islands, protect merchant ships and hold herself in readiness to intervene if France's interests were threatened. This involved patrol duties for about half the time, and staying in port at the ready for the other half. It gave La Pérouse and his friends a fair amount of leisure to attend receptions and balls and drop in at the theatre, and to observe colonial society. As was so often the case in the smaller colonies, this was split horizontally between the rich merchants and plantation owners and the shopkeepers, artisans and clerks. This distinction was plain enough to the officers of the *Belle-Poule* as they responded to the invitations of the locals. But what of the slaves?

A debate had been going on for some time in France over the ethical aspects of slavery. The eighteenth century was the century of the Enlightenment, of the *philosophes* who were debating how society should be constructed or reconstructed, and what a man's position and role should be in the country he lived in. Slavery had long disappeared in most of Europe, even though some might argue that the serfs who could still be found in a number of countries and the peasants who were everywhere subject to the customary privileges of the nobles, were effectively living as slaves. But then some people claimed that the blacks belonged to another species, and were not part of real society.

La Pérouse and his fellow officers discussed the works of the writer Charles de Secondat Montesquieu who had been something of a voice in the wilderness when he wrote that 'slavery is of use neither to the master nor to the slave'.[10] The colonists claimed that, without slave labour, the economy of the West Indies would collapse. Selfish or realistic or both, they had to cope with the flood of books about slavery and its moral and economic aspects that had begun to appear during the 1760s. The great *Encyclopédie* being compiled by Denis Diderot, Jean-Jacques Rousseau and other philosophers was boldly challenging ideas that had been taken for granted for generations.

There were also travel books, such as Jean-Baptiste Chanvalon's *Voyage à la Martinique* of 1763, and more controversial works, such as Claude Le Cat's *Traité de la couleur de la peau humaine* of 1765 and especially the Abbé Guillaume Raynal's recent and controversial *Histoire philosophique et politique des établissements et du commerce des Européens dans les deux Indes*. A new group of economists, known as the Physiocrats, which advocated freer trade, was subjecting economic forces to scrutiny and beginning to suggest that Montesquieu had been right all along, and that forced, unwilling labour was a costly and inadequate way of producing goods. Some held the view that even colonial possessions were of little economic value, costing the metropolis more than they gave it back in return. Thus Moreau de St Méry, a creole from Martinique and a councillor in Saint Domingue, in his book *Description de la partie française de St-Domingue*, calculated that 200 slaves produced a mere 150 tonnes of sugar, and that since half this so-called labour force consisted of children, old people and estate servants, the true productivity was little more than 1½ tons per head.

The visitors felt uneasy in the island environment, La Pérouse probably more than most. He was a Galaup, the descendant of merchants and local administrators whose gradual rise over the years was the result of cool objective analysis and a down-to-earth approach. He would experience the same unease when he went to Mauritius, and often wondered whether slave-owning was more a matter of status than of profit – it was impressive to own an estate with hundreds of black workers and their families, even though one might be able to make more money in other ways. And a similar argument could be applied to most colonial possessions, which many saw as an expensive drain on the home country's resources.

The *Belle-Poule* made her way back to Brest in October 1771. La Pérouse signed off on the 14th, and received a special commendation from the captain, whose report to the ministry mentioned 'La Pérouse. Very well read and knowledgeable. A young officer in whom one places great hopes.'[11]

He spent a few weeks ashore, calling on old friends and bringing himself up to date with the latest developments at Versailles. The Abbé Terray had moved on, and there was now a new Minister of Marine, Bourgeois de Boynes, a skilled and careful administrator who had successfully navigated his way through the troubled waters of the post-Choiseul period.

The appointment of De Boynes had been important for La Pérouse, because it had helped to bring Ternay back into full favour. Well regarded by De Boynes, he was named Governor of the Isle de France and Isle de Bourbon, known today as Mauritius and Réunion, in the Indian Ocean. He was also given command of the *Belle-Poule*. This meant he could choose his officers, and he wasted no time in appointing La Pérouse as one of them.

Part 3

DOWN IN THE INDIAN OCEAN

6. ARGUMENTS IN THE ISLE DE FRANCE

January–September 1772

THE *BELLE-POULE* left Brest on 22 January, put in briefly at Lorient for supplies and continued on her way across the Bay of Biscay towards Portugal and the coast of Africa. La Pérouse had sailed a few times across the Atlantic, but in spite of his sixteen years in the navy, the furthest south he had gone was Gibraltar and Toulon. Now, for the first time, he was to cross the equator and enter the southern hemisphere.

The Crossing of the Line was an occasion for feasts and mock ceremonials that provided a welcome break in the unending shipboard routine. The crew practically took over for the day, hanging decorations, preparing disguises and practical jokes of every kind. No one was exempt from taking the oath and suffering the ritual baptism, though the officers and passengers were spared the grosser slapstick and tricks that were visited upon the crew and the servants – usually in exchange for a few coins thrown into the mock collection plate passed around by the sailors. Crossing the Line created a sort of freemasonry of the sea, and the nonsensical ceremonies had an underlying value: they reminded the men that the sea might be stormy and moody, but down below there was rock and a solid world of its own, mysterious and threatening.

La Pérouse took the oath presented to him – 'never to make love to the wife of an absent sailor, to do unto others as was done unto you and to help sailors everywhere' – which was sealed by the sprinkling of water, a christening of salt water and the passing round of the collection plate. The ceremony was not unlike the medieval Feast of Fools before the beginning of Lent when a mock bishop rode around a city on a donkey, accompanied by a crowd of acolytes hurling mud and water at the crowd and singing parodies of hymns. Ternay had several barrels of red wine brought up from the hold so that the men could enjoy 'bacchic libations in honour of the neophytes'.

Then routine fell back upon the ship like a hot, heavy blanket. She went through a period of calms, a dreary time when the great grey sails hung down in the still air, and the heat caused waves of stench to rise from below decks. Most of the crew tried to sleep on deck, among coils of rope or in odd corners between the few remaining fowl cages and the gradually emptying pigpens. The dense blue of the tropical sea raised spirits a little during the day. There were strange phenomena to marvel at, such as flying fish skimming the waves or, at night, St Elmo's fire flickering around the tops of the masts. The older sailors explained these mysterious happenings, serving out old tales and superstitions to the wide-eyed ship's boys gathered around them.

It was a slow crossing – six dreary weeks from Gorée in Senegal to the Cape of Good Hope. The *Belle-Poule* spent a month at False Bay, on the eastern side of the Cape, for repairs and fresh supplies. It provided an opportunity for the men to stroll ashore and breathe in the 'land air' that was believed to be such a great cure for scurvy. What made the real difference, of course, were the fresh fruit and vegetables bought ashore to replace the standard daily ration of salt meat and dry biscuit.

The *Belle-Poule* reached Port-Louis, the capital of the Isle de France, on 21 August 1772. This was no ordinary occasion. It was not just one more ship coming into port, but the arrival of a new governor. Etiquette required Ternay to be welcomed with all due formality by the local officials, including the governor he was replacing, François du Dresnay Desroches. But no one on the island knew the exact date of the *Belle-Poule*'s arrival. There had been no way for Ternay to advise anyone of his date of departure from False Bay or of his landfall on the Isle de France; nor could anyone guess how long the crossing would take. So the frigate had to drop anchor outside the port and wait. La Pérouse used his eyeglass to scan the small town, built in a valley at the end of a long harbour, with steep hills on all sides and a jumble of hazy peaks in the distance. But there was no sign of Desroches or anyone else – the governor was on a farewell visit in the neighbouring island of Bourbon. An urgent message had been sent to him to return in a hurry, but meanwhile all Ternay and his officers could do was to stay on board and wait.

Finally, after they had been marking time for a full three days, everything was ready. The officers landed and walked to the Champs de Mars, an open square in the centre of the town, where 2000 soldiers from the Isle de France Legion were lined up. Drawn from four regiments, they wore white uniforms with blue, red or green collars and facings, made even more colourful by splashes of gold braid. The sergeants barked their orders and the men all stood at attention, banners flying in the warm breeze, with drum rolls and trumpet calls. Around them crowded almost the entire population of Port-Louis in their

Sunday best, the ladies bowing to each other under sunshades held by black maids.

Desroches stepped forward, with the *intendant* or civil administrator Pierre Poivre at his side. Each in turn welcomed Ternay, neither addressing a word to the other – they had not been on speaking terms for years. Desroches led the new governor to inspect the troops, while a gun salute thundered through the valley. Then, in a formal cortège, followed by the *Belle-Poule*'s officers and the local notables, they walked towards the church. The Apostolic Prefect, Father François Contenot, was waiting in the porch to lead them inside. There – not without some jostling, because precedence was a matter of constant bickering in the colony – they sat down for a solemn *Te Deum*. This done, they went on to the administrative offices for the formal handover. It took only a few moments. Ternay was now governor and commandant; Jacques Maillard Dumesle was the new administrator.

The next few days were taken up by formal calls from a succession of leading citizens and by the chores of moving out and moving in. There was a great deal to learn about life in the colony. Ternay gave up his command of the *Belle-Poule*, but La Pérouse continued to live on board for several weeks. He, too, had to get used to a new style of life, alternating between voyages in the Indian Ocean and periods on the island.

For many centuries, Mauritius had lain isolated and unknown in the western Indian Ocean. A few hopeful Arab traders may have landed on its deserted shores, but they soon sailed away in disappointment. Undisturbed, the turkey-like dodo waddled through the semi-tropical forest and fussed around its ground-level nest, where it laid its single, large egg.

A Portuguese navigator put Mauritius on the map in the early sixteenth century, but it was not claimed by any power until 1598, when the Dutch occupied it and named it in honour of the Stadtholder of the Netherlands, Maurice of Nassau. Even so, the island remained uninhabited until 1638 when a small Dutch colony was established, but that never prospered, and it was gradually abandoned during the early years of the eighteenth century. Mauritius reverted to its isolation and loneliness until 1715, when the Frenchman Guillaume Dufresne took over, renaming it Isle de France, but another six years went by before the first few French colonists arrived and began to build a colony.

The French India Company, in particular, appreciated its potential, and established a sound settlement, building the port and the township. Sugar plantations originally developed by the Dutch were restored, providing a solid basis for agriculture and trade. It was a promising colony, quite prosperous, a valuable port of call for ships on their way to India and the Far East. However, the end of French hopes in India, following the disastrous Seven Years War, put paid to its aspirations; the French India Company was almost bankrupt and in 1767, the French government was forced to take it over.

As local residents soon explained to La Pérouse, it had never been easy to govern the colony. An early administrator, Mahé de la Bourdonnais, had successfully built up the thriving sugar industry and organised the port as a reliable and efficient supply base, but as the colony developed, local interests began to clash with the company's. It was an age-old argument: should there be free trade or a single monopoly? So far away from France, it was not easy to enforce any monopoly or to arbitrate between rival commercial interests locked in bitter disputes. With a military and a civil administrator sharing power, the situation rapidly worsened.

General Daniel Dumas was appointed governor, with orders to look after the defence and maintenance of what Versailles regarded as an important strategic base. Pierre Poivre, 'a brown-eyed, round-faced Lyonnais, full of passion and intelligence, a man sympathetic to the expansion of agriculture and to horticultural experimentation',[1] took over as *Intendant*, and devoted himself energetically to the island's economic development. It was never easy to draw a line between the two jurisdictions, and the two fell out within weeks. What could in theory have been a uniting influence, the local residents' *Conseil Supérieur*, should have helped, but the colonists were more anxious to defend their own position against interference from either side, so that, if anything, they formed a third camp.

Dumas' problem was that the French government had no money to spare. Far from being given funds to strengthen the island's defences, Dumas was told to retrench. Poivre was all vision and drive. He wanted to develop coffee and cotton plantations, as well as a cattle industry. Above all, he wanted spices. The spice trade was a Dutch monopoly, jealously guarded. The Isle de France could only challenge it if the locals could obtain seed and plants. 'Bring us some spice plants. Go about it carefully, but bring some back', was Poivre's appeal to anyone who was about to sail through or near the Dutch East Indies.

Nutmegs, above all, could be a source of wealth. They were believed to have medicinal properties, warding off winter ailments and, even more important, keeping the dreaded plague at bay. Cloves were also prized: these small, dark-red olives also cured a number of ills and were effective against toothache, the common curse that affected every level of society. Extractions and any form of dentistry were excruciatingly painful in the days before anaesthetics, and one frequently saw people walking around with a hand against their jaw, or working with it wrapped in a bandage soaked in aromatic herbs. Nutmeg was also used for cosmetic purposes, as an ingredient added to perfume or soaps – at least, by those who could afford such luxuries. In addition, cooks sought out spices to flavour their meals with something more exotic and more exciting than mere salt.

Poivre never won his secret battle against the Dutch spice monopoly, and he was in despair whenever he heard rumours of a successful smuggling raid on an isolated Dutch plantation by some daring British captain. But he did a great deal for the island, encouraging trade with India and making every effort to beautify Port-Louis and its environs. In particular, he developed the magnificent garden of Pamplemousses, near his country home, Mon Plaisir.

All this meant clashes with the governor. Eventually, Poivre's manoeuvres and those of his allies on the island and in what remained of French India, helped to ease Dumas out of his position. The ministry back in France, which was responsible for both the navy and the colonies, came to the conclusion that they should have sent a naval man, not a general, to command what was primarily a naval outpost. They replaced him with Desroches, a *chef d'escadre* (roughly, a rear-admiral).

It was too late. Poivre had become set in his ideas and the clash of cultures between the military and the civilian administrators continued unabated. Versailles lost patience and decided to recall both Poivre and Desroches, replacing them with Ternay and Dumesle. It was at this point that La Pérouse arrived, not as an official, but as a naval officer who soon became part of island society. Within days, he was being dragged aside and warned by various residents about the underlying turmoil that had been affecting the island for years. Forget Paris, forget Brest, forget Albi, he was told, this is a different world. In reality, it was not all that different. The social divisions were not quite the same, but the provincialism, the petty jealousies and the sly undermining went on there as anywhere else.

There were the administrators, divided between naval and civilian, but also with their own social layers: senior officers, juniors, merchant sailors, senior clerks, petty clerks. The locals, too, had their social differences. They might be merchants, wealthy and influential, or struggling plantation owners, exporters or mere tavern-keepers – Port-Louis boasted no fewer than 125 of them, a number Ternay promptly reduced to 30, also introducing other reforms such as a ban on Sunday drinking and gambling.

Then there were the slaves and their owners. The 1776 census gives a total of 25,154 black slaves, as against 6386 whites. Most slaves had come from Mozambique and Madagascar, a few from India. At times, they escaped, fleeing into the hills, where they struggled to survive, often attacking isolated settlements. The roads were inadequate enough as it was. The danger of runaway slaves, known as *marrons*, attacking a passing traveller made them worse. Ternay would try to flush them out, but the island suffered from a chronic shortage of horses, and sending reluctant foot soldiers into the high country was not really effective.

La Pérouse had been given new quarters in the *Belle-Poule* that were a little more comfortable than on the cramped voyage out, but in September, when the frigate was making ready to sail back to France, he was required to move over to a small transport vessel, the *Africaine*. This did not mean that he never stayed ashore. Locals invited him to spend a day or two with them, in or near Port-Louis. It gave them a chance to try to get him on their side in one or other of the ongoing quarrels. They explained their difficulties and their point of view, and he responded with his usual courteous sympathy. He was a serious man, a good observer of places and people, calm and not easily given to unwarranted bursts of enthusiasm. He listened, nodded and kept his views to himself.

He had been able to gauge the local situation from the first day, when he entered the church for the *Te Deum*. The officers had their ranks, which dictated their order of precedence in the procession. Even then, there was always a subtle distinction between the nobles, the true 'reds', and those who were closer to the lower or professional classes. When it came to the locals, however, the jostling, although not noisy, was quite evident. The members of the local council wanted to assert their precedence over the senior administrative and military staff. Wealthy plantation owners made sure that they were not seated behind traders or merchant captains. Hostile looks, and other forms of body language, made it clear that there were groupings and rivalries La Pérouse could not as yet understand – the silent struggle between the supporters of Poivre and those of Desroches, in particular, was hard to appreciate in the milling crowd. In the days that followed, other silent moves were made at receptions and dinners, as the locals worked to ingratiate themselves with Ternay and Maillard.

Invitations to country homes, however, were freer and happier occasions. The countryside was indeed a place of joy and relaxation. There were shady valleys, quiet streams suddenly turning into cascades of clear water, the chattering of birds, and the intense blue of the sky, so different from the mists of Brittany and the storms of the Atlantic. La Pérouse began to feel at home in such an enchanting place.

The *Africaine* provided La Pérouse with a chance to visit the nearby island of Madagascar. He served as second-in-command to Captain Du Chayla – Claude-Joseph, Vicomte du Chayla de Langlade de Saint-Paul, to give him his full, resounding name. The two men got on well. The hardworking storeship had suffered some damage during the cyclones that had struck the Isle de France a few months earlier, but she had now been adequately repaired. She was sent several times to the east coast of Madagascar to bring back urgently needed supplies of rice and beef.

The French had had their eye on Madagascar for quite some time. It was a large island, larger than France, not far off the east coast of Africa, not quite on the route to India and the East, but with distinct economic potential. One could even envisage a triangle, Isle de France-Madagascar-Pondicherry, a French port in India that could become a dominant feature in the Indian Ocean. Its inhabitants, however, were fiercely independent and quite averse to the French settling on their land. Versailles, anyhow, was not really anxious to acquire it. Time and again, officials reminded the enthusiasts that colonies were costly affairs, a constant drain on funds, however impressive they might look on a world map. The most the government was willing to do at the time was to establish a trading post and see what developed.

They were not too hopeful about it. There had been one attempt back in 1643 when the Frenchman Jacques Pronis had founded Port Dauphin, on the south-east coast. It proved a sad failure, although for a while France ruled a strip of coast and a small offshore island, and called it Eastern France. It lasted about ten years. The Malagasy attacked it and killed most of the settlers: just a few managed to escape to the Isle de Bourbon. In 1750, a similar venture on Isle Sainte-Marie fared no better. In 1768, the Comte de Maudave established a small settlement; it lasted a mere two years. It was far simpler, and less costly in money and men, to maintain friendly relations with the local chiefs and show them the benefits of mutual trade. Thus La Pérouse was able to walk ashore and greet the Malagasy, buying food supplies and even acting as a peacemaker between warring tribes: 'The Vicomte Du Chayla and I, in October 1772, managed to persuade Yavid to make peace, even though he was winning, by telling him that these were the wishes and instructions of Mr de Ternay'.[2]

Ternay was now settling in at Port-Louis – carefully, to ensure that his reforms did not upset the local population. He got on sufficiently well with Maillard Dumesle for an adequate collaboration to develop between them. They each had their own residence and their own quarters in town, with their own officials and servants. Ternay used the navy's offices in Port-Louis, but he spent most of his time at Le Réduit, eight kilometres out of town – two teams of four bearers carried him there in a palanquin, taking two hours to cover the distance.

A respectable-looking manor house, built in 1748 by a previous governor, it was set in a large wooded area between two tributaries of the Grande Rivière. It was comfortable and substantial enough for official dinners and the occasional garden fête. Ternay had taken over the furniture left behind by Desroches.

way to compete w/ Britain

More correctly, he had bought it, together with the cattle, poultry, the farm implements and the black slaves who worked the estate. It would remain the official residence of successive governors, including the British after they took over the island in 1810.

Maillard's headquarters were the Hôtel de l'Intendance in the centre of Port-Louis. Like his predecessor, however, he seized every opportunity to go to Mon Plaisir. Pierre Poivre had bought this country house in 1770 and spent every moment he could spare developing its already extensive gardens. It was a homely house, built of timber with a long verandah onto which opened a spacious drawing room and two bedrooms. But it was the estate that had delighted Poivre: a vast expanse of some 70 hectares, with an ornamental garden laid out in the symmetrical French style, a small lake, a vegetable garden and an aviary. There were spice plants from the East Indies, rose trees from China, cherry trees from Japan, tea shrubs, mango trees, coffee plants and breadfruit trees. Today the estate has become the famed botanical gardens of Mauritius.

Maillard, however, had come not to develop, but to retrench. The French government's instructions had been clear on this point, and just in case Ternay had not quite got the message the ministry had reduced the governor's salary from 80,000 to 50,000 *livres* a year. Maillard, whose own stipend had been proportionally reduced, was in no mood to give out grants or express much sympathy to those who soon crowded his waiting rooms, clamouring for financial subsidies or the payment of old debts.

One famous victim of Poivre's departure was Philibert Commerson, the naturalist of the Bougainville expedition. When the navigator reached the Isle de France on the final leg of his circumnavigation, Commerson had been left behind, by no means unwillingly, at the request of Poivre and possibly to the relief of Bougainville. He had carried out botanical surveys in Madagascar and Bourbon, which Poivre was pleased to get done, but now he had no money and no employment. He got short shrift from the new administrators. Maillard Dumesle was not about to embark on unauthorised spending. In October, he wrote to the Minister of Marine about his decision: 'I showed him a letter from the Duc de Praslin in which it is stated that it is the King's decision that he should return to France and that his salary should come to an end. I further explained to him that this expenditure was not included in the new list of outgoings for the colony.'[3]

Fair enough. Maillard was a public servant with orders to cut down on expenses. Ternay was prepared to help by finding him a passage home, but Commerson's health was not up to the long voyage. He had previously been living in quarters provided by Poivre, but Maillard was reorganising the property. He told Commerson he had no room for him and his large collections of plants, shells, fish and other items; nor could he carry on providing board and lodging for him, his servant Jeanne Baret and the two black slaves he had recently bought. The fact that Commerson's servant was a woman, and that she had sailed with him on Bougainville's expedition disguised as a man, shocked the rather strait-laced and humourless *indendant* who referred to Commerson as a libertine. No one else in Port-Louis was prepared to take him in, and put up with his collection and 'the kind of stench that rose out of his plants and all his fishes, unbearable for anyone who was not passionate about the natural sciences'.[4]

Commerson moved into a somewhat rundown house in the old quarter of Port-Louis, and wrote to De Boynes for help. Getting a reply took months. Commerson's health recovered for a time, and so did his spirits. Always given to sudden bursts of enthusiasm, he began to plan an institute of learning, a mixture of a university and a research centre. With nothing much else to do with his time, he filled pages with his elaborate plans and showed them to anyone who was prepared to listen.

La Pérouse encountered him briefly. Commerson was always eager to meet new arrivals from France, especially someone who was serious and well-educated. He talked at length about his voyage around the world with the Bougainville expedition and the places they had visited on the way, and brought out his plans for an academy on the island. La Pérouse was impressed by the naturalist's knowledge and slightly amused by his enthusiasm, which was nevertheless flavoured with a touch of realism. Commerson was aware that he was only dreaming up something to pass the time away, although he always harboured the hope that some day there would be a glorious Institut de l'Isle de France. 'When one is building castles in Spain,' he said, 'it doesn't cost anything to make them large and beautiful.'[5]

However, some of the locals warned La Pérouse about Commerson's close association with Pierre Poivre. It might not do to appear too closely involved with a friend and supporter of the former *intendant*. It was no way, they warned him, to ingratiate himself with Maillard Dumesle, and Poivre's former local enemies would certainly not go out of their way to help any friend of the naturalist. As it turned out, Commerson's health soon suffered a setback. He moved again, this time to a quiet spot on the west coast, where he died in March 1773. Maillard Dumesle, in a letter notifying the minister of his passing, revealed once again his soured opinion of the unfortunate naturalist: 'People assure me that Mr Commerson was very knowledgeable in the area of botany, but he enjoyed little public esteem and had few friends. He was reputed to be quite debauched and was considered to be a very ill-natured person, capable of the blackest ingratitude.'[6] The *intendant* had been irritated not merely by Commerson's repeated requests for assistance, but his insistence that he was entitled to public support as of right. Maillard was not a man who forgave easily.

There were other members of the Bougainville expedition for La Pérouse to meet. Charles de Romainville had been the cartographer on board the sister ship *Étoile*. A military engineer, he had been transferred to the local regiment when Bougainville left for home on the final leg of his voyage. He was a cheerful, able man who spread out some of his charts and sketches for La Pérouse to study. He outlined the track the expedition had followed and its considerable achievements.

The myth of Davis Land had been finally eliminated: Bougainville's ships had simply sailed right across the stretch of ocean where it was supposed to lie. This had been followed by numerous discoveries, small atolls rising out of the sea where nothing was supposed to exist, and great islands that now bore French names, such as Choiseul and Bougainville. And if the expedition had not discovered the mysterious Southern Continent, it had proved that eastern Australia, which James Cook had christened New South Wales, was defended by a fearsome barrier of coral islands and reefs.

Above all, there had been Tahiti. Commerson had waxed lyrical about the island. It was a true South Seas paradise, the abode of the Noble Savage untainted by civilisation. Romainville had a more balanced point of view than the excited naturalist. He told La Pérouse that they had not discovered Tahiti. Samuel Wallis had got there just before them, and he had taught the islanders to beware of the white man's guns. The Tahitians now also realised what white people came for – fresh food, fresh water and relaxation, which they believed meant women – so they came up with coconuts, revealed the location of streams and made sure that plenty of their girls made the visitors welcome. They had a more relaxed attitude to sex than Christians. Commerson was right there, but the married women could not be expected to behave in the same way. There were far more restrictions on life than anticipated. Tahiti was not the simple society it was at first believed to be.

La Pérouse knew about the debate over Tahiti that had arisen in France and indeed spread through Europe. Some of the *philosophes* had sided with Commerson's view, inspired by Jean-Jacques Rousseau's writings, that human beings had changed over time from happy, simple folk, sharing everything in common, and had become acquisitive, greedy, oppressive and war-like. Most realised that, if that were true, one could hardly restore society to its primitive state, with everyone becoming either a peasant or a hunter-gatherer; instead they looked forward to a future in which society could be reorganised into a co-operative and selfless state.

Romainville was more down-to-earth. The Tahitians had not shown Europeans a new way of life: they had merely reacted as anyone else would to a strange new situation. Anyone who travelled into hitherto unvisited parts of the world had to be careful of the natives. Wallis was the discoverer, so he was attacked. The French had found this in other places they discovered, such as the Island of Lepers in Espiritu Santo and in Choiseul. Romainville asked himself what would happen if a shipload of strangers landed on French shores and behaved as if they were going to settle there. The peasants and fishermen would soon band together and try to drive them away.

La Pérouse agreed at least partly with his views. He, too, was a realist by nature, but he was even more interested when Romainville pointed out to him areas that had not yet been explored. A dotted line here and there on his charts reflected his uncertainty about the lie of the land, and some of his coastlines looked too straight: were there not bays, inlets, offshore islands that only a careful survey could reveal – the kind of painstaking surveys La Pérouse had carried out around Brest?

Romainville was also able to tell La Pérouse about French India where he had recently served in the Pondicherry regiment. French trade there was still restricted, but the situation was relatively peaceful. They had another lengthy discussion when La Pérouse was about to sail there.

Other members of the Bougainville expedition had stayed behind: a couple of *pilotes*, Jean-François Oury and Charles Oger, and the astronomer Pierre Antoine Véron, who unfortunately had recently died following an expedition to the Philippines and the Moluccas that was one of Pierre Poivre's last attempts to obtain spice plants from the East Indies.

There were also plenty of locals prepared to gossip about recent expeditions to the Pacific. La Pérouse knew already about the voyages of James Cook, who had returned to England in 1771, as well as the expeditions of Byron, Wallis and Carteret. What he could now learn about was the background to recent French voyages, including that of Marc-Joseph Marion Dufresne, who had hoped to return a young Tahitian, Ahutoru, to his native land.

Bougainville had taken him on board when he called at Tahiti. He was an eager young man whose great wish was to see for himself the homeland of the strange white-skinned visitors. He had been a great success in Paris and Versailles, enjoying the fuss made of him, attending the opera and even being introduced to Louis XV. Sooner or later, however, he had to be sent back to his home. As a first step, he had been provided with a passage to the Isle de France.

That was easy enough. There were always merchant and naval ships sailing down to the Indian Ocean that could take him on as a passenger and he was able to embark for Port-Louis, arriving in October 1770, but getting him out to the Pacific Ocean was another matter. No one on the island had been quite sure what to do with him. Ahutoru knew Commerson, but the naturalist was away on one of his botanical expeditions and, being more often than not short of money, was not likely to accept responsibility for him. Pierre Poivre was more amenable. The Tahitian had been especially recommended to the local authorities by the Duchesse de Choiseul, and Bougainville had made some provision for his sustenance – but there was little Poivre could do until a South Seas expedition could be organised.

Eventually, a deal was struck between Marion Dufresne, a man with considerable naval experience and a local landowner, and the administration. Dufresne was keen to lead his own expedition, hoping to combine exploration with commercial aims. With some help from the local administration, he could finance a voyage, earn the gratitude of the government and acquire fame. Ahutoru sailed with him in October 1771. Unhappily, he had contacted smallpox and he died shortly after his departure. Marion Dufresne carried on regardless – too much had already been spent to simply give up and go home. He made some discoveries in the southern Indian Ocean, not particularly promising from an economic point of view, but geographically valuable. He then continued on to Tasmania, and crossed to New Zealand, where he was killed with a number of his officers and men.

News of this event had not yet percolated back to Port-Louis. Nevertheless, the expedition, with two ships and strong local backing, was a matter of frequent discussion. The exploration of the Pacific by the French had now begun in earnest, and the Isle de France was becoming an important point of departure. Tahiti seemed to offer the possibility of a French outpost or even a naval base in the central Pacific.

Bougainville had sailed in the opposite direction to Marion Dufresne, but the last lap of his circumnavigation had brought him to Port-Louis. At much the same time, in 1769, another French would-be explorer and someone well known in the island, Jean-François de Surville, had gone from Port-Louis to Pondicherry and from there had begun a voyage of discovery in the Pacific. He had been in New Zealand at much the same time as James Cook, and from there he had set out to look for new islands, including Tahiti, which, somewhat confusingly, he seems to have identified as Davis Land. Like Marion Dufresne's, this expedition ended in its leader's death. But now there was yet another voyage under way, again with the Isle de France as its pivotal point: that of Yves-Joseph de Kerguelen-Tremarec.

This was certainly a major topic of conversation among the residents. They were divided between enthusiasts and doubters, because Kerguelen, on a first voyage, had claimed that he had discovered a large and attractive land far to the south of the Isle de France, a region which a fair number of locals were certain was much too cold to be of any interest to anyone. Others, pointing to Bougainville's recent settlement on the Falklands, did not see this as an obstacle to development and felt confident that a French outpost to the south, with an adequate number of colonists, farmers and whale hunters, would greatly increase the prosperity and importance of Port-Louis.

Kerguelen was an officer in his mid-thirties. He had considerable experience of the sea and, like most others after the end of the Seven Years War, had been looking for some appointment that would ensure his promotion. While visiting England in 1767, he noted that country's growing interest in the Pacific, and on his return to France he found that Bougainville had been entrusted with an important mission to the Pacific. Could he not also lead an expedition, to fly the French flag across waters that would otherwise be taken over by the British?

He did not know a great deal about the South Seas, and does not even seem to have read Charles de Brosses' important *Histoire des navigations aux terres australes*. He decided to consult a leading geographer, D'Après de Mannevillette, who suggested that the South Indian Ocean might be a more rewarding area to explore than the Pacific. The knowledgeable D'Après showed Kerguelen that a number of blank spaces still remained on the map of the world. The long-held belief in a great southern continent had been eroded in recent years by the voyages of Surville, Bougainville and Cook, each of whom had sailed across blank areas of the Pacific where earlier geographers thought this land might be. Even as early as 1642, Abel Tasman had rounded the south of Australia, gone on to New Zealand and north to Tonga, finding no indication of any continent. So it was not a question of searching again for what most geographers were now convinced was a mere chimera.

The southern waters of the Indian Ocean were another matter. As yet no one had ventured down there, apart from one Bouvet de Lozier, who had sailed on behalf of the French India Company back in 1738. Venturing far to the south, he found himself faced by 'an iceberg of enormous size, then a succession of smaller ones like so many floating islands'. But then, on 1 January 1739, a steep snow-covered peak, with land behind it, rose out of the mist. He named it Cape Circumcision, this being the day on which the church celebrated the feast of Christ's circumcision. He soon found himself again faced by icebergs, and then a heavy, cold fog came down. When it cleared after a few days, he thought he could still see land, although he began to have doubts: it looked more like a cloud bank. Everything was soon blanked out by more fog, a growing number of his crew had become affected by scurvy – 'or pretended to be' – and he decided to give up.[7]

He felt optimistic that he had discovered some land in the deep south and urged the directors of the company to finance a new voyage. He dangled before them the usual attractions unknown lands were believed to have – pearls, gold, even spices and slaves. He stressed that this could also open a new sea route. His report on the climate, however, made all this improbable. The company could see no benefit from any further search and they dropped the whole idea.[8]

D'Après told Kerguelen of an earlier discovery made by Binot Paulmier de Gonneville in January 1504. Trying to round the Cape of Good Hope, Gonneville had been driven off course by a wild storm and ended up on a pleasant shore, where the natives welcomed him. He had even taken on board a young chief, Essomeric, together with his servant, and brought them back to Normandy. No one was quite sure where this land, which became known as Gonneville Land, actually was, but it was widely believed to lie somewhere to the south of the Cape. Others thought it might be Madagascar; some even suggested Australia or New Zealand. A descendant of Essomeric, a churchman, had even petitioned the Pope for an expedition to Christianise his people.

Kerguelen saw there were possibilities in a programme that included a search for Gonneville Land and for whatever might be hidden around Lozier's Cape Circumcision. This vast area had at least been visited by French navigators over the centuries, and France would have a strong claim to whatever he discovered there. The French government accepted Kerguelen's proposal, and gave him the *Berryer* and enough supplies for fourteen months. When Kerguelen reached the Isle de France in May 1771, Pierre Poivre offered him two smaller ships in exchange for the large *Berryer*, as they would be easier to handle off an unknown coast and among uncharted islands. He had to wait until the southern summer before he could venture into colder latitudes, and sailed due south from Port-Louis in mid-January 1772.

He was back two months later with great news. He had discovered a new land, cold but with great potential. True, his consort, the *Gros Ventre* commanded by Louis Alesno de Saint-Alouarn, had disappeared, but this little setback was swept aside. Separated by fog and a storm from Kerguelen's ship, he suggested, Saint-Alouarn had probably stayed behind to continue the survey. Of course, something more tragic might have happened but, agreed the residents of Port-Louis, it was a risk all explorers took and many ships had vanished in distant seas over the centuries. What was important was to report the discovery as soon as possible to Versailles and organise a proper colonising expedition.

Kerguelen's enthusiasm was catching. The governor, Desroches, wrote to the minister that the land that had been discovered 'is intersected by woods and greenery, which indicates a country that is inhabited and carefully cultivated'. That it was fogbound and what could be seen of it looked bleak and barren was not mentioned. Pierre Poivre was even more enthusiastic in his report: 'Mr de Kerguelen has discovered for France, in the space of two months, a new world'.[9] In this, they echoed what Kerguelen himself was writing to the minister: 'I have had the good fortune to discover the southern continent', and telling his adviser D'Après de Mannevillette that all his hopes were now being realised because he had discovered 'Southern France', and that what he had had time to see was only at the centre of a mighty continental gulf. Kerguelen hurried back to France, where he was at once promoted and given the Cross of Saint Louis. One could hardly do less for a man who was presenting his country with a whole new continent.

He would have to return without delay and establish a proper settlement before another European power, undoubtedly Britain, tried to muscle in. He had already drawn up a plan, which the minister speedily accepted. What else could he do when faced with the glowing claims Kerguelen and his supporters were making? Kerguelen assured the minister that his proposal was financially sound: 'Before six years have passed, I am sure that it will repay with interest the services that will have been rendered to it and that, far from needing the assistance of our islands, it will begin to give in its turn a great deal of assistance, enrich their trade, and finally become their metropolis'.[10]

His enthusiasm ensured that he was given the leadership of the proposed expedition. However, some of the leading geographers and scientists began to express doubts. It all sounded too good to be true. The climate of Southern France, down in the colder latitudes, seemed hardly likely to be as suited for agriculture and trade as Kerguelen claimed. Bougainville had managed to build a small township and settle a small number of hardy French Canadians down in the Falklands, but the climate there was pretty harsh – and Kerguelen's land was even closer to the frozen Antarctic. Had Lozier not come upon icebergs? And had Kerguelen not mentioned heavy fogs in which he had lost sight of Saint-Alouarn's ship?

The plan as submitted was scaled down, in line with the natural caution of politicians and the tight financial situation of the kingdom, but Kerguelen did sail with two ships in March 1773. By then, however, the residents of the Isle de France had been shaken by the return of Saint-Alouarn's *Gros Ventre* and the news she brought back. No one had seen anything like a southern continent, and the sailors guffawed when they were told about the attractions and potential of 'Southern France'. It was a wretched windswept place they never wanted to see again.

So, whenever he spoke of exploration, La Pérouse found himself in the middle of countless arguments about Kerguelen's land and the location of a southern continent. He realised that these created yet more groupings in the complex web of local society – those who held on to their beliefs about Gonneville Land and Bouvet de Lozier's Cape Circumcision and those who dismissed Kerguelen as a fraud. His followers defended him as an overenthusiastic navigator who had returned too soon to find out what the deep south really concealed, but who would soon put everything right when he went back on a second voyage. But their number was dwindling. A growing majority felt that there was little of any value in the south – the future lay in the east. That was where the Dutch had time and again come upon a large expanse of land they called New Holland. And in fact Saint-Alouarn, in accordance with the original plan of the voyage, had sailed east, reached Cape Leeuwin and the island of Dirk Hartog in what is Western Australia. He had seen Aborigines and the dog-like dingo, taken some turtles and even buried a bottle claiming possession of the land in the name of France.

This was where Bougainville and Cook, sailing west across the Pacific Ocean, had discovered the Great Barrier Reef, and the English navigator had surveyed the land behind it, naming it New South Wales. Further south, both Abel Tasman and Marion Dufresne had been to Tasmania or, as it was then called, Van Diemen Land. So maybe, as Surville, Cook and others had now shown, there was no vast southern continent in the Pacific Ocean, but there were opportunities aplenty for further discoveries, including the mystery of New Holland itself. Was it a great island continent, possibly *the* continent so many had speculated about? Or did it consist of several large islands, some in the east, like Cook's New South Wales, some in the west, so recently visited by Saint-Alouarn, with a wide sea separating the two?

The enthusiasts, taking La Pérouse aside – and indeed any other new arrival who was prepared to listen – saw great possibilities for trade and settlements in the western part of this vast New Holland. The Dutch had never been really interested in it, but now that Saint-Alouarn had claimed it for France, a base should be established there. The triangle Mauritius-Pondicherry-Hartog Land would strengthen France's position in the Indian Ocean and create totally new trade routes.

La Pérouse became fascinated by the account of this voyage and his interest developed even more when he realised that the man who had recently claimed Dirk Hartog Land for France had links with Albi. It was Jean-Baptiste Mengaud de la Hage, the brother of his schoolfellow Charles Mengaud, who had stepped ashore and buried the bottle containing the all-important document.

There was so much to talk about, so much that was fascinating and enticing about the eastern seas and the vast ocean that lay beyond. However, dreams of exploration had to remain just that. All he was, La Pérouse had to remind himself, was an *enseigne* ferrying supplies from Madagascar to the Isle de France, much as he had done between Bayonne and Brest. He found this work interesting to begin with, but soon began to wonder what the future might hold in store for him. Fortunately, Ternay had not forgotten him. Early in 1773, he told La Pérouse that he had a new position for him. He would at last be given command of his own ship.

7. SERVICE IN INDIAN WATERS

April 1773–April 1774

THE *SEINE*, WHICH La Pérouse took over on 21 April 1773, was a solid ship of 700 tonnes, carrying 30 guns, with a complement of 110 officers and men. His quarters, although not spacious, were better than anything he had had as a mere officer. He could proudly head up his brand-new *Journal de la flûte du Roy la Seine* and add the words 'under the command of Mr de la Pérouse, *enseigne* of the King's ships'.[1] His orders were to sail to India, or at least to what remained of the French Indian empire: the ports of Mahé on the west coast, near Calicut, of Pondicherry, Karikal and Yanaon on the east coast, and Chandernagore, a short distance upriver from Calcutta.

First, he had to collect supplies from the island of Bourbon, since the Isle de France had still not completely recovered from the devastating cyclone of the previous year. He sailed from Port-Louis on 18 May and reached Bourbon without incident. It was a pleasant small island, only too happy to sell its surpluses to its larger and often domineering neighbour. Life there was usually quiet and peaceful, the few settlers – they had only begun to arrive in 1762 – developing gardens and sugar plantations, inevitably with the help of imported black slaves.

After a stay of four or five days, La Pérouse continued on to the Seychelles, a group of small islands north-east of Madagascar. Visited by the Portuguese in the sixteenth century, they had remained unclaimed and uninhabited until Mahé de la Bourdonnais, the administrator of the Isle de France, decided that they could form part of the French possessions in the Indian Ocean. They were at first referred to as the Bourdonnais Islands, a name soon changed to Seychelles. The name Mahé for one of the islands and of Praslin for another honoured both La Bourdonnais and the Minister of Marine, the Duc de Choiseul-Praslin. Impressive though these names sounded, the islands remained of little value, and recently had been more trouble than they were worth. They were in fact in a state that was pretty close to anarchy.

It was La Pérouse's task to bring some order to the tiny settlements. This required a mixture of tact and firmness. 'I trust you to settle the difficulties that seem to be besetting the Seychelles,' Ternay told La Pérouse. 'There is no provision in any budget for their upkeep or development. It is up to the colonists to work a soil that they tell me is fertile.' In other words, he knew very little about them and hoped La Pérouse would take that particular burden off his shoulders.

La Pérouse wrote to his father and to La Jonquière expressing his happiness and gratitude at being, not just in command of his own ship, but sent out on a voyage that included some exploration and some political or administrative duties. Admittedly, it did include carrying back some commercial cargo from India to Port-Louis, but this voyage gave him far greater status than anything he had done previously.

Even getting there required skill. The charts were at the best sketchy, and even D'Après de Mannevillette, though a skilled hydrographer and author of the greatly admired *Neptune Oriental*, was not too sure of their correct position. They were scattered over an area of 390 square kilometres, and they were seldom visited. La Pérouse would have to do his best to find his way there. Fortunately, he could talk to a number of acquaintances in Port-Louis, put together what knowledge they had and set off with a fair measure of confidence.

He had no chronometer to help him. The Englishman John Harrison had finally developed one that would work at sea and in the tropics, but it was not yet readily available and certainly not to middle-range officers in the French navy. La Pérouse had to rely on observations of the sun and the usual signs of land and currents used by captains of his day: floating branches or fruit, the flight of birds and the type of bottom – sandy, muddy, rocky or out of reach of the sounding line. He sailed slowly and cautiously, using his intuition to allow for currents and winds. When he finally did sight Frigate Island, the most easterly of the group, and compared his estimated position with the chart, he found that he had a difference from his estimated longitude of some 240 kilometres.

'It was something all navigators in this region can expect,' he commented. 'The charts are very inadequate, and to make up his chart, Monsieur D'Après was forced to rely on old Portuguese and Dutch maps, drawn in days when the instruments the navigators had were quite unsatisfactory.' It had not been an easy navigation, but it was incident-free. As the French admiral Maurice de Brossard wrote many years later in his biography of La Pérouse, 'One can only admire his shrewdness and his intuition.'[2]

He now made for the largest island in the group, Mahé. It had been granted as a concession to a resident of the Isle de France, Brayet, who sensibly had remained in Port-Louis, sending one Anselme to run it. Before the *Seine* had even moored outside the tiny settlement, a canoe came up with a settler named Silord, who pleaded urgently with La Pérouse to remove Anselme. 'There were problems indeed among these unfortunate people. I told them that I had come to bring them peace.'

The unfortunate people in question consisted of about twenty whites and a number of black slaves. The whites had split into at least three groups. A few sided with Anselme, who was cowering in a leaky hut, terrified by the threats being made by the dissidents. Others, rather more numerous, formed the Silord faction, and in addition there was an oddball priest named Montagnier 'who had alienated everyone'.

Not surprisingly, the settlement had made no progress. A few hectares had been cleared, but they were now overgrown with weeds. Rats were feasting on the stocks of maize that remained and scurrying around in the few wretched huts the settlers had managed to put together. 'Everyone is begging to be allowed back to the Isle de France.'

La Pérouse adopted a policy of firmness mixed with compassion. He had a ship's boy whipped for having threatened to kill Anselme, and he told the others that their complaints about Brayet not paying them were unwarranted, as they had done so little work. He told them that Anselme was no longer to be regarded as Brayet's agent, but as Ternay's direct representative. He then gave them a modest supply of food and equipment. More important, he took away with him Silord and his wife, as well as Father Montagnier and his black servant, with whom he had been cohabiting for several months, and a half-dozen troublemakers, men and women, who had done no work. He had to take steps to make sure these squabblers did not start fighting among themselves once they were on board the *Seine*. A mixture of threats and promises achieved adequate peace, and he sailed to the nearby settlement on Sainte-Anne, which· was far more successful. There the situation was calm, the crops had succeeded and there had been none of the famine the settlers at Mahé had complained about.

There were even a few spice plants, the result of Pierre Poivre's attempt to develop a plantation away from prying eyes. La Pérouse counted six nutmeg trees and one clove tree. 'The best of these shrubs is only about a foot high. If ever the Dutch try to carry away this treasure, they will need no more than a small dinghy ... Yet, their owner, Mr Gillot, is like one of these monks who show you some relic and are convinced that all the wealth that exists on earth is not worth as much as an old piece of the robe of their holy saint.'[3] Still, it was a start.

Poivre's hopes were gradually fulfilled. A spice trade of sorts did develop – until 1778 when a ship appeared, flying the British flag. Rather than let their precious plants fall into British hands, the settlers set them on fire. Unfortunately, it was a French ship that had hoisted the Union Jack. Its captain was worried that the British might have taken over, and he felt it wiser to approach as a friendly vessel and check out the situation. Flying false colours was a common trick in earlier days, but it often had unexpected consequences. Unmentionable words were exchanged, but it was too late: the spices had gone up in smoke. Today, the only spice of any importance grown locally is cinnamon.

La Pérouse loaded the *Seine* with sea turtles and coconuts, and on 26 June he sailed on for India. He could feel satisfied with his mission. The Seychelles had so recently been settled that teething troubles were unavoidable. Once things settled down, they could look forward to a peaceful and reasonably prosperous future.

The route to India involved careful navigation. From the Seychelles cautious manoeuvring was required to enter the famous Nine Degree Channel between the Maldives and the Amindivi Islands and reach the Malabar coast. The sea was rough and there were frequent fogs. La Pérouse knew how important it was to identify and avoid the small islands that make up a defensive and dangerous chain off the southern coast of India. It took time, but finally, on 9 July, 'the fog having cleared, we saw quite clearly the coast of Malabar'. He was bound for Pondicherry on the eastern side, and all he now needed to do was to follow the coast towards the south, make his landfall on Sri Lanka, round it and then veer north. He reached Pondicherry without difficulty on 21 July.

The port had been captured by the British in 1761 and practically destroyed. It was a symbol of the collapse of French dreams in India. A mere twenty years earlier, France had been a power to be reckoned with on the subcontinent – which meant that it was also a menace to British aspirations. The great Joseph Dupleix had skilfully capitalised on the fears of the powerful Indian rajahs threatened by the steady advance of British power. When the War of the Austrian Succession broke out in 1740, pitting Britain and France against each other, the struggle had its repercussions in faraway India as Dupleix seized every opportunity to build up an anti-British alliance, manoeuvring, cajoling, bribing, conquering when needed, until he controlled a vast stretch of territory from central India to the southern tip. Even Madras fell to the French in 1746. Dupleix's empire, however, was a house of cards, held together by his personality and his experience of Indian politics. It eventually collapsed before the superior generalship and greater resources of Robert Clive. When peace was signed in 1748, France's hold on the country was drastically reduced.

War broke out again in 1756. The remaining French possessions were once more at the mercy of the British. Supplies from Mauritius, and even coastal communication between the French ports, depended on the command of the sea, which the French did not have. They were lucky that, under the terms of the peace treaty, they were allowed to keep five ports and a few minor trading outposts. French agents still travelled to the courts of friendly rajahs, trade gradually recovered and Pondicherry was rebuilt, but the whole of India was slowly and inexorably sliding into what was to become the British Empire.

The French India Company had been practically bankrupted as a result of the war and the unremitting suspicion with which the British regarded any activity by the French. However, its British counterpart, the East India Company, was not having it all its own way. It had an uneasy relationship with the government back in London, and needed to juggle the interests of its shareholders with the expectation of the ministries that, now that the war had ended, administrative and military costs would be reduced. It also had to be wary of the local princes who, admittedly under British supervision, retained their rights as rulers.

Then Haydar Ali of Mysore rebelled and invaded the Carnatic, threatening even Madras. Any hopes of reducing military expenditure vanished. A famine in Bengal in 1770 and 1772 caused the deaths of an estimated one-sixth of the entire population. The East India Company's income was slashed; its shares slumped dramatically on the London stock market; unrest began to spread among the princes. The company, compelled by circumstances to turn into a military power, something London had long been uneasy about, appealed for financial help. The British government's reaction to these ongoing problems, apart from agreeing to an emergency loan of just over £1.5 million, was to pass the Regulating Act, which provided for the appointment of a governor-general with extensive powers. It represented the first step towards taking over the entire administration. This was the state of affairs when La Pérouse landed in Pondicherry. His main mission was to show the flag in these troubled waters and offer any help the French governors in each port might require.

Pondicherry was administered by an able and determined man, Jean Law de Lauriston. He was the nephew of a more famous – or, in the view of many, infamous – John Law, who had tried to introduce the idea of state banking and a state trading monopoly to shore up France's ever-tottering finances. It was a slightly different version of a scheme introduced in Britain by the Earl of Hartley back in 1711 to take over the national debt and gradually pay it off through import duties and trade monopolies in South America and the South Seas. This seemed to work so well and promised so much that public enthusiasm lifted the price of shares to dizzying heights. Profit-taking by some of the shrewder investors then followed, causing a rapid fall in share prices. The pricking of what became known as the South Sea Bubble ruined thousands in the process. To their cost, the British had discovered the cycle of stock exchange boom and bust.

In keeping with the axiom that people never learn from their mistakes, the French had followed suit. John Law, the son of an Edinburgh jeweller, was the driving force behind the idea of a state bank that would be backed by trading monopolies in Africa, America – notably in Louisiana – and the East. Law had been forced to flee England, not for any financial misdeeds but because of a duel in which his opponent was killed. He was charming, intelligent and persuasive. It took some time for his theories to be accepted by French ministers, but in 1716 he managed to get permission to open a bank.

A year later, he founded a *Compagnie d'Occident*, and in 1718 Law's bank became the royal bank. He then merged his company with others – the *Compagnie des Indes Orientales,* the *Compagnie de la Chine* and the *Compagnie d'Afrique* – creating one great *Compagnie des Indes*. In 1720, he was named Minister of Finance. Profits soared. Granted a monopoly on the tobacco trade, plus the right to collect duties and other taxes, as well as to issue banknotes and the broad control of trade in India and many other territories outside France, the new company seemed sure to flourish. Investors rushed to buy whatever stocks and shares they could, queuing outside the bank's offices, jostling in the streets, trampling over nearby gardens, until the guards had to be called.

Prices soared and stories of sudden wealth raced around Paris. A priest was said to have made 18 millions *livres*; a waiter even more; a chimney sweep 40 million; a street beggar, investing the generous alms joyful investors had given him, bought some stock, resold it and made 70 million. As the writer Montesquieu commented, 'Even God does not cause men to rise that swiftly out of nothing.'[4]

A dividend of 40 per cent was announced, causing great rejoicing – until people realised that this would be paid on the nominal capital, not on the inflated prices they had paid for their shares. Their investment would bring them only 3 or 4 per cent. It was wiser to sell out and make a capital gain. Once investors began to sell, the prices collapsed and panic ensued. The French bubble had burst. Many were ruined; a few had got out in time and made money. Tradition has it that a hunchback had made a small fortune by offering his hump as a desk for traders to sign documents, and wisely turned the tips he received into gold coins instead of paper money.

Law was forced into exile and eventually died in poverty in Venice, but members of his family were not ostracised and in time were forgiven. The nephew had risen to a combined position of administrator and entrepreneur, and had transformed Pondicherry, once again, into a promising French outpost. He welcomed La Pérouse, quickly brought him up to date on the situation in British India, and outlined the help he required from him in the coming weeks. For his part, La Pérouse landed his motley group of Seychelles troublemakers.

This done, he was able to rest a while, 'waiting for the bad season to come to an end in Bengal before continuing on my way north.'[5] There were several other French ships at anchor in the port, and three more arrived a little later from Europe. He was able to renew old acquaintances and get up-to-date news from France. Law, for his part, was eager to discuss the exploration of the Pacific, in which he had been recently involved as one of the promoters of the expedition of Surville's *Saint-Jean-Baptiste*.

Jean-François de Surville was a former captain of the French India Company who, like others in his situation, was planning to trade on his own account in eastern waters. When garbled news was received of a large and rich island discovered by the British in the central Pacific, which sounded like the fabled Davis Land emerging at last from the unknown, he decided to sail for it as soon as possible in order to prevent a possible British takeover. Law and his counterpart in Chandernagore, Jean-Baptiste Chevalier, agreed to back Surville and provide him with all the supplies he might need, including goods for trading with the islanders.

The Abbé Alexis Rochon, who wrote a fascinating book on his travels in the Indian Ocean, reveals the excitement that gripped Pondicherry at the time of Surville's departure: 'I was in Pondicherry in August 1769 when the rumour spread that an English vessel had found in the South Seas a very rich island where, among other peculiarities, a colony of Jews had been settled.'[6] It was nothing more than Tahiti, discovered by Samuel Wallis in 1768 and by Bougainville not long after. The name 'Wallis' had soon been transmuted into 'Davis', which led to the belief that Davis Land had been at last discovered.

Surville's bold venture ended in disaster, but Law was not too dismayed. There was still a great deal to be discovered and clarified in the great Pacific Ocean. If only France could establish a base on some island there, it would provide a foothold for further trade, especially – and this was the grand plan Law and Chevalier were cherishing – if Spain, a French ally, allowed traders to come and go in the Philippines and from there to China. A trading route from Port-Louis to French India, China, the Philippines and the Pacific held out great promise. One could almost hear echoes of the grandiose plans Law's uncle had in mind when he founded the *Compagnie des Indes*.

By August, the monsoon was abating sufficiently in Bengal for La Pérouse to leave. He sailed from Pondicherry on 27 August, sailed slowly north, flying the French colours as close to the shore as was advisable, and reached the mouth of the Hooghly at the beginning of September.

The British at Calcutta, who had been busy developing into a thriving port the villages they had bought from the Moghul emperor in 1698, kept a wary eye on the movements of any foreign ships. It was only fifteen years since Clive had recaptured Calcutta from the Nawab of Bengal, sadly too late to rescue the unfortunate prisoners held in the infamous Black Hole. Suspicion and mistrust were still rife. Any ship that sailed up to the Hooghly estuary had to wait for a pilot, long enough for a messenger to race up to Calcutta to advise the authorities. By the time La Pérouse approached the port, the British would know all about him.

The pilot certainly did not hurry. La Pérouse had to learn Eastern patience. 'At night, we set up lights and fired our guns.' No one seemed to take any notice. Two days went by with nothing to do but wait. Eventually, the pilot appeared and then began a slow struggle up the river towards the French settlement.

It took nine days. Nothing could be done to speed up the progress of the *Seine*, and it was not safe to try either – guided by the pilot, the ship manoeuvred her way through an unfamiliar world of muddy water, half-drowned islands, settlements built precariously over the river and a repulsive flotsam of decaying vegetation, dead animals and, occasionally, dead humans, bobbing their way downriver to the bay. As they moved away from the estuary area, they went past more prosperous villages, surrounded by extensive ricefields. La Pérouse checked the names against his chart: Raipur, Ulubaria, Nangi and Calcutta, with its now rebuilt and greatly strengthened Fort William.

Following the reorganisation of the British administration, Calcutta had become the capital of their Indian possessions. In just 75 years, the villages had coalesced into a busy city of half a million people, almost equal to the population of Paris, and growing by the day. The contrast with the nearby European settlements was striking. The Danes had a post at Serampore, just north of the city, but it was in ruins. The Dutch had theirs at Hooghly-Chinsura, a trading settlement, with a garrison of 150 soldiers, but it too was doomed. The Portuguese had once had a trading station at Bandal, but it was now abandoned. Only Chandernagore (Chandannagar, as it is known today) was reviving, thanks to the energy of Chevalier, though the recent peace terms under which the French had been allowed to stay, restricted its jurisdiction to an area contained within a periphery of no more than 16 kilometres. The boundary could be marked by a ditch – not a moat, just a shallow ditch and not more than 6 metres across. The garrison was limited to 200 sepoy soldiers and 20 European officers and NCOs.

Chevalier had argued that more ditches needed to be dug, not for military purposes, but for irrigation. The water should not be stagnant, useless except for breeding mosquitoes, but clear and running. This led to endless bickering and arguments with both the East India Company and the British administration, but Chevalier had a nose for intrigue, and he had gained enough concessions to maintain Chandernagore as an effective port. The French government gave him just enough money to run a modest office with a small staff. The same rule applied to Law, down in Pondicherry, but they were both resourceful men who soon found ways of increasing their budgets. First, they used some of their own money as seeding capital, engaging in private trading ventures. The profits from these operations were then used to repair and build up their city – with something left over for themselves.

Versailles neither encouraged nor discouraged private ventures. The Minister of Marine, whose area of responsibility included the colonies, simply shut his eyes to what was a sensible solution to a constant shortage of money. The only, unwritten, condition was avoiding excesses that might create a scandal. Any administrator who indulged in shady or corrupt practices was promptly disowned. And any losses that might be incurred were borne by the administrator. This was the case with Surville's *Saint-Jean-Baptiste* expedition: the administration helped with the preparations, as well as some advice and equipment, but Chevalier, Law and other investors carried the costs and shouldered the losses.

Able men like Chevalier and Law ran their little kingdoms with consummate skill. The profits far outweighed the losses, there were no scandals and rebuilding and expansion proceeded apace. La Pérouse soon learnt to appreciate Chevalier's talents and endless energy. Changernagore was now a viable port, sending ships out to the Near East and to China, and back to the Isle de France and Europe. Like others, Chevalier had his eyes on the vastly profitable spice trade, but the Dutch still jealously guarded their Indonesian empire against all outsiders.

He maintained close links with minor 'factories' or trading posts throughout India. The main one was at Kazimbazar, the centre of the silk trade; there were others at Patna in Bihar province, at Joudhia in the east and at Balasore in the west, each manned by a single French agent. Law had his own small network, and Chevalier hoped that others could be developed from the small French ports of Mahé and Yanaon. He showed La Pérouse his map of India and pointed out how a web of French trading posts could in time stretch across the entire subcontinent.

The British authorities thought along the same lines, and they were determined to make sure that the vision of Chevalier and Law was not realised. As soon as war broke out, in 1778, they marched against all the French-held ports and seized them. They would give them back in 1783, but retake them in 1793. Only when they were satisfied that the French had learnt their lesson – that the ports were to be no more than trading posts and keep within their boundaries – did they finally hand them back.

For the present, however, the mood in Chandernagore was one of optimism and active trading. Chevalier sent goods on board the *Seine* – 'a cargo of comestibles to be taken to the Isle de France as freight on behalf of private traders', as he reported to the minister.[7] When his visit came to an end, La Pérouse sailed slowly down the Hooghly, accompanied by another armed storeship, the *Étoile*, recently arrived from Lorient and Port-Louis, commanded by Trobriand. Their activities aroused the suspicions of the British, who sent armed soldiers in a small boat to investigate. Trobriand shouted down at them that the first Englishman who stepped on board would be thrown back into the sea. Wisely, the British sailors rowed clear of the French ships, but remained at a distance, watching them.

La Pérouse and Trobriand had expected them. Reports had been received while they were in Chandernagore that British vessels were stationed at the estuary to check on all river traffic, and that they planned to search all foreign vessels leaving the Hooghly. As they approached the Bay of Bengal, they came across several British warships, each with officers on deck, spyglasses trained on the two French vessels. Their purpose, though, seemed to be limited to close surveillance, which was just as well: La Pérouse and Trobriand had no intention of submitting to any search. These were their king's ships and no foreign nation had the right to interfere.

'I must confess, My Lord,' wrote Trobriand to the minister, 'that personally I would have been quite happy if they had started anything. I would have been helped by Mr de la Pérouze [*sic*], commanding the *Seine*, in whom I have the greatest confidence. We would have repelled force with force, and earned your gratitude and the King's favour.'[8] Having left Chandernagore in mid-December 1773, La Pérouse sailed down to the small French outpost at Masulipatnam and on to Pondicherry, where he dropped anchor on 17 January.

Law welcomed him, not just for the goods he brought, but out of a genuine sense of friendship. The two men had got on extremely well during the *Seine*'s earlier visit, and Law enjoyed discussing his ideas for Pacific exploration. La Pérouse had a long interest in the history of early voyages and was well up-to-date with the more recent expeditions. There was a great deal still to be done, and both men shared the view that France had to take a part in the work. Thus, La Pérouse's growing interest in voyages of exploration and the great potential of the Pacific was constantly being kept alive. The link he established with Jean Law was a lasting one.

The *Seine* left for the Isle de France on 3 February. La Pérouse had decided to sail south-east to avoid Sri Lanka, but once out in the open sea the old problem of unreliable charts, westerly currents and the remnants of the monsoon created uncertainty. Bird flights, anxiously watched throughout each day, seemed to be warning that land might not be too far away: 'We saw several birds of a type that does not stray far from land, and throughout the night we heard the cries of sea-swallows'. Was there an island close by? He began to suspect that he had developed an appreciable difference in longitude. There was an archipelago, the Chagos, somewhere ahead. It had to be avoided at all costs, though a distant sight of it would have helped to check the *Seine's* position. However, as La Pérouse recorded in his journal, 'Our horizon barely extends beyond a half mile.'[9] A growing sense of unease began to spread through the ship.

Finally, he came upon the island of Rodriguez, a lonely landmark, but a useful one because it told him it was time to veer west, and also because his men, greatly relieved that they had reached an area most of them knew well, were able to collect a few turtles. On 24 March 1774, the *Seine* dropped anchor in Port-Louis. She had been away from the Isle de France for ten months. It was time to renew old acquaintances and catch up with developments on the island. Nothing much had changed, except that Ternay and Maillard seemed at last to have restored confidence among the residents. The only problem was the constant shortage of funds.

There were no plans for any further voyages of exploration. People spoke with sorrow of the Marion Dufresne expedition, which had come to a tragic end, with heavy loss of life. The commander had been killed in New Zealand with a number of his officers and men; the financial losses exceeded 400,000 *livres*. Marion's land, furniture and slaves had all been auctioned off. Ternay was now arranging the sale of two substantial houses that Marion Dufresne had owned in Port-Louis. The total proceeds of all this were still not enough to clear the debts, and Dufresne's family was eventually declared bankrupt.

The Kerguelen expedition had fared no better. He had arrived at Port-Louis without the supplies he was supposed to bring from the Cape. This omission had greatly angered Maillard, but Kerguelen was more concerned about his voyage to 'Southern France' than about the Isle de France's food problems. He sharply dismissed Maillard's complaints, saying there were more important matters to worry about. This was no way to earn either the governor or the *intendant's* co-operation. Within a few weeks the two men were no longer on speaking terms. Ternay found himself forced to intervene, as Versailles would expect the local authorities to assist Kerguelen. He reluctantly supplied him with a small corvette, the *Dauphine*, to add to his *Rolland* and *Oiseau*. Kerguelen then sailed for the land he claimed to have discovered in February 1772. Most of the residents of Port-Louis now shrugged their shoulders when anyone mentioned this so-called discovery. His 'new land' or 'new continent' was nothing of the kind. As Saint-Alouarn's officers had reported, it was no more than a bleak, rocky, almost barren and uninhabited island. James Cook, when he sailed past it in 1776, would name it the Island of Desolation.

When Kerguelen returned to it, he was forced to admit that there was little about it that was appealing and nothing that might encourage even the hardiest of settlers. It remained fogbound for days. The climate was harsh – although this was midsummer, the cold was at times so bitter that sailors fainted on deck. His previous enthusiasm and his boastings had been foolhardy: there was nothing he could do but to turn round and go back to France. He chose not to return by way of the Isle de France, where his men could have restored their health but where he would have had to endure criticism and ridicule. Instead, he chose to sail to Madagascar.

The failure of Kerguelen's second expedition was not yet known in Port-Louis when La Pérouse arrived. All the locals could tell him was that Kerguelen had gone south with three ships to set up a colonial outpost on his famed southern land. Then, a fortnight later, the little *Dauphine* appeared. News of Kerguelen's failure spread like wildfire. Ternay and Maillard were not triumphant at the failure of a man they had found difficult to deal with, but furious at the resources they had wasted on the undertaking. Still, it was not their fault: they had received instructions to help Kerguelen as fully as circumstances permitted. Let Kerguelen explain himself in Paris.

He found this impossible. There had been too many absurdities, too many exaggerations behind his previous reports. A court martial was set up in Brest. Every book that could be thought of was thrown at Kerguelen. He was condemned for, among other things, neglect of his instructions, incompetence, private trade on his own account, including the buying of slaves in Madagascar for resale at the Cape, and the smuggling on board of a girl of doubtful reputation 'for his own pleasure'. He was sentenced to six years' imprisonment, of which he served four.

There would be no further French attempt to explore the southern seas or the Pacific Ocean for another ten years, and that expedition would be planned in minute detail and every instruction counter-checked – and its commander would be La Pérouse himself. For the present, Ternay told him to take some leave. After a few weeks, he planned to use him for a few minor administrative tasks at the *intendance*. Later, there might be another mission to India.

8. Introducing Eléonore Broudou

May 1774–September 1776

ABRAHAM BROUDOU LIKED to entertain visitors. He was a jovial man, well regarded in the Isle de France, where he had lived since 1768. Originally from Saint-Quentin, in Picardy, he had moved to the prosperous port of Nantes, engaged in the sea trade and become a successful shipowner. The recent war had not been kind to him, however, and he had been glad to accept a position in the Isle de France as manager of naval stores and supervisor of the hospital. It was a well-paid position, which enabled him to buy a house on the Plaines Wilhems, not far from the main road that led from Port-Louis to the smaller harbour of Port Bourbon in the north. It was only a short ride from the capital, a pleasant residence with spacious rooms for dinner parties.

Monsieur Broudou was always happy to invite visiting naval officers to his home. They could be sure of a warm welcome from a man who knew about the sea and, if truth be told, still yearned for life in France. In addition to which, he had daughters of a marriageable age. The youngest, Louise-Eléonore, was only seventeen when the thirty-one-year-old La Pérouse first met her.

As soon as the *Seine* had dropped anchor and La Pérouse had dealt with the more urgent business, he rode off to the Plaines Wilhems. Abraham Broudou was delighted to see him. His daughter had been genuinely attracted by the portly *enseigne* and the feeling was mutual. It would be a good match and it would make her happy. Any father would welcome such a combination, even though it was preferable to marry off the oldest daughter first.

Eléonore was no flirtatious little miss, not one of those teasers who fluttered their fans at attractive young officers. A portrait of her, painted some years later, shows a pretty, serious, gentle young woman. And La Pérouse was no *salon* Romeo. He was stocky, already beginning to give up his battle against an increasing girth. He was knowledgeable, and instead of the witty small talk that was the stock-in-trade of visiting officers he preferred to talk about voyages of exploration, the problems of longitude and the political situation in India.

But his manner was lively, his slight southern accent attractive, his laughter infectious and the appeal of his red and gold uniform quite irresistible.

La Pérouse was often accompanied by Charles Mengaud de la Hage, his old friend from Albi. Abraham Broudou noted with quiet satisfaction that his older daughter, Elisabeth, often paired up with Mengaud, without, however, engaging in too close a *tête-à-tête*. This preserved the proprieties, since neither girl was left alone with her beau for more than a few moments. He might have allowed himself to dream of a double wedding, but common sense told him that one match was as much as he should hope for. Though he was well regarded in Port-Louis and his position was healthily remunerated, Broudou knew that he could only provide a modest dowry for either of his girls. He was also aware that he belonged to the middle class and had no noble or even semi-noble relations to boast about. Some documents did bear the endorsement *vivant noblement*, but this meant that he was highly respected and worthy of being welcomed in the best circles, not that he could enter the ranks of the nobility.[1] A union between a Galaup and a Broudou would be regarded as a misalliance by most of their relatives and acquaintances. But if this was love …

It was, but La Pérouse adopted a cautious approach. This was the eighteenth century, when a father had the final say on his child's marriage, even when the son was approaching thirty-three. It was also a time when a naval officer needed the approval of his superiors before marrying. Even officers like La Pérouse, who came from the minor nobility, could not be allowed to undermine the navy's class structure by marrying beneath them. He needed to plan a strategy that would make a marriage to Eléonore Broudou acceptable. There were a few letters waiting for him at Port-Louis – not many, but enough to make him think of Albi and of his own future. He was still an *enseigne* (though in the senior cohort – equivalent to a British lieutenant) among many others, all hoping to be noticed and given a significant command and, above all, to be promoted.

The letters from home, especially from his sister Jacquette, seemed to hint that his return would be welcomed. His family recognised that an early vocation had drawn him to the sea, but there were also good opportunities in his home district. She gave him news of local events, marriages, plans for the purchase of more land. His uncle was now a senior church official, his younger sister Victoire was turning into a young lady, and his father, in his sixty-fourth year and gradually losing his eyesight, would certainly welcome his return to Albi – and perhaps his marriage to a local girl.

He hesitated before mentioning Eléonore Broudou in his own letters. He did not write to his father, but made a somewhat oblique reference to his attachment in a letter to Jacquette, and even then after some delay: 'I am a little in love with a young person from this island, and this affair might well end in a marriage, although nothing has been decided as yet'.[2] He knew that his letter would take about three months to reach Albi, and the same for a reply to come back. He meant with his tactful hint to test the waters; he had in fact sent a torpedo that would explode in Albi and cause a series of ripples.

When his son's letter arrived, Victor-Joseph de Galaup expressed his shock and anger, and immediately forbade the union. At the same time, to make sure no marriage took place on an island that was so far from France, he wrote to Ternay, formally appointing him his son's guardian and stating his formal and unwavering objection to any marriage that could be regarded in any way as unsuitable for a naval officer of his background. There had always been a strong bond of friendship and respect between Ternay and La Pérouse. Ternay was his protector, to whom in a tradition dating back to feudal times he owed a form of allegiance known as *fidélité*.[3] Now that his superior was also, so to speak, *in loco parentis*, his prospects for a marriage with Eléonore were bleak indeed.

That crisis, however, still lay in the future. After five months ashore he was again sent to India. It was once again one of those expeditions that combined public need and private trade. La Pérouse, on the *Seine*, was accompanied by the *Trois Amis*, a trading vessel commanded by a local merchant, one La Rochette. What could not be accommodated on the merchantman was stowed in the *Seine*. They reached Pondicherry in mid-September 1774, unloaded and went on to Mahé, by way of Calicut. La Pérouse spent a fortnight in Mahé, then sailed north along the Malabar Coast. This time, and on behalf of John Law, he was carrying arms to an Indian leader who was planning another uprising against the British.

Law was not just fishing in troubled waters – he was protecting the few French possessions that remained, in this instance the port of Mahé. Haidar Ali, the ruler of Mysore, was friendly towards the French because he knew them to be the traditional opponents of the British, but he was also powerful enough to eliminate Mahé altogether if his friendship was not reciprocated. Providing him with weapons and ammunition was a form of tribute to a local overlord.

Haydar Ali knew how to welcome an ally. When the *Seine* dropped anchor at Mangalore, he put on the kind of display at which Indian princes excelled: 'I was granted the honours normally accorded to an envoy extraordinary. Six thousand sepoys were lined up, presenting arms, I was invited to step ashore and the Governor made me the gift of a curved sword on behalf of his master.'[4] Reception after reception followed, each one attended by an array of guests in colourful costumes.

La Pérouse spent a delightful, if exhausting, ten days at Mangalore, then it was time to go on north, to the Portuguese port of Goa – where he received no welcome whatsoever. Portugal was an ally of Britain, and the arrival of the French, especially with their links with the Mysore ruler, was regarded with great suspicion. The *Seine*, as they well knew, since Portuguese, British, French and Indian spies were everywhere, had been taking goods to Pondicherry and Mahé, as well as muskets to Mangalore. This made her, in their opinion, a trading vessel, and as such subject to a check by customs officers.

At this point, however, the *Seine* had resumed her status as a naval unit. The King of France's ships were not to be subjected to searches by foreign customs officers, who were immediately sent back to their superiors:

> I promptly ordered them back to shore and went personally to see the viceroy and lay a complaint. He told me that he would follow his master's instructions. I replied that I was following the orders of *my* master and would not allow any of his employees on my ship, and that the first who dared to come up would fall victim of his obedience to the viceroy's instructions. From that moment on, not one was bold enough to show his face.[5]

Brave words, but the consequence was that the French could not go ashore. The *Seine* remained off Goa harbour for a full week, quite literally showing the flag, but nothing more. It was a stand-off position, with each side watching the other.

La Pérouse was forced to continue on his way north, making for Surat. And now, at last, he encountered action. It was 5 January 1755. He came upon a fleet consisting of three ships of forty guns and twenty-seven smaller vessels, most of them armed with eight to ten guns. He decided to sail boldly towards it, all guns manned: 'My decisive manoeuvre intimidated them and after a gunfight lasting two hours, I compelled them to return to their port of Coulages, which was not more than three hours away'.[6] This brief naval engagement was a welcome change from the somewhat demeaning task of ferrying trade goods from Port-Louis to India and back. It is likely that his opponents were not ordinary pirates looking for booty, as he first thought, but Maratha ships on the lookout for British trading vessels. The local situation in 1775 was extremely complex, with semi-independent states often fighting among themselves and certainly ready to fight the British or any other foreign-looking ship. That the *Seine* was flying the French colours was no guarantee of her true nationality: everyone knew that a flag could be hauled down at any moment and replaced with another ensign.

The conflict that was now starting would became known as the Maratha Wars, and it would continue, on and off, for another forty years. Getting entangled with the French was not part of the agenda. The incident may have been due to a simple misunderstanding, but La Pérouse may be forgiven the few triumphant notes that appear in his report: 'My men were not in the least frightened by the number of enemy ships we had to confront, and they all expressed their despair when the winds and the enemy's great speed worked together to form an insurmountable obstacle to the great wish I had of getting within a pistol's shot of them'.[7]

The *Seine* sailed on to Surat, a busy seaport and commercial centre in Gujarat state. She spent a couple of weeks there, then turned back towards Goa and Mahé. This time, the Portuguese in Goa made no fuss, and La Pérouse spent four days there, neither welcomed nor troubled. When he got to Mahé, however, he found to his astonishment that the port was under siege – and by an ally of Haydar Ali. An estimated force of 10,000 men was camped around the small French settlement, some of them possibly part of the very guard of honour that had greeted him a couple of months earlier. This army belonged to a Malabar prince, Sherikal, ruler of Kolatirri, to the north, and a rival of the ruler of Calicut. Unfortunately, the French had close links with the latter, and they now found themselves embroiled in one of the endless local wars. Mahé was in real danger. As La Pérouse commented:

It is scarcely more fortified than the village of Charonne [which was then close to Paris but has now been absorbed by the capital's growth]; a simple bamboo hedge forms the palisade, while a crumbling fort and a few other small batteries represent our power on the Malabar coast. The commander, Mr de Repentigny, is bedridden following a stroke, which has left him paralysed and helpless. All the inhabitants are extremely anxious. Only a small river separates them from the enemy army.[8]

It fell to him to take over the defence of the settlement. Still accompanying him was the *Trois Amis*. One small French ship, the *Galvette*, a galliot, was already at anchor. Together, they may have looked a little more impressive, but prompt action was required before Sherikal attacked. La Pérouse landed forty men and two guns to hold the riverbank – just in time, as it turned out, because the enemy launched their assault that very evening. Not realising that the river crossing had just been fortified, they were met by volley after volley of grapeshot.

The next morning, La Pérouse took steps to repair and strengthen the fort. He landed a further 50 men from his own *Seine* and 50 from the *Trois Amis*, all armed. He added two guns from the *Seine* so that any attackers would once again be met with grapeshot.

It was not a minute too soon. Sherikal had decided to throw everything he had at the fort. The attack came at dawn the very next morning. When the Indians found they were faced with the guns, they wavered and turned back, whereupon the French sent out two-thirds of the garrison – over 200 men altogether – in a counter-attack. It was completely successful:

> A great number of the attackers were killed during this pursuit. The sailors cut off at least 100 ears from the bodies and nailed them to the palisades. I did not regret this show of ferocity, because time was pressing. Soon the change of season would make the Malabar coast untenable for ships. And furthermore, mine was leaking and in no condition to stand up to a storm.

Some skirmishing followed for a few more days, but there was no other major engagement. La Pérouse had lost eight men, three Frenchmen and five Indians, but Sherikal was tamed, at least for the time being. Haydar Ali had known all along about Sherikal's siege, and he was happy enough to stay in the background and see what eventuated. But when he learnt of Sherikal's setbacks, honour required him to intervene. He sent an angry protest to John Law in Pondicherry, threatening to lead his own troops against Mahé if the French maintained their hostile attitude. Sherikal, he said, had merely tried to assert his dominance in the district, not to destroy the French outpost, but all he had faced was brutal opposition. This was no way to treat a friend.

Law did not waste his time arguing over the whys and wherefores. Indian politics were too intricate for him to try meddling with them. The Marathas were clearly manoeuvring in preparation for a major campaign against the British, and it was unwise to get in the way. He sent an immediate message to Repentigny: 'Negotiate'. The latter was still unwell, but he was ably assisted by La Pérouse and another *enseigne*, Robert de Closnard. A ceasefire was negotiated on 25 April. Sherikal could keep his troops in the area, but he had to agree that he would not attack Mahé or impede French traders coming in the port. Gifts were exchanged and the French assured the Marathas that they had every sympathy for their cause.

Three days later, the *Seine* sailed for the Isle de France, where La Pérouse stepped ashore in a joyful mood. The campaign had been a success from every point of view, and certainly more exciting that his previous voyages. He gave Ternay a detailed report, handed over the *Seine* to the port authorities so that they could begin on the much-needed repairs and sped off to see Eléonore.

Things now quietened down. Ternay, Law and others decided to see how things developed in India: there was no need for La Pérouse's services and he would not go back to sea for over a year. His duties were primarily office work. There were reports from captains and others to analyse, draft charts and maps to check, proposals on the development of the port to evaluate, and repairs to ships, including his own *Seine*, leaking and kept afloat only by two pumps working day and night, to supervise. But there were weekends and holidays, saints' days and other special occasions when work stopped and he could ride off to Plaines Wilhems.

His letter to his sister, hinting about a possible marriage, had now reached France. He wondered whether he had been wise to raise the issue from so far away, and whether it would not have been better to wait until he was back in France and able to argue his case personally. But how many months, or years, would he have to wait before he was posted back home? And Eléonore was barely twenty. Her parents were happy enough to let things take their course. They were satisfied that this was true love, but they also knew that the Galaups would not look very sympathetically at a marriage with a young woman from her class.

All they could do was wait – and the Isle de France was a place where time did not matter a great deal as the waters lapped around the cliffs and the green hills, the cane grew steadily in the warm air and business proceeded at its own pace. There were occasional storms, raging cyclones even, but in time the wild winds died down, the blue skies returned and repairs were soon carried out. And the fierce squabbles that had divided island society in the last days of Poivre and Desroches had settled down under Ternay. The old quarrels had left scars, to be sure, but these were beginning to fade. There was now a rising tide of mutterings about Maillard's administration and his policy of retrenchment, but much of this remained under the surface, at least for the time being.

There were other topics of discussion. In Europe, an entire world had come to an end. Louis XV had died after a reign of almost 60 years. Many islanders, like their compatriots in France, had been born, had married and raised families and gone to their graves knowing no other king. Now the unthinkable had come about, and a new ruler had ascended the throne. The name was still Louis, but Louis XVI was nothing like his grandfather.

He was only twenty, ill-trained – indeed, untrained – for a task that would have been daunting enough for a man of genius. And Louis XVI was no genius, merely a young man of moderate ability, unexpectedly propelled onto the throne of one of Europe's greatest powers by the deaths of his father and his two elder brothers, at a time when the country, indeed the whole continent, was being shaken by revolutionary ideas.

In 1770 he had married, or been married off to Marie-Antoinette, youngest daughter of the Austrian Empress Maria-Theresa. Politically, it was a sensible union. She provided a valuable link with some of the most powerful families in Europe. Furthermore, she was beautiful, charming, witty. She was also totally devoid of political sense.

Louis was not unintelligent. He was interested in technical advances: his hobby was tinkering with clocks and other mechanisms; he knew about the problems of timekeeping at sea and the consequent difficulty of working out a ship's longitude, and this had led him to read about voyages of exploration. He became quite knowledgeable about travels to faraway places, in the past and in recent times, and what still needed to be done.

He ascended the throne amidst a great deal of enthusiasm. The financial problems, the wars, the corruption and the squabbles that had plagued the last decades of Louis XV's reign had completely eroded the old king's popularity. In the early years of his reign he had been called 'Louis the Well-Beloved', but when he died, his corpse was driven away from the palace to the jeers of his lackeys. Now there was a new king, a young one, endearingly timid. Who could resist feeling a surge of sympathy for a monarch who invited a new Chief Minister to take up the reins of office by writing to him, 'I am only twenty'?[9]

The colonists in the Isle de France decided to celebrate this new reign by erecting an obelisk. As soon as the official period of mourning for the old king was over, Ternay led a week of celebrations. Messages of loyalty were read out, to the loud cheers of all those attending, and promptly forwarded to Versailles. There were banners everywhere, a series of banquets and a seemingly endless succession of toasts. The leaders of Port-Louis society jostled each other to make their speeches and glasses were raised endlessly.

The optimism seemed justified and peace assured, for some years at least. The new ministers had enough problems at home, particularly trying to balance the budget, without worrying about foreign ventures. The British had their own problems too. John Wilkes was agitating for parliamentary reform, irritating and unsettling the ruling classes; there was growing unrest in India and much worse in North America. In December 1773, a group of Boston citizens had protested against an import duty on tea by hurling crates of it into the harbour. The British Parliament had reacted by closing the port of Boston. There was much worse to come. Eight American colonists were killed by British troops near Lexington, heralding the coming uprising and War of Independence.

When this news reached Port-Louis, it was regarded as a sign that the British, having their hands full overseas, would not trouble the peace in Europe. As far as India was concerned, Ternay decided to let matters lie and not try to interfere. Haydar Ali had been pacified, and the French settlements were as safe as could be expected. The British could be left to handle their problems on their own.

With no immediate prospects of seagoing, La Pérouse decided to buy a country property not far from Port-Louis in Plaines Wilhems. It was sizeable, approximately 60 hectares, and situated by the Mesnil River, quite handy to the Broudou house. Since he had done this shortly after telling his sister about Eléonore and the possibility that he might marry her, it looks as if he was turning his mind to settling down on the Isle de France, and possibly giving up the navy altogether. If his father did oppose the marriage, as he half suspected he might, he could even cut his ties with Albi. He had put aside a fair sum – 90,000 *livres*, he told his sister – but not quite enough, so he purchased the property in association with his friend, Charles Mengaud de la Hage. They had always got on well, and the Wilhems estate might lay the foundations for a joint business enterprise.

For a few months, life continued calmly and happily. Then came the letter from his father, while political developments suggested that life on the island might not turn out to be quite so peaceful and rumours arrived from France that trouble was brewing because Versailles was unofficially supporting the American colonists, to the growing irritation of the British government. War was becoming a distinct possibility. Naval officers like La Pérouse would soon be called back to duty.

In addition, cracks were again appearing in Port-Louis society. Maillard Dumesle had fallen out with a well-known naval officer and hydrographer, Jacques-Raymond Grenier. The latter, commanding the *Belle-Poule*, had been sent to rescue the men of the *Fortune*, which had been wrecked near Fort Dauphin in Madagascar. This should have been a relatively simple operation but, as usual, trade and naval operations were interwoven in the expedition. Maillard had supplied goods, including muskets, for Grenier to sell in Madagascar and thus cover the cost of buying food for the men of the *Fortune*, but none of the French traders in Madagascar was interested in buying the weapons. Maillard's local agent insisted on cash or bills of exchange, something Grenier did not have. There would be no food for the men, and certainly no profit left over when the *Belle-Poule* returned to Port-Louis. Grenier was forced to sail to another French outpost, Foulpointe, where much the same problem arose. Grenier and his officers then decided to take over and meet the costs of the expedition out of their own pockets. Firstly they bought the muskets and the other trade goods themselves. Next, they sold the guns and the other goods privately, wheeling and dealing a little beyond that, and bought local goods and supplies to get their investment back and a handsome profit on top.

When they returned to Port-Louis, Maillard insisted that the profit – no one disputed the fact that a profit had been made – should go into the island's coffers. The island administration had provided the guns and other trade goods, and any surplus left from their sale and subsequent deals belonged to it. Grenier pointed out that he and his officers had brought the goods for ready cash, and that any profit they might have made was their own business.

It was a fairly sordid affair, of the sort that is not unexpected when official and private business become intertwined. Ternay tried to adjudicate, but only added to the rancour – and to his own irritation about the argument. These squabbles were all too frequent and quite unbecoming. He was a naval officer and a nobleman, not a trader. Unwilling to be involved in the affair any longer, he referred the matter back to the Ministry of Marine in France. The salons of Port-Louis gleefully divided into a pro-Maillard and a pro-Grenier faction. There was a ripple of excitement as some wondered how this might affect La Pérouse. Since he was a naval officer, the residents took it for granted that La Pérouse would support Grenier, and that Broudou, as a member of the civilian administration, would be in Maillard's camp. If this happened, the gossips gleefully calculated, Jean-François and Eléonore would find themselves cast as leads in a Romeo and Juliet operetta. Fortunately, Broudou was a cautious man and, living in Plaines Wilhems, he was able to distance himself from the rival camps. The ministry would adjudicate in the matter, he pointed out. No one in the Isle de France needed to take sides.

Another subject of contention was the future of Madagascar. It offered good prospects as a possible colony, but the local Malagasy were still fiercely defending their independence. Allowing the French to trade from a few coastal outposts was as far as they were prepared to go. It was profitable for them and for traders in Port-Louis. Maillard agreed with those who felt this was good enough. Anything more would cost a great deal of money and upset the local business people.

Others believed that more needed to be done. If one Malagasy tribe allowed the French to establish one or more trading bases, might not another allow the British to do the same? Madagascar was a large island. There was room for more trading posts – and the British were known the world over for steadily and craftily expanding their settlements into neighbouring districts. This had happened in North America and in India, as well as in Africa. If France was not careful and Britain got a foothold in Madagascar, a new British colony might soon develop and overshadow the small islands of Mauritius, Bourbon and the Seychelles. There had already been one British attempt to establish a beachhead of sorts on Madagascar, even though this was back in the days of Charles I.

The Port-Louis settlers were divided between hawks and doves. There were probably many more of the latter, but strategic considerations were important. Versailles had never been totally opposed to taking over Madagascar, essentially to keep out the British. Looking at the maps, the various ministers had realised how easy it would be for Britain to gain full control of the route to India and the Far East, and to cut across French trading lines. But the problem was how to achieve these aims without upsetting London.

One way of gaining a new colony without getting too closely involved was to allow a friendly third party to do it. When a Polish nobleman offered to found a French settlement on Madagascar, the French government readily accepted. It would not be a costly enterprise and it was not really an official government move. If he succeeded, he would be in France's debt, he would certainly need further assistance and gradually his settlement would be taken over. On the other hand, if anything went wrong, it could simply be shrugged off.

The suggestion had been made by Auguste de Benyowski, a man on whom fate had showered gifts and flaws in equal measure. Above all, he had charm – and when had Versailles ever resisted charm? He told colourful tales of his early years in Austria and Poland. The courtiers listened to him entranced and were even more entertained when he outlined his plans for a faraway place practically none of them had ever heard of. It seemed a good move for the administrators to give him their support.

His first idea had been to set up a French colony on Taiwan, then known as Formosa – the Beautiful One. This proposal did not impress the officials. It was too distant from any existing French bases, and earlier but unsuccessful attempts to colonise it had been made by the Portuguese, the Spanish and the Dutch. It was not an easy place to capture or hold and, worse still, it was claimed by China, which would challenge any attempt by a would-be colonial power. They suggested to him that Madagascar would be a safer bet. Benyowski had no objection: Madagascar it would be. He had never actually been there and knew very little about the place, but he sailed happily enough from Lorient in March 1773, with his wife, his sister-in-law, one maid and four servants, plus a mixed bag of 237 volunteers.

He first made for the Isle de France, where he planned to obtain supplies and possibly a few more settlers. He had already been to Port-Louis in the days of Desroches and had made a good impression on him. Local society had listened with amazement to his tales. Born in Austria, he had fought in the Seven Years War as a fourteen-year-old. After the death of his father, who was a general in the Austrian army, he was adopted by an uncle in Poland. Following more adventures in wartime Europe, he joined the Polish forces fighting against the Russians. Taken prisoner, he escaped, was recaptured and sent to Siberia.

Charming the governor of the fortress of Bolskeretsk-Ostrog, and his daughter, he led a rebellion, captured the fortress and fled with other prisoners and the young woman. They made their way from Kamchatka across the Bering Sea to Alaska, then sailed to Japan and Macao and eventually ended up in Port-Louis. It was impossible to distinguish between truth and fiction in his stories, but they were always exciting and entertaining.

He was only thirty-one when he met Desroches, who described him favourably and mentioned that he spoke French and German as well as Polish and Russian. 'He has some knowledge of every science. He is covered with the scars of old wounds, some of which disfigure him or cause him to limp. Nevertheless, he has retained a powerful appearance of health and vigour. His features are pleasing and his wit sparkled.'[10] Benyowski had quickly dazzled the rather provincial society of Port-Louis and Desroches had rightly surmised that he would do the same in Versailles. He supplied him with letters of introduction and sent him on his way with all his best wishes.

Now he was back, but Desroches had been replaced by Ternay, who was not too sure what he should do next. Colonising Madagascar was a far more complex affair than Versailles suspected or cared to worry about. Looking at the couple of hundred men Benyowski had brought with him, 'scruffy mustachioed troopers with daggers and long swords dragging along the ground', marching around Port-Louis with drums banging and trumpets sounding, he felt that they might frighten the Malagasy for a while, but he also worried that they might not make the best type of pioneering settlers.[11]

Maillard Dumesle, as usual, was concerned about the financial implications. Benyowski had brought letters of recommendation from the ministry, and he expected to be helped with money and with supplies. Maillard's attempts to cut down on the local budget would not be helped by spending thousands of precious *livres* on an attempt to colonise the largest island in the Indian Ocean.

Traders in the Isle de France had their own misgivings. They knew there were opportunities for commerce and initiative in Madagascar, and they had private arrangements for occasional deals, but caution and tact were required at all times when dealing with the Malagasy. The appearance of an interloper, with his odd crowd of followers, was not something they welcomed. Ternay, however, felt he had to follow instructions from France and do something for him. Maillard and many of the merchants considered the whole colonisation plan premature and ill-advised. Amid a rising chorus of grumbles, Ternay eventually provided Benyowski with a ship and sent him on his way.

The adventurers landed at Antongil Bay on the north-east coast. It was a deep inlet and well sheltered, but the coast was humid and marshy. Benyowski set to with energy, building a fort, some storage sheds and huts, and laying out the outline of a town. Then fevers struck down many of his men, and the local tribes began to show their displeasure at his presence. Unfortunately, he lacked enough supplies or trade goods to pacify them.

At this juncture, Yves de Kerguelen appeared, on his way back to France. Meeting Benyowski was a godsend – not necessarily for his men, fourteen of whom died of fever – but to repair his image. Here he could support a French settlement that had the blessing of the Minister of Marine. Helping Benyowski to give France a promising colony could make up for his failure to set one up in southern waters. The very presence of Kerguelen's two ships, the *Rolland* with her 64 guns and the *Oiseau* with her 32, was enough to quieten the Malagasy. A mixture of firmness and the distribution of some of the trinkets he had taken on board to trade with non-existent inhabitants of his Southern France did the rest.

When Kerguelen sailed for France, he felt confident that he would earn the minister's gratitude for his intervention. He took with him a letter of thanks from Benyowski which he could show around as evidence of his good work. In exchange, he had promised to give the minister a favourable report on the struggling settlement, coupled with a request for 600 more settlers and one million *livres*. This was passed on to the Controller-General of Finance, Robert Jacques Turgot, a noted *philosophe* and a renowned economist. His main task was to try to cope with France's chronic financial deficit, not to start spending large sums on new ventures. The fact that Kerguelen had brought the request did not help: the man was in disgrace and about to face a court martial. Turgot decided to wait and see.

He had a better opportunity to get a second opinion on the Madagascar venture. John Law was due to be replaced, and a new governor, the Maréchal Guy Léonard de Bellecombe, was about to sail to Pondicherry. It would be easy enough for him to look in at Antongil Bay on his way to India, and report back to France. He knew the region, having once been governor of the island of Bourbon, and he could be trusted to supply the minister with a sound and reasoned report.

Bellecombe arrived at Port-Louis in August 1776. He asked Ternay for an escort ship to accompany him to Madagascar; he would send it back to Port-Louis with his report while he continued on his way to Pondicherry. Ternay agreed. The Benyowski affair, coupled with Kerguelen's by-passing of the Isle de France, was causing too much local dissatisfaction. Local merchants felt that the trouble at Antongil Bay was jeopardising their own attempts to trade. Maillard, already embroiled in the Grenier affair, was urging Ternay to ignore Benyowski altogether. It was all becoming too much. Getting Versailles to decide the future of the Madagascar settlement, and provide the funds if it wanted something done, was the best way out. All Ternay needed do in the meantime was to send an up-to-date report to France.

He supplied Bellecombe with the *Iphigénie*, a small locally built trading vessel which, like so many others, was used in the King's service when the need arose and for trade for the rest of the time. And, as her captain, he chose La Pérouse. It was a good choice. La Pérouse had been to Madagascar before, and he had not been to sea for almost eighteen months. The prospect of settling down in the Plaines Wilhems and turning into a colonist, if that had ever been his intention, no longer appealed. The island was too small, too provincial. He felt at times like an outsider, dragged one way and another by local quarrels, and he realised that he was not made for commerce or agriculture. He and Mengaud had already sold their property and moved back into Port-Louis.

So La Pérouse took over the *Iphigénie* and accompanied Bellecombe's frigate, the *Consolante*, to Madagascar. They reached the small settlement of Foulpointe on 17 September. It was in a parlous state.

> The population of this village is down by half of what is was. The wars and the discouragement that has resulted from the drop in trade have destroyed agriculture. When I was here three years ago, I saw ten vessels here, all laden with rice, but now there are not 300 pounds of it in the chief's enclosure. We couldn't obtain any in the village. The blacks are subsisting on roots and wild fruit.[12]

Bellecombe organised a ceremony to bring peace to the warring tribes. An end to tribal warfare was essential if Benyowski's settlement was to survive. The oath of reconciliation was marked by the drinking of a potion 'made up of brandy, to which gunpowder has been added, together with sea water, a piastre and the tip of a lance'.[13] The ceremony may have been heavy with symbolism, but the potion does not sound too palatable.

The ships then sailed on to Antongil, where Benyowski had his headquarters. He had named it Louisbourg; the fort was called Fort-Louis, the bay Port Choiseul. The names were impressive, the settlement quite the opposite. His headquarters consisted of a single-storey building constructed of tree trunks, planks and straw, divided into three rooms by planks and sackcloth: one for his sister-in-law, one for himself, one serving as a store and office.

There were a few wooden shacks nearby, most of them in a state of collapse. The fort, holding three guns, was also built of tree trunks and planks dug into the sandy ground and rising little more than 1.2 metres above soil level. The streets laid out by Benyowski were simply overgrown paths; the few fields were invaded by weeds. Everything was damp and rat-infested. Fever had laid low many of the Benyowski Corps, as he called it, and several white crosses in a nearby field testified to the growing cost in lives.

To be fair to Benyowski, many pioneer settlers landing on undeveloped land in North America, and later in Australia, New Zealand and parts of Africa, faced similar conditions. He had serious problems, such as the climate, endlessly hot and humid, which weakened the colonists and encouraged fevers, the local Malagasy, who resented the arrival of the French, and insufficient funds and supplies.

Above all, he had his own boisterous and impractical nature to deal with. His high-flown ideas included building up an administration when there was still nothing to administer. He had appointed an administrative officer, an *ordonnateur*, with a notional annual salary of 6000 *livres*, a treasurer at 2400, a port captain at 1800 and even a port pilot at 900. Bellecombe expressed his astonishment.

> It would be hard to meet a more extraordinary man, both in his ideas and in his conversation. He is driven by the desire of being in command and of fighting. The prospect of using his sword often excites him, but his character and strength of purpose are certainly unusual. Let us remember what he has been during his lifetime: a priest, to begin with, then a page, then a marine; he has been in the service of the Austrian Emperor, then of the King of Poland, then fought with the confederation of rebels; taken prisoner by the Russians, he was sent off to Kamchatka. Let us take note of the quite remarkable manner in which he escaped from that place of exile, the good fortune he has enjoyed so far in coping with the climate here, and we must conclude that this Hungarian [sic] colonel, now aged 37, is indeed made for great adventures.[14]

He certainly was. He had met an old Malagasy woman who declared that he was nothing less than the descendant of a king of Mananara province, Ramini. The local belief was that one day such a person, infused with the spirit of Ramini, would rule over the province. Benyowski waited for Bellecombe and La Pérouse to leave, and the moment they sailed away, he accepted the mantle of Ramini, and the Mananara chiefs gathered to proclaim their allegiance to him.

La Pérouse had tried to discuss money with him. Benyowki had bought supplies on credit from several traders in Port-Louis, who had pleaded with La Pérouse to do what he could to collect their debts. The answer to that was nothing. Benyowski had no money to spare. He insisted that France should provide the couple of millions that he needed to transform Madagascar into a prosperous colony. The merchants of Port-Louis would benefit in due course. Meanwhile, they would have to wait.

The crossing from the Isle de France to Madagascar had taken a week. The ships had then spent a fortnight on the island. Bellecombe was now ready to hand over his report to La Pérouse, to be taken back to Ternay, while he went on to take up his post in India. Unfortunately, the weather turned bad and the two ships became separated during the night. Bellecombe waited a while, then went to Bourbon, hoping that La Pérouse would join him there. Three weeks went by with no sign of the *Iphigénie*. Bellecombe was worried, but he decided to sail to India and send his reports to Ternay by another trading vessel. He mentioned how concerned he had become: 'Mr de la Pérouse's old ship has not been careened for five years and was leaking badly'.[15]

Ternay and Maillard waited, but there was still no sign of the *Iphigénie*. Finally, nearly two months after La Pérouse's departure from Antongil, Maillard felt that he had to send on all the reports to the minister in Paris and tell him what everyone in Port-Louis was thinking, that the *Iphigénie* had been lost. But just as he was sealing his letter, a messenger rushed into his office, and Maillard joyfully added a dramatic postscript: 'The vessel *Iphigénie* has just arrived'.[16]

It had taken La Pérouse forty-eight days to complete a crossing expected to take a week, but he was lucky to get back at all. The ship was leaking through all her seams, the timber was cracked, and the sails had split in the storm that had driven her off course. The sailors were exhausted after weeks of working the pumps, bailing out the water that was seeping into every corner, filling up cracks with whatever they could find and endlessly manoeuvring to save the rotting canvas.

Ternay welcomed La Pérouse with open arms and told him to forget about the *Iphigénie*. Whether she was to be repaired or scrapped was none of their concern – that decision could be left to his successor, Guiran de la Brillanne, who had now arrived from France. He was all packed to go home, and La Pérouse was to come with him.

Within a week, La Pérouse had settled into the *Belle-Poule* that was to take him back to Brest. He joined a distinguished set of officers: Cillard de Suville, who would captain the ship, his friend Mengaud de la Hage, Robert Sutton de Closnard, who would one day join him on his great voyage of exploration, and Nicolas Pierre Duclos-Guyot, who had sailed around the world with Louis de Bougainville. There would be many opportunities during the voyage home to discuss navigation and exploration, as well as the worsening situation in the North American colonies.

There were the inevitable ceremonies to go through before Ternay could leave. The official handover took place on 2 December, with a solemn trooping of the colours and a march past, and a *Te Deum* in the Port-Louis church. There were also many friends to farewell, including the Broudous. Then, on 16 December, the *Belle-Poule* sailed out of Port-Louis. A fortnight later, another ship left for France. Among the passengers was Eléonore Broudou.

Part 4

THE AMERICAN WAR

9. BACK IN FRANCE

May 1777–June 1778

THE VOYAGE HOME was time-consuming. First, there was the mandatory call at the island of Bourbon, with a few farewells, fortunately less formal than at Port-Louis, after which the *Belle-Poule* sailed on to the Cape. The French spent a month there, paying a few visits, but mostly laying in stores and carrying out much-needed repairs. After this, there was a stop of a few days at Ascension Island, where they caught a number of turtles. Above all, nearer the French coast, there was a threat from an English privateer that turned into a thirty-six-hour chase.

Ternay and La Pérouse finally landed at Lorient on 7 May. They went first to Nantes, where La Pérouse wrote to his father, announcing his safe return, then continued on their way to Paris, briefly reported to ministry officials and hurried off to visit relatives and friends they had not seen for years.

And at last La Pérouse was promoted. Appointed *lieutenant de vaisseau*, backdated to 4 April 1777, he was also made a knight of the Order of Saint Louis, the distinguished order founded by Louis XIV in 1693. He nevertheless felt that he had been neglected over the years and almost forgotten while he was serving in the distant Indian Ocean. He did not hesitate to speak his mind in a letter to the Minister of Marine. Formally thanking him for the promotion and the decoration, he added: 'But if I had remained in Europe, I would have been able to lay claim to it three years earlier'.[1] The minister ignored the letter, but three weeks after sending it, La Pérouse was granted an additional salary of 300 *livres* a year 'in appreciation of services rendered in Indian waters'. He could read into that whatever he liked – it was as close as he would ever get to an apology. And it was an appreciable sum, payable for as long as he stayed in the navy.

La Pérouse found that there was not a great deal for him to do in Paris. Ternay took him with him to visit friends and officials, renewing old and valuable links with influential people. Everywhere they went, the talk was about the situation in North America. It was really time that they caught up with what was happening across the Atlantic. Port-Louis had always received its news second-hand, which the locals embroidered with rumours, gossip and speculation. Reports about the signing of the Declaration of Independence on 4 July 1776 had reached the Isle de France by October, but some saw in it nothing more than an attempt by disgruntled settlers to formalise a wave of rebellion that George III was determined to quell. Not everything had been going the rebels' way, and Louis XVI was determined to act cautiously. Supporting the colonists against London could only cause trouble. On the other hand, as Charles de Vergennes, the Minister of Foreign Affairs, reminded him, France's colonial interests in the West Indies and elsewhere needed to be protected. It was important to ensure that any British ships manoeuvring in Caribbean waters as part of their campaign against the insurgents respected the sovereignty of France's remaining possessions. The King agreed, as long as it did not involve an open confrontation with London.

That remained France's official position but, as La Pérouse and Ternay paid their courtesy visits to officials and *philosophes*, they began to realise the extent of the French government's unofficial support for the colonists. A strange collection of agents and operators was collecting funds and arms for them. Pierre Beaumarchais, the author of the recent theatrical hit, *Le Barbier de Séville*, was a leading figure in this cloak-and-dagger world. He was given a million *livres* 'to help in protecting French interests abroad'. That could mean anything. Beaumarchais was being given a free hand, but he could be dropped like a hot brick if any problems arose. Then, a couple of months later, he received another million from the Spanish authorities, to look after their interests.

Bankers, businessmen and arms dealers became involved in complex deals to assist the colonists, and turn a handsome profit for themselves. Also active in this shadowy world was Silas Deane, the unofficial representative of the fledgling American Congress. He worked in various ways, mostly covert, to recruit French volunteers to fight on the colonists' side, but far more prominent in this particular task was the flamboyant Marquis de La Fayette, who was to become a major figure in the War of Independence. Deane was anyhow soon eclipsed by the more impressive and better known Benjamin Franklin, who had arrived in Paris at the end of 1776 and rapidly gained the ear, not just of the *philosophes* and other sympathisers, but of Vergennes himself. It became apparent that France was now willing to listen, openly and almost officially, to an agent of the American rebels. It was a startling development, promptly reported to an increasingly angered British government.

Neither Ternay nor La Pérouse had any doubts that war was imminent. They were entitled to some long leave after their lengthy period of service in the Isle de France, but how long depended on the political situation. They made quite sure that officials and people of influence knew they were back and available, and only then did they go home to visit their families.

When La Pérouse went down to Albi in August, he had not seen his family for five years. He was welcomed home, almost as a prodigal son, and shown the improvements that had been made to the family house in Albi and to the country property at Le Gô. The fields and the vineyards were doing well, everything seemed peaceful and welcoming in the warm summer weather. For his part, he unwrapped the presents and the souvenirs he had brought from the distant East, unrolling colourful cloths from India, passing around intricately carved boxes and all kinds of curios, giving rise to a chorus of exclamations and thanks. Around the dinner table, surrounded by friends and family, he answered questions about his travels and his adventures, about the romantic Isle de France and the strange worlds of Madagascar and India.

But he had no success with his father concerning a marriage with Eléonore. The old man was now almost completely blind and, knowing that death could not be too far away, he worried about the future of his family. He was proud of his boy's achievements, even prouder of the recent recognition he had received, but promotion and a medal did not make up for a son who would be prepared take up the reins and look after the property, the farms, the vineyards. What good was an absentee landlord, sailing in faraway oceans?

After a few weeks, he had a serious talk with his son. A compromise was not impossible: Jean-François could continue with his chosen career, but he did not have to cut his ties with Albi. The Galaups had lived there for generations; they belonged to the upper gentry, and they had intermarried with others of equal or higher rank. A suitable marriage could be arranged without difficulty. He had various prospects in mind, and he knew that the parents of the young ladies he mentioned would welcome the match.

The heart-to-heart discussion soon became acrimonious. Jean-François loved Eléonore and he had no wish to marry anyone else, especially someone he had probably never met and who knew nothing about him or his life in the navy. His father retorted that the Broudous were unknowns, tradespeople, clerks, northerners. What would the local people think of such a marriage? How would it affect his naval career? He conceded that men like La Jonquière had married outsiders, creoles, ladies born in one of France's overseas colonies, but what they may have lacked in respect of their birth was compensated for by their fortune. Without this, these gentlemen would not have demeaned themselves by marrying them. But what dowry would Eléonore Broudou bring? The old man was staring angrily with his dead eyes, hammering his words out on the arms of his chair. Jean-François left the room to rejoin his mother and his sister, waiting in the drawing room, both averting their eyes and awkwardly trying to discuss other matters.

He left a week later for Brest, a destination that handily took him on the way to Nantes, where Eléonore was staying with her mother. The crossing from the Isle de France had been uncomfortable for her, and she was not in good health. He could not cheer her with the news he had hoped to bring – that his family was likely to accept her as a daughter-in-law – but he promised to remain faithful to her, in the expectation that his father would eventually come round. She responded that she did not want to tie him down and prolong a rift with his family. Their understanding was not an engagement, and he should feel no obligation towards her. It would be better for his career, and for his family situation, if he looked for someone else, or accepted whoever his father might select for him. He protested again that he wanted to marry her. It was merely a matter of time, he told her. She was not well and no doubt depressed. She needed rest and time to rebuild her strength, and he needed time to wear down his father's opposition. Meanwhile, his duties called. He continued on his way to Brest, promising to return to Nantes as often as he could.

Brest was a hive of activity, loud and bustling. Ships were being readied, stores loaded, crews trained. France was still not involved in any war, but the preparations for a looming conflict were obvious. As small coastal vessels sailed busily and confidently in and out of the bay and around the coast, La Pérouse could feel some satisfaction for all the rather dreary surveying and beaconing work he had carried out in earlier years. For the time being, he did not have a great deal to do, apart from giving some advice to a few captains on navigation in the Indian Ocean and the complex situation there. He strolled about the town, renewing a few acquaintances, gathering the latest news from near and far, but no specific task was assigned to him. He was still, to all intents and purposes, on leave.

He was just about to leave for Paris to join Ternay, when a letter arrived from Albi, written by his sister on behalf of his father. Not only had the old man not weakened in his attitude, but he wanted to express his opposition in terms that left no further room for manoeuvre. A marriage to the Broudou girl was quite out of the question:

[The thought of it] makes me tremble. You are cold-bloodedly contemplating something that would disgrace you in the eyes of the Minister [of Marine] and cause you to lose the patronage of powerful friends. You display contempt for the opinions of your friends; you will lose, together with the rewards of twenty years of work, the esteem you have acquired and which you seem to have deserved by the elevation of your sentiments. We had felt flattered by this, but by lowering yourself you would humiliate all the members of your family and all your friends. You are planning to bring nothing but sorrow on us; you are sacrificing your fortune and the respectability of your condition in life to a frivolous beauty and so-called attractions which maybe exist only in your imagination.[2]

There were clear hints that Jean-François would be ostracised from Albi and indeed from Languedoc society, and that he would lose all his important protectors. There was even the suggestion that he might be disinherited, difficult though that might be for a father to achieve with his only son.

La Pérouse was devastated. He went down to Nantes and told Eléonore that there was no possibility of an early marriage, but that neither of them should lose hope. Time and the strengthening of his position in the navy would help. Ternay, while careful not to take sides, decided to help. He took the younger man on as his personal assistant, and together they called on senior officials, especially the gifted and influential Claret de Fleurieu, recently appointed director of all the French naval bases and arsenals, a position roughly equivalent to that of naval chief of staff.

It was the first time La Pérouse and Fleurieu's paths had crossed and they found that they had much in common. They would remain firm friends and associates. Fleurieu was a learned man, who numbered among his interests the problem of timekeeping at sea and the study of the newly developed chronometers. It was said that he could read a new sea chart as quickly as he could scan the pile of letters that, day after day, landed on his desk.

Ternay had been asked to work on a plan for offensive-defensive operations in the Indian Ocean once war broke out. This double-headed policy was intended to pacify those who, whether aristocrats worried about the social consequences of an all-out effort to help rebels with republican ideas, or business people concerned about another costly war, were opposed to a head-on conflict with Great Britain. Ternay and La Pérouse were not asked to plan a campaign in eastern seas, but merely to ensure that, when war broke out, France's possessions were not endangered. With La Pérouse, Ternay went through all the reports that had come in on the situation in the Indian Ocean, pored over maps, drew up lists of the stores and men that might be required, and totted up the likely strength of the protagonists.

La Pérouse acted as secretary, and it was he who drew up the final report submitted to Fleurieu. It was a straightforward summary of the situation, and of what needed to be done. Pondicherry, on the Indian subcontinent, would have to be fortified into an impregnable base; the Isle de France needed strengthening as the pivot of French operations in the Indian Ocean, so that French ships could sail from there for India and the East 'as fresh as they are when they leave French ports'[3]; and in addition the Malabar coast, where France had local allies, would provide shelter and supplies of rice and other necessities. Fleurieu was pleased with the report, which he filed with all the others being sent to him. It still exists today in the French Naval Archives, complete with Fleurieu's annotations and comments.

For the time being, however, any plans concerning the eastern seas had to remain in the background. The Atlantic had to take priority, and Louis XVI would reject any proposal that might draw too many resources towards other areas. When Fleurieu presented his comprehensive plan to Gabriel de Sartines, the Minister of Marine, to be sent on to the King, he proposed that 65 of the available 90 French and Spanish warships should operate in the North Atlantic and the West Indies. Only a small squadron could be devoted to the Indian Ocean.

He also rejected the idea of a purely defensive strategy. War was now clearly unavoidable and any such strategy would be counter-productive. If France and Spain were to help the Americans, they would have to go ahead and challenge the British wherever they could, and do so without hesitation. Defensive wars, he wrote in his preamble, are bad for morale: 'A defensive war is not French: it humiliates the nation, it freezes courage, it destroys energy and initiative; it is not compatible with the ardour and the impatience of the French military.'[4]

The final recommendations, drawn up by the Duc de Broglie, endorsed these views. France and her Spanish ally would have to concentrate on the Channel and Atlantic seaways. Louis XVI studied the proposals and gave his full agreement. Broadly, the plan had three main sections: aid to the Americans, co-operation with the Spanish in accordance with the so-called 'Family Pact' between the two Bourbon powers, and active patrols in the English Channel to protect France's northern coastline.

As the year 1777 ended, the three powers were ready for a showdown. From the Franco-Spanish point of view, the situation was quite favourable. British forces under General John Burgoyne had marched down from Canada in June and scored a number of victories against the rebels, but then had been stopped and finally defeated at Saratoga in mid-October. Meanwhile, La Fayette's French volunteers had landed, symbolising, though in a small way, France's involvement in the American revolution.

Versailles could not sustain the policy of 'sympathetic neutrality' by which it had tried to help the colonists without too openly challenging the British. It had created absurd and not entirely honourable situations – witness the instructions issued to Captain Duchaffault de la Roche of the *Magnifique* who had just led a squadron to the French West Indies with the following instructions:

> Should a ship from New England belonging to the Insurgents that is being pursued by an English vessel seek the protection of the French flag, Sieur Duchaffault shall grant it this protection, and should the English vessel still attempt to capture the Insurgent ship, Sieur Duchaffault shall prevent it by using the forces that H.M. has given him, but only after he has hailed the English vessel and told it that his King has ordered him to extend the protection of his flag to any ship that may ask for it, and to prevent by every means any violence from being carried out against it.[5]

As men like Duchaffault and his fellow officers told anyone who would listen, this was nonsense and could in no way be regarded as neutrality.

The British had no doubt about it either. War might not have been formally declared, but no one could argue that some form of phoney war was going on. To prove it, they did what they had done just before the outbreak of the Seven Years' War: they carried out a pre-emptive strike against French shipping, capturing an estimated 150 merchant ships, large and small, either in English ports or on their way to France.

A few days later, on 6 February 1778, Versailles signed a secret treaty of friendship with Benjamin Franklin, thereby granting him full recognition as the representative of the Thirteen Colonies or Provinces, as they were variously known until the term United States became generally accepted. Secrecy was not easy to maintain, and rumours about Franklin's new status began to spread around the corridors of power and the foreign embassies, until 20 March, when Franklin was formally received at court with the full pomp usual for the reception of new ambassadors. Vergennes led the way, then Franklin followed by Silas Deane and another agent of Congress, Arthur Lee, and two others. They walked up the great stairway, flanked on both sides by a row of Swiss Guards in full uniform. They stopped as a drum roll began. Two guards opened the door to Louis XVI's appartments, and Vergennes announced: 'The representatives of the thirteen United Provinces'. Louis XVI, seated, with Marie-Antoinette at his side, welcomed them. Watched by the assembled courtiers, he spoke of France's friendship towards the American people. It was a brief ceremony, but it implied recognition of American independence. The next morning, the British ambassador, Lord Stormont, left for London.

The die was cast. La Pérouse and Ternay, now back in Brest, were preparing for the coming war. On 24 February, La Pérouse was given command of the *Serin*, a corvette of fourteen guns, and almost at once set off for the English Channel. He spent three weeks patrolling the sea from Ushant to Falmouth and endeavouring to train his small crew. Not one of them, he discovered, had any knowledge of gun handling, and he was grateful that he did not have to challenge a British ship or even fire at the lonely privateer from Guernsey that made a brief appearance before fleeing back home.

The *Serin* – the name means 'canary' and also, in common parlance, 'greenhorn' – was far from impressive. It was only ten years old, but needed a proper refit after having made a number of crossings to the West Indies. La Pérouse wrote to his superiors, expressing gratitude for the command he had been given, but expressing his regret at not being provided with a larger ship. He had enough seniority and experience by now to command 'a frigate like the *Belle-Poule* or the *Iphigénie*'.[6] Writing to the top, he had discovered, could be productive and prevent an officer from being lost in the crowd. You merely had to be circumlocutory and express gratitude for a small mercy while hinting that it was small indeed. The administrators would remember you next time and try to improve matters when the opportunity arose. He spent a little more time ashore – and visiting Eléonore – while the *Serin* was being repaired. Then war broke out in earnest, a conflict sparked by the *Belle-Poule*.

Commanded by Bernard de Marigny, she had set out from Brest to take Benjamin Franklin back to America. Two British ships were waiting. Marigny successfully warned them off. This was the king's ship and France was not at war. They moved away, but the weather intervened: a sudden storm forced Marigny to return to Brest and set Franklin back on shore. The frigate was repaired and set out again on 15 June, this time captained by Chadeau de la Clocheterie. The British were still waiting, and HMS *Arethusa* sailed up to challenge the French. 'She hailed me, calling out in English,' reported La Clocheterie. 'I replied that I did not speak that language. Then they used French to instruct me to report to their admiral. I refused and received a broadside. I fired back. The battle lasted six hours.'[7]

Successfully driving off the *Arethusa*, the *Belle-Poule* limped back into Brest to a rapturous welcome. The Duc de Chartres came on board to congratulate the officers and crew. La Clocheterie, although wounded, was invited to Versailles. This was the great age of rococo, with all its flamboyant embellishments, in paintings, furniture and even hairstyles. Fashionable ladies wore high elaborate wigs, and hairdressers seized the occasion to create the 'Belle-Poule style', a tall wig complete with a tiny model of the warship nestling between the curls. French honour had been defended in the face of an unwarranted attack, and all France was celebrating.

The attack also signalled the beginning of the war. Merely arguing that the French king's ships did not have to answer to British vessels was out of the question. The British clearly would not listen. On 10 July, Louis XVI instructed all his captains that henceforth any British vessel they came across should be attacked without parleys or arguments, and he told his ministers to set their war plans in motion. La Pérouse at last got his frigate.

10. THE AMERICAN CAMPAIGN BEGINS

July 1778–February 1780

LA PÉROUSE HAD to travel to Saint-Malo to take over his new command – an impressive brand-new ship, the *Amazone*, of twenty-six guns. It gave him a great feeling to stride along her deck, with the smell of fresh paint and wet tar still in the air. Supplies were being loaded from the local arsenal, and he wanted to make sure that there would be no shortages when he set out to join Ternay on what he thought would be an expedition to the Indian Ocean. The final preparations took almost a month – which meant that he missed the first major engagement of the war, the Battle of Ushant on 27 July. It was counted as an early French success. No ship on either side was actually lost, but the Western Squadron under Admiral Augustus Keppel suffered heavier casualties – 1196 killed and wounded against 680 among the French – and it marked the end of Keppel's career as a commander.

La Pérouse's opportunity came soon. By August, when the *Amazone* was ready, he joined Mengaud de la Hage, in the *Gentille*, and a small cutter, the *Guêpe*, and they went scouting about into the North Sea and around Britain. They brought back no fewer than twelve prizes, most of them small, but it was a gratifying result and a form of revenge for the British pre-emptive raids of the previous year. The French could hardly believe their luck. 'The British flag was no longer seen on these seas where, only a few months earlier, it had been flying as a symbol of mastery or aggression.'[1]

It would not last: Britain was busily fitting out new ships and the French were still too overawed by the reputation of the British Navy. It was enough, however, to satisfy La Pérouse as he waited for orders to sail to the Indian Ocean. As far as he knew, the plans he had drawn up with Ternay had been accepted, and before long they would set out together to challenge British supremacy in the eastern seas.

But the British had been quicker off the mark. Pondicherry was already under attack and after a siege lasting over two months Bellecombe had been forced to surrender. This was the strongest of France's posts on the subcontinent and its loss sounded the death knell of the others. Gone were any dreams they might have had of adopting an offensive posture and boldly flying the French flag along the coast of India. It was obvious that for most of the time they would be on the defensive and at a disadvantage. As far as Versailles was concerned, none of this really mattered – it was more important for France to mobilise her forces in the American theatre of war. Worse still, in spite of all their planning, neither Ternay nor La Pérouse was chosen for the Indian Ocean. Instead, the government sent out the Comte Thomas d'Orves with a mere two ships to the Isle de France, essentially to strengthen the island's defences. Anything else was being shelved, at least for the time being.

It was a bitter blow, but as a kind of consolation, Ternay was promoted to lieutenant-general and supplied with a fresh new ship of the line, the *Annibal*. He might also have derived a little wry satisfaction from seeing D'Orves' little squadron limping back into Brest after being attacked by English privateers off the coast of Portugal. He had succeeded in driving one away and capturing another, but the smaller of his two ships had suffered serious damage and it was unwise to continue any further.

During his stay in Brest La Pérouse was invited to join the Freemasons. For a long time, the movement in France had been regarded with some suspicion by the authorities, especially by the church. A mere forty years earlier, Pope Clement XII had issued a bull condemning it. However, the papal directive had not been registered in France, so Freemasonry remained a legal institution in the kingdom, although always under a cloud. Rather than the modern form of Freemasonry – groups of businessmen and public servants helping each other and engaging in quiet programmes of social work – the French system promoted gatherings of like-minded intellectuals and social reformers, mostly from the upper bourgeoisie. As the eighteenth century – the Age of Reason – progressed many leading figures signed up, including Voltaire, the scientist Joseph Lalande and La Fayette. Lodges were also set up for women, with the Duchesse de Bourbon as Grand Mistress. The local lodge which received La Pérouse was named the *Heureuse Rencontre* (Fortunate Encounter).[2] Freemasons were to play an important role in the rise of the revolutionary movement, although as the French Revolution turned into the Terror, a number of them fell victim to the oppressive rule of Robespierre. La Pérouse's entry into the lodge was in line with his affinity with the *philosophe* movement and with his growing sympathy towards constitutional monarchy and social reforms.

The war in America was put firmly in the limelight when, in February 1779,

La Fayette landed in Brest from Boston. He was welcomed like a hero and went straight down to Versailles to seek increased French help for the colonists. He had a strategy all written out for the ministers – twenty-six pages of it. According to his plan, France could land its forces on friendly or potentially friendly territory: Florida, Louisiana, Canada. The latter offered great prospects, as he expected the French Canadians to rebel against the British occupiers whose conquest of their homeland was so recent. There had already been one attempt by the American insurgents to recapture Quebec City; it had been unsuccessful, but this time, with French help, they would succeed.

His enthusiasm was impressive, but Louis XVI still disliked the idea of being drawn into a great new North American conflict. He had bowed to public opinion and political pressure to give his support to the non-royalist insurgents; he might be persuaded to provide them with troops and supplies, but he was determined not to go too far. He had other pressures to contend with – some of his advisers were pushing for an invasion force to be sent across the Channel while Britain's attention was turned towards her rebellious colonies. It looked easy enough on paper, but it could lead to a full European conflict, because Britain, which was probably not as unprepared as some thought, would quickly call on her allies for assistance. He decided to move cautiously – La Fayette would get his troops and personal promotion for himself, but not much more.

He was also concerned about other matters, such as protecting French overseas interests. This was becoming urgent, because now France's Indian outposts were already either in British hands or being besieged. In addition, the island of Saint Lucia in the West Indies had been captured. Louis XVI knew there were some defensive moves he could make that would satisfy his European allies that France was not embarking on grandiose adventures, but merely fighting back against an aggressor. Posing as an aggrieved party, rather than an ambitious young monarch thirsting for new conquest, would earn him friends and ensure the neutrality of others.

Part of these plans came into operation early in 1779. La Pérouse, Ternay and four other commanders and their ships were told to leave Brest for the outer roadstead. They were to stay close to the open sea, ready to sail out as soon as orders reached them. Officers and crews were cut off from easy communication with the shore, thus ensuring that no one would gossip and that the British were kept in the dark. Ternay was given sealed instructions which he was not to open until life on board had settled down to a routine. He and La Pérouse still hoped, especially with the setback D'Orves had recently suffered, that the squadron would be told to make its way to Rio de Janeiro, obtain more supplies and then sail out for the Indian Ocean. But on 25 February, when Ternay opened his secret instructions, he found that his real destination was the West Indies. He could forget about the Indian Ocean, at least for the time being.

Worse still, he suffered a fall and was forced to seek medical treatment ashore. This meant giving up his command. There were more delays, but the squadron finally set out on 1 May. The new commander was Toussaint-Guillaume de La Motte-Picquet, a tough, experienced sailor in his late fifties who had twenty-two campaigns to his credit, the latest being the Battle of Ushant the previous July, when he had shown what could be done once the French shrugged off their sense of inferiority about the British Navy. La Pérouse was despondent about not going to the Isle de France, but excited at the thought of being part of a major expedition.

La Motte-Picquet was in no mood to waste time. Once off the coast, he was joined by more warships from Lorient and a number of merchant vessels from La Rochelle that had to be escorted to the West Indies. They made up a massive convoy of some 60 ships, large and small, that needed to make its way across the Atlantic, avoiding any lurking English corsairs or warships. Under La Motte-Picquet's watchful command there were no incidents, and they reached Port-Royal in the island of Martinique on 27 June. The Comte Charles d'Estaing, commanding the French forces in the Antilles, was overjoyed at seeing them. Supplies had been running dangerously short, and the recent loss of Saint Lucia had depressed everyone's spirits. Now a great cheer went up. D'Estaing was delighted, and he promptly wrote to the minister to express his gratitude: 'The convoy has arrived! Those four words say everything that is needed ... The King's forces all gathered together present a new spectacle for America. This achievement on your Ministry's part will immortalise it. We are now equal to the English.'3

But while D'Estaing sent his fulsome thanks to the minister, he also ignored the sealed instructions Vergennes had just sent him through La Motte-Picquet. These ordered him to return to France as soon as possible, taking with him a dozen warships and four frigates. But he had other plans in mind. History has given prominence to the moment when Nelson put his telescope to his blind eye and declared that he could not see his commander's order to withdraw. This was the French version: D'Estaing simply put the letter in his pocket and later said that he had forgotten about it.

He wanted to recapture Saint Lucia, the loss of which he considered a blot on his record, but this was not going to be easy with the British forces on their guard. He thought the island of Barbados, standing somewhat on its own to the south-east, might be much easier to capture before Admiral John Byron and others, who were somewhere to the north looking after a British convoy, could react. He sailed without delay, leading a strong fleet of twenty-five ships, including La Pérouse's *Amazone*. The winds, as usual, decided otherwise:

blowing from the east, they drove the French fleet away from Barbados. However, Grenada stood to the south-west, a rather lonely outpost, and D'Estaing decided that this British possession would be as good as any to make up for the loss of Saint Lucia. Versailles would be more than happy and would forgive him his delay in coming home to France.

Early on 2 July, the French troops started to land, 2000 of them facing a mere 700 redcoats defending Fort St George. The British defenders fired a number of salvoes at the French ships, but one set of targets was fixed, while the other could manoeuvre at will. The French fleet sailed past and returned time and again, each time firing at the town and the fortress. By the time dawn broke the next morning, Grenada was ready to surrender. La Pérouse recorded his delight in his journal: 'At last came the daylight I had been waiting for with such impatience, and I saw the white flag flying over the batteries and the fort. We shouted Long Live the King for a quarter of an hour.'[4] Some mopping-up was needed, but it was soon over, and the French could enjoy their victory.

However, the celebrations were short-lived: Byron's fleet was speeding to the rescue. The French sighted the enemy sails as dawn broke on 6 July. Should they fight or flee? Holding onto the island while his ships stayed at anchor off the coast would place D'Estaing's men at a disadvantage. His ships would be in exactly the same situation as the British had been earlier: Byron could sail past, fire his salvoes and manoeuvre at will while the French turned into sitting ducks. It was wiser to get out of the way, let Byron move in and then turn back on him from the open sea. This, however, took time. 'Our frigates sounded the alarm before full daylight came … The General ordered us to weigh anchor,'[5] wrote La Pérouse, but there was not enough time to raise all the anchors. A number of boats and longboats were still ashore, tied up or pulled up on the silty beach. Hoisting them all back on board in a mood of near-panic was impossible.

D'Estaing ordered any ships still struggling with their moorings to cut their cables and sail. The boats that were still ashore would have to stay there, and their men could join the French soldiers in the town. The pressure of time created chaos on land and disorder at sea. Orders were being shouted in every direction, men were running along the shore, trying to get to their ships or to get the batteries ready for the coming fight. D'Estaing was no great organiser, but he had dash and daring. He got fifteen of his ships sufficiently under sail to make straight for the enemy. La Pérouse recorded the pros and cons of this chaotic situation: 'Our General sailed towards the enemy, and we were so close to them that it was impossible, as we sped towards them, to arrange ourselves into any order of battle. But the daring nature of our manoeuvre increased the confidence of our crews and no doubt reduced that of the enemy.'[6]

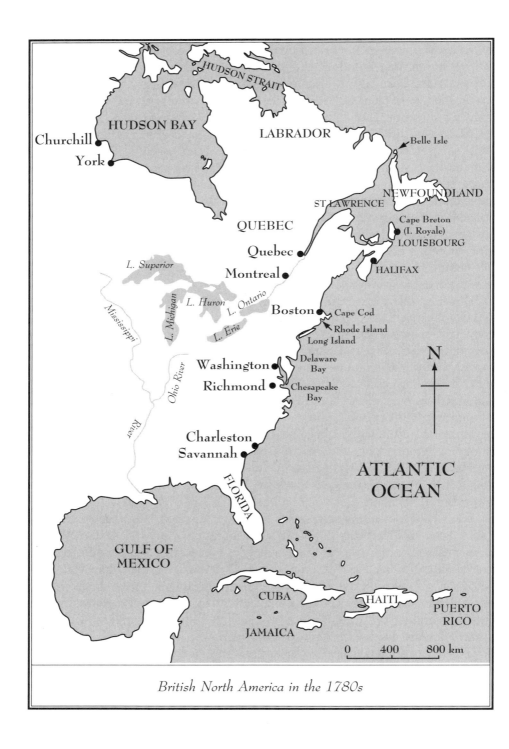

HUDSON STRAIT

HUDSON BAY   LABRADOR

Churchill   ● Belle Isle

York

NEWFOUNDLAND

ST LAWRENCE

QUEBEC   Cape Breton
(I. Royale)
LOUISBOURG

Quebec

Montreal   HALIFAX

L. Superior

L. Huron

L. Michigan   *L. Ontario*

Boston   Cape Cod

L. Erie   Rhode Island
Long Island

Mississippi

Washington   Delaware
Bay
Richmond   Chesapeake
Bay

Ohio River

River

Charleston
Savannah

FLORIDA

N

ATLANTIC
OCEAN

GULF OF
MEXICO

CUBA   HAITI
PUERTO
RICO

JAMAICA

0   400   800 km

British North America in the 1780s

Byron may not even have realised that Grenada had fallen to the French, and when the batteries of Fort St George let fly at his ships, with yelling French gunners firing their salvoes at him from the ships as well, he was forced to change direction urgently, exposing his ships' flanks to further gunfire from both the shore batteries and the returning French warships. He reorganised his fleet as quickly as he could and led a counter-attack. A fierce battle began, which lasted all the morning, costing several hundred lives and a thousand wounded, among them La Motte-Picquet himself, whose thigh was crushed by a cannon ball but who continued to direct operations lying on a mattress on the deck of his *Annibal*.

By mid-afternoon, Byron's only concern was to get away and avoid suffering further damage and casualties. He sailed north to a British base, where he could land his wounded and repair his ships. Grenada would remain French, at least for the time being. D'Estaing would be criticised later for not having chased the enemy while the British vessels were in a state of disarray. How easy this would have been is open to argument: the French still had a number of men and boats on Grenada. He could not sail off and leave them to fend for themselves. They needed protection, and D'Estaing had had no time to organise the island's defences properly. He had captured a British colony and won a sea fight; surely this was enough for the time being – especially as he was supposed to be on his way back to France.

La Pérouse's rôle during the battle had been to ensure that D'Estaing's signals were seen and correctly understood. His *Amazone* spent most of the day manoeuvring between the ships of the French fleet, not quite out of range of the enemy guns, but lucky not to suffer any serious damage. It gave him the chance to observe the battle, which he felt had gone very well. Eager for a greater success, he was one of those who wished D'Estaing had taken greater advantage of Byron's disarray. D'Estaing's ships, the *Amazone* included, went back to Grenada, made arrangements to ensure that the island would be well defended in case the British returned, and sailed to Martinique and then on to French Guadeloupe to carry out some urgent repairs and take on replacements for the men they had lost.

There were reports that Byron's ships had gone to Antigua, but D'Estaing was not sure what other British ships might be around. He prudently decided not to investigate and made instead for Santo Domingo, where he received a tumultuous welcome. He was greatly relieved that Spain had at last decided to enter the war on the French side. However, the Spanish had not sprung immediately into action, so that their help did not greatly affect the early fortunes of war, but on the map at least the situation looked very promising. Spain held Puerto Rico, Cuba and the Florida ports as well as Santo Domingo, which represented half of the large island of Hispaniola; the other half belonged to France.

The British were now outnumbered and D'Estaing, like La Pérouse, believed that London would be satisfied to hold onto its remaining possessions in the West Indies and concentrate the British campaign on the American continent. The Caribbean, delightful under an intense blue sky merging with an even bluer sea, seemed ready for a long spell of peaceful summer days.

But George III had no intention of turning his back on the West Indies. There was growing pessimism throughout Britain about the future of the land war, with a number of critics favouring a peace treaty at almost any price with the rebellious colonists. The American war was proving too costly, and it was time, some felt, to cut their losses. But if the American insurgents got their independence, the settlers in the West Indies might want to go the same way. And after them might come Ireland and even Scotland. The final result might be the economic ruin of Great Britain. There is nothing modern about the domino theory. George III urged his ministers to continue the struggle on every front: this was a fight for survival.

Meanwhile, confident that the French and Spanish islands were safe, D'Estaing prepared to sail north to America. Representatives of the insurgents and their French sympathisers, who had been pressing him to act, were overjoyed. Neither they nor his officers had any idea that he had received orders to go back to France. On 16 August 1779, he ordered his fleet – twenty-two ships of the line, nine frigates, two corvettes and two storeships, plus fifteen merchantmen, large and small – to sail for South Carolina. La Pérouse was delighted. He had been worried about a suggestion that he should be sent back to France to report to Versailles. Instead, he was once again to take part in a naval engagement.

By 1 September, the French fleet was preparing to land on the coast of Georgia, south of the British-held town of Savannah. The plan was to march up to it and catch the British defenders by surprise, but the terrain put paid to that idea. The troops found that they had to struggle through some 20 kilometres of marshlands and muddy creeks, dragging up their guns and other equipment, which brought them into range of the British defences. Stormy weather out at sea did not help matters, because food and other supplies could not be landed. Giving up any hope of catching the defenders off their guard, D'Estaing and the American General Abraham Lincoln reluctantly got down to a siege, but time was not on their side. A steady shelling in early October did little damage to the British defenders, who were comfortably dug in among sandhills. There was also the ever-present possibility that Admiral Byron, having repaired his ships, might appear at any moment and engage the French vessels anchored off the coast and desperately struggling to support the troops on shore.

The only solution was a frontal attack, a dose of the famous *furia francese*. On 9 October, the combined French and American forces launched a dashing full assault. It failed: the well-entrenched British troops shot the attacking columns to tatters. The French lost 1250 men killed, with 370 wounded including D'Estaing himself. On the 20th, it was decided to lift the siege and return to the ships. The moment the weary troops were back on board, a wild storm struck the French ships, scattering them in every direction. Some sailed south back to Martinique, others made for the Chesapeake, and D'Estaing, at last obeying the instructions that must have by then been burning a hole in his pocket, sailed for Brest.

La Pérouse had not taken part in the Battle of Savannah. He had been ordered to escort a number of merchant ships to French-held Charleston, further north in South Carolina. It looked as if he was back on humdrum duties, but on his way there, at dawn on the 9th October, he was involved in a solo battle of his own:

> I sighted a vessel so far away from me that I could not estimate its strength; but since the ships I was convoying had no further risks to run before they sailed into Charleston, I gave chase to the vessel I could see. It was making towards me, so that I was soon convinced that it was a frigate... At eight o'clock, we were only half a league away; she then raised the British flag and fired a shot by way of confirmation. I also raised the British flag but without confirming it, and the frigate at once veered off, wind astern and all sails out. I followed, similarly letting out all my sails ... At 10 o'clock I was within a pistol shot. I hoisted the French flag and fired a gun. The vessel, which had only twenty 9-pounders and six 4-pounders, fought with a bravery that cannot be praised too highly.[7]

The battle lasted a little over an hour. The British frigate, which was the *Ariel* commanded by Thomas Mackenzie, had all her masts smashed before she finally surrendered. La Pérouse lost twelve of his men, with a further thirteen seriously wounded; his mainmast had been pierced by a cannon ball and threatened to come down at any moment; the sails were in tatters, their shrouds or ropes cut through.

He limped into Charleston on the 11th, towing the *Ariel*, to the cheers of his friends and of the hard-pressed Americans. It was a small victory in the broader conflict, but it could not have come at a better time.

The autumn was approaching, and with it came storms and heavy rains. Repelled at Charleston and wounded in one of the skirmishes, D'Estaing had sailed for Brest. For him, the war was effectively over. The Nelson touch earns praise only when it results in some glorious victory. D'Estaing could claim a few successes, but he also had some failures to answer for. He had taken a gamble and lost, and he sat out the rest of the war like an unwanted guest at the dinner table. Years later, he returned to action and a moment of glory when the outbreak of the French Revolution propelled him to the rank of vice-admiral, with the task of reorganising the sorely tried French Navy. And then the Terror sent him to the guillotine, aged 65, where, like so many others, he threw out a final challenge. His last words were: 'When my head has fallen, take it to the English. They'll give you a good price for it'.

La Pérouse took his *Amazone* not to Brest, but by a roundabout route to Cadiz. With him went the *Sagittaire* and a recently captured prize, the *Experiment*, a ship of 50 guns and too good to be left behind, since aboard her had been found General George Garth and £650,000 in silver, as well as quantities of supplies and clothing. The latter had been especially welcome, as most of the French sailors still wore their light and worn-out summer clothing, so that when the ships reached Spain a number of them were dressed in a strange motley of British uniforms. There was another prize, a small British corsair, the *Tiger*, captured by La Pérouse during the Atlantic crossing. It was not particularly valuable, but it gave him a feeling of satisfaction.

The small squadron reached Cadiz on 15 December 1779. They needed a few days' rest, La Pérouse above all. He landed his sick and wounded at the local hospital, had a few makeshift repairs made and prepared to sail to Lorient, the *Sagittaire* with the *Experiment* deciding to go to Toulon. On 28 February 1780, he dropped anchor in Lorient harbour. Ternay was waiting for him, impatient to set out on another campaign: he had orders to escort a large French force to assist the American insurgents. There was no time for La Pérouse to relax. No sooner had he set foot on land than Ternay sent him off to Versailles to finalise the preparations with Claret de Fleurieu.

The town of Albi, Languedoc, as it was in the eighteenth century.

Le Gô, the country house of the La Pérouse family, where Jean-François was born.

The home of the La Pérouse family in Albi.

The fort at the naval port of Brest, where Jean-François began his career as a cadet.

'The Battle of Quiberon Bay: the Day After', a painting by Richard Wright.

Jean-François de La Pérouse.

Eléonore Broudou, who waited eight years to marry Jean-François.

Louis XVI and his minister the Marquis de Castries give their final instructions to La Pérouse before he leaves on his long voyage, 29 June 1785. Painting by Nicolas Monsiau.

Members of the expedition meet the inhabitants of Easter Island.

The two expedition frigates off Maui, Hawaii.

Disaster befell the expedition when two boats capsized near the dangerous harbour entrance at Lituya Bay, Alaska.

The French meet the natives at the Baie de Langle, on the present-day Russian island of Sakhalin.

The attack at Tutuila, Samoa.

Botany Bay, with the monument to La Pérouse's expedition.

The inscription on the monument at Botany Bay.

The tomb of Fr Receveur at Botany Bay.

Statue of La Pérouse at Albi.

11. THE STRUGGLE CONTINUES

March 1780–April 1781

WHILE D'ESTAING was struggling to save his reputation in the West Indies, Ternay had been working hard to get a fleet together. At the start, it had not looked too difficult, but the task seemed to be growing day by day. The French government had shed all its inhibitions about challenging British power on the high seas and on the American continent. It was now all or nothing, and Versailles was determined to be on the winning side – too many wars had been lost during the century, but now was France's opportunity.

And the American cause had wide support in France. The *philosophes* and their supporters were enthusiastic about the insurgents' ideals, now enshrined in the preamble to the Declaration of Independence: 'We hold these truths to be self-evident, that all men are created equal'. To the new generation of French men and women, brought up in the atmosphere of the Enlightenment, with the challenging theories of Jean-Jacques Rousseau and Voltaire, but kept back by a class-ridden social system, this sounded like a clarion call. The further suggestion, that 'Governments are instituted among men, deriving their just powers from the consent of the governed', was an equally exciting challenge to the rule of an aristocracy that derived its powers from their birth and from feudal traditions. Even the divine right of kings, who claimed to rule with the consent and approval of the deity, was challenged by such statements. Those who worried that supporting the men who had drafted such a declaration would undermine their privileged position consoled themselves with the thought that the real losers in all this would be the British, and that European societies were unlikely to be affected by the American storm.

So a major programme was under way to assist the insurgents. A French army would sail to America and make sure that Britain's hold on the continent was broken. La Fayette may have seemed like the obvious choice to lead it. He had served successfully in the French Army, rising to the rank of captain before going over to America where Congress had given him a commission

121

as major-general. But however successful and popular he might be, he was still only twenty-two, and an officer with greater seniority and experience was needed. The onus had fallen on Jean-Baptiste, Comte de Rochambeau, a 55-year-old veteran of numerous campaigns. A soldier since the age of seventeen, he had fought valiantly in Holland, Germany and Austria and, more recently, in Minorca. Better still, he was a true professional soldier, uninvolved in the seemingly endless court intrigues of the time, and satisfied, as some said, to serve the army and his country.

At first, the plan had been to send 1000 men with artillery and other support. Rochambeau swept this aside: if France was to play an honourable part in the conflict, much more was needed. He asked for 12 divisions, which meant 6000 men. Versailles agreed. The more realistic officials at the Ministry of Marine pointed out that they lacked the resources to send such a large expeditionary corps across the Atlantic. The figure was brought back to 5000. Very well, but he would need cavalry, insisted Rochambeau. His wish was granted.

Ternay knew how difficult it would be to take all these men and their equipment across the Atlantic, a distance of 4500–5000 kilometres. Transport ships were inevitably slow and heavy, dependent, as always, on wind and weather. Ternay would have to protect them from enemy raiders and guide them along the way. As Rochambeau was granted more men and facilities back in Versailles, the problem of getting enough ships and crews together became more difficult. He was told that there was no time to waste, but Versailles seemed oblivious to the challenges that Ternay had to face. La Pérouse's arrival was a godsend. He had been to America and knew what was required to get Rochambeau and his army over. When La Pérouse landed, looking for at least a short period of leave and a little time with Eléonore, Ternay told him to forget about it and hurry to Versailles to discuss the massive logistical problems with Claret de Fleurieu.

La Pérouse was happy enough to travel overland and renew his acquaintance with Fleurieu. They had so much to talk about, in particular recent developments in Pacific exploration, which almost seemed to be a British monopoly after the three voyages of James Cook. Only Louis de Bougainville had succeeded in earning any glory for France in those distant seas.

But there was no time for leisurely conversation. The amount of equipment being gathered for the Rochambeau expedition was impressive. Montbarrey, a War Ministry official, had drawn up detailed instructions to ensure that Rochambeau's corps was suitably equipped. It was a seemingly endless list, which included 10,000 shirts, 10,370 pairs of shoes, 1200 greatcoats, 4000 blankets, 1210 tents, 1000 cooking pots and a similar quantity of mess-tins, cans, bill-hooks, shovels, axes and pickaxes. All this and the stocks of food were to be 'carefully packed and stowed'. It was the king's property, as Montbarrey reminded everyone, to be used in the king's service and not squandered.

Drawing up a list – or several lists, as more followed – was easy enough. Finding the ships was another matter. The war effort had by now almost drained the country's naval reserves. The transport vessels they could use were scattered from Le Havre to Bordeaux, others were already away ferrying troops and supplies to the West Indies or to American ports, and those that were readily available were in a poor condition. In addition, there were not enough men available in the ports. This was evident in Brest where merchant captains, themselves hard pressed, were trying to tempt men off warships onto their own, supposedly safer, vessels. Most days, one could see patrols, drums rolling and guns at the ready, going through the streets, clearing out the taverns and driving laggards back to their ships. A kind of emergency reserve had been gathered on the ship *Fine*, but they scarcely totalled 100.

The situation in Brest was not made any easier by the steady flood of troops arriving from various regiments. The roads were particularly muddy, often turned into quagmires by the early spring rains, and most of the soldiers were covered with mud. They could be set to work cleaning their uniforms, but apart from that all they could do was wait for the ships to be made ready. Meanwhile, they had to be kept in makeshift camps and prevented, as far as was humanly possible, from visiting the local taverns, where fights between them and the sailors were all too common.

The warships needed repair. Fleurieu agreed with La Pérouse that copper-bottoming the naval units was desirable if they were to manoeuvre safely close to the American coast and engage the enemy, but there simply was not enough copper sheeting available. He sent La Pérouse on to Nantes and Lorient to check with the heads of the local arsenals and shipyards to see what could be found, and to bully them into finding men and supplies. A chorus of complaints greeted him: 'We can't conjure supplies or sailors out of thin air. It's easy enough for the government to grant Rochambeau's requests and sign the authorising documents, but what do all these landlubbers in Versailles know about the navy's difficulties?' It was a tiring, strenuous mission, but he was the best man for the job: he knew the navy and the naval yards, knew their problems and their petty jealousies, and he could also explain what would be required for the crossing and for the navigation along the American coast.

Back in Brest, La Pérouse went almost daily with Ternay to talk things over with the Comte Charles Jean d'Hector, the director of the arsenals and shore installations, a sympathetic and able man who was doing all he could to help, even though he daily struggled with a tidal wave of orders and counter-orders.

La Pérouse would remember the month of March 1780 as one of the most exhausting he had lived through. But it was a fruitful one. By 9 April, almost all the shipping that could be got together was ready, starting to weigh anchor and making its way into the Brest roadstead – getting away from the quayside helped to prevent last-minute desertions or, at the very least, the endless carousing that went on in the taverns when the men had nothing to do.

Ternay and Rochambeau had to decide which port to make for. 'Obviously,' wrote Ternay, 'we cannot land on a point of the coast where the enemy disposes of superior forces.'[1] He favoured Cape Henry, the southernmost point of Chesapeake Bay, where he hoped to get in touch with La Fayette, who had sailed from Brest a couple of weeks earlier. Failing that, they could make for Rhode Island, which they knew was controlled by the insurgents.

Ternay called a general meeting on 12 April to outline the plan and issue his final instructions. He had taken over command of the *Duc de Bourgogne*, a ship of 80 guns. His fleet consisted of two ships of 74, four of 64, two frigates of 32, as well as four *flûtes* or storeships. They were escorting a total of twenty-eight transports, crowded with men and supplies. La Pérouse was in command of his faithful *Amazone*.

They had expected to be joined by the *Charmante*, commanded by Charles Mengaud de la Hage, but on her way from Lorient, she struck a rock near the Ile de Sein. More than two-thirds of the complement were drowned, some 200 men in all. And one of these was her captain, La Pérouse's great friend from the Isle de France. It was a sad blow for him. Mengaud was one of the few who knew of his continuing attachment to Eléonore Broudou, still patiently waiting for him in Nantes. Only a few days earlier, La Pérouse had been able to spend a little time with her when he was in Nantes, and they had fondly shared memories of Mengaud and the property they had bought in Wilhems Plains. Eléonore was in tears when he left – now he had to write a letter of farewell and give her the sad news.

On the 17th, everything was ready. The ships were crammed with soldiers – four regiments of them: the Bourdonnais, Soissonnais, Saintonge and Royal-Deux-Ponts – plus 500 German auxiliaries, in addition to labourers and military police. As always, one had to wait for a favourable wind. 'When God pleases,' sailors used to say. Days went by, an irritating delay relieved by news that a storm was blowing up in the Channel. 'Rain over Portsmouth is always good news,' Ternay told Rochambeau, by way of consolation. 'It keeps the British ships in port.' Finally, on 2 May, the fleet began to emerge out of the Goulet and make its way south and west.

La Pérouse was now effectively acting as *capitaine de vaisseau*; his rank was formally confirmed a year later. His task during the slow crossing, which took two months, was to sail around the clumsy merchantmen, rather like a hardworking sheepdog making sure the laggard ewes keep up with the flock. In this, he was assisted by the other frigate captain, Cillard de Villeneuve. At least it kept them busy, not merely chafing at the convoy's slow progress. The dictum about the speed of a convoy being equal to the speed of its slowest ship was once again proved correct.

Inevitably, given the crowded conditions, scurvy made its appearance. Biron de Lauzun, who had to his credit the recent recapture of the French outposts in Senegal and who was now leading his men to America, grumbled about unsympathetic naval officers and the conditions of his soldiers 'crammed, six or seven hundred of them per ship, unable to move about, drinking water that is so old it has taken on a reddish colour, eaten by lice, bugs and fleas'.[2] All he could do to alleviate the boredom was to organise impromptu concerts by the collection of musicians he had brought with him – fifes, trumpets and drums.

Boredom vanished on 10 June when a sail was sighted, an unlucky cutter on her way from Halifax to the West Indies with a cargo of cod, herring and oil. La Pérouse's *Amazone* gave chase, easily capturing her. The crew were taken prisoner and the boat sunk, but not before her cargo had been shared among the various warships. It created a scene of chaos: 'Each warship was allowed to send a boat to collect its share of the booty. The men fought among themselves and during the mêlée a sailor fell overboard. Unable to swim, he had to be rescued.'[3] This episode lightened the mood a little, as the soldiers guffawed for days about sailors who could not swim.

A week later, as they neared the Bermudas, another sail appeared, this time a corvette of twelve guns from Charleston, also on her way to the West Indies. It was Cillard's turn to give chase and capture her. From her crew, Rochambeau and Ternay learnt that General Sir Henry Clinton had captured Charleston a month earlier and that the British, now well entrenched, both there and at Halifax, knew about the French convoy and were waiting for it. Worse still, British ships were patrolling the approaches, looking for it.

This made Ternay cautious, especially when six ships were seen on 20 June approximately 160 kilometres south-west of Bermuda. His officers were eager to take on the enemy, whom they comfortably outnumbered, but his instructions were to see Rochambeau's troops safely landed, not to take risks and delay the convoy with a naval engagement. The officers argued that the odds were so much in their favour that they could quickly cut off the enemy, which consisted of only one frigate and five smaller vessels. He compromised by allowing an exchange of shots. There was always the possibility that the enemy, realising it was outclassed, would quickly surrender. This did not happen: there were a few casualties on both sides, night fell and Ternay called off his ships. When dawn broke, there was no further sign of the British.

La Pérouse had stayed back to protect the convoy in case one of the enemy ships broke away to fire a few shots at some of the slower transport vessels, so he was not involved. Ternay had to face a fair amount of criticism over what some of the officers called his excessive timidity, but Rochambeau was full of praise. Ternay, he said, had been man enough 'to prefer the preservation of the convoy to the personal glory of capturing an enemy ship'.[4]

Ternay was aware that Admiral Thomas Graves's fleet was looking for him and that the situation was becoming more perilous as the convoy neared the American coast. There was another alert when, one night, a couple of British frigates, mistaking the convoy for one of theirs, tagged on behind. Discovering their error, they lobbed a few shots as they veered back as quickly as they could, throwing a few guns and masts overboard to lighten themselves. The *Amazone* and the *Surveillante* started to give chase, but Ternay signalled them back. They were too near to the end of their mission to compromise it with unnecessary captures.

They had sailed in a wide curve across the Atlantic, starting as if they were going to the West Indies, then heading north just off the American coast past areas where the British were active or in actual control. They went well beyond New York towards Newport, Rhode Island, which they reached without problem on 11 July. This was the end of their mission; Rochambeau and his senior staff transferred to La Pérouse's *Amazone* for the final few kilometres.

When he landed, Rochambeau felt both disappointed and puzzled. He had expected to be welcomed as a liberator and a friend. Instead, he found a small town only recently freed from British rule and still divided between loyalists and supporters of the Revolution. A fair number were not anxious to see their streets overrun with loud, hard-drinking and, above all, Roman Catholic soldiers and seamen, to say nothing of the 1000 scurvy cases who had to be accommodated in makeshift hospitals. It took some time for the locals to thaw – the northern colonies were peopled by icicles, shrugged Rochambeau as he set about the task of assuring the townspeople that he had come to help La Fayette and Washington, to bring a quicker end to the war and thereby ensure the future prosperity of the port. Gradually, the stiff New Englanders relaxed, and by the 20th men and stores were safely ashore.

It was not a day too soon. The very next day, the fleet of Admiral Graves, sent out from Portsmouth specially to track down Ternay's convoy, appeared off Rhode Island. Rochambeau heaved a sigh of relief that the landing operation was over, but Ternay's ships were effectively bottled up. When La Fayette arrived on the 25th in excellent spirits, keen to organise a march on British-held New York, he was dumbfounded. He had sailed from France ahead of a convoy which he had been told would bring 6000 men to help the Americans. Now Rochambeau told him the true number was 5000 and that 1000 of them were sick. Furthermore, he needed at least 2500 men to hold Newport against an expected attack by Graves and, in view of recent reports that General Sir Henry Clinton was on the march, the rest would be needed to defend the town from that quarter. Clinton's troops attacking from the landward while Graves' warships shelled the town from seaward was precisely what the citizens of Newport had feared.

La Fayette wrote hastily to Washington. His strategy was for Washington to come to Rochambeau's aid, clearing Clinton's troops from the countryside, after which the French would be able to join him in an all-out campaign against the British. But Washington rejected the idea as absurd. The situation was becoming worse than if Versailles had not sent any troops at all, and he certainly had no troops to spare to reinforce Rochambeau. The situation was saved when General Clinton decided to ignore Newport. Instead, he landed his troops at New York, feeling that was safer. He had no information about the French troops which, he believed, numbered 6000, possibly more. Let Admiral Graves keep them occupied. He would later be blamed for missing a great opportunity. Clearing Louis XVI's troops from the American continent would have been a superb psychological victory – but military campaigns are always easy in hindsight.

It took time for Rochambeau to be sure than Clinton had bypassed Newport, and even more to feel confident that Admiral Graves's ships were not going to attack. Plans were made and unmade on both sides during an oppressively hot August. The convoy had brought some food for the men, but it was beginning to run out. Rochambeau issued strict orders that nothing was to be taken from the inhabitants without their consent and anything received should always be against payment. The penalty for looters was a prompt hanging. As a result, food was rationed, with slightly larger rations going to the sick, whom Rochambeau needed back on duty as soon as possible. Prices soared. The harvest could not begin soon enough.

A great deal of time was also wasted in correspondence. Rochambeau and Ternay decided to meet Washington at Hartford, Connecticut, in mid-September for a full discussion. The French had set up an efficient organisation around Newport and the scurvy cases were recovering, but the autumn weather would soon hamper military operations. It was no time to be rash. Both sides agreed to wait and ask Versailles for more help, so that a joint anti-British offensive could start in the spring and be effective enough to turn the tide of war. Meanwhile, both Rochambeau and Washington would dig in for the winter.

If any justification was needed for the policy of proceeding with caution and seeking more assistance, it was provided by the unmasking of Benedict Arnold, the commandant of West Point, the key to the Hudson River valley. He had been in touch with General Clinton for several months and had agreed to surrender the fort to the British in exchange for a commission in the British forces. Among the reasons for his betrayal was a dislike of the Franco-American alliance and of Roman Catholic France. He fled to the loyalist side a mere two days after the Rochambeau-Washington meeting, thereby becoming the United States's most famous traitor. A skilled general, with a detailed knowledge of the terrain and of the insurgent army's tactics, he now became the scourge of his former friends.

Rochambeau's appeal to Versailles needed to be made by an influential representative and one free from any self-motivation or the petty jealousies of the service. It would not be an easy mission. He had come to America with all the support France could muster, and he had really very little to show for it. Knowing that family influences were always important, he chose his own son, the Vicomte de Rochambeau, a colonel in the expeditionary force. But time was of the essence, and he had to be conveyed as quickly and as safely as possible to France. The captain selected for this task was La Pérouse.

The *Amazone* sailed on 28 October, accompanied by Cillard de Villeneuve's *Surveillante* and Louis-René de Latouche-Tréville's *Hermione*. These were bound for Boston, but together they would make up a force strong enough for any British vessel patrolling the approaches to Rhode Island to veer off. As it turned out, a wild north-westerly gale, bringing down the first warnings of a harsh winter, scattered any of Admiral George Rodney's fleet that might be guarding the coast. La Pérouse did sight a few enemy vessels, but he crowded on sails to get away from them as quickly as he could. There was a price to pay for carrying too much canvas in a high wind – his main topmast broke – but all three got away safely. Just as they were about to separate, La Pérouse going on to France and the other two veering west for Boston, they came upon an unfortunate British merchantman carrying a cargo of port wine. It was captured with little difficulty and Cillard took it to Plymouth, a small port south of Boston, where he exchanged the port for more humdrum but urgently needed supplies which he then took down to Rochambeau's army.

La Pérouse completed the crossing to Brest without incident and relatively quickly – just over five weeks. As soon as the *Amazone* was tied up, he and Colonel Rochambeau hurried to Versailles. They had just learnt that there had been a government reshuffle a couple of months earlier and that the new Minister of Marine and the Colonies was the Marquis de Castries. This was more important news for them than the death of Maria-Theresa, the Empress of Austria and Marie-Antoinette's mother, in late November. The French court was in mourning but the political processes were continuing. The appointment of Charles de la Croix, Marquis de Castries, was excellent from La Pérouse's point of view. Born in Paris in 1727 but orphaned from the age of two, he had been brought up under the supervision of his uncle, Armand Pierre of Castries, who was Archbishop of Albi. Not only was La Pérouse able to reminisce with Castries, but one of the new minister's tutors turned out to have been Jean-François' own grandfather, Father Jean-Antoine, canon of the cathedral. Young Rochambeau was also in luck. Castries' son, the Comte de Charlus, was serving in America as part of Rochambeau's expeditionary force. He also happened to be a good friend of La Fayette. Castries, glad to have first-hand news of his son, welcomed both envoys formally and informally.

La Pérouse and Rochambeau were greatly cheered by the new political situation. Castries promised to do everything he could to help. La Pérouse was instructed to return to Brest as quickly as possible and sail back to America, to assure Ternay and Rochambeau that reinforcements and supplies would be sent as soon as practicable. This was fair enough, but young Rochambeau, a realist, stayed behind to make sure that these promises were carried out. It was a wise move. Money, as always, was tight and Castries would have to argue his case with the Comptroller-General of Finance, Jacques Necker, who was compiling a detailed *compte-rendu*, or financial statement, showing that France had very little cash to spare for foreign ventures unless – and this would give rise to howls of protest – realistic forms of taxation with no exceptions for the privileged classes were introduced.

Still, Castries was able to back his promises with some immediate tangible aid. Soldiers and their equipment would take time to assemble, but getting his hands on ready cash was easier. He was, after all, a new minister with a great deal of goodwill to his credit, and officials were eager to please him. So La Pérouse was entrusted with 1.5 million *livres*, a substantial sum that would put an end to the endless haggling the French had had to face on the American continent. Glad that he would not land empty-handed at Newport, La Pérouse hurried to Brest. There another tangible expression of Castries' goodwill awaited him: a brand-new frigate of thirty-two guns.

She was called the *Astrée*, a name loaded with romantic and patriotic associations. It was the title of a lengthy and immensely popular seventeenth-century novel, which depicted love as an honourable sentiment, of which virtue, modesty and above all constancy were the leading characteristics. Various episodes showed love conflicting with duty and the call of what others would regard as honour. Many of these aspects, as he cannot have failed to point out to Eléonore and her brother during a hurried visit, echoed their own situation. The name was not totally inappropriate for a warship: the novel contained several battle scenes, in one of which the hero is wounded, as well as a traitor one could, with a small effort, identify with Benedict Arnold. More important, the frigate was well equipped, copper-bottomed and ready to sail. It was far superior to the now tired *Amazon* that required remasting, new sails and a general cleaning and repainting. Practically all her officers and men were promptly transferred to the *Astrée*, which sailed from Brest on Christmas Day 1780.

It was a rough midwinter crossing that lasted 64 days, a severe test for the new frigate, which withstood the storms without serious damage – although La Pérouse made sure that Castries was aware of the troubles she had encountered. He wrote a few days after his arrival in Boston:

> Never have I encountered weather as bad as what we endured between the 2nd and the 17th of February. I was then a hundred leagues east of the Newfoundland Bank. I was forced to sail south down to the 25th degree, otherwise I would have lost all my crew. The 'tween-deck hatchways had to stay shut for a fortnight and any sail that caught the wind was immediately carried away. Finally I reached Boston without any serious damage, having lost only two men, but I have 25 of them sick … during the crossing I met only two Dutch vessels, which I hailed, and one that I believe was English cruising along the latitude of the Chesapeake; my instructions forbidding me to investigate, I did not go close enough to identify it, nor do I believe that I was recognised myself.[5]

The big shock on arrival was to be told that Ternay had died – 'The best friend I had in the entire world; he had been like a father to me from the time I joined the Navy'.[6] This was no empty sentiment. La Pérouse had always depended on the aristocratic naval officer who had taken him under his wing years earlier, and he felt closer to him than he did to the stern patriarch back in Albi. Ternay had not died of frustration at his enforced inaction and the petty squabbles that surrounded him, as some have suggested, but from the typhoid epidemic that had been ravaging the town.

He had been succeeded by the Chevalier Charles René Destouches, a *capitaine de vaisseau* and the most senior of the captains of the small Rhode Island fleet. Eager to put an end to the winter of inaction, he had, with Rochambeau's agreement, organised a small force to assist La Fayette, who was now threatened by detachments of redcoats led by Benedict Arnold. He was disappointed that La Pérouse had not brought with him the much-awaited reinforcements, but remained hopeful that they would arrive soon. He decided to continue the struggle against Arnold's men and lead a raid up Chesapeake Bay.

La Pérouse was asked to go up to Boston and make sure than no enemy ships roamed into Massachusetts Bay. It was routine work, policing well-known waters where few British ships were about. Meanwhile, on 16 March, Destouches engaged the enemy on land. His eight ships came upon a similar number of vessels from Admiral Graves's fleet. There was a fierce exchange of gunfire, with 100 casualties on each side. Graves turned away and Destouches went back to Newport to land the dead and wounded and repair his ships. It was a victory of sorts, and the American Congress, glad the French were active at last, sent him a message of congratulations.

La Pérouse played no part in all this, beyond keeping an eye on the waters further north. Things brightened up a little in April when he was told that an attack was being planned on Penobscot Bay, north of Boston. The British had a well-defended fort there, but a French force, with the advantage of surprise and moderately superior numbers, should be able to capture it without too much difficulty. Rochambeau agreed to provide 820 men, just to make sure. La Pérouse's *Astrée* had been on patrol off this coast and he had every hope that he could play a major role in the expedition. Unfortunately, the operation was not likely to have much effect on the overall situation. General Clinton was solidly ensconced in New York and planning to lead an offensive at any moment, while further south General Charles Cornwallis was marching into Virginia, raiding at will and destroying the sorely battered insurgent colony. La Fayette was hurrying on his way to help the insurgents in the south, and a French raid on a northern outpost like Penobscot would make little difference to the campaign. If anything, being a mere 160 kilometres from British-held Canada, it could turn out to be a liability, costly to hold for very little advantage.

In the end Rochambeau decided to stay put and wait for the promised reinforcements. Good news arrived on 6 May when his son reached Boston in a fast frigate. He brought news that a large convoy had left France on 22 March, led by the Admiral François de Grasse. It was a massive fleet – over 30 warships escorting 100 transports. Leading the vanguard was the 'Blue Squadron' led by the famous French circumnavigator Louis de Bougainville. Crowds had lined the quays and from the heights all along the famous Brest Goulet, peasants and sailors' wives had cheered wildly. Even the Minister of Marine had come up from Versailles to wave the ships off. No one now had any doubt the war would finally swing in the Americans' favour.

But the convoy was bound for the West Indies. The French Caribbean possessions had to be protected, first and foremost, and the men would need to be rested and reorganised before they were ready for a military campaign in the unfamiliar surroundings of colonial America. The waterways of Rhode Island were certainly not a safe place to bring them, and Boston was still too insecure and ill-equipped. The French island of Martinique would be their first port of call, after which, probably with Spanish reinforcements, they could sail to the continent. A few ships were being detached from the main convoy to join Rochambeau's forces, but not enough to make any difference.

12. Triumphs and Defeats

April 1781–May 1782

La Pérouse felt happy enough to be involved in the various manoeuvres, political and naval, going on in France and in America, but he also felt a little uneasy about the way things were developing or, rather, dragging on. The repeated delays affecting the French troops and their naval escort were threatening to undermine a mission he had been secretly entrusted with in Versailles – a raid on northern Canada.

He had planned this with Claret de Fleurieu during his recent visit to France, and it had been promptly approved by both Castries and Louis XVI. The idea was to sail into Hudson Bay, which had long been the preserve of British traders. This vast expanse of ice floe-cluttered waters had been discovered by the English navigator Henry Hudson back in 1610 during a search for the so-called North-West Passage, the dream of so many explorers, which they hoped would lead them from the Atlantic to the Pacific. The *Discovery* had become trapped in the winter ice and after months of extreme suffering the crew had mutinied and set Hudson adrift in a small boat with his son and seven others. Some of the mutineers survived to reach England – and prison – but Hudson was never seen again. In 1670, Charles II had granted exclusive trading rights to Prince Rupert and seventeen other noblemen and gentlemen who had formed the Company of Adventurers of England, trading into Hudson Bay. They still controlled the vastness of the bay, obtaining furs and skins, mostly from the local Indians.

It was an immensely profitable business, though it had suffered for some years from competition by French fur traders to the south. The conquest of French Canada had largely restored the company's monopoly. Fleurieu and La Pérouse saw an unexpected attack on the bay settlements as a resounding challenge to British supremacy in a war that had seen too many moves ending in a stalemate. They also saw advantages from a geographical point of view: anyone sailing into those waters would test the reliability of the British charts, always a little suspect when a business monopoly was involved (as was the case in the Dutch East Indies), and this would be valuable should a French attempt be made to explore the road to the supposed North-West Passage.

They realised that the French Navy would be unable to spare more than a couple of ships for the enterprise, but this would be enough for their purpose. They would have no hope of success, however, if the British were forewarned. Secrecy was paramount. Castries gave La Pérouse private instructions that would override the authority of whoever was in charge of the French naval forces in America, but this did not mean that he could do anything that interfered with political or strategic considerations in the West Indies. He could go as and when circumstances permitted, but no sooner. On the other hand, once he was in a position to proceed, the local authorities would have to help him.

He had his own ship, but a second one had to be found, and that was easier said than done. He was promised the *Sagittaire*, which was expected to sail from France in early February, but weeks had gone by with no sign of her. La Pérouse became increasingly despondent. It was possible to enter Hudson Bay and get out safely during the months of June to early August, but after that, the ice would block them in. This meant that he would need to sail from Newport or Boston in early May – but when the *Sagittaire* finally reached New England, limping into Salem harbour, it was 4 June. She had been battered by almost daily storms, the crossing had lasted 75 days and she had 150 sick on board, mostly scurvy cases. It would take a month to ready her for a new expedition and she needed an entirely fresh crew. La Pérouse now had no hope of reaching Hudson Bay before the first ice made its appearance, and certainly none of getting out again.

Sorrowfully, he put his instructions away among his personal belongings and waited for other orders. Ternay's replacement, Admiral Louis Jacques de Barras, found something for him to do: he sent him off, together with the *Hermione*, under Latouche-Tréville, to patrol the estuary of the Saint Lawrence River to chase off any British vessels he might come across. And on the way he could escort a convoy of six transports ferrying supplies from Boston to Martha's Vineyard.

By now, it was early July. The war was swinging wildly from side to side. General Cornwallis had recently defeated General Nathanael Greene at Guildford in North Carolina, and he was now threatening Virginia, organising raids against Charlottesville and almost capturing Thomas Jefferson in the process. However, his campaign had meant depleting the loyalist troops holding New York under General Clinton, which led Washington and La Fayette to seriously consider an attack on this key city. Rochambeau's men had begun to advance – cautiously because this was territory they knew little about – but to capture New York they would need the reinforcements that France had sent over under De Grasse. And those were now in the West Indies. Barras sent out urgent pleas to bring up the French and any troops he could spare, together with anything the Spanish could muster. It was De Grasse, he was sure, who held the key to final success.

Cornwallis realised that his lines of communication were overstretched. Greene was once again on the march, eager to avenge his recent defeats. On 21 June, Cornwallis evacuated Richmond – 'a devastated town', wrote La Fayette,[1] who rode through its ruins the next day. British forces began to concentrate around Yorktown near the mouth of the Chesapeake Bay. From there, Cornwallis could keep in touch with Clinton's forces in New York and form a united front. Rochambeau realised that if De Grasse could move up to the New England coast, the British would be entering a trap that the French could slam shut.

So where was De Grasse? He had first tried to take the British-held island of Saint Lucia, but failed and had to satisfy himself with the island of Tobago. Knowing Admiral Rodney was looking for him, he had made his way back to the safety of Martinique. It was there that the frigate *Concorde* found him; she brought another pressing request from Washington for ships, men and money. Her captain was persuasive. De Grasse promptly mortgaged his extensive properties in the West Indies and pressured the Governor of Cuba for additional funds, raising a total of 1,200,000 *livres*. He then set sail, manoeuvred his way through the Bahama Channel and reached Cape Henry at the head of the Chesapeake at the end of August.

The British ships guarding the Chesapeake fled at his approach, not prepared to risk an unequal fight, but they sped away up the bay, thus becoming effectively bottled up by De Grasse's fleet. La Fayette's troops meanwhile were marching up to join up with the newcomers. Everything was going to plan – until Rear-Admiral Graves's fleet, consisting of twenty-two warships and ten frigates, was sighted on 5 September. A showdown was inevitable.

De Grasse gave orders to clear the decks for action and sail towards the enemy. As usual, the strategy was for the opposing fleets to sail past each other, firing broadsides as they went, then veer back for another go. Masts and rigging came crashing down, legs and arms were carried off by cannon balls, sails were torn, hampering ships' movements, smoke obscured everything, shouted orders could scarcely be heard above all the shots and the screaming of the wounded.

After three hours, Graves realised that the battle was over and led the remnants of his fleet to New York. Casualties from both sides exceeded 600, and Graves had lost HMS *Terrible*, an imposing warship of 82 guns. De Grasse was triumphant. He had brought Rochambeau his much-needed reinforcements and driven off the British ships. Even more important, he held the entrance to Chesapeake Bay, while Cornwallis was completely blockaded in Yorktown. Day by day, the French and American troops increased their pressure. On 19 October, Cornwallis was forced to surrender. The loss of Yorktown was the final turning point in the war. Britain was now being driven out of her American colonies.

La Pérouse missed the Battle of the Chesapeake. He spent all of July and much of August cruising with the *Astrée* and the *Hermione* in the St Lawrence estuary. They were off Aspy Bay in the northernmost part of Cape Breton Island, Nova Scotia, when, on 21 July, they sighted a convoy of twenty British transports escorted by several warships, mostly frigates. This was a great opportunity for a sensational raid, but two of the protecting frigates and one corvette veered and made straight for them, thus giving the convoy a chance to seek the shelter of the bay. Then three more warships veered back to face the French. La Pérouse, with only two ships at his disposal, had to manoeuvre himself into a favourable position. It was already late afternoon and the defenders did all they could to gain time – once night fell, the convoy would be safe. They wove about skilfully enough to leave La Pérouse and Latouche-Tréville facing a line of five warships, with one hovering around in the background, while the transports continued their route into the bay.

> I had been far too anxious during that day to engage the enemy to be put off by the situation, however determined the English might be. I made for them, all sails out. I did not have a moment to lose ... The *Hermione* was within hailing distance, and I instructed Mr de la Touche to sail close astern of me, as we were about to attack. He was as keen as I was, and our men and officers were moved by the same feelings. Our sole, our unique regret was that we could not prolong the daylight and had a very sombre night to fear. The *Astrée* and the *Hermione* sailed to windward of the enemy so as to destroy any hope they might harbour of fleeing wind astern.[2]

It was a fierce but short engagement. The French warships each outgunned the individual British vessels – the *Astrée* carried 32 guns, whereas the largest of the enemy, the *Charleston*, had only 28 – but altogether the British disposed of well over 100 guns. It was a matter of boldness, not to say rashness, as the French sailed past the British line, firing everything they had as they went. The *Charleston*'s topmast came crashing down, the *Vulture*, twenty guns, veered out of line, the smaller *Jack* was forced to haul down her colours. In failing light and unsure of the situation, the other two decided to sail back to the convoy, while the sixth ship that had been watching from a distance vanished.

As La Pérouse turned back towards her, HMS *Charleston* seemed to have thought better of it and hauled down her colours. It had been a brief engagement, lasting just over an hour, but La Pérouse could feel satisfied with the result – at least at first:

> I was unrigged to quite an extent and I was also afraid that soon, in spite of my night glass, I would be unable to see the runaways. I decided to alter course [and not to follow them] and to take at least the *Jack* and the *Charleston*, which remained at the rear and represented the only certain fruits of my victory which the enemy might have contested, attributing to their manoeuvres and their valour a salvation which they owed entirely to the darkness.[3]

But he found that the *Charleston* had only pretended to strike her colours, to divert his attention. As he approached, she began to slip away, seizing the moment when the French sailors were taking over the *Jack*, their one sure prize. La Pérouse was furious at what he considered a breach of the law of the sea and of the rules of combat. Seeing the *Charleston* haul down her ensign, he had held his fire and turned away. But it was normal practice to fly a different flag from one's own when approaching an unidentified vessel or a port that might be held by enemy forces, or to indulge in similar subterfuges. War was hardly a duel between two irritated noblemen defending their honour, and crashing yardarms or snapping ropes may well have forced the *Charleston* to rearrange her flag.

When daylight returned there was not a ship in sight and, to make matters worse, a thick fog began to roll in. La Pérouse was left to count the cost. He had suffered fifteen casualties, his masts and rigging were damaged and the *Hermione* had fared no better. It was time to return Boston for repairs.

He was welcomed back by the authorities, American as well as French. His mission had been quite successful. He had been at sea for 56 days during which, in addition to the *Jack*, he had captured the *Thorn*, a corvette of 20 guns, as well as three merchant ships. He was told that the British had considered him to be a real threat and had dispatched three vessels to hunt him down. He also learnt that Captain Evans of the *Charleston* had died of his wounds.

Since his *Astrée* and her companion ship needed extensive repairs, Admiral Barras placed La Pérouse in charge of the port of Boston while he led the French fleet to join De Grasse off the coast of Virginia. La Pérouse therefore missed the critical Chesapeake campaign that ended with General Cornwallis's surrender 'at Yorktown. Instead, after Barras had sailed from Newport on 25 August, he enjoyed the relative quiet of a New England coast largely abandoned by the British, who were more concerned with holding the approaches to New York and maintaining their Saint Lawrence River lifeline to Canada and Maine.

There was only one incident. On 27 August, the *Magicienne* sailed from Portsmouth harbour, escorting a transport to Boston; she was attacked soon after by HMS *Chatham*, a powerful warship of 62 guns. La Pérouse hastened to her rescue, but to no avail: the *Magicienne*, outgunned, was forced to surrender.

La Pérouse felt despondent about this loss, but the Marquis de Castries sent him a letter of commendation that more than made up for his disappointment:

> I have read with pleasure the detail of your manoeuvres in Boston Bay on 31 August and 1 September. I note that you were prevented by circumstances from coming to the aid of the frigate *Magicienne* when she was forced to surrender to the ship *Chatham*; it is unfortunate that the wind was against you, but I cannot praise too highly the ardour you displayed in trying to reach the enemy ... I have drawn to the King's attention your fight against six frigates on 22 July. His Majesty was perfectly satisfied with your behaviour and that of Mr de la Touche who assisted you.[4]

Praise from the Minister of Marine was welcome enough, but a pat on the back from Louis XVI was an unexpected extra. La Pérouse was overjoyed. He had, after all, been lucky: if he had been sent down to join De Grasse's fleet, he would in all probability have been lost among all the other vessels manoeuvring in accordance with the admiral's orders. In the Saint Lawrence estuary he had been his own master and could claim any successes as his own.

He was also now formally promoted to *capitaine de vaisseau*, and Castries promised his future patronage: 'I will not miss any opportunity of drawing attention to your services; it will always be a happy occasion for me to once again advise you of the satisfaction of H.M. who has always noted the wisdom and the bravery that you have shown in such circumstances.'[5] Behind all the flowery language was a clear statement: Castries knew that the late Chevalier de Ternay had been La Pérouse's patron; he was now taking over.

For the next few weeks, La Pérouse stayed in Boston supervising the repairs to the two ships and enjoying a well-earned rest. Officially, he was still looking after the important but essentially untroubled waters between Boston and Nova Scotia, but there were no more incidents to disturb his peace. Collecting news from the Chesapeake and New York areas, and adding whatever other information he could gather from inland, he sent regular reports to Paris. His letters were welcome, carefully filed away – and he was not forgotten.

The British were keen to intercept De Grasse. Admiral Samuel Hood had sailed to the Chesapeake, but seeing no sign of a French fleet, he assumed that it must be on its way to attack New York, which was defended by Graves. Hood accordingly sailed north, but there were no French vessels in that area either – De Grasse reached the Chesapeake just after Hood had left. The two British admirals joined forces and hurried down from New York, while General Clinton organised a force to come to Cornwallis's aid.

A major engagement between the two enemy forces was now inevitable. The fleets came face to face on the afternoon of 5 September 1781. They must have looked formidable across a seascape ruffled by a strong breeze: a total of 1410 British guns against 1800 French ones, though some of the latter were inadequately manned because a number of men had been left ashore when De Grasse gave his hurried order to sail. The British, however, suffered from an early setback, when confused signals caused a number of Hood's ships to manoeuvre away from the main body. The battle lasted some three hours. The British suffered rather more in casualties and damage to their ships, and as daylight began to fade, they sailed off towards the open sea – not an easy manoeuvre as the breeze had dropped.

Meanwhile, Barras was landing his reinforcements and linking up with Rochambeau. There were further indecisive manoeuvrings at sea, and after a few more days Hood decided to give up and sail for the Hudson River. Admiral Graves needed to repair some of his ships, too damaged for any further engagement and a liability to the rest of the fleet. Clinton's troops were still not ready to sail to Cornwallis's assistance. When they were, on 24 October, it was too late. Yorktown had fallen five days before. In a final touch, Cornwallis's troops did not surrender to Rochambeau, as they had planned. Just as General Charles O'Hara, delegated by Cornwallis for the formal ceremony, was about to present his sword to the French commander, one of the senior officers, Matthieu Dumas, intervened and pointed out that the commander-in-chief was George Washington. He should be the one to receive the symbolic sword. George III's army was not surrendering to its traditional enemy France, but to the leader of his own rebellious colonists. Dumas, a man with republican tendencies who would one day arrest the fleeing Louis XVI, probably relished the moment as much as anyone present.

For the next eight months, France held the mastery of the sea, in the Atlantic if not in the East. The peace party was gaining ground in London, and what mattered was the terms it could obtain in the coming treaty. Lord North, the prime minister, remained in favour of continuing the war, to be in a better situation during the negotiations, but his majority fell to a single vote. In the House of Commons, Sir James Lowther moved that no further troops be sent out to America: he lost by a mere forty-two votes.

The continuation of the war pleased La Pérouse because it meant the Hudson Bay plan did not have to scrapped. He would have to wait, of course, until the winter had passed, but he could still make his preparations and sail as soon as the weather improved. For De Grasse, more war meant that he could go down to the West Indies to secure France's position there, or even to improve it – and to protect his own interests. He sailed for Martinique in November, but without La Pérouse whom he sent up to Boston to escort a convoy of transport ships down to the West Indies.

This included the *Résolue*, commanded by La Pérouse's friend Paul Fleuriot de Langle, which had recently arrived from France bringing a subsidy of over 4 million *livres* granted to the American Congress. The other escorting vessels included the *Sagittaire* and the cutter *Espion*. In their charge was a convoy of ten transport ships. The move had to be carefully organised, as some of the ships needed repairs and all of them had to take on extra cargo. They were ready by the end of November, but wild storms lashing the coast kept them in port until 7 December. The challenging winter voyage took just under a month, but the safe arrival of the ships at Martinique earned La Pérouse another commendation for his growing file at the Ministry of Marine: 'We have learnt of the arrival of his convoy, and we find in the report further evidence of the same intelligence and the same zeal that he does not cease displaying'.[6]

Meanwhile, De Grasse was working hard to strengthen his position and, if possible, confront Admiral Hood's fleet, which was sheltering in Barbados. He had been foiled in his attempt by continuing bad weather, but the Marquis François de Bouillé had at least been able to capture the small island of Saint Eustatius in the Leewards, which he handed over to his Dutch allies. It still forms part of the Dutch West Indian possessions to this day.

Nearby was the island of Saint Christopher, more generally known as Saint Kitts. Discovered by Christopher Columbus in 1493, it was settled by the English in 1623, who lost it to the French in 1666 and having recaptured it lost it again in 1689. Its chief port and capital bore a French name, Basseterre (Lowland), although confusingly one of the two main islands in the French archipelago of Guadeloupe, some 160 kilometres to the south, is called Basse-Terre, with a port of the same name. Saint Kitts had often been a pawn in the endless struggle between the great powers and it could not escape this time. De Grasse and Bouillé decided to take it. The attitude of the inhabitants reflected the island's chequered history: they made no effort to resist the landings

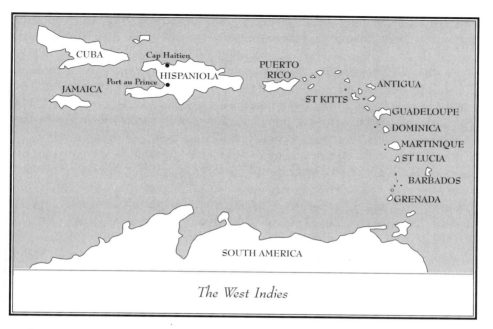

The West Indies

and promptly swore allegiance to Louis XVI. The British garrison, however, barricaded itself in the fort – a modest redoubt. De Grasse and Bouillé landed their troops, an impressive 6000 men, and settled in for a quiet siege. It was at this stage that La Pérouse arrived in the *Astrée* to place himself under De Grasse's orders.

The admiral felt that he had sufficient forces at his disposal. The garrison, as La Pérouse wrote, 'was being vigorously attacked',[7] and it should soon surrender, so De Grasse had no need of his services, and he sent him off to assist and escort out of the way a merchant ship from Marseilles laden with sugar and coffee. While La Pérouse was away on this modest mission, Admiral Hood appeared, leading 22 warships and a force of 2400 men. It was 25 January 1782. De Grasse had enough warning of Hood's approach to raise anchor in time and sail out to face him.

Hood followed a cautious line. Once he realised that De Grasse was not going to be trapped between his fleet and the port, he manoeuvred about, more swiftly than De Grasse as his ships were all copper-bottomed, then he decided to sail off to Barbados, where he planned to meet Rodney and his fleet. There would be no battle this time. The Saint Kitts redoubt surrendered on 13 February and De Grasse left at the end of the month, by which time La Pérouse had joined him. They made for Martinique, but on the way captured the small island of Montserrat. Discovered by the Spanish back in 1493, it was first settled by the British in 1662. France took it from them in 1666 and held it for four years; now it changed hands once again. But it was, like Saint Kitts, a small place with a few thousand settlers and slaves, mostly engaged in farming.

De Grasse celebrated his success when he reached Martinique, combining this with the official celebrations over the birth of Louis XVI's son. It was quite a grandiose affair, with a *Te Deum* in the church, a great ball at the governor's, and fireworks and streamers for the populace. The messages of congratulations and loyalty sent to Versailles were accompanied by a report on the capture of Saint Kitts and Montserrat, boasting of more possessions taken away from George III. But Versailles was not too impressed. These were pinpricks at most, specks on the world map, not significant enough to affect the peace negotiations. What would make a real difference was the capture of a substantial island, such as Jamaica, the largest of the islands held by Britain in the West Indies, third in size after Spanish Cuba and Spanish-French Hispaniola.

De Grasse was told that Jamaica should be his real target, and since Spain was now an ally of France, Admiral Serano's fleet, based in Santo Domingo, could join him. The Spanish should be only too pleased to help take Jamaica away from the British: it had been a Spanish possession from 1509 to 1655. Serano's ships added to De Grasse's fleet would help to maintain a superiority of numbers, and make up for the ships of Admiral Rodney, who had now sailed down to link up with Hood. And the Spanish troops he could supply would bring their total forces to over 20,000 men.

Politically, it was a sound idea. If a joint landing on Jamaica succeeded, the French negotiators back in Europe would have one more card to play. For La Pérouse, however, this presented a problem. He would have to take part in the campaign. The attackers might well become bogged down and need help and protection by naval units. This, in all likelihood, would involve ferrying supplies back and forth, and with his experience he would certainly be called upon to assist. It was already March and it could take a month or so for De Grasse to finalise his preparations. The Jamaica campaign might not start until May, the time La Pérouse had set himself to get ready for the Hudson Bay expedition. His secret orders, just as in D'Estaing's case, were still burning a hole in his pocket. Worse still, there was growing talk of peace. In London, Lord North's government had finally fallen and with it the Earl of Sandwich, First Lord of the Admiralty. There were further reshuffles during the following weeks, but it was clear that the hawks were giving way to the doves. The Marquis of Rockingham, who became prime minister, had always been sympathetic towards the American colonists, and had predicted that Lord North's hard-line policies would only lead to more trouble. Rockingham died in office after a few months, but the doves still dominated the cabinet.

Peace treaties were usually signed in the autumn, after the final summer campaigns and before the troops were forced to dig in for another winter, so La Pérouse might still have time to sail with De Grasse and then prepare for Hudson Bay. He prayed that the latter would get on with his planning. His prayers were answered: De Grasse was ready to move by early April. The first stage would take him to Haiti, as long as he could get past the waiting fleets of Rodney and Hood. He worked out a sensible strategy: part of the French fleet would sail out to draw Admiral Rodney's closest ships away, and the heavier transport vessels – a total of 100 or so ships – would slink away by night.

La Pérouse was given the task of sailing out towards Rodney's watching ships in the hope of drawing them into Saint Lucia Channel. He left Fort-de-France Bay on 6 April and veered south. Meanwhile, the transports were hoisting in their boats and getting ready to sail north the moment evening began to fall. Escorted by the remaining French warships, they would then begin their slow trek to Haiti.

According to early reports, only a couple of Rodney's ships had followed La Pérouse; the others were still watching the port. This caused De Grasse to call back the convoy. La Pérouse himself was driven back on the 7th, chased by two frigates and two ships of the line. As their quarry sped back to harbour, those on board the British frigates clearly saw the transport ships in the bay, some of them under sail. Now quite sure of what De Grasse had in mind, Rodney moved his fleet closer in.

De Grasse decided he had no option but to go ahead. His ruse had failed, but he still had the numbers because Admiral Hood's fleet had not yet caught up with Rodney's. He decided that the transports would sail north, the naval units would manoeuvre around and at the rear. Nature decided to join in as well: the winds dropped, leaving the French and British wallowing in a dead calm, though occasionally light breezes blew up to add to the confusion. On the 9th, the French convoy sought refuge in Basse-Terre, Guadeloupe, while De Grasse's warships manoeuvred as best they could off the small islands of the Saintes, between Guadeloupe and Dominica.

There were some exchanges of fire, but they were inconclusive. De Grasse could not make up his mind whether to take Rodney full on, or whether he might still get away with the convoy while the British were struggling with unfavourable and inconstant winds. Rodney was facing a similar dilemma. He was not a man to take undue risks when the winds were so changeable, and he knew that, with his superior numbers, De Grasse could inflict severe damage on any of his ships that floundered within reach. Indecision on both sides and an unreliable breeze kept both fleets from each other – and then Hood's ships arrived. De Grasse was now outnumbered, 37 British ships to his 30, or 30 guns to his 2246. To make things worse, the winds at last gathered strength and started to blow steadily from a direction that favoured the attackers.

Communication between the fleet and its commander was a perennial problem, especially once a battle started and smoke began to hide the ships from each other. La Pérouse was sent with the *Astrée* and the frigates *Amazone* and *Richemont* to observe the movements of the British and report back, 'forming a kind of chain behind the fleet'.[8] Noticing that two of his ships were missing, De Grasse in the *Ville-de-Paris* sent La Pérouse to investigate and report back. He found that they had been caught by the calms and were struggling to catch up in the failing light. He escorted them until they had all joined up with the main body, barely visible in the moonlight.

Early on the 12th, De Grasse dispatched La Pérouse to help a ship that had been making distress signals. It was the *Zélé*, which had collided with the *Ville-de-Paris* and lost a couple of masts. It took three attempts to get a boat across to her and hook up a cable to tow her along in a perilous situation. 'Daylight was breaking. We found ourselves surrounded by enemies, with the French ships three leagues away and the English very close. There was even one frigate that was getting ready to fire a few guns at us and interfere while I was seeing to the cable.'[9] He managed to get the *Zélé* away towards Basse-Terre in Guadeloupe, a distance of some 25 to 30 kilometres, all the while being chased by several British warships. De Grasse sailed back towards them, whereupon a full naval engagement began.

To some extent, La Pérouse provided the spark that started this major battle, subsequently known as the Bataille des Saintes, the Battle of the Saints. De Grasse could not allow the enemy to capture not only the *Zélé*, but La Pérouse's *Astrée* as well; he felt responsible for letting La Pérouse get into what had become a dangerous situation. He also realised that he would have to fight sooner or later, and this seemed to be as good a time as ever. The first shots were exchanged around 8 a.m., with the two fleets evenly matched. It was the wind which, by veering to the south, gave Rodney his opportunity. The French ships were forced to manoeuvre constantly, reducing or increasing canvas to cope with the wind. This caused them to break their line of battle, leaving gaps through which the British could now sail.

Rodney boldly took his flagship, HMS *Formidable*, through a break in the French centre. Five ships followed him, raking De Grasse's vessels with gunfire as they sped past. In the ensuing confusion, De Grasse's *Ville-de-Paris* and his close supporting ships became isolated from the rest. Hood took him on, concentrating the fire of his 90 guns on the French commander. The chaos rapidly worsened. Casualties mounted, masts and spars collapsed, sails tore into shreds, fires broke out here and there. As the sun began to set, De Grasse, faced with truly enormous losses, was forced to surrender. Four other ships of the line were also captured – the *César, Hector, Ardent* and *Glorieux* – and several smaller ships. The casualties, killed, drowned and wounded, were equally disastrous. On this day, the French naval threat to the West Indies came to an end and Britain won back control of the Atlantic. Not surprisingly, the Battle of the Saints has been called the Trafalgar of the West Indies.

La Pérouse struggled to piece together the events of the day from the little he could make out during the battle and from various items of information he gathered over the following days. This enabled him to write up a detailed report which he presented two years later to the court martial set up in Lorient to consider the Battle of the Saints and allocate responsibility among the various, by then squabbling, commanders.

> The French squadron was still fighting courageously, and the smoke and the distance prevented me from seeing which side had the advantage. Nevertheless, I had the greatest hope that we would win as I could see fifteen or sixteen enemy ships disabled and no longer able to fight; but shortly after, I sighted three frigates and a cutter hugging the wind and tacking along the Saintes, a league and a half to windward of me. I soon identified them from our numbered signals as the *Galathée*, the *Amazone* and the *Cérès*. The latter signalled that the enemy had the superiority of numbers. I then realised that M. le Comte de Grasse's forces were in a serious situation since the frigates had presumably been forced to abandon him.[10]

He was right. The battle had degenerated into a state of total confusion. The signals were hard to see, sometimes appearing contradictory or meaningless, so that that no one was quite sure what was happening beyond the direct neighbourhood of the ship. La Pérouse could only try to rally a few ships around him and hope that some reliable information might come forward.

> I signalled to the cutter *Clairvoyant* to come up within hailing distance, and to the three frigates to join me. They came up a little, but always kept half a league to windward. The cutter passed astern, we both hove-to and her commander, M. D'Aché, came aboard. He told me that the *Glorieux* had been dismasted and had fallen into the hands of the enemy, although he thought they had not yet secured her and that she still seemed to be to windward of the other ships. First of all, I conceived the plan of going to her rescue if the enemy did not present too much of an obstacle [but]

coming closer I saw that the *Glorieux* was completely dismasted, that the enemy were close to her and in the process of securing their prize.

As night was now about to fall, I sailed on, intending to join the ships, including the *Caton* and the *Jason* that had sailed from Basse-Terre, hoping that the next day we might be able to recapture the *Glorieux* if she had been left in charge of a weak escort … we all tacked about in the Saintes Channel during the night.

His hopes were dashed when, about 8 p.m., they sighted a fire to the south. It blazed up fiercely, reflected on the dark waters. La Pérouse feared that the *Glorieux* had been set on fire, a fear soon confirmed when a mighty explosion rent the night sky.

When the 13th dawned, he looked around, surveying the pitiful aftermath of the battle. Ships manoeuvred painfully, their sails flapping uselessly in the weak breeze. 'As we were on the field of battle, we saw the sea covered with floating debris of broken masts and spars.' It was some consolation to see that the British were also struggling to keep together. 'I had lost all hope of doing anything useful during that day, and I suggested to Mr de Framont, commanding the *Caton*, to return to Guadeloupe and discuss with Mr de Bouillé and Mr D'Arbaud what might be the best thing to do in our situation.'

Nearby were half a dozen ships, mostly frigates, which were able to sail slowly with La Pérouse down to Basse-Terre. The next day, they saw Admiral Rodney's ships limping north, presumably bound for Antigua. Rodney would be criticised for not pursuing the defeated French more energetically, but he, too, had suffered heavy damage and the winds were too weak and changeable for him to manoeuvre successfully – a warship becalmed was no more than a helpless giant.

The Marquis de Bouillé, left in charge by circumstances, decided to check whether the British, though victorious, might not be more vulnerable than some thought. In the evening, he sent La Pérouse in his *Astrée*, accompanied by the small cutter *Clairvoyant*, to find out what the situation really was. With any luck, the remaining French ships might yet go out and capture a British frigate or two. Alternatively, if the coast was clear, the French could set off together for Santo Domingo and rejoin the rest of the fleet.

The weather, however, was infuriating. An occasional breeze came up, so that the ships could begin to manoeuvre, then it fell back to dead calm. Bouillé decided to send a few more ships, and six of them went out to join La Pérouse. Though the latter was acknowledged as the most experienced officer when it came to careful coastal and offshore navigation, the captain of the *Caton*, Framont, was senior to him and he took over command of the small squadron.

It was a slow struggle, but by the morning of 18 April they were in sight of the southern tip of Puerto Rico. They went on their way, keeping together as best they could, until the 20th when they saw, in the distance and to the south, a dozen sails, which they soon realised were enemy vessels.

They had now reached the south coast of Puerto Rico, far enough to make for the wide channel, La Mona, that separates the island from Santo Domingo. Framont decided to enter it, hoping to lure the English into it while he sought refuge with the other vessels in Bahia de Aguadilla. The Spanish batteries in the port of Aguadilla would keep the enemy at bay and possibly drive them off. Meanwhile, La Pérouse in the faster *Astrée* could go on straight to Santo Domingo, where some believed De Grasse might have taken refuge and where the main Spanish fleet was supposed to have gathered for the planned attack on Jamaica. Then the remaining French and Spanish vessels could hurry east towards Puerto Rico and catch any British ships struggling in the channel.

It was a good plan, and La Pérouse did his best to sail towards Santo Domingo. He was lucky: there was more wind out at sea than in La Mona. Framont was less fortunate – as soon as he turned Cabo Rojo, the southwesternmost tip of Puerto Rico, and veered into the channel, the wind failed altogether. With no hope of carrying out his plan, he turned back to sea – and came face to face with the British who, further south and still away from the shore, had just enough wind to manoeuvre towards him.

Framont opened fire the moment they came within range. The British split up, eight ships advancing to attack him, the others going after La Pérouse. It was a close-run thing. The fact that La Pérouse was about 10 kilometres ahead and making full sail to reach Santo Domingo kept him reasonably safe, but even so only the wind, which strengthened in the late afternoon, saved him:

> I was being energetically pursued by a large warship driven by a strong breeze, whereas I was only making a couple of knots. She was coming up to within range, and there was no doubt that she was about to come within reach ... Being wholly becalmed just at that time, I lowered my larboard studding sails and set my canvas to receive whatever wind might come from the north-east. Fortunately it started to blow at half-past five. I did not have a moment to lose as she was rapidly gaining on me. The squall enabled me to make seven and a half knots within a quarter of an hour and I gained almost a league. Three other ships had now joined the first hunter, so that I had four vessels giving me chase, the other eight having remained to deal with the *Caton, Jason, Aimable* and *Cérès*.

Fortunately for him, the English had their own problems. Some had suffered damage and some casualties during the battle, and the constant manoeuvring forced on them by the weak and unreliable breeze was proving too much of a strain. One gave up the chase at five o'clock, another an hour later. There were still two left to pursue him, one closing up the gap on his port side, the other on the starboard. Night and a freshening wind saved him. He made good progress, wound his way carefully into the strait and, when morning came, found himself alone – not a ship in sight, French or British. He went slowly on his way, emerging without any further danger into the Atlantic, and veering west along the northern coast of Santo Domingo. It took him another two days to reach Cabo Viejo, and then he sighted ahead of him a squadron of some twenty ships, which soon raised their colours. This was part of the French fleet he had been seeking.

La Pérouse went on board the main ship, where he was welcomed by Monsieur de Vaudreuil. 'I have come to join M. de Grasse's fleet,' he told him. 'There are other French vessels that I hope will be joining me shortly.'

'Admiral de Grasse is now a prisoner of the English,' Vaudreuil replied. 'The *Ville-de-Paris* has also gone, as have four others among our largest warships. I have taken over as senior commanding officer.'

This was when La Pérouse discovered the true outcome of the Battle of the Saints. Vaudreuil was now trying to decide whether to proceed with the Jamaican campaign, with the help of the Spanish naval units that were nearby, waiting for orders. The French forces had been weakened, not merely by the loss of the ships, but by casualties among the officers and crews of the others. A number of ships had already left for France or elsewhere, including Louis de Bougainville's squadron.

Vaudreuil led his ships, La Pérouse's *Astrée* included, to the port of Cap Français – known today as Cap Haïtien – and checked each unit for fitness and suitability. The last thing he wanted was to be associated with a failed attack on Jamaica. Having culled out those vessels he deemed unsuitable and ordered repairs to others, he realised it would be unwise to risk everything on a campaign against the powerful British colony. Hanging over his planning was uncertainty about Admirals Hood and Rodney, who might come back at any time or, worse still, sail north in an attempt to attack Boston or some other mainland port.

He concluded that the Jamaican venture would have to be postponed until he knew more about the situation elsewhere and until fresh supplies had arrived from the mainland. It was a sensible move. Most of the other commanders shared his views and the Spanish had always been lukewarm about the plan. This was no time for more risky adventures. Peace negotiations were continuing in Europe and a treaty might be signed in the autumn. If the negotiations broke down, the Jamaican campaign could be revived some time in October or November. In the meantime, Vaudreuil decided, his men could take life a little easier and start repairing their ships.

La Pérouse then promptly brought out the Hudson Bay plan, to which Vaudreuil had no objections, considering it to be well conceived and quite practicable. He could certainly spare a couple of ships over the coming months – and the instructions La Pérouse showed him made it quite clear that he was expected to give all the help he could. 'This is the beginning of May, an ideal time. But you need a better and fresher ship than the *Astrée*,' Vaudreuil told him. 'You may transfer to the *Sceptre*, a ship of 74 guns, launched a mere couple of years ago, copper-sheeted and in very good condition.' The *Astrée* would still go with him, after it had been cleaned and repaired. Her captain would be Fleuriot de Langle, former commandant of the *Résolue* and the *Expériment*. La Pérouse was also provided with a third ship, a fairly old frigate, the *Engageante*, commanded by Lieutenant André Charles de La Jaille.

The preparations for the Hudson Bay campaign had to be carried out in total secrecy, so that the British were not forewarned and did not attempt to intercept the small fleet. Speed was the other requirement – spring was now well advanced and La Pérouse had only a few weeks in which to reorganise his crews and lay in all the stores he would need for what promised to be an arduous and dangerous campaign.

13. THE HUDSON BAY RAID

May–November 1782

HUDSON BAY IN the eighteenth century was one of the loneliest corners of the world. Even today, with modern forms of transport, including a railway connection, to the interior, the population along the shores of Hudson Bay struggles to reach 5000. Yet this enormous inland sea covers an area of over 600,000 square kilometres – three times the size of the Black Sea – and is fed by numerous rivers, large and small. In La Pérouse's day, there were just a few outposts along the rivermouths, homes of employees of the Hudson Bay Company, with a handful of trappers and traders who disappeared for weeks into the frozen hinterland, collecting furs and trading with the scattered Indian tribes. France had once sent its own traders towards James Bay and Rupert's Land, fiercely competing for full control of the fur trade, but the Treaty of Utrecht of 1713 put an end to the rivalry by granting full control to Britain. The fall of French Canada in 1763 had extinguished any lingering French hopes of a return to the trade, but the reputation of Hudson Bay as a potential source of wealth remained. There was also the persistent belief that it held a way through to the mysterious North-West Passage.

The plan evolved by La Pérouse and Fleurieu was not one of conquest. It was basically a show of force, a challenge to British supremacy comparable in spirit, if not in scale, to the defiance shown so successfully by the American colonists. It did, however, contain an element of exploration. This region was so little known that geographers and cartographers hankered for any information about it. Fleurieu may have looked at the project as part of an overall military and naval strategy, but the geographer in him was also curious about an area so sketchily shown on most charts.[1] The Hudson Bay Company had its own maps and outlines, but it did not make them available to outsiders, and certainly not to the French. As La Jaille wrote to his mother when he told her of the *Engageante*'s voyage: 'One can truly say that for all purposes we were going to explore a country of which the only thing we knew was the name'.[2]

Fleurieu and La Pérouse had consulted all the works they could find on the region. Though few enough, they seemed adequate for the purpose. There had been publications in London about some of the navigators who had ventured into those bleak regions, such as Martin Frobisher who had made three voyages in the sixteenth century, hoping to find the North-West Passage or, failing that, discover gold or other minerals. Very little of the literature produced by these endeavours had been translated into French, but it did give them an image of the bay and its approaches.[3]

La Pérouse knew that he could expect to find himself in a vast expanse of freezing water, relatively shallow, swept by wild northern winds that could cause the temperature to drop sharply in a matter of hours, or at other times invaded by cold, thick banks of dense fog. The shore could be dangerous, as it was mostly low with hidden mudbanks near the rivers, especially along the west. It was an alien silent world for most of the year, but during the brief summer it gloried in a sudden profusion of wildflowers, mosses and coloured lichen, with balsam, spruce and poplar along the southern shores. Back in the forests or in the plain were caribou and musk oxen, with a multitude of ducks and loons along the riverbanks, and overhead the soulful honking of Canada geese. And for most of the year, one could expect to find the waters teeming with cod and salmon, and with porpoises and whales.

But La Pérouse had little precise information, as he reported, later, to his mother in Albi:

> I must tell you that I had neither a chart nor a pilot. Not a single Frenchman in the last hundred years had come within three hundred leagues of this bay. The English, who considered that the difficulties of such a navigation were their best form of defence for these settlements, had forbidden the publication of any charts, and I can swear that they were justified in thinking that no one would think of coming to look for them so far away.[4]

There was little he could do to improve his knowledge. It was too risky to consult any of the other French officers since this would give rise to gossip and it was all too easy for a spy to sneak across to one of the British-held Caribbean islands and earn himself a good reward.

Even taking on winter clothing could arouse suspicions. La Pérouse gambled on the summer up in the far north being mild enough for his crews – and officers – to cope. He could not even tell his own officers about the destination. Only Vaudreuil knew and he was wise enough to keep the secret to himself. It was sufficient for him to note in his records that La Pérouse would be leaving for France with three ships, possibly with a call at Boston or Newport. This would explain why he would be sailing north – not that anyone would be particularly interested in what route he intended to follow. It was still wartime and questions were not encouraged. Not even the other two captains were told. Fleuriot de Langle and La Jaille were handed their orders in sealed envelopes and told that they were not to open them until the three ships had reached 45° north – the latitude of Nova Scotia, a point where they would normally have expected to veer off on their crossing to Brest or Lorient.

The preparations were spread over a fortnight. Supplies were loaded, not just for the crew, but for the detachments of soldiers, approximately 300 of them, mostly from the Auxerrois Regiment. Most of them expected that they would be landed in America as additional reinforcements for La Fayette's forces, as would the mortars and light guns being stowed on board.

They sailed from Santo Domingo on 31 May 1782, going north. It was a warm early summer in the West Indies and quite pleasant until they passed the latitude of New York and Maine. The nights got noticeably cooler as they continued on their northerly route, instead of starting to sweep out into the Atlantic as almost everyone expected. There may have been a psychological effect on morale after De Langle and La Jaille opened their secret instructions and told their officers that they were bound for the far north. The shock was increased by the realisation that so few had extra clothing to put on once the thermometers began to drop and ice appeared.

By the beginning of July, having sailed almost 3200 kilometres and reached the coast of Labrador, they were faced by a troublesome heavy fog hiding all kinds of hazards, including the first signs of floating ice. Pierre de La Monneraye, second-in-command to Fleuriot de Langle and one of several who have left us useful accounts of the expedition, underlined the dangers they were coming across:

> We kept the *Sceptre* in sight as best we could, and when we got lost in the fog she would sound her bell, beat the drums and fire her guns. It was then that our navigation became dangerous: the thick fog greatly limited the range of our horizon; we ran the risk of dashing ourselves against some mountains of ice, prodigiously high, floating on the sea here and there as the winds drove them; they often have reef-like outcrops on which one can get smashed up as easily as on rocks.[5]

The weather grew colder day by day and the mountains of ice ever more fearsome. For many of the French these icebergs looming out of the mist were both strange and terrifying. The sailors crossed themselves and prayed to their various saints. Frobisher's men, a couple of hundred years earlier, had reacted in much the same way, falling to their knees and praying – their officers had not criticised them for it, accepting their belief that divine intervention might be all that could save them. The lookouts, freezing in their thin clothes, yelled down warnings and directions. The ships manoeuvred constantly to avoid the icebergs, but the most dangerous time was at night when they were only just visible in the eerie white gloom. La Monneraye, however, allowed himself to wax lyrical in his descriptions:

We were hauling along ice mountains of an incredible size. If the sun shone down into their crevasses, great reservoirs of thawed ice would collect in them, which then would pour down with a mighty roar in cascades or sheets of water. The sun sending its rays down onto those voluminous waterfalls varied infinitely their colours, completing the picture. At times, these mountains of ice would close off our horizon; their different heights, their quite varied shapes seemed to build up the impression of a fortified city, with its towers and belfries, and its palaces of rock crystal. At other times, it looked like a vast army of three-decked ships, all laid out in battle formation. This field of illusions presented an infinite set of varying spectacles.

On 18 July the fog began to lift and eventually vanished, revealing the entrance to Hudson Strait. But the great icebergs still dominated the scene. As La Pérouse wondered how to deal with these obstacles and whether there was a way around them, they parted briefly – just long enough for the French ships to make their way through. Then, like a prison gate shutting slowly behind a group of newly arrived convicts, the pack ice closed again. To add to their discomfort, a freezing wind swept down from the north. The sailors huddled down together, their gloveless hands clasping their shoulders. La Monneraye decided that moving about was a better way of coping with the cold: 'We went climbing onto those uneven ice surfaces, which enabled us to communicate with our comrades from the *Sceptre* and the *Engageante* without the need for boats. And to warm ourselves, we made snowballs, as children do, and fought battles.'

Fortunately, the ice began to break up, with floes and small icebergs drifting away on the tide. At this point, the French were making their way north-west, fairly close to a coastline. The country looked totally deserted, but for the first time they saw a group of inhabitants coming towards them: Eskimos or, more correctly, Inuit, their word for people. The term Eskimo actually means one who eats raw meat. It was not just their human company that delighted the French, but the fact that they were friendly traders eager to sell furs and sealskins. A brisk market developed: here at last was a supply of warm clothing. The furs were not made up into anything like jackets or trousers, but ingenuity soon took over, with the sailors wrapping fox, beaver or even bear skins around themselves or stuffing them into their vests. 'It was a highly comical spectacle to see our men thus clothed, climbing into the rigging and the yards, looking like bears or seals.' The French, some of whom were beginning to suffer from frostbite, were not interested in the likely commercial value of the furs and in no mood to haggle. These locals were welcomed like the saviours they were and there was a great deal of laughter and back-patting.

Soon, La Monneraye was able to go ashore and visit one of the small local settlements, a collection of temporary pointed huts made of branches and leaves. When he returned, the talk on board took on a philosophical or sociological turn. Were these people examples of Natural Man, the *bon sauvage* who was so much a topic of debate in eighteenth-century Europe? Certainly, their society seemed to lack the complications of modern civilisation, such as private property, with theft, exploitation and jealousy, and bitter divisions between rich and poor. Rousseau had stated the problem with resounding clarity and more than a little bias some thirty years earlier in his essays on the origin of inequality in society and the role played by the sciences and the arts. Man in his primitive state, he had stated, was free and happy until property owning had begun to corrupt him. Were these Inuit, seemingly happy and friendly in what was clearly a harsh environment, examples of uncorrupted original man? La Monneraye, however, was quite convinced that Europeans would find nothing to envy in this society:

> Let Rousseau, the man of paradoxes, praise all he likes the freedom and independence of savage man, for my part I much prefer the loss of part of my freedom, which civilised societies require of us to ensure the happiness and safety of each one of us. Our *philosophes*, men of such renown, have worked out their principles and their systems simply out of their imagination, and if I had been with [Voltaire] or [Rousseau] I could easily have argued with them and showed them the contradictions within their ideas.

Few of his fellow officers were prepared to disagree. Comfort and survival were easier to achieve in civilised societies, even though there might be a price for pay.

La Pérouse had worked out from the sketchy charts that they had landed on

Baffin Island, which forms the northern limit of Hudson Strait. Frobisher had called it *Meta Incognita*, the Unknown Limits. It was an unappealing place, a stony, arid shore, barren of trees except for occasional patches of stunted greenery huddling within the shelter of grey rocks. It was useful as a landmark, and for the furs the French obtained there, but it was a dangerous coast, with ice still floating past and the ominous threat of cold fogs. Hudson Strait is relatively wide, but it is long – over 320 kilometres in length – with freezing winds and dangerous currents. By 1 August, however, Baffin Island had vanished into the northern mist and the French began to make their way into Hudson Bay.

It was still cold, but at least they could now veer south, towards relatively warmer temperatures, and mercifully the bitter northern wind began to drop. The inhabited parts of Hudson Bay lay mostly on the western shore – and even so they consisted of only two small fortified settlements, Prince of Wales Fort on the Churchill River and Fort York on the Hayes River. Once he had entered Hudson Bay, La Pérouse had merely to sail south-west, crossing the bay with little likelihood of meeting a boat or a trader who might warn the British of his arrival. When the three ships appeared off Prince of Wales Fort on 8 August, each flying the French white ensign, they achieved their aim of total surprise. As La Pérouse told his mother, the British never expected anyone to come this far to threaten them.

Surprise was a great asset, but when he landed with the first French troops in the morning he discovered how ill-defended the fort really was. It had been well designed and looked quite formidable from the bay, but the masonry was patchy and much of it was crumbling away. There were 42 guns, but not enough of a garrison to man them – most of the inhabitants were traders and company clerks. Its real defences were isolation and the pack ice. Once these were breached, the fort could only surrender. There was no need to fire a shot.

The British commander was Samuel Hearne. Then aged thirty-seven, he was a man notable for his exploration of the area, during which he had suffered great hardships, including the loss of his toenails to frostbite. He had to his credit the discovery and naming of the Coppermine River in the far north, and many years of experience working for the Hudson's Bay Company.

After the surrender terms were agreed upon, the French dined with him and, according to La Monneraye, found him a charming and learned host, 'a handsome man, well educated and with a wide knowledge'. La Pérouse later helped him to make his way back to England in a small ship, the *Severn*. 'When we returned to France,' wrote La Monneraye, 'we learnt with pleasure that he had safely reached England.' Later, Hearne returned to the Churchill River, struggling to restore the trading post until he decided to build a new one further up the river. It turned out to be one the harshest winters he had known and he endured great privations: 'All my wine froze and split the bottles and casks that contained it. Our salted provisions froze so solid that we could not separate them any more than the hardest ice.'[6]

Civilised socialising between conqueror and conquered was all very well, but La Pérouse had come to eliminate the company's two main posts. Accordingly, the traders and employees were taken on board with their personal belongings and the stocks of fur were stowed away, 'mostly mink, bear skins, lynx, white and blue foxes'. In addition, there were over 17,000 goose quills – invaluable writing implements in those days – and 135 kilograms of goose feathers. All in all, these stocks were worth, by the company's own reckoning, more that £14,000. The financial loss caused by the French raid was quite substantial, and the company was unable to pay a dividend until 1786.

The food stores the French discovered were more than welcome: dried fish, a few pigs, and butter from Ireland preserved in sealed double jars, the outer one consisting of brine. Best of all were the stocks of clothing, lengths of cloth and sheets that were rapidly turned into shirts and trousers for the officers and crew, all too happy to be able to discard their odd coverings of bearskins and untreated furs.

The guns were then spiked, the few cannon balls stacked near them were hurled into the water and the fort was blown up. The soldiers were about to set fire to a scattering of ramshackle huts when La Pérouse realised that they were not company property, but had been built by predominantly Cree Indians who stayed in them when they brought their furs to exchange for company goods. He also remembered the trappers and traders who were out in the forest, as well as a handful of men who had fled into the woods when the French landed. They would be returning before long with the furs they had trapped or bought, only to find the little settlement in ruins and autumn fast approaching. He ordered the buildings to be left as they were, to provide some shelter, and even had them stocked with dried fish, flour and other food for the winter. He decided also that some muskets should be left behind with enough ammunition for them to do some subsistence hunting. There was plenty of fish in the river, including salmon, so at least they would not starve.

La Pérouse did the same at the next outpost, Fort York, saying, 'If the king was here, he would endorse my actions.' In fact, both Louis XVI and the British government would praise him for his humanity. Samuel Hearne, settling as many of his men as he could get into the small *Severn*, was the first to thank him for his actions. Some of the British, unable to fit into Hearne's ship, were allocated to the *Sceptre* and the *Astrée* and incorporated into the crews. 'We treated them just as we did our own men; they were excellent people as adept at working on the ships as our own sailors.'[7]

Fort York or York Factory on the Hayes River was more difficult to reach. To get to Fort Wales, La Pérouse had only needed to sail across the bay in deep water, but now he had to follow the coast, without any charts to help him. Samuel Hearne and his companions refused to provide him with any information – and La Pérouse could only agree that it would have been wrong for them to do so. There were shoals and rocks to beware of, day and night. It took a week to reach the fort, and when the men went ashore they had to wade through marshlands. Then a series of wild storms blew up, causing the two frigates to lose two anchors each. Fortunately, the fort surrendered without difficulty. It was already 24 August. Hearne confirmed that an early winter could make its appearance any time in the month of September.

The French hurried, taking all the stores and furs they could store, but there was very little space left on board. More British had to be crammed into the *Severn* and a few more into the two frigates. Fortunately, the Hayes River and the nearby Nelson River led into an area of lakes and waterways that joined up with Lake Winnipeg and Lake Superior, so that some of the small garrison and the traders had escaped to safer places further south. La Pérouse ordered that some of the outbuildings and provisions be left for those who might return. And then York was burnt down and its defences blown up.

The weather did not improve. 'In the storms, bears, apparently carried off to sea by the violent rush of the swollen rivers they attempted to cross, came around our ships; often exhausted by having to swim this far, they climbed onto our cables to rest.' So reported La Monneraye, while another noted two cables broken and the tiller bar snapped. On 30 August, there had been thunder, lightning and rain. Several Canada geese landed on the deck, exhausted, as did some smaller birds. The next day they experienced a 'strong gale with clear weather. In the afternoon, we saw several flights of wild snow geese of different species, flying in amazing numbers, preparing to leave these shores.'[8] It was time to follow their example. Sickness was now affecting the crews, as the English noted: 'Many people on board this ship are eaten up with the scurvy and otherwise unhealthy, which makes it look dismal to a stranger'.

On 2 September, all the ships got under way. A British pilot agreed to lead them out of the bay – the *Severn*'s men were as anxious as the French to avoid getting trapped in this bleak world by the closing ice. Fortunately, the breeze, west-north-west, was favourable and it took them only four days to cross the bay and reach Hudson Strait. Working their way through it was not too difficult, and this time the British could see no reason to refuse when asked for advice.

On the 10th, the French were sufficiently advanced to farewell the *Severn*. Hearne and thirty-two others took their leave off Resolution Island, off the tip of Baffin Island, known in Frobisher's day as the Queen's Foreland, where the strait opened out towards the Atlantic. The French wished them well as they started on their voyage home by way of Stromness in the Orkney Islands. At the same time, La Pérouse parted from Fleuriot de Langle, who sailed for Brest in the *Astrée*. As for himself, he decided to make for Cadiz, where a milder climate would enable his exhausted crew to recover. It was also quicker – a mere thirty-three days.

It was indeed time to rest his men. The *Sceptre* had a complement of 355, as well as 181 soldiers. Out of this total, 70 had died and 400 were ill. By the time he was sailing across the Atlantic to Spain, he had only 60 men fit enough to work the ship. La Jaille's *Engageante* had fared no better. She had lost 15 men of scurvy by the time she left Hudson Strait, over 100 were too sick to work and all the others were affected by scurvy or some other illness.

As La Pérouse wrote to his mother, it had been 'the hardest campaign ever undertaken', adding 'Now that I know that country, I shall never return to it'.[9] As for himself, he assured her, he was in good health and quite keen to continue playing his part in the war. He hoped to join a new assault on Gibraltar, which had been under threat since 1779. The problem was the condition of his two ships.

The *Engageante* needed extensive repairs. Her masts were so split and rotten that they were threatening to break if too much canvas was put out, the mizzen mast had already snapped and the stem had been cracked by knocking into ice floes. As a result seawater had been seeping in for weeks, ruining and rotting a lot of the smaller timbers. The *Sceptre* was in a better condition, but nevertheless required a week or two of work.

This did not prevent La Pérouse from offering his services to the Comte de Guichen, who was organising the attack on Gibraltar. He was willing to serve on another ship if need be while his own was being refitted and men were recruited locally to replace those he had been forced to send off to hospital. Both his offer and the Hudson Bay campaign earned him the thanks of his superiors, but Versailles was not enthusiastic about the attack on Gibraltar. The war was almost over and the attempt to capture the Rock had been agreed upon more to please France's Spanish ally than for any tactical or negotiating advantage.

The American colonists were anxious to negotiate the terms of peace with Britain. In London the Shelburne ministry was equally prepared to end hostilities. Strictly, under the terms of the Treaty of Paris, the colonists had agreed not to negotiate a separate peace, but war-weary and faced with setting up a new form of administration to cope with future problems, the Americans were not interested in such diplomatic niceties. The French government, anyhow, was quite happy to let them go ahead while they negotiated the best terms they could get for themselves. By November 1782, so-called provisional articles were signed, constituting an effective peace treaty between Britain and her former colonists.

Under it, Shelburne and the British peace party agreed to give away the Old North West – the area between the Saint Lawrence River and the Ohio, and all the land south of the Great Lakes, with boundaries extending to the west of the Mississippi River and down to the edge of Florida. In exchange, Britain obtained full recognition of her rights over the whole of Canada, including Newfoundland and Nova Scotia. Benjamin Franklin and other American negotiators in Paris thus signed away without a second thought any hopes the Canadian French still harboured for the return of 'New France', a land that had been theirs until a mere twenty years before. The British loyalists who were forced to leave the new United States made their way to Canada, thereby strengthening Britain's hold on the territory.

France's turn came in January 1783, when discussions began over a full treaty. She managed to get a few rewards for herself: the islands of Tobago and Saint Lucia, fishing rights off Newfoundland, secured by the small island bases of Saint Pierre and Miquelon, Senegal in Africa and the return of her old trading posts in India. It was not a great deal, but France had entered the war more to weaken Britain than to expand her own possessions. Support for the American insurgents had, to begin with, been fairly limited, restricted to the *philosophes* and various liberals, but it had grown steadily as the government saw that the American Revolution was developing into a major movement and pressure mounted throughout France for more backing. France's real reward, apart from the sense of satisfaction that arose out of Britain's humbling, was the creation of an independent country on the American continent, that could challenge Britain while remaining indebted to France for generations.

La Pérouse continued to supervise the repairs to his *Sceptre*. The Cadiz shipyards were busy and the work was not finished until March 1783. He had time to rest, to write letters, to pay visits to a few acquaintances and to local geographers. The mail from France brought him the government's congratulations for the Hudson Bay expedition, expressed in useful concrete terms by an increase in his salary of 800 *livres* a year. He was now financially secure, while his reputation grew day by day. Jean-François de Galaup de La Pérouse, confirmed in his rank of *capitaine de vaisseau*, had become a well-known figure on both sides of the Channel and across the Atlantic.

Before long the American Congress would recognise his wartime help by appointing him a member of the Society of the Cincinnati, founded by officers of the American Revolutionary Army in May 1778 to commemorate the hardships and the triumphs of the War of Independence, an exclusive order of which George Washington was the president, its badge an eagle suspended by a white and blue ribbon 'emblematic of the union of America and France'.

In April 1783, he took the *Sceptre* to Brest. He was formally welcomed by the port authorities, handed over his ship and saw to the proper discharge of his faithful crew. Then, within a few days, he was on his way to Paris. There were pressing matters to decide, the most important one being his marriage.

Part 5

FAMILY BUSINESS

14. Marriage at Last

April–October 1783

THE COURTSHIP OF Jean-François and Eléonore had been marked by long breaks owing to his campaigns abroad, but now he was back, it was peacetime and he was entitled to a long period of leave mixed with occasional duties ashore. It was the perfect time for them to settle down.

Not surprisingly, over the six years, there had been periods of strain between them. Knowing how much the Galoup family disliked their friendship and how cool a reception she could expect from Albi society if she ever went down to visit his hometown, Eléonore had at times offered to break off their notional engagement. For his part, the ceaseless battle between his duty to his family and the dictates of his heart cast a shadow on much that he did and thought. He had not visited his family for almost six years, and he felt guilty about it for, though his father had greatly upset him, he dearly loved his mother and his sisters.

The death of Ternay should have freed the two lovers a little, but they both remained aware that the navy presented a serious obstacle to their union. If they announced their intention to marry his father could contact another senior officer, or even the Minister of Marine, the Marquis de Castries, who was after all a man from Albi, and have a fresh *caveat* imposed. Whatever their rank or age, naval officers needed official approval for a marriage, to ensure that their red status was not weakened – and a connection with the middle-class Broudous would certainly endanger that status. Nevertheless, by the beginning of 1783, La Pérouse's increased reputation would have made it difficult to forbid his marriage under the pretext that the bride was not a suitable match for a naval officer. He was now in Paris, meeting Claret de Fleurieu, Castries and a number of senior officers almost on a daily basis. He was a major and influential figure in naval circles.

His father, however, had upped the ante. He had arranged a marriage for him while he was away, with Elaine de Vésian, the young daughter of a respected aristocratic Albi family. He discovered this when he reached Cadiz and began to sift through the mail that had been sent on to him. One might have expected La Pérouse to rebel against what his parents had been planning during his absence. He was forty-two years of age, a senior officer in the royal navy, respected at court and in the world of *philosophes* and scientists, a knight of the order of Saint Louis and a member of an exclusive American order. He had been in love with the same woman for almost ten years. And yet he now bowed to his father's wishes and agreed to marry a girl he could not even remember having ever met.

Tracing La Pérouse's love affair with Eléonore is not easy. Their relationship was kept private, partly because of the attitudes of the time, partly because of his career. She was careful not to put herself forward, leaving him entirely free to act towards his family as he thought fit. Time, they believed, was on their side: old Victor-Joseph might weaken and eventually allow the match even though he considered it unsuitable. 'Are you not aware, or are they not aware, that you are under my authority, that you are not free, and that anything you may have promised is worthless?'[1]

Victor-Joseph remained adamant. And inevitably, this led to some strain between the two lovers – and one can suspect that Abraham Broudou and his wife began to feel anxious that their daughter might remain unmarried and lose any chance of ever finding a husband. The life of an unmarried, almost penniless spinster was not an enviable one in the eighteenth century. Indeed in 1782 Abraham Broudou made arrangements with his wife to provide Eléonore with a dowry of 2000 *livres* a year should she marry. This would make her a more attractive match.

In the earlier stage of their relationship, Jean-François and Eléonore had written to each other in close personal terms, using the *tu* that implies close friendship and familiarity. Later, when she had returned to France, they were using the more formal *vous*. This could be interpreted as a cooling of their friendship, but it may indicate little more than a return to formality once they were back on European soil. La Pérouse's father and mother both wrote to him using the *vous* form – the *tu* is found only in letters between Jean-François and his sisters.

When he was about to sail to America in the *Astrée*, La Pérouse had felt that Eléonore had been cool and formal towards him. When he wrote reproaching her for this, she replied at once, protesting her love: 'How could you misread my true feelings for you? The pain I suffered when I learnt of your impending departure you took for coolness. You badly misinterpreted the efforts I was making to keep back my tears lest the sight of them should increase your own sorrow.'[2] But when he reached Cadiz and discovered the arranged marriage, he did not protest. Was he finally bowing to his father's wishes? Or was he giving way with every outward expression of courtesy, while waiting for an occasion to extract himself from a situation neither he nor the young Mademoiselle de Vésian wanted.

His letter to Madame de Vésian is a masterpiece of *double entendre*:

> Your daughter, brought up by you and educated under your care, must be like you; I know her through having once seen her when she was still a child, and I can swear to you that if I were the most perfect man in the world, with every possible advantage, I would prefer her to all other women ... Born with a very sensitive nature, I should be the most unhappy of men if I were not loved by my wife, if I did not have her deepest trust as is due to her best friend, and if living within my family and hers too, among her children (if we have any) did not fill her heart with happiness ... I hope one day to consider you as my mother, and I wish from this very day to regard you as my best friend; so I open my heart to you: consult your daughter; it is up to you to see whether we are suited to each other. Love us sufficiently to say *No* if that is your opinion ... I owe you my closest confidence, and so I authorise my mother to tell you the story of my former love. I was only thirty (my heart has always been a novel) ... but I never forgot the respect I owed to my parents and to their wishes; they are the ones who stopped me ... I hope that I shall soon be free, and if by then I have your reply and, better still, your assurances that I can make your daughter happy and that my character suits her, I shall fly down to Albi.[3]

He sent this letter while he was still in Cadiz. One suspects that he wanted to save Eléonore from the shock and the pain of learning about the arranged marriage, and if Mademoiselle de Vésian was at all hesitant about marrying a much older man she could hardly remember having ever met, and her parents gave in to her, all he would need to tell Eléonore was that the Galaups had arranged a match for him, but that he had rejected it.

To make quite certain the Vésians knew the situation, he also wrote to Monsieur de Vésian. It was a shorter letter, but it made the same points: be quite sure that your daughter does want to marry me, and I have someone else I love. And for good measure, he added that he would not be free for a couple of months – to which any sensible father would add the words 'or longer':

> I assure you that my feelings would suffer if I owed your daughter's hand to nothing more than the fact that you had chosen me, and that she was merely obeying her parents. I do beg you therefore to place no impediment in the way of Mademoiselle de Vésian's affections, and to

consider that if both of us are to be happy there must be no reluctance to overcome. I must inform you, sir, that while my eagerness has not allowed me to delay any further in communicating with you, I do have a certain matter to settle, which does not yet allow me to dispose entirely of myself. My mother will give you the details. I hope to be free in six weeks or two months.[4]

There was, naturally, no letter for Mademoiselle de Vésian. It would not have been quite proper and, in truth, what could La Pérouse add to what he had already told her parents? He was gambling on her having some other suitor in the wings, possibly someone she loved. But her parents still felt that the now renowned naval officer, even though he was twenty-five years older than her, was the best match. They replied in sympathetic terms, without going so far as to claim their daughter was attracted by him. How could she, when she hardly remembered meeting him? But they did look forward to his visiting them all in Albi, when everything could be arranged …

By the time he got their reply, he was in Paris. He wrote back, assuring them that he could hardly wait to go down to Albi. But Eléonore was also in Paris, boarding at the Convent Saint-Antoine. His hopes that Mademoiselle de Vésian might persuade her parents to forget about the reluctant lover were dashed, but he still hesitated about going to see Eléonore and breaking the news to her.

He tried another tactic with the Vésians. They were of a noble background, with excellent connections among the local nobility, and of a higher social level than the Galaups. This was no doubt what made the match so attractive to old Galaup: his family would move up the social ladder, and his son's reputation as a naval officer, combined with the Vésians' own connections, would give the La Pérouse family an unchallenged position in Languedoc society and beyond. La Pérouse, quite aware of this, decided to sow some doubts about his suitability in the Vésians' mind. He stressed that he was a plain man, honest and blunt, used to a hard life at sea, with no trace of snobbery. They already knew that he had fought for the republicans in America and was being granted the republican Order of Cincinnati. He underlined his plainness – no doubt, deliberately – in a letter from Paris to Madame de Vésian:

You are too good a mother to force [your daughter's] inclinations, and I have too much delicacy to try to marry a young person against her wishes. For my part, everything that I remember of Mademoiselle de Vésian pleases me greatly [but] *I want to love my wife as a peasant does* [author's italics], have in her so much confidence that I can entrust her, together with my mother and yourself, with all my business.[5]

These words cannot have failed to arouse more disquiet among the Vésians. What sort of a man was he? After all, they themselves scarcely knew him. Only Madame Galaup's charm and persistence allowed the negotiations to continue.

But the weeks went by and the Vésians must have expressed their growing impatience to Madame Galaup, who wrote to her son pressing him to end his affair with Eléonore. Back in November, he had told Monsieur de Vésian that a couple of months would be enough to settle things, but almost six months had passed and nothing had happened. Would he be down in Albi by summer? It was already late May. And what of Eléonore, still in Paris and waiting for a visit from him? As the hoped-for withdrawal of the Vésian family from the marriage negotiations failed to materialise he began to feel that he could no longer put off contacting Eléonore. The excuse that he had pressing matters to settle with ministry officials after his return from America was wearing thin.

He went halfway towards keeping his promise to Madame de Vésian: he sent a friend, Lecoulteux de la Noraye, a banker, to see Eléonore with hints that he was not sure whether she wanted him to keep to his notional engagement with her after such a long period of time. He could offer her the option to break it off if she now had second thoughts about him. If she wanted to, he would free her from her promise and give her monetary compensation – 20,000 *livres*, he later claimed – so that she could settle down and marry anyone else she wished. Lecoulteux was also to hint that La Pérouse himself had begun to harbour some doubts about their relationship. It was to be a tactful, highly diplomatic interview, in which he was to test the waters.

Her reaction was immediate. She wrote that she still loved him, that there could be no one else and that she did not want any money. If she did not marry him, she would enter the convent as a novice and withdraw from the world. La Pérouse rushed to the convent to see her. They fell into each other's arms and he vowed to marry her without delay, regardless of what his parents or anyone else might think. It was a dénouement that would have fitted well into the popular sentimental dramas of the time, known as *comédies larmoyantes* – tearjerkers.

He wrote almost immediately to his mother. He had done the best he could to follow her wishes, but he could no longer conceal his true feelings. Underlying his letter is a hint that both her and the Vésians shared part of the blame because they had failed to read between the lines:

Madame de Vésian had foreseen it, my dear mother: she knew my own heart better than I did myself ... I have seen Eléonore ... I could no longer fight against the remorse that was devouring us. My excessive attachment for you had led me to break what is the most sacred promise a man can make: I was forgetting the oaths I had made, the wishes of my own heart, the protests of my conscience. I had spent 20 days in Paris, and faithful to the promise I had made to you I had not been to see her … [but] I received a letter stained with her tears … [it contained] not a single reproach, but a deep sense of pain pervaded it. The veil tore at once … my situation filled me with revulsion, I could see all my guilt; I was nothing but a perjurer, unworthy of Mademoiselle de Vésian, to whom I was bringing a heart eaten up with remorse and worn out by a passion that nothing can extinguish, and unworthy of Mademoiselle Broudou, whom I had been weak enough to think of forsaking. My excuse, dear Mother, lies in the desire I have always had of pleasing you: it was for you alone, and for my father, that I was agreeing to marry.

I was stifling the remorse I was feeling. I thought that I was sure of myself, but I was breaking the laws of God and of man. Virtue, innocence and gentleness were being sacrificed to the framework of devotion that I had built up to enable me to always follow your wishes. But, my dear mother, this motive, however commendable, would be merely weakness if I pursued the course I was on. I was imprudent when I contracted this engagement without your prior consent, but I would be a monster if I broke my word and took to Mademoiselle de Vésian a heart that was withered and a conscience that was torn with remorse. I can belong only to Eléonore. I hope you will give your consent … but I shall come to Albi only when Mlle de Vésian is a married woman.[6]

This done, he took up his quill once more to write to Monsieur de Vésian. It was not an easy letter, but it had to be done, and without any more prevarication. He told him quite clearly that he could no longer contemplate marrying his daughter, who was a total stranger to him, as he now stated quite clearly: 'Never having had the honour of meeting her'. He went on to express his regret at losing the opportunity of 'belonging' to the Vésian family. What else could he say, indeed? He could – and did – let slip that he had recently discovered that the Vésians had another suitor in mind for their daughter, should the Galaup de la Pérouse arrangement fall through: 'I am in every respect inferior to Monsieur de Sénégas'.[7]

Whatever explosion of anger there might have been in the Galaup family, the Vésian family took his refusal quite calmly. A mere two months after they received La Pérouse's letter, Mademoiselle de Vésian married the Marquis de Sénégas. It was a good match, linking her family with a member of the local aristocracy.

By then, Jean-François and Eléonore were already husband and wife. He had no intention of wasting any more time on futile arguments with his parents, and he may even have suspected that they had other brides in mind for him. A *fait accompli* would bring them to their senses and close the matter once and for all.

Jean-François and Eléonore were married on 8 July 1783 at the Church of Sainte Marguerite, in Rue Saint Bernard, not far from the Bastille. The customary marriage contract had been earlier signed before a local lawyer, Monsieur Piquais. Only the witnesses required by law were present at both ceremonies. He was forty-two; she was twenty-eight. They spent just over a month in Paris. He then took his new bride down to Albi to meet his family, staying at Le Gô since it was now summertime. Not surprisingly, she was worried about the reception she would get from his father and mother, who for so long had bitterly opposed the marriage.

She need not have worried. The Galaups were not about to allow the local wagging tongues to gossip about the Vésian fiasco and the Broudou mismatch. They organised a solemn nuptial mass at the cathedral, followed by a reception worthy of a leading local family. All who wished to attend were made welcome and it went off without a hitch. All their friends were charmed by Eléonore, whom they found modest and gentle, and they were impressed by the show the Galaups had put on. It was high summer, a time for light dresses, for quiet gatherings in the shade of the narrow streets and the cobblestoned courtyards, and for a relaxing time in the country.

There was still one task for La Pérouse to carry out in the quiet shady reading room of Le Gô. He had to notify the navy that he had married without the prior permission that tradition and the rules required. It called for tact on his part, and a fair dose of diplomacy. The wording, however, suggests that this was little more than a formality, and that unofficially the naval authorities had been advised and had already given their agreement. His letter, a request addressed semi-formally to 'The Minister of Marine', was a lengthy, somewhat emotional communication sent, one suspects, largely for the record.

The great kindness you have shown towards me requires me to make a confession which I address, not to the King's Minister, but to the Marquis de Castries: I am married and have taken my wife from Paris to Languedoc. My story is a novel, which I implore you to be good enough to read. The Princesse de Bouillon had been told and may have spoken to you.[8]

The mention of the Princesse de Bouillon, a member of one of the leading aristocratic families of the time, makes it clear that, somewhere in the highest circles, someone had already spoken on behalf of La Pérouse. During those strain-filled weeks of May and June 1783, he had been in almost daily touch with Claret de Fleurieu and other senior officials – five days a week, he says himself – and it seems unlikely that his close collaborators did not know about his personal problems. If Fleurieu knew, and the Princess knew, how many others also knew? Castries was probably quite aware of what was going on, if not officially. La Pérouse could hardly seek the ministry's approval for his eventual wedding to Eléonore while he was still negotiating with the Vésians. But clearly, someone had been told that he had no intention of marrying Mademoiselle de Vésian and that he intended all along to marry Eléonore Broudou – and La Pérouse must have been advised unofficially, presumably by the Princesse de Bouillon, who seems to have acted as an intermediary, that Castries had no objection.

His letter was couched in terms calculated to soften all but the most hard-hearted:

> Eight years ago in the Isle de France I fell madly in love with a very beautiful and charming girl. I wanted to marry her. She had no money. The Chevalier de Ternay opposed it. My parents had given him full authority over me by a legal document. He added their power to his own and remained unshakeable, telling me that love was a passing fancy and that one did not feel any consolation in poverty after one was married. We left the Isle de France shortly after that. I was still in love. I told the young lady to go to France, where I would marry her … her father, who was very keen that I should become his son-in-law, sent her to Europe on a ship that left a fortnight after mine.

Ternay's arguments and those of his parents, who looked forward to the possibility of arranging 'a great marriage' for him, had some effect on his passion, and the war further delayed his plans. La Pérouse went on to describe the Vésian affair, and the approaches he had made to put an end to his links with Eléonore.

> Then I learnt that the young lady had been in tears since the end of the war and that she was thinking of entering the religious life. I went to see her. I could not resist. There was not a single reproach, merely a pain that was the decisive weapon against me. I remembered that I was 30 when I had made her a promise and that she was 15; I felt that it was my solemn duty to keep sacred promises that had been made at an age when flightiness is inexcusable. The young lady was totally honest, virtuous

and gentle … I then broke the engagement that my parents had made on my behalf for a union that would have been beyond all my expectations …

My proposal was accepted. The young lady was at the Convent of Saint Antoine; I was married in the parish of Sainte Marguerite with no other witnesses than those needed for the formalities. I have taken her down to Albi, where I was welcomed as handsomely as if I had won some battles.

He closed with an offer that tells us indirectly how advanced France's plans were for a major expedition: 'I have agreed with her to make amends in the Service, and I am ready, my Lord, to go round the world for six years if you order it.'

The letter was written for the record, with the possibility in mind that the breach of naval regulations by a senior officer might require the case to be referred to Louis XVI personally. If we assume that Castries already knew and had no objection, the long narrative of this love affair could be shown to the king, who presumably would be moved by it, and then it would be filed away in the official records.[9]

Castries replied within a fortnight, formally approving La Pérouse's actions:

I understand perfectly all the different feelings you have had, as well as the sentiment that has been driving you. And since this commitment will not take you away from the service, you can count on the King's approval.

If the lady you have taken as your wife is a worthy person and justifies the preference you have shown for her, you have made a good match; the truest proprieties are those one finds in our feelings and I shall always feel more favourable towards this kind of union than one motivated by self-interest.

Enjoy the pleasure of making someone happy, and the tokens of honour and distinction you have received from your fellow citizens; they are well deserved, and as a former resident of Albi I join them with all my heart.[10]

Jean-François and Eléonore spent a few happy weeks in the warm and tranquil countryside but, as she knew only too well, the call of duty would soon separate them again. A court martial concerning the Battle of the Saints was being set up in Lorient: La Pérouse would be expected to testify. And there were the complex and still secret plans being drawn up in Paris for a major voyage of exploration. As his letter shows, La Pérouse was reasonably confident that he would be asked to lead it, but the decision had not yet been made. He needed to be around, continuing his work with Fleurieu and others, not hidden away in Albi and in danger of being overlooked. As summer turned to autumn, he left Eléonore in charge of his mother and made his way back to Paris and Versailles.

Part 6

THE GREAT VOYAGE

15. An Inquiry in Lorient and Plans in Paris

October 1783–May 1784

THE ADMIRAL DE Grasse had not taken his defeat easily. While a prisoner in England he had multiplied criticisms and accusations against the captains who had served under him during the battle. They had not followed his orders, they had not come to his help, and they were the real cause of the disaster.

La Pérouse, as captain of the *Astrée*, knew only too well how hard it was to make out other ships' signals among the smoke and the chaos of a sea battle. He had found it difficult to assess what was actually happening during the battle, and he had not realised that De Grasse had been taken prisoner until he reached Santo Domingo and met Vaudreuil ten days later.

François-Joseph-Paul, Comte de Grasse du Bar, had always been a difficult person to deal with. He was a southerner, hot-blooded and hard on himself and others. He was a colossus of a man, well over 1.8 metres in height and built in proportion. He belonged to the nobility, was proud of his lineage and had no intention of accepting any blame for the defeat. Now aged 60, he could claim that his experience outclassed all those who had been involved in the Saintes affair. He had spent forty-five years at sea, fighting against the British Navy, Turkish pirates, Algerian raiders, anyone and anywhere. He had defeated Admiral Hood off Tobago in 1781; he had sailed to the Chesapeake to enforce French naval supremacy; he had played a vital role in the capture of Yorktown; he had captured the island of Saint Kitts in 1782. He took pride in being a professional sailor, a nobleman who had no time for the niceties and political games of the court. He had won battles through using his own judgement when others advised caution. Often ill-tempered and impatient, he had trodden on many toes and was unpopular with many other senior commanders. He knew this and had no intention of accepting the blame he knew they would try to pin on him.

Both Vaudreuil and De Grasse had their highly placed supporters. When De Grasse was taken to England, he was warmly received and almost hailed

– but then he did acknowledge that he had been fairly defeated and praised the superiority of the British Navy, the quality of its guns, as well as the ability of men like Hood and Rodney. But the atmosphere that surrounded him in England did not mellow him. If anything, it made him more angry about what he considered had been a lack of support from his captains. Even as he was being taken to England, he had drawn up a letter of complaint for his superiors in Paris.

Now, he turned to composing a more comprehensive report on the Saints, exculpating himself and showering blame on everyone else. This he sent to Louis XVI and the Minister of Marine, Castries, as well as to George Washington and General Rochambeau. The thought of this report being sent to Washington, who was not only a foreigner but a republican as well, however technically correct it may have been since he was the commander-in-chief, caused something of an explosion of fury among the aristocratic naval officers.

And not everyone shared his opinion, not even in England. De Grasse was granted an audience by George III, during which he could not resist repeating his complaints about the poor support he had received. He included in his criticisms Louis de Bougainville, who was highly regarded in Britain as a gifted mathematician and navigator, the first Frenchman to have completed a circumnavigation, and a Fellow of the Royal Society. To De Grasse's astonishment and embarrassment, George III said that James Cook was a great sailor, but Louis de Bougainville was an inspired one. This led De Grasse to moderate his criticisms for a while, especially when he realised that other British naval men and scientists shared their monarch's opinion, and that some of those he was criticising had strong supporters and close acquaintances on that side of the Channel.

It was much the same in France. De Grasse had his enemies, and those he was attacking had their own friends. Louis XVI became increasingly disturbed by the continuing argument. His first thought had been to let tempers cool down so the dispute would die a natural death, but De Grasse's broadcasting of his attacks to all and sundry made this difficult.

The situation worsened when Vaudreuil returned to France in June 1783. Not long after, De Grasse was freed on parole and came home to launch a fresh series of broadsides. Castries advised him to relax and keep away from Versailles, at least during the summer months. But nothing could stop De Grasse. He was not going to shoulder any of the blame for the Battle of the Saints and he wanted full justification. This meant passing the blame onto his subordinates, including La Pérouse, although he does not seem to have mentioned him by name. Nevertheless, La Pérouse was told to be ready to defend himself.

It was Bougainville, speaking on behalf of most of the other officers directly or indirectly criticised by De Grasse, who formally asked the Maréchal de Castries for permission to defend himself publicly. This could be achieved only with a court of inquiry. He denied, in a letter of 4 November 1783, that he wanted this – 'God knows that I have no wish to indict the general'[1] – but he knew what he was doing. He really had no other option: De Grasse would continue to blame others unless a formal investigation was set up.

Louis XVI had become quite irritated by the whole affair – Castries' hint to De Grasse to keep away from the court was more than a friendly suggestion: it was meant to avoid the king showing his annoyance and the smirking courtiers around him causing another explosion from the irate admiral. A court martial seemed inevitable. It would cause more accusations to fly in every direction. It was regrettable, but the King had to placate public opinion.

La Pérouse and his fellow commanders were told to report to Lorient during November, so that if the court of inquiry wanted to hear their testimony it would not have to wait for them to come up from Paris or the provinces. As is usual with such hearings, there were preliminary arguments that caused endless delays. 'A total waste of my time,' commented La Pérouse,[2] a sentiment echoed by most of his fellow officers. Fortunately for his own temper, he was allowed to spend December and part of January in Paris.

There, he continued his work with Fleurieu. That there would be a major voyage of exploration was now taken for granted. As always, the problem was money. The American war had strained France's finances to the edge of bankruptcy. It was a familiar story, but it was not just the war that had proved costly. Maintaining a court at Versailles, Compiègne and elsewhere was expensive and Marie-Antoinette was enjoying life, spending lavishly on grandiose receptions, with elaborate dresses and expensive jewellery – after which she complained that all this was exhausting her and she needed a quieter time in the country. The court could not move away from Versailles when it was not midsummer – the palace was not just a royal residence, but France's top administrative centre – so the solution was to build the queen a 'hamlet', the Petit Trianon, in the vast grounds of the palace. There she and her close friends could play at being shepherdesses and, when they were bored with that, stroll around the newly designed English-style garden. Servants in picturesque costumes attended to the sheep, as well as to the ladies, ensuring that the latter were comfortable and that the former always snow-white and well combed.

So there would not be an expedition of any kind until the financial administrators felt a little less anxious, La Pérouse and others talked about what might eventuate, and drew up plans, but they were frustrated. Then he received orders to return to Lorient in the New Year. He had already handed over his journal of his time in the West Indies and off the American coast, but the Comte de Breugnon, who was chairing the inquiry, again insisted that all the officers concerned should remain close at hand.

It was a boring period. There was practically nothing to do in Lorient, apart from endlessly discussing the events of the recent war. Not surprisingly, tempers rose. Breugnon began to worry about squabbles developing – 'a fermentation of spirits among these gentlement'[3] – especially when De Grasse arrived. When a rumour emerged that De Grasse had actually named La Pérouse among those who had let him down, the latter flew into a fury and dashed off a letter to Breugnon, with a copy to Castries. He wanted to be heard, right away if possible, and to defend himself. He asked Breugnon to tell everyone concerned that he totally denied all the charges. He asked Breugnon to send a copy of his protests to De Grasse, to the public prosecutor, the commissioners and all the judges. However, it was only a rumour. Breugnon told La Pérouse to calm down and refused to bother anyone else with his protestations. La Pérouse's angry letter would not be circulated. There were already too many claims and counter-claims to deal with as it was. Castries endorsed the decision: 'Approved, if he is not involved, that his note be rejected.'[4]

La Pérouse calmed down, but his sense of futility and boredom continued. Though it was early spring, the weather seemed to reflect the general mood of grumpiness. There were frequent grey days with a cold drizzle coming in day after day from the Atlantic that made it unpleasant to go outside, while the few drawing rooms he visited were filled with backbiting and rancour. He unburdened himself in a letter to a cousin in Albi, in terms not very different from his frequent letters to Eléonore and his mother:

> I hope that this unending business in Lorient will soon allow me to see again that region, that family, those parents that I love so much, and where I so earnestly wish to spend the rest of my life. I don't know any more what Fate had in store for me, because as I had to defend myself fairly heatedly against Mr de Grasse, against whom there is now a wide feeling of contempt, I may have somewhat upset Mr de Castries, since it was he who had appointed that commander. But this is still only a slight suspicion which the high opinion I hold of that Minister does not really allow me to entertain.[5]

He was worried, and bored, by the drawn-out affair. Fortunately, Breugnon decided that he did not need La Pérouse in Lorient any longer, and he was allowed back to Paris in mid-May.

It may have been around this time, probably while he was still filling in time in Lorient, that La Pérouse decided to write down his thoughts on the reorganisation of the French Navy, *Mémoire sur la réorganisation de la marine*, reprinted in the centennial edition of the *Bulletin de la Société de Géographie*. It is a valuable document, which shows La Pérouse holding a middle position – possibly just a little right of centre – in the continuing and often bitter argument between the blue and red officers.

Officer rank had always been the preserve of the nobility. Sons, usually younger sons, served in the king's navy, *La Royale*, just as their brothers had served on land since feudal times, following their lord and leading their own retainers on lengthy campaigns. The noblemen accepted that in wartime larger fleets were needed, resulting in a greater and urgent demand for more officers, and that these could come only from the merchant service, which was largely staffed by the middle and lower middle classes. The nobility insisted that these men be given temporary commissions, and wear a distinctive blue uniform. When the war ended, they should return to the merchant navy, though some, who had particularly distinguished themselves during the various campaigns, tried to get themselves accepted for permanent naval service. The government was torn between the need to keep these talented men for when a new conflict broke out, and the traditions of the navy.

The nobility had its own social differences. There was the upper nobility, known as the *grands nobles* – not many of whom wanted a full-time naval career – the landed nobles, whose families owned substantial estates, the gentry, whose estates were much smaller, and the *noblesse de robe*, what one might call the administrative nobility, owners of medium-sized or often quite modest properties. The land enabled them to add the critical *de* to their name. The aristocratic officers all knew that this was a growing practice among well-to-do families, and that these landed titles were being accumulated. Thus Jean-François, whose family name was Galaup, had added La Pérouse to his name, and was now entitled to add yet another landed title, De Brens, as an additional estate had recently been purchased. Jean-François Galaup de La Pérouse de Brens might have sounded impressive, but it would not have fooled his fellow officers, who knew precisely the background history of most of their friends and relatives.

The end of the American war had once again highlighted the problem. And how long would it be before another war flared up and the navy would once again have to send out a hurried call for the help of middle-class officers? There was also the problem of running a growing overseas colonial empire. The French Navy would not become a stable and efficient force until 'the cause of our past misfortunes' was properly addressed, he wrote in his report. La Pérouse did not hesitate to face the class structure that underlay the problems of recruitment and retention. 'They have their roots in the present structure of the Navy.' By saying this, he was boldly venturing into dangerous territory. He did not go so far as to advocate the end of the privileges of the nobility, but he highlighted the weaknesses inherent in what another age would call 'the old boy network', and put forward the view that birth does not guarantee ability:

> [Under the present system] every officer, from a captain down to the most recently appointed lieutenant, belongs to the same class. The first and second officers have often been *gardes de la marine* together, as has the man in command, and they have established that familiarity that comes from age and an equality of birth, and which an ephemeral appointment to command a ship cannot extinguish.[6]

His solution was a two-tier system, with the captain and his first officer coming from the aristocracy, and the other officers from the merchant service. The latter should never be disregarded or cast aside, and their loyalty and continued devoted service could easily be assured by better recognition. There was no need to look for any revolutionary measures: these were men 'for whom the command of a fireship and the Cross of Saint Louis bestowed after twenty-five years of service would represent a very great reward'. He knew that, though most of the red officers would reject his proposal with anger and contempt, there were plenty of officials back at the ministry who would appreciate his suggestion of creating a class of 'devoted and grateful servants'. His memoir got nowhere – it was ahead of its time, but would soon seem much too conservative and class-based.

Among La Pérouse's ideas, there was one other minor, but interesting suggestion: naval officers who had given years of service – usually from their teens as *gardes de la marine* – should be guaranteed promotion to senior rank by the age of forty-five. They could thereby look forward to a rewarding career and be encouraged to give their best throughout their early working life, without having to lobby powerful patrons for promotion. When he wrote this, he was forty-three.

The court martial finally began its open proceedings in Lorient in May 1784. Each commanding officer was questioned in turn. Vaudreuil, who had had time to think the situation over and to talk to Bougainville, had already withdrawn his criticism. The inquiry dragged on for days, and La Pérouse's part in it was quite minor. When it ended Vaudreuil and most of the captains, including La Pérouse, were exonerated from any blame. Bougainville's squadron suffered more: though the criticism directed at him was quite mild it resulted in a formal public admonition. Captain Poulpiquet, who had been in charge of the 74-gun *Hercule*, and Renaud d'Aleins, the captain of the *Neptune*, were also formally admonished. Gouzillon, of the smaller *Ardent*, was suspended from any command for three months, for having lowered his colours too early. Cavel, the captain of the *Scipion*, had fought well, but he had failed to hand over command when he was wounded and clearly no longer able to carry on, leaving his officers in total confusion; he may have shown courage in the face of great personal suffering, but his first duty was to his ship and his overall commander.

De Grasse fared worst. Not only did the inquiry reveal that he had shown a serious lack of judgement but, as Castries wrote back, 'all your accusations of disobedience to your signals and of failure to assist the admiral ships, have been disproved by the verdict of the court-martial. The result is that you have compromised, by your ill-founded accusations, the reputation of several officers, in the hope of justifying in the eyes of the public your role in an unfortunate affair.'[7] De Grasse was exiled to his country property, where he died four years later.

La Pérouse could now return to Paris, and Fleurieu welcomed him back. The two men knew what they wanted – a full-scale voyage of exploration into the Pacific – but they still had to bide their time. Money remained short and too much haste and eagerness might bring about a rebuff. It was better to work on quietly, and let things settle down.

But Eléonore was still in Albi. Depending on the weather, dashing down to see her might mean a three- to four-day journey. Spending a week with her would mean an absence of three weeks from Paris. But bringing Eléonore up to the capital was not the simple solution it might appear to be. She would need to stay in some apartment that would need furnishing and equipping. A maid would be required. And who did she know in Paris apart from a few nuns and La Pérouse's own friends? Her husband would be away most of the day at the Ministry of Marine or at Versailles. Introducing her to his colleagues' wives would involve time-consuming, etiquette-laden formal visits. It was much simpler for her to stay among his family who, to his great relief, had been kind and welcoming. She was charming, modest and unfailingly helpful. It had not been difficult for her to make new friends and be welcomed into their homes.

Yet Paris had so much to offer. La Pérouse would have liked to show his wife what was going on, such as the first experiments with hot air balloons. Everyone was talking about the Montgolfier brothers who had sent one up into the sky at Annonay. Even bolder, a balloon rose with a man beneath it in a basket. The Marquis d'Arlandes had actually sailed in one over Paris, while in England, Vincent Lunardi had made the first rival ascent, and François Blanchard was preparing to sail through the air across the English Channel from Calais to Dover. Children everywhere, and adults as well, were playing with balloons, large and small, in every open space, although some conservative-minded clerics shook their heads at what they suspected might be a sacrilegious, if puny, attempt to imitate birds and interfere with God's orderly world.

There were plays and concerts they might have gone to. A new composer named Mozart, who not long ago had lived in Paris, was increasingly popular. Beaumarchais' much talked-about play, *Le Mariage de Figaro*, was finally being performed after being banned for six years for its subversive plot, and there were even rumours that Mozart planned to turn it into an opera.

La Pérouse could console himself with the thought that the approaching summer months would bring a relaxation in society activities. Louis XVI was only too happy to leave the court and go hunting, a number of the courtiers retired to their own estate to escape the heat of Paris and the oppressive atmosphere of the corridors and drawing rooms of Versailles. (And in those days when bathrooms were few and bathing infrequent, and body odours had to be concealed by generous applications of eau-de-cologne, those passages and rooms were also pungent.)

Life down in Albi was much more pleasant, especially at Le Gô. La Pérouse did manage to make a couple of quick visits himself, but as Admiral de Brossard calculated in his biography, he could have spent only about three months in all with his wife between their marriage and his departure on his voyage of exploration. He had confided his disquiet to a friend in Lorient, who wrote back to him in late May or early June:

> I find your anxiety to go back to see your wife perfectly natural, especially when you are married to such a charming and pleasant person, but you should be able to ascertain without too much difficulty before you go what the Minister has in mind for you. It would not be natural that a married man who may have to go overseas for five or six years should not be allowed a few months to settle his affairs.[8]

So he went down to Languedoc, but not for anything like the few months his friend mentioned. There was too much going on in Paris and too much at stake for him to risk not being on hand in case some urgent question arose. Few people were in the know and he remained totally discreet, but the plans that Fleurieu and others had been working on were far more advanced than anyone suspected.

16. PARIS: THE FINAL PLANS

September 1784–June 1785

SOME TIME IN the autumn of 1784, an official at the French embassy in London was in touch with William (or Wilhem) Bolts. A strange, ebullient character, Bolts was a less swashbuckling version of the Baron de Benyowski, but no less given to drawing up plans for distant expeditions. Born in the Netherlands, though claiming to be of German origin, he had gone to England in 1749, sailed to Calcutta ten years later and worked for the East India Company. Later he fell out with his employers, possibly as the result of private deals he seems to have carried out for Austrian commercial interests, but also because of his distress at the way the locals were being exploited by the company. He was sacked in 1768, and avenged himself by writing a book criticising the administration of Bengal. This solid three-volume work, entitled *Considerations on India Affairs, particularly respecting the present state of Bengal*, was published in London in 1772, and translated into French in 1778.

At the time, the East India Company was under fire and about to lose its privileged status as a private trading company – it was effectively taken over by the British government, following legislation passed in 1773. The company's supporters promptly fired a counter-salvo in the form of a book by Harry Verselst, entitled *A View of the Rise, Progress and Present State of the English Government in Bengal, including a reply to the misrepresentations of Mr Bolts and others*.

Bolts became involved in a number of costly libel suits, which effectively ruined him. He was employed for a while by the Trieste Company in Coromandel, but decided to leave India altogether, and make his way to the Isle de France. He was there in early 1780, carrying out various business transactions. What he was looking for, though, was something to absorb his energy and, above all, end his dependency on trading companies that always looked upon him as a brash and irritating outsider.[1]

Back in England, however, he realised that his reputation as a troublemaker was preventing him from finding possible backers, and that there was now also a fair amount of suspicion over his links with Austria and the French in Mauritius. He turned to the French, with embassy officials reporting on his ideas to the Minister of Marine, Castries, until he was invited, informally, to travel to Paris.

On 25 January 1785, he sent a detailed seventeen-page proposal for an expedition to the North-West Coast of America. The covering letter makes it clear that he had been working for the French for some time, and that his report had been expected: 'I would have fulfilled this task a long time ago, in accordance with the promise I made to Your Highness, but a voyage to Flanders prevented me.'[2] It is clear that either Castries or Fleurieu had arranged for him to move to Paris in October or November 1784, so that they could consult him tactfully about his ideas. Now they could use him for their own ends, to promote their plans and submit a proposal direct to the king.

William Bolts's plan was for a straightforward, if well thought-out, trading voyage, during which the French ships would sail to the North-West Coast of America, buy furs and sell them in China, pick up a cargo of goods there and make their way back to France, or possibly back to America for further trading. All this would allow a thorough exploration of the coast, with the possibility of discovering the longed-for North-West Passage from the Pacific to Hudson Bay and thence to the Atlantic. In this way, France could complete the work begun by the late James Cook and establish important strategic and commercial outposts.

Armed with these proposals, Castries approached Louis XVI, who turned them down flat – ships of the French navy could not undertake commercial enterprises of this kind. There were other tasks to carry out, more dignified and more appropriate for a leading European power. The King also outlined his own ideas, adaptations, no doubt, of suggestions previously made by Castries and others, and from then on he took the closest interest in the planning and execution of the voyage.

Castries and Fleurieu had won. The expedition was now to proceed by the King's will – it was almost the old absolutist motto, *Le Roy le veult*. Every obstacle could be swept away. The effect of the Bolts report can be gauged by the date. It was dated 25 January; less than a fortnight later, on 5 February, La Pérouse was still champing at the bit, writing to Éléonore: 'I am still in the same state of uncertainty. Nothing is decided. Mr de Castries showers me with kindness and favours, but he does not finalise anything, and I am wasting time and money far from those I love.'[3] But the very next day, Fleurieu told him that everything had come right and that Castries was putting his name forward to command the expedition.

Bolts was kept in the background, with the usual diplomatic assurances needed to maintain his silence. His expenses were paid and more, with the funds coming from the navy's secret funds.[4] He had moved to a private house on Place Saint-Michel, from which he wrote to Fleurieu that 'my secretary is writing out copies of various items that could be useful for the exploration of the islands and the continent in question'. The next day, he wrote from Versailles to Castries, urging a search for an island discovered by Laroche in 1675 that could be useful as a whaling station and a port of call for French ships – this was South Georgia, in a fairly frigid latitude. By then, there were enough rumours, true and false, circulating for Bolts to realise that the expedition that was being planned had little to do with him. Paid off, he gradually dropped out of sight, though he may have carried out some investigations for French officials in Europe and almost certainly in Scandinavia.

Louis XVI's role could easily be viewed as a monarch taking a benign interest in the work of his officials, but he had always been interested in geography and cartography. His tutor had been Philippe Buache, the eminent Royal Hydrographer, who had taught, first the heir apparent, the Duc de Bourgogne and, when the young lad had died, had moved on the Duc de Berry, the future Louis XVI. He used the same text that he had written for his previous pupil, *Instruction historique*, as well as Guillaume Leblond's *Arithmétique et géométrie de l'officier*.

In 1769, aged fifteen, the young duke had drawn an impressive, careful map of the environs of Versailles, in full colour.[5] It included blank areas of the kind found on early explorers' charts, labelled 'Places that have not been surveyed'. The quality of this work makes it clear that it was not his first attempt:

> The Dauphin exceeded Buache's expectations. A passion was aroused in him for hydrography, for the navy and for the geography of discoveries, and it never left him. He could understand all the great geographical questions of his day, and discuss them intelligently.[6]

Louis XVI's role in promoting and planning the expedition has led to the suggestion that La Pérouse was acting on his behalf, carrying out a great voyage of exploration that Louis would have loved to lead, had he not been the King of France. This idea was boldly expressed by Paul and Pierrette Girault de Coursac in the title of their 1985 book: *Le Voyage de Louis XVI autour du monde: l'expédition La Pérouse*. However, Fleurieu, Castries and their assistants rapidly took over, carrying out the king's wishes, but at the same time setting in motion the plans they had been mulling over for so long.

The scientific world received its instructions – to draw up proposals for research in the areas of geography, physics, astronomy, botany and zoology – and responded enthusiastically. There was so much to do, so many gaps to fill in every area of research. Castries wrote officially to the *Académie des sciences*, France's equivalent of the British Royal Society, and to the *Société de médecine*. Fleurieu and La Pérouse approached individual scientists, all of them leading figures in French and indeed in European circles. La Pérouse contacted Buffon, who was by then in his seventy-ninth year but still highly influential. Fleurieu discussed issues of geography and cartography with Jean-Nicolas Buache de la Neuville, navigational problems with Jean-Charles Borda and the problems of Pacific exploration with Louis de Bougainville.

The scientists reacted speedily. The chemist Antoine Lavoisier organised his colleagues into committees. The Abbé Tessier, regent of the Paris faculty of medicine, started work on a study of the corruption of water on board ships. It had baffled chemists and doctors for centuries: was it to do with long-term storage, with the spontaneous generation of harmful larvae or, as he thought, the eggs of insects that had fallen in the water or otherwise made their way into the casks? It was a daring advance to the brink of bacteriology, which he wanted La Pérouse to test by the use of twenty different barrels, each of them having come into contact with different insect species. It was hardly practical, but it reflected the enthusiasm of many of the researchers. There had been so few opportunities to try out their ideas, so little official assistance for their work. Botanists and zoologists were particularly enthusiastic, a number of them offering to join the expedition. It was a chance to gain immortality by discovering some new plant or new animal and naming it, adding an adjective to the name to ensure future generations would remember them.

It was no longer possible to keep the expedition a secret. La Pérouse told Éléonore in late February. The full scale of the enterprise remained hidden throughout March, when two ships were allocated, the *Portefaix* (the Porter) and the *Utile* (the Useful). The latter turned out to be too small and too slow, and was soon replaced by a larger one, called, equally unsuitably, *L'Autruche* (the Ostrich). Changing the names was left until they could be formally transferred to the naval service. Until this happened, the British could be left somewhat in the dark, although by the end of March, London's naval information services cannot have been in any doubt: the French were preparing a major voyage of exploration.

La Pérouse and Fleurieu were selecting solid, heavy vessels similar to James Cook's *Endeavour*, which had been a mere collier. The two ships selected for La Pérouse were stout storeships of 450 tonnes, providing ample space for stores and the crews. They were 39 metres long and eight wide – not impressive warships by any means, but serviceable and manoeuvrable. Registering them as naval units made up for their fairly low status. Cook's ship had been listed as a Royal Navy barque; La Pérouse's two storeships were registered as frigates. The names were changed at the same time. The *Portefaix* became the *Boussole*; the *Autruche* re-emerged as the *Astrolabe*.

British naval authorities were still not sure what the French were up to, and Fleurieu and Castries tried to keep them in the dark for as long as possible. This led to a serio-comic mission by Paul Monneron to London. He had sailed with La Pérouse to Hudson's Bay and was appointed *ingénieur-en-chef* in late February or early March. La Pérouse suggested that he should travel to London, collect information about James Cook's efforts to keep scurvy at bay, and buy whatever scientific instruments he could. With any luck, Sir Joseph Banks could be approached and would provide a few valuable introductions. But to conceal his true mission, Monneron invented the character of one Don Inigo Alvarez, a wealthy Spanish trader who intended to send merchant ships to the Pacific coast. He did his best to keep up the pretence, but at times got his 'I propose' and 'he proposes' mixed up. It was not altogether a successful ruse: senior members of London naval and scientific circles did not go out of their way to help a Frenchman supposedly working for a Spanish merchant. He was more successful with second-line officials and with the painter John Webber who had sailed in Cook's *Resolution* and painted a famous full-length portrait of the explorer.

One way Monneron gained Webber's confidence was to ask him to paint his portrait: 'In order to see him more often, without interfering with my own affairs, I have decided to get myself painted, for the first time in my life'.[7] Webber was delighted, chatted to him at length and took him to the British Museum to show him artefacts and other items from the South Seas. Even better, he introduced Monneron to booksellers and instrument makers in Fleet Street. Among the books Monneron brought back to Paris were two copies of James Cook's narrative of his second voyage, and two separate editions of the third. In addition, he purchased James Lind's *A Treatise on the Scurvy* of 1753 and two copies of David Macbride's *An Historical Account of a New Method of Treating the Scurvy*. Several cases of anti-scorbutic remedies were shipped to France on his orders: 2 cases of spruce essence, 68 of malt essence, 20 of molasses and 6 of preserved fruit. He spent an estimated 8000 *livres* during his stay, and made a list of further items that an official back in Paris, one Jean-Claude Piquet, ordered separately. On the other hand, Webber's portrait of Paul Monneron has never been found – it was probably little more that a pencil sketch. The artist, however, was not fooled for long. Monneron's conversation and his purchases made it clear that he was not working for any Inigo Alvarez and that there was probably no such person.

After no more than a few days, the British authorities realised what Monneron was doing. With information now trickling in from Paris and an investigation into Monneron's background, it was easy to put two and two together: Monneron was working for the French Navy and collecting material for the rumoured voyage of exploration. The British were in no way upset by his small subterfuge. Sir Joseph Banks came forward, ensuring that the Royal Society lent Monneron two dipping needles, instruments that had been used by James Cook himself. It was not something Banks would have done for an obscure Spanish merchant.

Monneron was back in Paris by mid-April, his departure watched and recorded by the spies who had begun to dog his footsteps. Their counterparts in Paris reported that Monneron, immediately on arrival, had made for the offices of Fleurieu and La Pérouse. Everything was now falling into place.

William Pitt and Lord Howe, by now First Lord of the Admiralty, were not concerned about the French moves. They held La Pérouse in high regard – he had always proved himself a gallant and humane enemy, and once the rumours that had surrounded Bolts's plans for developing the fur trade along the North-West Coast disappeared, they could feel satisfied that the expedition was essentially a scientific one, a voyage of exploration that would complement James Cook's great work. This was confirmed when official advice was received on 5 May from Lord Dorset, the British Ambassador to Versailles, that La Pérouse would shortly sail from Brest on a great voyage that would include a call at New Zealand.

When Monneron landed in Paris, he found the preparations in full swing. Work was going on apace in the ports of Rochefort and Brest, appointments were being made daily, and the king himself was at work on the likely route and the research to be done on the way. The scientific societies came forth with their reports. The *Académie des sciences*, under Buache's supervision, completed a twenty-six-page report, with lists of what was required in the fields of geography, astronomy, physics, mechanics, chemistry, mineralogy, botany and zoology, each of these sections the painstaking work of various sub-committees. The *Société de médecine* drew up its list of the problems it wished investigated, twenty-three pages long. With various appendices, notes, memoirs, and associated reports, some of which found their way into the instructions, all this came pretty close to 200 foolscap pages.

La Pérouse had written to his wife and his family in early April, bringing them up to date on the planned voyage and his role in it. Éléonore was distraught. She had expected him to go on some expedition, possibly to Mauritius or America, but this would take him away for years. Had he not said that his dearest wish was to settle down with her and his family, who had made her so welcome? Alas, it was something he had said when promotion seemed to drag and time hung heavy with indecision and doubt. His mother tried to console her, reminding her that neither she nor his sisters had seen him over long periods, receiving the infrequent letters that were the norm in days when the postal service was almost non-existent. He sent presents and letters from Brest and Paris, but this was no consolation for his absence. He may have managed a hurried visit down to Albi, staying no more than a couple of days, but even that is uncertain.

Recruiting officers and scientists to take with him on the voyage took up most of his time. Parents, ambitious for their sons' future careers, called on him, stressing the boys' talents and pulling whatever strings they could to ensure an appointment. A few cranks also dropped in with suggestions about the route the ships should follow and the discoveries, largely of imaginary islands, they could make.

There was little difficulty in selecting the top officers. His friend Fleuriot de Langle, with whom he had sailed to Hudson's Bay, was an obvious choice to command the companion ship, the *Astrolabe*. Neither Fleurieu nor Castries had the slightest hesitation in endorsing the nomination. Indeed, De Langle was so well known in naval circles that the rumour began to circulate that he had originally been considered for the leader's position. He was highly experienced in navigation and had a solid scientific background. This led the gossip writers, carrying on the work of the late Louis de Bachaumont, the author of *Mémoires secrets pour servir à l'histoire de la république des lettres en France*, to record that La Pérouse was a second choice.

Admittedly, De Langle was well connected and married to Georgette de Kérouartz, the niece of the Comte d'Hector, lieutenant-general of the naval forces and commander of the port of Brest. But if this speculation was based on the idea that better connections lead to greater preferment, then it should be remembered that La Pérouse was the close collaborator of Fleurieu and a *protégé* of the Marquis de Castries, the Minister of Marine and a fellow Albigeois. In addition, La Pérouse was older by four years and the more experienced naval commander.

As his first officer on the *Boussole*, La Pérouse picked Robert Sutton de Clonard (or Closnard), who had been his first officer on the *Serin* back in 1778. Though only thirty-three, Clonard had a wide experience. He had served on ships of the French India Company, fought and been wounded at Mahé and earned the Cross of Saint Louis for his valour. Next, he fought in the American

War, was taken prisoner in October 1779; freed, he had served on the *Glorieux* at the capture of Tobago, and received his first command, that of the *Diligente*, not long after. Lively, not to say impetuous, he was knowledgeable, efficient and above all enthusiastic.

He was seconded by a colleague and friend, Charles Gabriel d'Escures who, like him, had served in India and during the American War, taking part in the capture of Grenada and the siege of Savannah. He was first officer on the *Sibylle* at the Battle of the Saints when her captain, Kergariou, was too badly wounded to carry on, but he was eventually defeated by the *Centurion* and taken prisoner. He too had received the Cross of Saint Louis for his deeds.

La Pérouse's junior officers were also veterans of the recent war. Charles Boutin, the son of a powerful *intendant des finances*, had been present at the capture of Grenada and the siege of Savannah. An officer in the ill-fated *Cérès*, he had been taken prisoner, but on his return had been given minor commands, as well as the Cross of Saint Louis. His friend Ferdinand de Pierrevert had fought in the same battles, served in the *Solitaire*, which had been involved in three major naval battles, and gone home for a well-earned period of rest; he was highly connected, being a nephew of the great admiral, Suffren de Saint Tropez.

So La Pérouse surrounded himself with men he knew and could depend on – compatibility and friendship are essential in situations where everyone is confined in a small ship for months on end. Even among the younger *gardes de la marine* he included two he knew, Henri Mel de Saint-Céran, the son of the *Receveur-Général des Finances* at Montauban, near Albi, and Pierre Armand de Montarnal, who was related to him on his mother's side. Montarnal was drowned on the North-West Coast, causing La Pérouse to write that he had now lost 'the only relative I had in the Navy, to whom I was as tenderly attached as if he had been my own son'.[8]

But another relative, a brother-in-law, also sailed in the *Boussole*, as a *volontaire*. How much of a volunteer he was is not easy to say: young Frédéric Broudou was a hot-tempered and unruly character whose family was keen to see out of the way and under control. Back in March 1782, he had been arrested for threatening his sister Elzire with a loaded pistol; he then disappeared to serve on privateers, but in April 1784 he got into more trouble, causing his mother to make an official request to have him incarcerated in the Mont Saint-Michel island prison near Saint-Malo. Shipboard discipline and the privations endured during the long voyage seem to have straightened him out, and La Pérouse had no complaints to make against him. He eventually received a junior lieutenant's commission.

The other *volontaire* was Roux d'Arbaud, a student at the *École militaire* recommended on the grounds that 'he was a prodigy in the field of astronomy'. His appointment raises the fascinating question of whether Napoleon Bonaparte might have been selected in his place. This possibility was raised in a book published in Paris in 1954, which quoted comments by another student at the school, Alexandre Jean des Mazis:

> Buonaparte was in the mathematics class ... Messrs Dagelet and Monge, two men of distinction, were our teachers ... During 1784, the question arose of the voyage of Mr de la Pérouse. Messrs Dagelet and Monge were granted the favour of joining as astronomers ... Buonaparte would have liked this opportunity of displaying his energy in such a fine enterprise, but D'Arbaud was the only one selected.[9]

It is tempting to speculate on how European history would have turned out had Napoleon joined the navy and been lost at sea while he was still in his teens. However, Mazis is not a very reliable source. He gets the date wrong – no one knew anything about the expedition in 1784 – and he had no idea that behind young Napoleon lurked the formidable persona of Letizia Bonaparte. When he went to the school at Brienne, the young Corsican found that training was being provided, with some overlapping classes, for young men who were planning to be army officers as well as for those who were studying for the naval service. He enjoyed the mathematics courses and the navigational classes, and liked to discuss the problems of cartography. Letizia received a report that classified him as 'highly suitable to become a naval officer'. She was having none of that: his true prospects lay with the army, not the class-ridden old naval service. She firmly told the school authorities that her son was destined for an army career, and that she wanted no further reports on his suitability for the navy. Napoleon may have told Roux d'Arbaud that he envied him the great adventure for which he had been selected, but nothing more.

Fleuriot de Langle's task was to choose officers for his *Astrolabe*, submitting his nominations to La Pérouse, Fleurieu and Castries. To second him, he picked on Anne Georges Augustin de Monti, a veteran of the American campaign who, like a number of others had fought at Grenada and Savannah, and also like other senior officers, a *chevalier* of the Order of Saint Louis. He was an excellent choice, painstaking, tireless, patient and dependable.

Among the *enseignes*, Prosper Philippe d'Aigremont, aged twenty-four, already had a fine career behind him. He had taken part in the various campaigns off the coast of America and the West Indies, including the disastrous Battle of the Saintes when he was taken prisoner and sent to England. When he got back to France, the government gave him 1000 *livres* to make up for the belongings he had lost, and a further 800 as a reward for his bravery. Lieutenant Blondelas is a more shadowy character, but no less brave or involved in naval battles. A report in the naval archives refers to him as an 'excellent officer, with a modesty that makes him most interesting'.[10] This cryptic comment suggests that he may have been a blue officer who kept his distance from his more aristocratic fellow officers.

There were two sons of a prominent, well-to-do court banker and tax collector, Jean-Joseph, Marquis de Laborde, a friend of the powerful Choiseul brothers, a patron of the arts, interested in geography and exploration. He was too successful for his own good and, as part of the loathed circle of tax collectors, would lose his head on the guillotine during the French Revolution – as did the world-famous chemist Antoine Lavoisier. The eldest son, Édouard de Laborde de Marchainville, sailed as an *enseigne*; the younger, Ange Augustin Laborde de Boutervillier, as a *garde de la marine*. Both were already experienced sailors, with a fine record during the recent war.

All these men knew each other, and all were known to La Pérouse and Fleuriot. The best example of this close-knit world is Jean Guillaume Law de Lauriston, the twenty-year-old son of the Governor of Pondicherry whom La Pérouse had met on several occasions in India and whom he had long admired. Lauriston had sailed in the *Solitaire* in 1783 and been taken prisoner in December. Freed, he had served in several ships, where he had met Sutton de Clonard and Laborde de Boutervillier. His parents were delighted by his appointment to the expedition, and they at once set out to provide him with everything they thought he might need. His father sent him a library of books, including the narratives of the voyages of Cook, Byron, Wallis and Carteret. His mother packed a crate with 18 kilograms of chocolate, over 100 tablets of concentrated anti-scorbutic broths, and nine kilograms of lemon concentrate. To this were added spare clothes – seventeen shirts, twelve pairs of cotton socks, one pair of black stockings – a full medical kit to deal with bandages for wounds, salves to cure the bites of venomous snakes, and medicine to fight scurvy, dysentery and stomach upsets, as well as a box of mathematical instruments.[11]

Then came the selection of the scientists. The expedition was not being planned simply as a voyage of exploration into little-known waters; it represented a major undertaking of the Age of Enlightenment, carrying the hopes and aspirations of savants of all types. The specialists who were to sail with La Pérouse had to be carefully selected, and they had to fit in with all the others. As Louis de Bougainville insisted in the advice he gave, there was no room on board for prima donnas or obsessive botanists or zoologists. On his own expedition, the naturalist Philibert Commerson had soon fallen out with the others, and everyone knew of the problems James Cook had faced with Sir Joseph Banks who, unable to get his own way on the second voyage, had walked out on the expedition. Clashes between savants and officers could easily occur. The former wanted the ships to spend more time at anchor, so that they could go ashore and look for new species of animals or plants and other specimens, whereas the officers were often pressed for time, either because of the timetable they needed to keep to, or the dwindling stocks of food.

Selecting the right men from the motley groups of scientists, amateurs and enthusiasts who began to manoeuvre around the expedition's organisers was easier said than done. Louis Monge and Joseph Lepaute Dagelet were obvious choices, but Monge fell seasick from the start and got no further than Tenerife, summoning enough courage for a sea journey back to France and a career on *terra firma*. Dagelet was a gifted watchmaker and proved invaluable in calculating and checking the ships' constantly changing positions. He had already sailed with Kerguelen and avoided the arguments that plagued that voyage. He was, as La Pérouse has stated, 'a charming man', serious, hard-working and apparently strait-laced − life on board was too rough for him: 'In our sailor's world, one sings, swears, smokes, drinks and talks of women, all within the space of half an hour … For my part, as you know, I recognise love only when it is veiled by modesty, and I constantly suffer in those conversations.'[12]

Jean André Mongez (or Monges) shared his views. A typical example of the scientific *philosophe* of his day, he possessed a wide knowledge of ornithology, entomology and chemistry, on all of which he had written learned papers. He was the editor of the *Journal de Physique* and a member of numerous scientific societies, including the prestigious *Société d'histoire naturelle*. But he was also a priest, a canon regular of the Church of Sainte Geneviève, and had friends among several Spanish religious orders. He could therefore double up as chaplain, so La Pérouse was delighted to appoint him to the *Boussole* and satisfy the church authorities that the expedition's spiritual needs were being catered for.

A similar appointment was that of Claude François Joseph Receveur as chaplain to the *Astrolabe*. He came from a modest but well-respected family living on the Swiss border. One of his brothers became mayor of the village, another became a priest, vicar of Clerval, and his grand-uncle had been a Jesuit missionary in China, serving as an adviser to the emperor Kang-Si. Claude became a Franciscan brother, later joining the Grey Friars in Paris under the name of Brother Laurent. But he was a tireless naturalist, carrying out a number of scientific 'missions' and contributing numerous papers and reports for the *Académie des sciences*. La Pérouse and Fleuriot were both delighted by the contributions of this gentle soul, so full of energy and always ready to go off collecting plants and other specimens.

La Pérouse was not so lucky with two scientists of noble birth, Jean Honoré Robert de Paul de Lamanon and Joseph Boissieu de Lamartinière. The former, who specialised in geology, had travelled through much of Europe with his distinguished brother Auguste. He knew most of the *philosophes* and *encyclopédistes* of his day, including the mathematician Marie Jean Antoine Nicolas de Caritat Condorcet, whose *salon* was frequented by the best of French society. Imbued with the spirit of the Enlightenment, he was certainly an enthusiastic supporter of the ideas of Jean-Jacques Rousseau. He wanted to join the expedition and made his first approaches, but he was still only an amateur, and La Pérouse had his doubts about Lamanon working with a team.

Lamanon began to pull strings. He asked Condorcet to talk to Fleurieu, then he got the Duc de la Rochefoucault to back his request. Fleurieu still had reservations, but a duke's recommendation could not be swept aside. He agreed to meet Lamanon, and was forced to admit that the man had talents which would be useful on the voyage. The study of rocks and land formations was an essential part of the expedition's work, and Lamanon also had a sound knowledge of meteorology. The sticking point was money: Lamanon discovered how much men like Dagelet were being paid annually, and insisted on being paid as much or even more. An expedition split by problems of salary relativity could turn into a nightmare. Fleurieu skilfully used Lamanon's own snobbery as a weapon. 'A man of his status should not be paid an annual wage,'[13] he wrote to Castries. An overall cash grant for his expenses would be more in keeping with his rank and his role on the voyage. Lamanon was offered a flat sum of 12,000 *livres* (possibly with a hint of 'take it or leave it'), which he promptly accepted.

Lamartinière turned out to be a different type of nuisance. He was a doctor, a graduate of the famous Montpellier University, with a great reputation as a botanist and a friend and correspondent of most of France's best-known scientists. A gardener had been appointed to the expedition, Nicolas Collignon, a hard-working and talented young man of twenty-four, specially recommended by André Thouin, a professor at the national botanical gardens and Buffon's assistant. Collignon's approach to his task was simple: he was directly responsible to Thouin, and sent him reports and packets of seeds from every port of call. Lamartinière, for his part, considered that this mere gardener should work as his assistant and take orders from him. Collignon complained to Thouin and asked La Pérouse to adjudicate. The captain's solution was simple: he appointed the two men to different ships, so that they would seldom meet and Collignon could keep out of Lamartinière's way.

Paul Monneron, when he went to London, had been asked to find 'an Eskimo interpreter'. Practically nothing was known about the tribes and languages of the North-West Coast, but the French assumed that a former or current employee of the Hudson's Bay Company might be available and be useful as an adviser and guide. Monneron had to act so discreetly that he failed to find anyone. La Pérouse thought a Russian interpreter might be the next best thing, and that careful advertising in Paris might bring forth a former servant of a Russian diplomat or trader. Fleurieu thought it better to ask the Lieutenant-General of Police, Jean Le Noir, but this was equally unsuccessful – and La Pérouse was not too sure that recruiting someone from the police files was a wise move.

At this point, the young son of the French consul general in St Petersburg, Barthélémy de Lesseps, arrived at Versailles with dispatches from his father. Castries was told about him and wasted no time in appointing him. Still only barely nineteen, he had been brought up in St Petersburg, spoke Russian fluently and was delighted by the invitation to join the expedition. There was one minor problem: his father's permission was required and there was no time to send a message to St Petersburg and get a reply back before the expedition sailed. Castries simply appointed Barthélémy vice-consul, to succeed his father in due course. Instead of returning overland to St Petersburg, Barthélémy would take a roundabout route – through the Pacific with La Pérouse, on to Kamchatka and overland by Siberia. It took him three years. La Pérouse got his Russian interpreter, and, better still, a gifted, able, helpful young assistant.

Time was pressing. Preparations were continuing at a feverish pace. As young Lauriston wrote to his parents at the end of May: 'I am on board the ships from five in the morning until seven at night, which does not leave me a second for myself'.[14] The target date for the departure was mid- to late July. In June, Castries gave the scientists a farewell dinner at Versailles, after which they made their own way to Brest. Most of the officers and men were already there.

Lord Dorset, the British Ambassador, picked up some fascinating rumours which he transmitted to the Foreign Secretary: 'I can now inform Your Lordship, from good authority, that 60 criminals from the prison of Bicêtre were last Monday conveyed under a strong guard and with great secrecy to Brest, where they are to be embarked on board Mr de la Pérouse's ships.'[15] Convicts sentenced to hard labour were indeed sent at fairly regular intervals to the main ports, where they were set to work, but 60 of them being taken on board the *Boussole* and the *Astrolabe* during a voyage of exploration was unlikely. Even Lord Dorset felt it necessary to suggest a purpose: La Pérouse planned to sail to New Zealand and the convicts were 'to be left to take possession of that lately discovered country'. London wisely ignored Dorset's report.

There remained the important matter of the instructions. Fleurieu and his advisers had been at work on them for weeks, incorporating as many suggestions as possible from the scientific societies, but above all following Louis XVI's recommendations. Copyists were constantly at work, carefully rewriting drafts to be discussed and amended. Finally, the work was done and submitted to the king for his approval. It is an impressive document, over 300 pages long, with appendices and notes of every kind. Even then, the King made a number of marginal comments that confirmed his close personal interest in the expedition.

On 28 June, La Pérouse had his final audience with Louis. This official meeting is the subject of a famous painting by Nicolas Monsiau which perfectly interprets the relationships between the various participants. A large world map, backed by a globe, is spread out on a table, and the king, with Castries behind him, is pointing to some geographical feature; La Pérouse, deferentially leaning forward, takes note of what the king is saying, while a lesser figure, in all probability Fleurieu, watches from further back in the shadows. The painter has flattered La Pérouse somewhat, who was considerably more portly than the man depicted by Monsiau.

Two days later, Castries took La Pérouse to meet Queen Marie-Antoinette at her Trianon Palace. After this final formal interview, La Pérouse set off for Brest, where he arrived on 4 July to check on the final preparations and attend the official welcome on board the ships, with the officers, scientists and men lined up on deck. The great expedition he had dreamt about was at last coming true.

17. South and North to Alaska

August 1785–June 1786

THE FINAL ORDERS were given. The last men rushed up the gangways, which were then pulled back, and there was a frenzy of activity on board the two ships as the mooring ropes were released. Four longboats started to tug at the towlines, and the vessels, slowly but finally, began to move away from the quayside. A great cheer went up from the crowds that had gathered to see them leave – friends, officials and porters, with, further back, layabouts and ships' women waving and yelling. The *Astrolabe* and the *Boussole* creaked slightly as they moved towards the middle of the harbour, away from the other naval units, traders and ferries still moored to the wharves. They let out just a little canvas to catch enough breeze to make their way majestically towards the open roadstead. More cheering was heard from the shore, and some of the ships gave a one-gun salute to speed them on their way. The sun shone, the intensely blue waters shimmered, the white ensigns with their fleurs-de-lys fluttered softly.

That at least is how Hollywood might picture the scene as the *Astrolabe* and the *Boussole* raised anchor on 12 July 1785, ready to start on the voyage to the Pacific. But the reality was infuriatingly different. In the days of sail, men proposed and the winds disposed. And the winds were either stubbornly blowing towards the land or failed altogether. It was close to midsummer, warm and tranquil, great for relaxing but vastly irritating for all on board. The ships were towed out a little distance and tied up to buoys. The longboats rowed back to shore, and everyone waited and waited.

Inaction created problems. Usually working in three eight-hour shifts, the crew could sleep down below while the others worked or idled above. Now that there was so little for them to do, finding somewhere to rest or pass the time became a problem. The Comte d'Hector sent out a spare storeship to anchor between the two frigates and serve as a dormitory, thus reducing the overcrowding while they waited for the wind to change. It also helped to keep an eye on the men who might be tempted to desert or to smuggle themselves ashore for yet another wild night on the town.

The scientists found the conditions on the waiting ships almost unbelievable. The decks looked like farmyards: there were five cows tied around the mainmast, 30 sheep in one longboat, 20 pigs along the companionways, 200 hens clucking away in cages along the poop deck. Fish hung down from the shrouds, slowly drying in nets. Down below, every nook and cranny was crammed with food supplies – sacks of flour, potatoes, beans, fruit, salads, cabbages. Hay was stashed everywhere and anywhere, as long as it was easily accessible to feed out to the cattle and sheep, which meant that it was in everyone's way. Further down, there were spare ropes, pieces of canvas, lengths of timber, caulking material and water casks.

The cabins were small and cramped, but space had to be found for the *savants* and their equipment. The main council room in each ship, often a place for socialising and meetings, had been partitioned into small cabins; one or two areas separated by lengths of rough sailcloth were designated as studies. On the *Astrolabe*, the space allocated for D'Aigremont, Lamartinière, Prévost and Dufresne was pompously christened *Chambre des Savants*. At the start, the ships, though noisy, smelt fresh. This would not last very long, and it would take time for some of the landlubber scientists to come to terms with the odours that filled the areas below deck.

They had to spend nearly three weeks at anchor, hoping for a favourable breeze. It finally came on 1 August 1785, which became the official day of departure. To shouts of 'Long Live the King' and to friendly waving from a few of the nearby ships, the *Boussole* and the *Astrolabe* made their way slowly but gratefully along the Goulet and out into the Atlantic.

The weather now smiled on them. A smooth blue sea, with moderate but steady breezes, enabled the frigates to lay out all their canvas and present an impressive spectacle to any passing ship. Even the Bay of Biscay, renowned for its temper, let them through without trouble. Certainly, there was movement: ships, especially sailing ships, constantly creak and sway with the steady swell of the sea, as poor Monge soon discovered, but there were no blustering gales, no angry rain squalls, nothing that could spoil a straightforward and easy summertime voyage off the coast of western Europe.

The first call was at Madeira, where the French were warmly welcomed. La Pérouse had hardly lowered his anchor when a boat came up laden with fruit sent by an English trader. The governor and other local notables invited all the officers and scientists to dinner. The British consul, Charles Murray, and his wife organised an al fresco lunch at their country estate – 'she played the harpsichord and made us welcome in her home in a most dignified manner'. Everyone knew about their expedition because the English residents had received letters from people in England 'recommending us …, letters which surprised me greatly as I was unacquainted with the people who had written them'.[1] Less satisfactory was the price of local wines, which La Pérouse had planned to buy there. The export trade with Britain had caused prices to rise to levels he considered unreasonable, but his hosts made up for his disappointment with generous gifts: 'a prodigious quantity of fruits of all description, a hundred bottles of Malmsey wine, half a barrel of rum and some candied lemons'.

They went on to Tenerife in the Canaries, a mere three days' sailing away. Again the locals welcomed them, and since their stay included France's national day, the Feast of Saint Louis, the whole town decided to celebrate it with gun salutes and a minor fiesta. The crews were issued with double rations of food and wine, and the festivities went on for most of the night. Wine was available and reasonably priced – La Pérouse bought on an estimated 24,000 litres – but delivery was slow, forcing the ships to stay for ten days.

The scientists had seized the opportunity to go ashore at both Madeira and Tenerife. Indeed, Lamartinière wrote to Thouin that, when he landed on Madeira, he felt a mad desire to run up the mountains. He still had not come to terms with life on a small, crowded ship, and he missed his usual exercise of walking around Paris to see friends or to inspect the latest additions to the *Jardin du Roi*.

But in Tenerife it was Lamanon who caused the first clash by deciding to climb the famous Peak. Mariners had used it for years as a landmark, and astronomers and cartographers had always based their calculations on its longitude and latitude. Looking up at it, Lamanon decided that he could not go home and tell his colleagues that he had not bothered to climb it. He planned an expedition that would enable him to complete, on the summit, all the observations and calculations he had in mind. He hired mules and porters to carry his equipment and supplies, but La Pérouse had to tell him that no financial provision had been made for this, hinting also that there was not a great deal new to discover about such a well-known geographical feature.

Grumbling about unco-operative sailors, Lamanon cut back on the cost, which he finally decided to pay out of his own pocket. It was undoubtedly an acrimonious exchange, and La Pérouse vented his own spleen in a private letter he wrote to Fleurieu:

Lamanon is full of zeal, but as ignorant as a monk on anything other than systematic physics. He thinks he knows better than Mr de Buffon how the world was formed: I am quite sure that neither of them has any clear idea about it, but there isn't a fifteen-year-old girl in Paris who doesn't know more about the globe than this doctor, who has been aiming his spyglass at the Tropic ever since the apprentice pilots told him that it could be seen from a hundred leagues off … He is a hothead and displays a meanness of character that hardly fits the disinterested man the Baron de Choiseul had described.[2]

The Peak was an arid place, with practically no vegetation on its upper reaches. Monneron, who also went up, was forced to give up when the muleteers rebelled. Their animals had not had anything to drink for nearly three days, and neither pleas nor offers of money could persuade their drivers to stay any longer. Lamanon was also forced to come down, irritated by the locals' attitude and complaining that they were worse than the sailors.

His chances for any further observations were doomed: the ships were about to sail, and this time right across the Atlantic. They left at the end of August and saw no more land until mid-October. Crossing the equator on 29 September was uneventful, with only the giggling apprentice pilots enjoying the event as they slyly watched to see whether Lamanon would direct his spyglass at the waves in the hope of seeing the line itself.

Three weeks later, they reached the lonely island of Trinidad. The scientists were keen to go ashore and start exploring this little-known place, but the local governor panicked when he saw two ships in full sail making for his poorly defended settlement. It had already been attacked twice in less than a decade, and the fact that they hoisted French colours did not reassure him – raising false colours being such a common trick in wartime. He calmed down a little when he realised that the ships were really French and not on a warlike mission. Even so, he would not allow Lamartinière, Receveur or any others to venture inland. They were forced to pick up a few stones along the shore, anxiously watched by a few Portuguese guards.

The governor assured them that he could provide neither food nor water, and that there was no point in lingering there. He was clearly worried about the French discovering the poor condition of the fort and settlement, telling either the Spanish or the British, and setting in motion yet another raid. La Pérouse did not insist but made instead for the island of Santa Catarina, closer to the coast of Brazil.

All he wanted was to take a few fresh supplies on board, especially fresh water, rest his men a little and give the naturalists a chance to examine the area and collect a few specimens. He did not want to call at a major port, as this would entail official visits and functions, and merely waste time. His men, fortunately, were in good health: 'I had neglected none of the precautions that experience and caution advised, and in addition we had taken the utmost care to ensure that their spirits remained high by making the crew dance every evening, weather permitting, between eight and ten'. Hornpipes and plentiful food, not forgetting Spanish wine, had paid handsome dividends. However, supplies at Santa Catarina were cheap and plentiful, the governor was friendly and La Pérouse bought oxen, pigs, poultry, 500 oranges and vegetables, all 'at a very modest price'.

A boatload of sailors collecting firewood in a cove capsized, and 'the locals who helped to save it insisted on our sailors having their own beds, themselves laying down on mats in the middle of the room'. It was just one more example of the friendliness of the locals, and it would have pleased everyone, men and scientists alike, if La Pérouse had tarried there for a while, but time was pressing, and on the 16th, after a little more than a week, he raised anchor.

He had intended to look for a few islands in the Southern Atlantic, but he decided to restrict his searches to the Isle Grande, reported in 1675 by Antoine de la Roche, a merchant on his way back from Chile. No one had seen it since then, but it was included in a number of the works by historians such as Charles de Brosses and James Burney. It was probably some outlying island belonging to the South Georgia group, which La Roche had discovered, and the search proved both futile and time-consuming:

> I gained nothing from my plan and after 40 days of fruitless searching, during which I encountered 5 squalls, I was forced to set sail for my next destination ... I am quite certain that the Isle Grande is like [Ambrose Cowley's] Pepys Island, an imaginary land that has never existed ... As I had by then passed the position assigned to the island of La Roche on all the charts and the season was very advanced I decided to follow only the route that would get me W, as I was anxious not to round Cape Horn in the bad season.

Going round Cape Horn avoided the wearisome navigation through the Strait of Magellan that had cost Bougainville so much time at the beginning of his circumnavigation. 'We were about to sail through fog in seas reputed to be stormy.' La Pérouse and De Langle needed to be careful, since there was always the danger that they might lose sight of each other in a bad storm. With no means of communication other than visual signals, they could easily become separated and waste precious days sailing around trying to meet up again. To avoid this, they arranged a series of rendezvous, where they could sail independently and without delay. La Pérouse told De Langle that, if they became separated, he should make for Le Maire's Strait, through which he intended to sail, and that if he still did not find the *Boussole* or the separation occurred after they had gone through the strait, he should sail for Tahiti and wait there.

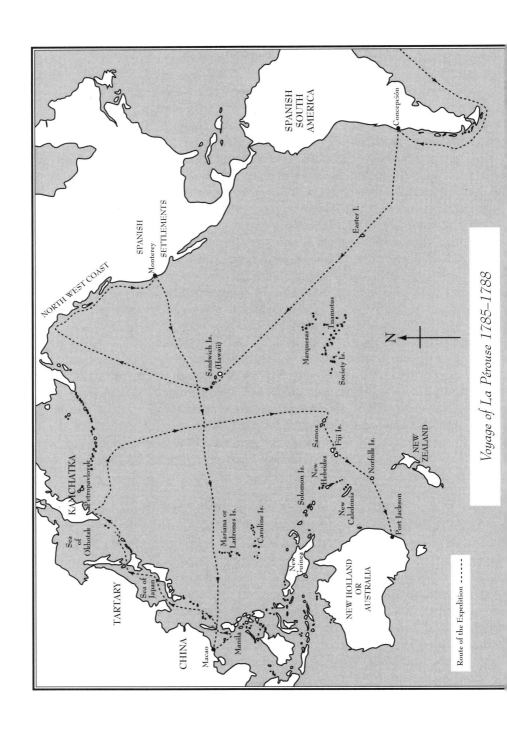

Voyage of La Pérouse 1785–1788

SPANISH SOUTH AMERICA

Concepción

SPANISH SETTLEMENTS

Monterey

NORTH WEST COAST

Easter I.

N

Sandwich Is. (Hawaii)

Marquesas Is.

Tuamotus

Society Is.

KAMCHATKA

Petropavlovsk

Sea of Okhotsk

Samoa

Fiji Is.

New Hebrides

Norfolk Is.

NEW ZEALAND

Solomon Is.

New Caledonia

Port Jackson

Mariana or Ladrones Is.

Caroline Is.

New Guinea

NEW HOLLAND OR AUSTRALIA

TARTARY

Sea of Japan

CHINA

Macao

Manila

Route of the Expedition - - - - -

This shows that, at this point, La Pérouse still intended to follow his original instructions which would have seen him sailing across the Pacific, roughly following the track of Bougainville's expedition, and making for the New Hebrides and Australia. But there was no separation. There was some fog and a land haze, but Cape Horn did not live up to its evil reputation. This being the southern hemisphere, it was midsummer, with only partly cloudy skies and a reasonably heavy swell. 'I rounded Cape Horn with far more ease than I would ever have dreamt.' By early February, the ships were sailing into the Pacific, which, for once, fully justified the name of peaceful ocean bestowed on it by Magellan.

The French sailed over an area where some charts still showed 'The Land of Drake'. La Pérouse, in common with most navigators, did not believe it existed and he had no trouble in confirming his opinion: there was no sign of land. 'Ever since my departure, I have thought of little else than the routes of the old navigators … geographers who are not sailors are generally so ignorant that … they drew islands that did not exist and which, like phantoms, have vanished before the new navigators.'

By now, he had decided to make use of the freedom given to him by his instructions. There was no real point, he felt, in simply retracing Louis de Bougainville's old route. It was better to sail right away for the North-West Coast. By the time he got there, it would be late spring or early summer. So he sailed rapidly north along the coast of Chile, and on 24 February dropped anchor in the Bay of Concepción. His men could now have a proper rest before the hard period of exploration in cold latitudes, and the scientists could botanise and collect specimens to their hearts' content.

The city had been destroyed in an earthquake in 1754 and rebuilt on a different site, 13 kilometres away. So little was known about the area, largely because of the Spanish policy of exclusiveness that kept away all foreign trading ships, that La Pérouse's maps were outdated and practically useless. Fortunately, Madrid had advised all its colonial governors about the French expedition and instructed them to provide whatever help it might need. Fruit, vegetables and fresh meat were brought out in small boats, and Spanish officers offered any other assistance the French might require.

The *Boussole* and the *Astrolabe* stayed three weeks. This sojourn gave everyone a chance to rest and enjoy themselves ashore, while for the townspeople it offered welcome relief from the crushing boredom of life in a small isolated port. Concepción was a provincial backwater, but it was transformed by the excitement of the French visit. There were receptions, dinners and balls, and every day seemed an occasion for a joyful fiesta. Not surprisingly, two men deserted. La Pérouse did not bother to get them back: he did not want any reluctant sailors with him. If the country appealed to them so much, let them stay. He noted wryly that in the fishing village of Talcahuano, near which the frigates were anchored, 'every house is a tavern, and the women are as obliging as those of Tahiti'.

The military commander had been away when the French arrived, leading one of his endless campaigns against the restive Araucanian Indians, but he hastened back to welcome La Pérouse and join in the revelries. He was Ambrosio O'Higgins, who would soon be appointed Governor of all Chile. His son Bernardo later entered history as *El Libertador*. The official reception involved all the notables and every local inhabitant of any standing. It was an impressive affair, which the French authorities could report back to Madrid to the credit of the locals:

> Mr Higgins came to meet us a league from town and led our cavalcade to his residence where a table was laid for a hundred guests ... The healths of the kings of France and Spain were toasted to the accompaniment of gun salutes. Each course was marked by a Franciscan improviser reciting verses celebrating the unity that reigned between the two branches of the House of Bourbon and their respective subjects. There followed a great ball during the night where all the ladies came dressed in their finest attire. Masked officers danced a very fine ballet.

Just before the expedition left, La Pérouse organised an open air reception for all the people of Concepción. 'A vast tent was erected along the sea shore: there we entertained a hundred and fifty people, men and women, who had been good enough to undertake the three-league journey to respond to our invitation. This dinner was followed by a ball, a fireworks display, and finally a paper balloon large enough to provide a spectacle.'

This was probably the first appearance of the aerial balloon in Chile.

Chile proved to be a great place for taking on supplies. Grains, fruits, fresh meat were brought on board by grateful traders and farmers. There was a surplus of all such goods, which they were delighted to sell at knock-down prices. This meant that there was no point in sailing to other settlements, such as Valparaiso or Monterey, and the voyage of exploration could begin in earnest. On 17 March 1786, the *Boussole* and the *Astrolabe* sailed out of the bay on their way to the North-West Coast. There were two places on the way that La Pérouse and the scientists wanted to see: Easter Island and the Hawaiian Islands. He sailed directly for the former.

This would be their first Polynesian island, a place of mystery and ancient tragedy. They all wanted to see the great statues, most of which looked out enigmatically at the ocean around them, and the scientists hoped for a few finds, although the place was now treeless. La Pérouse's instructions stated that, on every occasion, he should 'behave with the utmost gentleness and humanity towards the various people he will visit during his voyage. He will display zeal and consideration in everything that can improve their standard of life, by supplying their country with vegetables, fruit and other useful trees, teaching them how they should be sown and cultivated ...' He stayed less than a day at Easter Island, but he went ashore with goats, pigs, sheep, and seeds of orange and lemon trees, maize and other cereals. Collignon travelled inland to look for a fertile sheltered spot, and sowed cabbages, carrots, pumpkins, beet, showing the islanders crowded around him how to plant the trees. They laughed, cheered – and stole whatever they could lay their hands on.

These gifts, offered in the king's name, were meant to raise the islanders' standard of living – civilised Europe's aid to primitive societies. But this was the Age of Enlightenment, when the *philosophes* were arguing about the benefits of European civilisation and what man might have lost once he had left his earlier, simpler way of life. Rousseau had argued that the ownership of property was a major corrupting factor, and that the 'noble savage' would not gain from contact with Europeans. What they could bring to distant and so-called primitive societies was not new social structures and commercialism, but simply new crops that could raise their standard of living. La Pérouse was no Rousseauist. He was a down-to-earth, practical man, a sailor with no time for theories evolved by philosophers, academics and drawing-room geographers. He never stopped being sarcastic towards those who pontificated without any first-hand knowledge. Man was man, warts and all, wherever he lived. Kindness need not be blind: La Pérouse had already taken a dim view of the goodness of primitive people when, towards the end of the American War, after destroying some British forts in Hudson Bay, he left food and weapons for the defeated enemy lest they fall defenceless into the hands of the Indians.[3]

The Easter Islanders were such shameless thieves that he could not help laughing at their impudence. He took no punitive action. Indeed, seeing them stealing hats from the sailors, most of them rough, quick-tempered men, he told them that he would replace their losses, and that they should on no account get angry and start fights to get their property back. An engraving published in the 1797 account of the voyage shows the French socialising with the locals around a couple of statues. The scene is highly romanticised, but it shows an officer, possibly La Pérouse himself, with a hand on a statue, talking to someone, probably a scientist, taking notes, while an islander, half-hidden behind the statue, is busy stealing his three-cornered hat.

His attitude was based on realism, not any philosophical theories or even on any religious ideas of tolerance and forgiveness. Though educated by Jesuits, La Pérouse verged on the agnostic, but inclining a little more towards the idea of original sin than of innate natural goodness. He saw no reason to assume that native people in distant islands were any different from his own men, rogues and drunkards many of them, kept under control by a stern but paternal discipline, simple, hardworking, credulous Bretons, praying to saints no one else knew much about, or rascals who had fled their homes in search of adventure, quick to wench and brawl.

So he took his precautions, kept an eye on his men, laughed at the Easter Islanders' antics, dispensed gifts and forgiveness in equal doses, but harboured no illusions and took no reprisals, not even shaking his fist at the cheekiest of the thieves. As he sailed away in the darkness, however, he made a comment that reveals a gentle touch of naivety: 'I flattered myself that when, at dawn, they saw that our ships had gone, they would attribute our prompt departure to our just displeasure over their activities, and that this thought might make them better men'.

The ships were now making for the Hawaiian Islands, then known as the Sandwich Islands, from the name James Cook had given them. La Pérouse felt a little uncertain about the kind of reception he might get, since this was where the famous English navigator had been killed only seven years earlier. The murder was puzzling, because only a few days earlier the Hawaiians had fêted the great navigator. Something, no one in Europe was too sure what, had caused this fatal turnaround, and anyone approaching the islands should be very much on their guard.

So when, on 30 May 1786, La Pérouse landed on the island of Maui, he was protected by forty watchful soldiers. He need not have worried: the islanders welcomed him with every sign of enthusiasm and friendliness. They brought him pigs and coconuts, and he in turn gave them axes, lengths of iron and other gifts, including some of the commemorative medals that had been specially struck to mark the expedition. There was no theft: this was barter. The reception was so friendly, open and honest compared with what he had found at Easter Island that he began to wonder what Cook had done to get himself killed. This was a charming, beautiful country, with coconut palms fringing golden beaches and crowds of islanders coming up to him with gifts and gestures of welcome. 'I had not expected such a gentle and considerate people.'

De Langle had rashly allowed them to clamber on board the *Astrolabe* and he soon found himself swamped by 100 or so excited islanders. He gestured helplessly to La Pérouse, but the Hawaiians quickly understood his dilemma and they returned to their canoes. La Pérouse had been more cautious but he soon allowed a number on board – 'they did not make a single move without our permission'. He admitted that he had been prejudiced against them because of Cook's murder, but he now queried the general verdict of a noble man suddenly attacked by a bunch of wild natives: 'It is more natural for navigators to regret the loss of so great a man than to assess coolly whether some imprudent action on his part did not, in some way, compel the inhabitants of *Owhyhee* to have recourse to justified self-defence'.

He went ashore, visited a village and with a small guard of six soldiers ventured further inland. Several of the scientists came with him, but he warned them to be careful to avoid anything that might arouse suspicion or upset the locals. Even gathering botanical specimens might be seen as a threat or a breach of some protocol. When he returned to his ship, he found that Clonard had entertained a chief, bought a cloak and an ornamental helmet from him, as well as pigs, bananas, sweet potatoes and a host of other items.

Maui had not, so far as La Pérouse could tell, been visited by any European before him. This meant, technically, that he could have laid claim to the island in the name of Louis XVI, but he considered such a practice 'too ridiculous' and immoral. What right had Europeans, he asked, to claim as their own lands that the local people had worked with the sweat of their brow and where their ancestors lay buried? The *philosophe* in him went a step further and added: 'It is fortunate for these people that they have been discovered in an age when religion is no longer a pretext for violence and greed'.

The stay on Maui was meant only as a brief stop to take on as much fresh food as might be available before starting the exploration of the cold latitudes. After forty-eight hours, sailing along the west coast of the island, La Pérouse passed through Kaui Channel, north of Oahu, and set a course almost due north towards the more austere Alaskan coast. Day by day, the weather got colder. Fog hid much of the horizon, surrounding the ships for at least part of each morning, damp and clinging. The sailors' clothes were cold and wet, 'with never a ray of sunshine to dry them', but at least they were winter garments. 'When we sailed to Hudson Bay, we could not take on appropriate clothing,' La Pérouse told Clonard. 'The men sailed in light summer clothes and they suffered greatly as we neared these frigid latitudes.'

By and large, the crew were cheerful, well fed and with few worries. The surgeon suggested that adding quinine to their morning grog would be good for their health, but it had to be done in secret, otherwise they would have refused to drink it. James Cook had faced much the same problem with his anti-scorbutic remedies. Then early on the morning of 23 June, the fog began to clear, revealing a long line of snow-covered mountains. 'We identified Bhering's Mount St Elias, its peak visible above the clouds.' This was the point the Russian Vitus Bering had reached in the *St Peter* back in 1741. The French should have rejoiced at making this landfall, but the place was far from attractive. 'The sight of land, which ordinarily makes such a pleasing impression after a long navigation, did not have that effect on us. The eye rested painfully upon all this snow covering a sterile and treeless land … a rocky plateau a hundred and fifty or two hundred *toises* in height, black as though burned by fire, lacking trees and greenery of any kind.'

Still, this marked the beginning of the North-West Coast. The exploration could now begin in earnest.

18. ALASKA TO CALIFORNIA

July–September 1786

THE MYSTERIOUS NORTH-WEST Coast, where William Bolts had wanted France to go trading for furs, was now a place all the great powers were vying to control. Russia could lay a reasonable claim to it, following the brief visit of Bering, but the navigator had died on the way home, having done very little charting, and all his exhausted and sick crew could report was that it had a dense population of fur-bearing animals – sea otters, Alaskan seals, blue and white Arctic foxes. It was enough for a number of Russian captains to try their luck along the Alaskan coast, but they were more interested in trading than in exploring.

Their incursions began to worry the Spanish, who claimed the entire Pacific coast of America. They controlled it from Cape Horn to California, but they recognised no northern limit to their possessions. To confirm this, they started sending ships beyond the ill-determined boundaries of northern California. In 1774, Juan Perez sailed to Queen Charlotte Islands; a year later Juan Francisco Bodega reached the site of modern Sitka in southern Alaska. But then in 1778 James Cook came on the scene, staking a British claim as he proceeded to chart the coast with his usual precision. He bestowed English names on numerous natural features, much to the irritation of the Spanish and the Russians. And now a French expedition was coming in to complicate the situation. Spain had accepted that it was first and foremost a scientific voyage, but the Russian Empress, Catherine the Great, came to view it as a direct threat to Russian interests in the North Pacific.[1] Just a year earlier, in 1785, the Russians had begun to settle in the Aleutian Islands, a clear indication of Russian plans for the control of the Bering Sea and further advances into Alaska.

La Pérouse, clearly, was more interested in hydrography. Even after Cook's careful survey, a number of gaps and question marks remained on the charts. There were innumerable inlets and bays still unexplored along this deeply indented coast – and there was always the possibility that one might lead into the interior, linking up with lakes and waterways, and forming the famous

North-West Passage that would lead from the Pacific to the Atlantic. La Pérouse was no great believer in its existence, but he could not discount it.

The problem was the everlasting curtain of fog. It opened up from time to time, offering a tantalising glimpse of the coast, then closed again. To be safe, the ships had to sail out to sea for a few hours, then cautiously turn back to land. On 26 June, the French sighted a bay that looked promising. La Pérouse sent three boats to explore it, but it led nowhere. As the Chevalier de Monti had led this reconnaissance, La Pérouse called it *Baie de Monti*. The first French name had now joined the Russian, Spanish and British ones; it was probably what is now known as Yakutat Bay.

Cook's map was unclear about this stretch of coast. His problem had been the fog and foul winds. La Pérouse slowed down, to avoid missing any features not seen by his predecessor. 'Calm but foggy … the winds constantly changing … the coast very hazy.'[2] It was slow, irritating work, but gradually he was filling the gaps in the charts.

On 1 July, the French were just west of Mount Fairweather. Time and again, they lowered their boats to send them on small but valuable surveys. Dagelet worked feverishly to check every reading. The next day, an opening appeared, a bay that was shown on none of their maps. There was still haze about, but it was possible to discern a wide opening, with still waters behind it. It was certainly a new discovery: 'If the French government had any plans for a trading post in this part of the American coast, no nation could claim any right to oppose it'. La Pérouse confirmed this by naming it *Port des Français*. Its present name is Lituya Bay.

He sailed in, to find what turned out to be an excellent anchorage, a true harbour. The problem was the entrance, which had rocks not far below the surface and could be dangerous if the winds shifted suddenly. 'Never in the thirty years I have spent at sea have I seen two ships so close to destruction.' But that danger over, the French settled in for a stay of almost a month. A camp was set up on a small island; the scientists put up their instruments on it, so that it became known as Observatory Island. The men went off collecting firewood and fresh water.

La Pérouse rapidly organised the exploration of the tortuous inlet. It was more or less T-shaped, with two basins opening roughly north and south. There was plenty of fresh water running from these into the bay: this could mean the estuary of a river further up and possibly some way inland. But the water came, not from rivers, but from the melting of great glaciers, five or them, grinding their way slowly from steep bare mountains, the silence broken only by the cries of lonely wild birds and the occasional fall of enormous blocks of ice: 'It was at the back of this bay that we had hoped to find channels by which we could enter into the interior of America. We assumed that it might lead to some great river running between two mountains, and that this river might well have its source in one of the great lakes of northern Canada.'

Alas, there was no way through, so that 'we completed our trip into the interior of America in a few hours'. And if this was midsummer, how dismal a spot would Port des Français be when winter came? Could anyone really contemplate building a settlement in such a spot, even with the rewards that could be gained from the fur trade? There were natives about, who came forward to barter fish and furs for clothing, nails and implements, but mainly to steal – they would hardly be of any help to European settlers. Lauriston and D'Arbaud, on duty at the observatory, were robbed of a musket, their spare clothes and a notebook in which the astronomical observations had been recorded. 'I am willing to admit,' commented La Pérouse, 'that it is impossible for a society to exist without some virtues, but I am forced to admit that I did not have the skill to notice any here.' He was even less chivalrous towards the women, whom he dismissed as 'repulsive'.

In spite of his personal views about Europeans landing in distant lands and claiming them for themselves, he agreed to a suggestion from a man whom he took to be the local leader to buy Observatory Island. Without the 'Eskimo interpreter' the French had hoped to bring with them, it was not easy to communicate with him. In fact, even if an Inuit speaker had been found, it would not have been easy to make themselves understood: the locals were the Tlingit.

In all likelihood, the invitation to 'buy' the island was no more than a suggestion that the French would be welcome to use it any time they came back to trade. The Tlingit had originally taken the strangers to be visiting servants sent by Yehlh, their bird creator. It was only after an elderly warrior had ventured on board that they realised that the newcomers were nothing more than men sailing some gigantic form of canoes, and not spirits at all. From that moment, the French became fair game for thieves – strangers towards whom no hospitality was due – as well as potential source of profitable trade. And so, with the exchange of a few gifts, *L'île de l'Observatoire* became a legal French outpost.[3]

It was soon time to get back to exploring the coast, and La Pérouse began to ready the ships for departure. Monneron and Bernizet hurried to complete their charting of *Port des Français*, and the scientists started to bring their instruments back on board. Then disaster struck – 'a disaster more cruel than sickness and the thousand other events of the longest voyages'. D'Escures was sent out to take soundings in the bay, so that Monneron could show the various depths on his chart. La Pérouse warned him not to venture too close to the rocks near the pass, which had proved so dangerous when the ships had first entered. But apart from that, they could go anywhere, take soundings at leisure and, if they wanted to, go ashore to hunt or picnic. 'It was as much an outing as it would be useful.'

But D'Escures misread the signs. There was always a steady outpouring of water towards the sea, but the high tide had now turned and a wild tidal race had developed. First his boat, then the *Astrolabe*'s pinnace, were carried away helplessly. As they reached the fatal bar and the open sea they both capsized. It was all over in ten minutes. Six officers and fifteen men were drowned, including D'Escures, Pierrevert, La Pérouse's young cousin Montarnal, Flassan and the two Laborde brothers. Boats rushed to the rescue, landing search parties along the shore to look for survivors and bodies, but they found no bodies washed ashore, heard no cries for help; there was only the implacable sea breaking on the black rocks.

This appalling tragedy affected La Pérouse for a long time. When he was forced to the conclusion that no one had survived, he sat down for the painful task of writing to all the men's relatives, telling them the sad news. There was also an official report to prepare for Castries, a less formal one for Fleurieu, but an especially sad letter for his family in Albi and for Éléonore to tell them about the death of young Montarnal. He erected a small cairn on the island, which he renamed Cenotaph Island, burying a bottle underneath it setting out the tragic event and listing the dead. Lamanon added his own inscription: 'At the entrance to this port, twenty-one brave sailors perished. Whoever you are, mix your tears with ours.'

The blame lay with D'Escures. To defend his own position, La Pérouse felt the need to copy out the precise instructions he had given him, including the clear warning about not venturing too near the pass. D'Escures had rather dismissed his warnings as unnecessary – 'Do you take me for a child?' And indeed this was a man of thirty-three; he had joined the navy as a volunteer and had first met La Pérouse when he served on the *Belle-Poule* in 1751. His devotion and talents had been recognised the previous year by the award of the Cross of Saint Louis.

The death of the two Laborde brothers was particularly upsetting. They were promising, enthusiastic young men with a sound future ahead of them. On 3 May 1787, Lord Dorset reported the tragedy to his superiors in London: 'The two sons of Mons. de la Borde (formerly the Court Banker) were unfortunately drowned on this occasion, to the great grief of their family who are inconsolable at the loss of two very promising young men'.[4]

The disaster delayed the departure for several days. Apart from the writing of reports and letters while the events were still fresh, there were changes to be made to the duty rosters. The belongings of the dead men had to be moved, some to be stored, others to be auctioned among the crew. The officers' cabins were rearranged to provide a little more space and comfort for the others. And there were promotions: this was when Frédéric Broudou became a *lieutenant de frégate*.

The two ships sailed out on 30 July, their colours at half-mast. Everyone fell silent as they went though the pass and down the coast, still watching the shore in the forlorn hope that there might be some remains or debris on the shore. There was nothing that might cheer their spirits or help to focus their sense of mourning.

They continued on their way south, to carry out as much of the coastal survey as they could. La Pérouse had now realised what an impossible task he had been set. The countless bays and narrow inlets would need months of exploration if the riddle of the North-West Passage was ever to be solved or the coastal charts completed to the geographers' satisfaction. But he had been allocated less than three months for his survey of the Alaskan and northern Canadian coasts. His timetable now required him to press on, so that he could devote the next summer to exploring the north-western Pacific: 'All my plans had to be subordinated to the absolute necessity to reach Manila by the end of January, and China in February, so as to be in a position to spend the next summer surveying the coasts of Tartary, Japan, Kamchatka and the Aleutian Islands'.[5]

The Lituya Bay tragedy had cost him precious time, so a period of extraordinary activity followed. Everyone was mobilised, charting, surveying and checking, though a number of minor bays and inlets could not be examined in detail – it was too time-consuming and they had to cope with the ever-present morning fogs. La Pérouse dropped any further plans to search for the North-West Passage. It was simply a theory evolved by those who believed that somehow the world had to be symmetrical, and that if there was a southern strait linking the Atlantic and the Pacific Oceans, then there had to be a northern one as well.

On 4 August 1786, the fog dissipated to reveal what was obviously Cross Sound, marking the beginning of the Alexander Archipelago. There were now more coves, bays and passages than ever before. The sea was fairly quiet, with a steady gentle swell, but the winds were contrary. It took the French almost a day to cover a mere 16 kilometres. The area offered tantalising possibilities – 'Here, I am convinced, we could find twenty different harbours' – but progress was too slow. Then a new inlet opened up before them. This was Sitka Sound, followed by Baranof Islands, which had so many headlands and hills 'that it is enough to change our position just a little for an island to change its appearance'. Christian

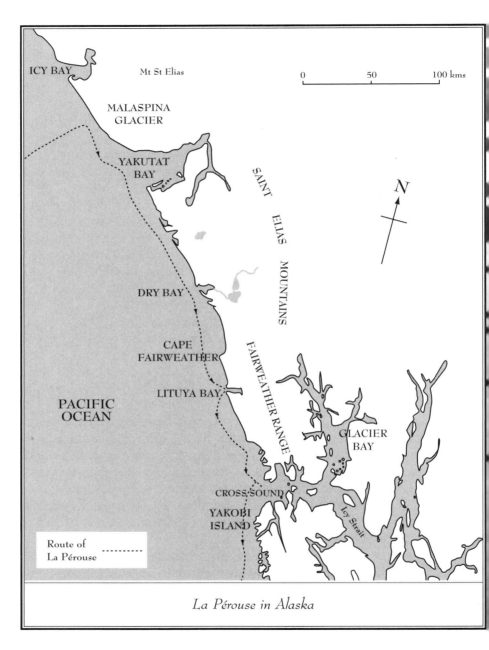

La Pérouse in Alaska

Sound, 'a great opening', marked the southern part of the archipelago with the clusters of islands that lie offshore from Prince of Wales Island like so many faithful retainers protecting their master. The breeze became more helpful, though the strong currents constantly flowing from various passes and inlets drove the ships time and again towards the open sea. This was a region known to the Spanish, but their charts were of little help. Somewhere around here the navigator Francisco Maurelle had carried out surveys, but 'I have found nothing in his map or in his account that could enlighten me'.

As the ships continued their survey, a number of features received French names. The Count d'Hector, who had been so helpful back in Brest, had his name bestowed on the northern tip of Queen Charlotte Islands. Fleurieu's was given to the northern point of Vancouver Island. Earlier, a mountain had been named 'after my friend, the Comte de Crillon'. (This was Félix, François Dorothée de Berton, Comte de Crillon.) La Pérouse decided not to enter Queen Charlotte Sound and Juan de Fuca Strait. He would have been able to clear up many vague notions about these inlets and make his mark on the local hydrography, but the decision saved him from the danger of getting bottled up in the narrowing straits behind Vancouver Island and wasting even more time. The problem was still the fog, swirling around, hiding features that might have guided the French along the coast and into new areas. And August was now coming to an end. The weather was still pleasant, but the first signs of the coming autumn were becoming increasingly evident. La Pérouse even had difficulty in finding James Cook's Nootka Sound, which he reached on 25 August, as 'a very thick fog rising up at about five in the afternoon hid the land altogether'. The fog continued for another five days. The coastline was changing as they sailed away from the Canadian coast and along the Oregon coastline. There were fewer bays, but violent coastal currents made navigation difficult and dangerous. But there was work to be done in this area, as Cook had not charted this part of the coast in any detail. It was a challenge for the French, but it turned out to be slow and dangerous work, coping with fogs, wild currents and sudden calms.

This work took up the first half of September. The scientists did not mind the fog, which gave them an opportunity to rest and put their work in order, but the sailors were becoming increasingly exhausted, forced to tack, struggle up the cold, clammy rigging to change the sails, making sure that the two ships did not become separated in the gloom or, worse still, come too close and collide. The maps, fortunately, were now more helpful, and La Pérouse could mark off the headlands as he identified them. Each one was like another prayer answered along a string of rosary beads: Cape Flattery, Cape Lookout, Cape Blanco, Cape Mendocino, Point Arena – and at last the wide, welcoming expanse of Monterey Bay.

When the *Boussole* and the *Astrolabe* dropped anchor on 15 September 1786 they were expected, their arrival promised but long delayed. The Spanish port authorities promptly sent out pilot boats to help them and the fort of Monterey fired a welcoming salute. They were the first foreign vessels to enter the bay, the first Frenchmen to visit California, not just sailors but men of education and talent, some of whom had even visited Spain. And, they brought news and information from the northern coast.

The settlement of Monterey was a mere fifteen years old. The bay had been discovered back in 1602 by Sebastian Vizcaino, but knowledge of the area was so limited that when the colonists and soldiers arrived in 1770, they had difficulty in identifying it. In those first years the harsh environment almost forced the inhabitants to give up. It was not until 1773, when a track was blazed to link Monterey with Mexico and the rest of Spanish America, that morale improved and they began to appreciate what a delightful spot it was. There were problems, however, with troublesome Indians, unruly soldiers and erratic supplies. The Franciscans had come and established a mission station, San Carlos, but they decided that moving to the Carmel River, a few kilometres away, would make life easier. More Franciscans came, but most of the settlers were soldiers, glad enough to leave the army, marry and start farming a small strip of land in this fertile area.

The arrival of the *Astrolabe* and the *Boussole* was a welcome break in the sleepy routine of the small town. Apart from the squabbles of minor officials, religious festivals and the occasional threat of an Indian raid, Alta California slumbered away in pastoral simplicity. The area, however, was fortunate in having an energetic administrator. Somewhat grandly called Governor of the Two Californias, Pedro Fages had worked tirelessly and efficiently to build up an administration. Europe – including, one suspects, the Spanish back home – knew very little about this corner of America, and La Pérouse's journal, filled with detailed comments on the local administration and the missions, provides an invaluable outsider's report.

He held Pedro Fages in high regard, and not just because he pressed gifts of all kinds on the French, sent supplies on board and fêted them on land.

His government covers an area of more that eight hundred leagues in circumference; his real subordinates are 292 cavalrymen who have to supply garrisons for five small forts [known as *presidios*] and squads of five or six men for each of the twenty-five missions established in the old and the new California. Such small means are enough to control approximately fifty thousand Indians who roam this vast part of America, of whom approximately ten thousand have embraced Christianity.

The Christianised Indians were under the control of the Franciscans, who represented a state within a state. Coping with them required all of Fages's skills, and by and large they co-existed satisfactorily. Mission industries were being set up to diversify the agriculture-based stations, artisans were coming in from Mexico, the Indians were being taught carpentry, house-building and a wide range of new trades. The organisation and aims of the Franciscans impressed La Pérouse: these were no obscurantist priests living like lords of the manor on tithes and benefices or collecting rents, but missionaries concerned with improving the standard of living of their flocks. Admittedly, their system was essentially paternalistic, but to a Galaup this was a sound and sensible way of developing society, far better than the romantic sentimentality of the Noble Savage and family-based subsistence farming:

> It is with the happiest sense of satisfaction that I can make known the pious and wise behaviour of religious who so perfectly serve their sovereign's wishes; I will not hide what struck me as reprehensible in their internal administration, but I shall proclaim that they are in each case a hundred times better than the rules laid down by their superiors ... The replies the religious gave to our various questions, left us in no doubt about the system of government of this kind of religious community, for no other word can be used to describe the legislation they have established; they are its temporal as well as its spiritual directors; the products of the soil are entrusted to their administration. There are 7 hours of work every day, 2 hours of prayers and 4 or 5 on Sundays and on feast days which are days of complete rest and divine services.

La Pérouse's no-nonsense approach saved him from viewing the Indians too romantically, but it made him equally clear-eyed about the Spanish. This was a land of 'inexpressible fertility' held back by an economic and political structure that belonged to past ages. The policy of exclusiveness and military control was counter-productive. There was no trade, no spirit of enterprise, no ambition. The missionaries impeded the Indians' intellectual development, while the Spanish policy of exclusiveness isolated California from the rest of the world and even from the other Spanish colonies. It was a charming, welcoming spot, but inertia reigned supreme.

Inevitably, the outside world would soon force California into a new, turbulent way of life. There were already signs of change: during the ten days they spent there, the French were questioned about the possibilities of developing a fur trade along the northern coast. The settlers hoped that before long they would be able to buy otter skins from the northern *presidios* and the mission stations. Spanish traders could then take them across to China, and then Monterey would become a prosperous commercial centre. An official, Vincento Vasadore y Vega, was due to leave as soon as he could for China in order to 'sign a commercial treaty relative to the sealskin trade'. But as La Pérouse and the others realised, there were obstacles that might be too difficult to overcome: the Franciscans were opposed to outside influences weakening the Indian missions, and there was, as ever, the spirit of *mañana*. The consensus among the locals was, 'One day maybe, but not yet'.

The French sailed from Monterey Bay on 23 September 1786, assisted by Spanish sailors who guided them through the main channel and cheered them on their way. 'I can only inadequately express my gratitude to all the local people,' wrote La Pérouse. 'They have all rendered us a thousand services.' In return, Collignon had planted potatoes and other seeds, but there was little that was lacking in this delightful spot – 'the gardens of the Governor and of the missions are filled with an infinity of vegetables'. Both ships were laden with fresh supplies of all kinds, mostly gifts to help them during their crossing of the Pacific. 'How can one repay such generosity?' The route that lay ahead would lead them almost due east to China. Then the second half of the great voyage would begin.

19. Across the Pacific to China and

the Philippines

October 1786–March 1787

THE VOYAGE ACROSS the Pacific was straightforward. La Pérouse decided to sail north of the Hawaiian Islands, so that he could search, in a fairly relaxed way, for the lost island of Nuestra Señora de la Gorta. It was one of these semi-legendary places that had cluttered the charts over the years, though this one at least was now being omitted by most geographers. No one was quite sure who had first reported its existence, warning other sailors to be careful when they approached its supposed location. Robert de Vaugondy, the eminent cartographer who had drawn a detailed map of the Pacific for Charles de Brosse's famous *Histoire des navigations aux terres australes* of 1756, had not bothered to include it. But some of the Spanish firmly believed in its existence, and La Pérouse had promised to look for it. He altered course a couple of times to make sure, but there was nothing to see.

On the other hand, he did make a discovery, to the north-west of Hawaii, of one small island, which he named Necker, in honour of the famous Minister of Finance who had tried, unsuccessfully, to reform France's chaotic tax system. His ideas had not appealed to the majority of French taxpayers, and his island was similarly unattractive. 'It is really only a rock about a thousand yards long ... There is not a tree to be seen ... the sides are steep, like the side of a well, and the sea breaks wildly all around it.' Still, it needed to be shown on the charts because, as he said, 'It might be fatal to navigators.'[1] The island has kept its name, a lonely spot practically on the Tropic of Cancer, and still a danger for the unwary.

A few evenings later, on a fine warm night, with only a steady moderate swell, the best evening they had enjoyed since leaving Monterey, the lookout on duty up in the mast yelled, 'Reef ahead!' Everyone leapt into action and the ships altered course just in time, for there, in the pale moonlight and a mere 300 metres away, stretched a long low reef of evil-looking rocks over which the waves were silently breaking. As the *Boussole* and the *Astrolabe* sailed past, the depth fell to a mere 9 fathoms – some 15 metres. The reef had appeared so suddenly, looking so eerie in the silent night, that La Pérouse wondered whether it had been a mere illusion.

This was how ghost islands got reported and placed on charts, to puzzle generations of later navigators, for few captains would bother, or have the facilities, to make the astronomical observations that would help to pinpoint their location. But La Pérouse did not want to be blamed for reporting what might have been a mirage, or to give only an approximation of the reef's position. So in he morning he veered back and there it was, a rocky islet surrounded by reefs and sandbanks extending for several kilometres in every direction. It was, he said, like a circle of diamonds around a medallion – possibly attractive in daylight, but a serious threat at night. He named it French Frigates Shoals, a name it has retained.

The route now led straight towards the Mariana Islands. There was not a great deal left to discover about them; they were simply markers along the way. But they were tropical islands, offering a promise of refreshments, especially fruit. Asunción, one of the most northerly, came into view on 14 December. The names sounded attractive and after weeks on an endless ocean the French imagined that they were approaching one of the famed Polynesian islands, warm and enchanting under a tropical sun, with a long sandy beach fringed by coconut palms. The reality was a bitter disappointment:

The most vivid imagination would have difficulty in conjuring up a more horrible place:

> after such a long crossing, the most ordinary appearance would have seemed delightful to us, but this, a perfect cone the entire side of which, up to 40 *toises* [80 metres] above sea level, is black as coal, could only depress us and make us rue our expectations, because for several weeks we had been talking of the turtles and coconuts we were confident of finding on one of the the Mariana Islands.

Actually, once they looked a little more closely, they did find a few trees on Asunción and collected about 100 coconuts – not even one each, and this not without difficulty and getting dusty and muddy in the process. That was all. They went on, disappointed and disgruntled.

The strain of the long crossing was making itself felt in other ways. After being at sea for almost three months, all they had seen was the empty sea, Necker Island and French Frigate Shoals, and now this unattractive Asunción Island – a dreary trio indeed. Shipboard life, boring as it was, could be endured by the sailors and the officers because it was part of their standard routine, but the scientists had no duties to keep them occupied. They had written all their reports, they had sorted and resorted their specimens, checked over once again the library books they had become so familiar with over the previous year, and now they were waiting, day after day, for something to happen. The astronomers could at least help the officers by taking readings, but the naturalists were utterly bored.

Inevitably, this created tensions. Lamanon, ever proud and rebellious to naval discipline, had clashed several times with La Pérouse, and he became the leader of a small group of equally dissatisfied passengers. He was dismissive of naval routine and traditions and made a show of ignoring them: 'He expressed his opinions very freely, never attended the Sunday service – it was a day when he stayed in bed from eight in the evening until nine or ten in the morning, boasting of this challenge to the general practice'.[2]

When the ships finally arrived at Macao on 1 January 1787, Lamanon and several others simply walked off and took lodgings ashore, not even bothering to tell the captain where they were staying. So when receptions were held, as was usual whenever naval units put into a port, they were not sent invitations. Lamanon, Lamartinière, Monges and Father Receveur wrote a letter of complaint about what they considered to be a deliberate slight, but La Pérouse replied that he did not know where they lived and so had been unable to contact them. They replied that it would have been easy enough to find their addresses ashore if he had only bothered to make a few simple enquiries. Angered by this act of insolence, he told them that it was not a captain's job to hunt down his officers or passengers, and he had them brought back to their ships and kept under arrest for twenty-four hours. It was time they learnt who was in charge and what naval discipline involved.

The affair smouldered for days. Each side wrote to officials and friends in Paris, putting their side of the case. La Pérouse unburdened himself in a letter to Fleurieu. 'I must admit that these, Lamanon and Monges, have wearied me of all these makers of systems … They are so pretentious, especially Lamanon; they have such a high opinion of their day-dreamings and are in fact so ignorant that in the long run it is all so boring. These so-called savants are devilish fellows who test my patience to its very limit.'[3] Dagelet, the mild, busy astronomer, he could stand, and Receveur was normally a quiet man. But, as Dagelet wrote to a friend, they all needed a break from the dullness and confinement of life on board: 'We have just completed a voyage lasting a hundred days. It has seemed like a thousand to us, and like all on board I need a landfall; but now that it is all over. I will settle down on land among the Chinese and in that way I hope to get back to normal within a few days.'[4] The Marquis de Castries wisely had the letters filed away and got on with more important matters. He knew that by the time these complaints reached him, the arguments would be long over and generally forgotten.

Macao was a strange place, a peculiar toehold on the great landmass of China, surviving on sufferance, the target of official contempt mixed with fear of the alien Europeans. It dated back to 1757, but it was not even a Portuguese outpost, merely a Chinese possession leased to Portugal, where outsiders could trade with China without polluting the Chinese way of life.

It was a source of wealth for both the Chinese and the Europeans. When La Pérouse arrived, he counted forty-one foreign ships at anchor, twenty-nine of them British and five Dutch, but only two from France. This fairly accurately reflected the relative positions of the great powers in the region. One of the French vessels was the *Marquis de Castries*, newly arrived from Manila, part of a small force commanded by Bruny d'Entrecasteaux. Its task was to protect French interests in the East, which was not easy given the constant vexations of the Chinese administrators and the haughty jealousy of the East India Company. Still, it was a pleasure to meet French officers for the first time after so many months, and exchange news of home and gossip about the navy. But there was no mail from France. It should have been there, in Macao, having made its way down the Atlantic and into the Indian Ocean, but the ship bringing it was still on its way from the Isle de France.

The Portuguese governor tried to make up for their disappointment by entertaining the officers and the scientists from both ships – including in time the few who had decided to board ashore. He had been in the Portuguese settlement of Goa on the Indian coast twelve years earlier when La Pérouse was in command of the small *Seine*. The governor's wife made a charming hostess: 'Nowhere in the world could one find a more delightful picture: the most beautiful of children surrounding the loveliest of mothers'.[5]

The Chinese authorities ignored the new arrivals, and La Pérouse made no effort to contact them in Canton. All he really wanted was to get rid of the stock of furs he had bought on the North-West Coast. Buying furs was not really part of his mission, apart from testing their availability in a general way and pleasing the Tlingits, who expected him to purchase what they brought him. The original instructions had provided for the possibility of a merchant ship joining the expedition in the early stages, in which case La Pérouse would have offered her his protection, but none had appeared. He certainly did not want to encumber his ships during the next stage of exploration with otter or seal skins.

But selling them was not all that easy. Rather than waste valuable time, he landed the lot in the care of the naturalist Dufresne, who was only too delighted to leave an expedition he does not seem to have wanted to join in the first place. His presence on board was something of a mystery – even his Christian name is not recorded. He had been one of the last to arrive at Brest, with a recommendation from the powerful financial administrator, Charles Alexandre de Calonne, and from his own brother Bertrand Dufresne, financial controller for naval and colonial matters. He was a quiet, able man, who kept out of the way and helped La Pérouse with record-keeping. He had tried to get off in Chile, but failed, and seized this second opportunity with both hands. He could take his time and, helped by the local French consul, could start bargaining with the hard-headed dealers who controlled Macao's trade. Bargaining with traders would have been quite *infra dig* for a senior naval officer like La Pérouse.

So, on 5 February, the *Boussole* and the *Astrolabe* sailed for Cavite, on Luzon in the Philippines. With them, they took six Chinese sailors for each frigate, to make up in part for the losses sustained at Lituya Bay.

They were not sorry to leave. Macao had provided a welcome four-week break after a tiring crossing, and it was a new experience, but it was a claustrophobic world, almost a walled city in unfriendly surroundings. There had been a chance to rest, some pleasant interludes, a few receptions, but no strolls in a pleasant countryside, no excursions along a quiet seashore. Instead, there had been vexations and arguments both among themselves and with the town's traders. Even the climate had not smiled on them: 'Most of us had a temperature and heavy colds which disappeared when we reached the more pleasant climate of Luzon'.

Three weeks later, on 28 February 1787, the two ships dropped anchor in Cavite, the port of Manila Bay. Before that, they had stopped at a small island to buy wood, which they had been told would be much more expensive in Manila. This call provided at last an opportunity to walk ashore amid peaceful surroundings:

I went down to the village at around midday; it consists of some forty bamboo houses, roofed with leaves, and raised about four feet above the ground. These houses have bamboo floors, with gaps, that make one think of bird cages; one climbs up by a ladder and I do not believe that the entire house, including the roof timbers, weighs two hundred pounds.

'But why stop at Cavite? Life is so much more pleasant in Manila.' That was the first question the Spanish authorities asked the French, whose arrival they had been expecting. Why the dull neighbourhood of Cavite instead of the colour and social life of Manila where the population was close to 40,000? The governor had been eager to give La Pérouse an official welcome, but Cavite made this more difficult. La Pérouse, however, knew what he was doing: this was where the shipyards were situated and the vesels could be repaired easily and more cheaply. Also, there were not the taverns and brothels to tempt his sailors away and encourage desertions.

There were some opportunities for visits to Manila, in spite of a mediocre road and the great heat. The Spanish very sensibly disappeared from sight to take their lengthy midday siesta, but the French found it hard to accustom themselves to the practice. They left their ships as soon as they could in the morning, but they could hardly pay their calls and return to Cavite before late afternoon. La Pérouse had all the time he needed to appraise the state of the colony and pass his usual down-to-earth judgement on its administration and prospects. The beauty of the scenery, the blue expanse of Manila Bay, the colourfulness of the busy streets, the exotic blend of races, might enthuse the romantics among his officers, but his own objectiveness was never impaired.

For one thing, the Philippines were not a colony in the true sense of the word, a place like California where colonists were encouraged to settle. Luzon was more a feudal dependency of the King of Spain who had divided most of it into large estates, a number of them allocated to religious orders. Consequently, the Philippines were 'still like the landed estates of great noblemen that remain fallow but could make a fortune for several families'. This was feudalism with a vengeance, and not likely to appeal to a friend of the *philosophes*.

It was disappointing, because Manila was excellently situated to become a great trading centre. There was a number of reasons why it was not. First there was the Spanish policy of exclusiveness that protected their American possessions at the expense of the Philippines. An edict of 1593 had banned direct trade between the Philippines and Spain; goods, in theory at least, had to be shipped to Europe by way of Spanish America, consequently crossing the Pacific. The aim was to prevent calls at ports in China, India and the Cape, which would no doubt have led to some unauthorised trading, but the route across the Pacific and then overland to the Atlantic was absurdly uneconomic. And even then, there were restrictions: gold and other precious goods could be sent by only one ship a year – the famous Manila Galleon – but even then with a limit on the value of its cargo: not more than 750,000 *pesos* in all. Contraband and false declarations helped to raise this total – the *San Jose* in 1784 had taken almost three million *pesos'* worth – but it still throttled the economy of the Philippines.

In addition, Spain lacked the foothold in China that Macao represented for Portugal, and consequently Manila's geographical advantage could not be exploited. Indeed, the reverse occurred: junks from China came each June for the Manila Fair, bringing silks, tea, jade and porcelain. To benefit from this important commercial event, Spain would have needed a much larger and unrestricted merchant navy and to have given Manila the right to send ships home by the Cape of Good Hope route. Instead, only luxury goods were traded, to fill the Manila Galleon, and the great opportunities offered by the eastern trade fell to the English, the Dutch and the French.

The governor who welcomed La Pérouse was Don Basco y Vargas, an enlightened man who had been struggling since 1778 to change the ingrained attitudes of Madrid. He was on the verge of success. A Company of the Philippines had been set up, to trade in competition with the monopolistic annual galleon. Success came in 1789, when Madrid finally agreed to turn Manila into a free port. It could have become the main emporium of the East had this move been made earlier. As it was, though Manila's trade boomed – there would be 50 trading vessels in Manila by 1795 – it was too late. The influence of Great Britain was rapidly becoming overwhelming.

The climate had it drawbacks, particularly at the beginning of the hot season, which normally lasts from April to July. The French spent March and early April in Manila Bay, and they discovered what often happens at this time of year with the temperature rising into the 30s (90s Fahrenheit). The colds and fevers from which they had suffered in Macao were replaced by stomach cramps. In the case of Lamanon and d'Aigremont, these developed into dysentery. Local remedies were of little avail. The stifling heat made the narrow cabins unbearable. On 25 March, d'Aigremont died. Apart from a servant who had died of tuberculosis during the crossing to Easter Island, this was the expedition's first case of death from illness.

In the meantime, Bruny d'Entrecasteaux himself had reached Canton on his flag-showing mission, but he was too late to meet La Pérouse, who had left for the Philippines. So he hurriedly sent the frigate *Subtile* to bring him news from France and his own offer of help. The news was stale – over ten months old by now – but the help was welcome. La Pérouse took one officer and four men for each of his ships. Pierre Le Gobien, an officer in his early twenties, joined the *Astrolabe;* Pierre-Louis Guillet de La Villeneuve, a couple of years older, joined the *Boussole.* These gains were balanced by the departure of young Mel de Saint-Ceran, whose health was giving serious concern. Rather than risk losing a second officer in Manila Bay, La Pérouse sent him home. While in Macao, the *Boussole* had taken on Gabriel de Bellegarde, a young man from the storeship *Maréchal de Castries,* so numbers were adequately balanced. Nothing, however, could be done to compensate for the tragic losses sustained in North America.

By the beginning of April 1787, La Pérouse was anxious to begin his exploration of the north-western Pacific. It was a cold region with a fairly short summer, and surveying the largely unknown coastline would take him months. He needed to get there by June at the latest and to get away by mid-September. After that, ice and snow would begin to close off the area and prevent his ships from getting away. The Spanish governor warned La Pérouse that the north-east monsoon would continue for another month, impeding his progress towards the north, but he decided to take the risk. He farewelled all the friends and acquaintances he had made and sailed on 9 April. His plan was to go north towards Taiwan and Japan, examine as much as he could of these closed worlds and go on towards Siberia.

20. THE PHILIPPINES TO KAMCHATKA

April-September 1787

'FORMOSA, THE BEAUTIFUL' the Portuguese and the Spanish had called it. And beautiful it was – deep forests, a fertile soil, fruits of all kind, warm weather. The Chinese called it Taiwan, but for centuries it had been semi-independent, partly occupied by Japanese, then claimed by the Portuguese, the Spanish and eventually the Dutch. By the seventeenth century, the Chinese claimed it as part of their empire, maintaining an uneasy hold that the locals, both aborigines and immigrant Chinese, kept on challenging. Vargas warned La Pérouse that one of the frequent uprisings against the mainland Chinese was in progress, and that the waters around it could be dangerous.

The weather at least was on the side of the French. The *Astrolabe* and the *Boussole* sailed north along the coast of Luzon with no difficulty until they reached its northern extremity, Cape Bojeador. Then the monsoon came on the scene to show how wrong the French had been and how much wiser were the Spanish. Implacably, it blew from the north-east, keeping Formosa out of sight until 21 April.

Hoping the wind might be less strong and regular in Formosa Strait, the French sailed up along the west coast of the island. It was a dangerous decision. Somewhere to the north was a Chinese fleet, landing troops to put down the rebellion. La Pérouse thought it wiser to stay away from the coast of China, which was closed to all foreigners and would be even more dangerous in times of war. This meant sailing past the Pescadores Islands, which were shown only roughly on his charts. Almost everything went wrong. The winds did not abate. The weather was truly frightful, but nevertheless as the frigates entered the little-known Penghu Channel they could not avoid lowering some of the boats so that they could check the depths. The Chinese fleet was straight ahead, almost in sight – busy, admittedly, with its own concerns, but there was always the possibility that its commander might send two or three vessels to find out what these strange ships were doing down in the south. Uncharted rocks appeared, seemingly closing the channel. The sea was so wild it was not possible to tell whether the waves were breaking against rocks or were merely whipped up by the gale. 'Never in my life have I seen heavier seas.'[1] La Pérouse turned back. There was no alternative: he would have to sail up the east coast of Formosa, though it was more open to the unpredictable Pacific Ocean.

By then, it was May. He might as well have stayed in Manila waiting for the monsoon to change. But all had not been wasted. The astronomers had been able to survey part of the coast and clarify some points on the rough charts. And now, as if endorsing his decision, the winds generously turned to speed them on their way north.

Passing through the Sakishima group, La Pérouse entered the East China Sea, sailing almost due north until 21 May when he sighted Cheju-do, which guards the entrance to the Korea Strait and thus access to the Sea of Japan. No other expedition had ever ventured into these waters. Certainly, none was welcome. Korea was a land totally forbidden to foreigners: anyone shipwrecked on this coast could expect to spend the rest of his life as a slave. The Japanese, on the eastern side, were scarcely more welcoming. Foreigners were likely to face death or imprisonment, unless the head of the Dutch trading post at Nagasaki, itself kept under strict control, could intervene in time and strike a deal with the authorities to ransom the intruders.

La Pérouse preferred to sail close to the Korean coast, which offered better opportunities for hydrographic work. No boats ventured near, even though the frigates were within 10 kilometres of the shore, but they were shadowed by two small vessels hugging the coast behind them. 'It is more than likely that we have aroused some concern on the coast of Korea because, during the afternoon, we saw fires being lit on every headland.'

Having sailed along the south coast, and finding that the shore was beginning to trend north and west, La Pérouse veered east towards Japan. It was 27 May. A small island hove into sight that was not shown on any of the charts. It was, as far as European geographers were concerned, a new discovery. He named it Dagelet Island 'after our astronomer who saw it first'. It is modern Ullung-do, a distant possession of South Korea. Naming a geographical feature after a member of the expedition was always a matter for celebration. Dagelet, normally a retiring modest fellow, was toasted on the *Boussole* and, as soon as Fleuriot de Langle was told, on the *Astrolabe* as well. The officers raised their glasses to his 'geographical immortality', amid much laughter and ribbing. The sailors were not forgotten: there was a little extra for them as well.

La Pérouse decided to send Boutin in a boat in the hope of finding an anchorage or buying a few supplies, but the few inhabitants he saw fled into the hills. It was too dangerous for them to try to talk to the alien French, and even more to engage in any barter. There was no point of taking any risk at this stage of the voyage. Boutin wisely turned back.

What mattered was fixing the position of some feature of the Japanese coast in order to have some precise reference point for further hydrographic work, but the French were plagued by recurring fog patches. Closeness to the shore spelt danger not merely because of uncharted rocks and islands, but also because of the continuing presence of other vessels. They might be friendly or neutral towards the visitors, but no one could be sure. On 2 June, two Japanese ships were in sight, one so close that they could hail her, but since neither side understood the other's language the encounter was more comic than useful:

> It had a crew of twenty men, all wearing blue cassocks like those of our priests … . They had a small white Japanese ensign with words written vertically on it; the boat's name was on a kind of drum next to the flagstaff. The *Astrolabe* hailed her as she went by – we no more understood their reply than they had understood our question – and they proceeded on their way south quite eager to announce their meeting with two European vessels in seas where none had gone before us.

Two days later, the French counted a total of seven ships; the next day there were ten. Extreme caution was required. Fortunately, a cape appeared, which they identified as Cape Noto, the prominent headland of central Honshu. Ten days spent fixing its longitude and latitude with great care enabled them to assess with final accuracy the width of the Sea of Japan and, by using a previously known position for the eastern coast, work out the width of Honshu. Although bothered by the fog, La Pérouse was able to get close enough to the coast of Japan to see 'the trees, the rivers and the landslips' and a little further up the coast a number of houses and 'a kind of castle'.

As for landing, that was totally out of the question. After early missionary successes, Christianity had been banned by a series of edicts issued between 1633 and 1636, which had been enforced with great brutality. Japan had effectively closed its doors against the world. Even trade with China was cut back drastically – by the time La Pérouse reached Japanese waters no more than ten Chinese junks a year were entering a major port such as Nagasaki. A few trading vessels were sent out from Japan to Manila, Cochinchina or Siam, but under such strict control that in practice no Japanese were allowed out of the country. And if any subject of the empire took it into his head to escape, he could expect only death or slavery in the most accessible country, Korea. Further north the cold, bare lands of Sakhalin and the Kurile Islands constituted an inhospitable and uneasy no-man's-land between Japan and

Russia. The Dutch, being Protestants and traders rather than missionaries, had been allowed a small foothold through Deshima, in Nagasaki, but it was no more than a hatchway through the cultural wall that defended Japan from the influences and the ambitions of the outside world. Through it passed small quantities of cloth, spices, sugar and ivory, in exchange for Japanese porcelain, silks, lacquer boxes, copper and camphor. Any deviation from this strictly regulated pattern could mean death.

At best, shipwrecked adventurers such as Benyowski could, with the help of a glib tongue and a good story, receive some help before the inevitable expulsion. Benyowski had told the Japanese that Russia was moving south into territory nominally claimed by Japan. The Minister in charge, Tanuma Okitsuga, was sufficiently persuaded to send an expedition which had returned shortly before La Pérouse's appeared off the coast. It had found nothing to substantiate Benyowski's tale, but the glib adventurer had talked himself out of the country before his story could be challenged. But for one who got away, there were dozens who were enslaved or brutally put to death.

The French veered back to the Asian continent. 'Our landfall was precisely the point that separates Korea from the Tartary of the Manchus.' This is where present-day Vladivostok is situated. Tartary held a host of romantic and less romantic associations for eighteenth-century Westerners. It was the end of the enormous Eurasian landmass that begins on the Atlantic with the Breton peninsula and dies away in the mysterious Sea of Japan. Little was known about it, so that imagination had free reign. The name raised visions of a world of darkness – for was not Tartarus the lowest hell of antiquity, far below Hades itself? What was known of its people was unflattering – the naturalist Buffon made allowance for them on account of the harshness of the climate 'uninhabitable for any other nation', and Voltaire basing his views on the little he had heard about them wrote them off as 'rough, stupid and brutal'.[2] The missionaries sent back reports that were usually based on vague rumours, the infrequent Russian travellers brought back information that was a little more reliable, but essentially Tartary was a mysterious land, ill-traced on the maps, unappealing to the imagination. The average reader would not be attracted by a utopia or an imaginary kingdom set in such a bleak and frightening environment.

Still, entering Tartary in 1787 did present the French with an illusion of suitably theatrical dimensions. As the *Astrolabe* and the *Boussole* sailed towards the land, La Pérouse reported:

> We could see the mountains, the gullies, in a word all the details of
> the terrain, and we could not imagine where we could have entered

such a strait … but soon these bluffs and gullies disappeared; the most extraordinary fogbank I have ever seen had caused this error: we saw it dissolve: its shapes, its colours rose up into the clouds, and fortunately we had enough daylight left to ensure that no doubt remained about the non-existence of this fantastic land. I sailed all night over the sea space it seemed to have occupied, and at daybreak nothing could be seen.

It was, as he said, the most complete illusion he had ever seen in all his sailing days, and it explained how easily non-existent islands could find their way onto explorers' maps. The fog then swirled in like a curtain, but when it parted it revealed a steep coastline on which no landing was possible. The scientists were impatient to go ashore and the officers to complete their survey. 'This was the only part of the globe that has escaped the attention of the tireless Captain Cook.' They had to wait until 23 June, when they dropped anchor in a small bay, which La Pérouse named Ternay Bay after his great mentor and friend. No toasting was required on that occasion, but some thoughts were spared for friends back home. Ternay acquired some geographical immortality on that day: Ternei Bay can still be found on most modern maps.

Other features on the mainland received French names: Pic Receveur, Cap Lesseps, Cap Monti, Pointe Vaujuas, and across on the island of Sakhalin, Pointe Boutin, Pic Lamartinière and Pic Lamanon. Not all these have survived, but each one helped meanwhile to fill out the chart of an area that was almost unknown to geographers – and it created a feeling of achievement and friendliness on the two ships that was good for morale.

There were animals about – deer and bears – but no inhabitants, or at least none that were alive. A tomb on the edge of a brook contained two bodies, wrapped in bear skins and wearing small skull caps, surrounded by some small artefacts, a few tools and a bag of rice to see them on their journey to the next world.

Four days later, the two ships sailed north, hugging the coast, surveying the headlands and coves, plotting the small rivermouths, but still seeing no inhabitants. On 4 July, a bay was explored and named, ephemerally, Suffren Bay. The Sea of Japan was being left behind and they were sailing into the Tartary Strait. On the starboard side, the coast of Sakhalin was moving closer. La Pérouse edged towards it and on the 12th dropped anchor in a bay which he named after de Langle but is probably modern Tomari. And at last he met the natives.

A sketch by Duché de Vancy recorded this meeting, on 13 July 1787. From it, a famous engraving was made, quite faithful to the original, with only a slight overlay of romantic exoticism and the inevitable addition of artistic balance and perspective. In both, La Pérouse is shown with the middle three buttons of his uniform undone and the lower ones struggling to hold back his paunch. The long months of arduous navigation had done nothing to reduce his waistline. The poverty of the natives is transformed by the engraver, who embellished their clothing and gave several bystanders the appearance of Romans in a classical tragedy. But La Pérouse's pleasure at the meeting cannot be exaggerated. Poor though they might be, they were not thieves and had to be pressured into accepting gifts. Their leaders, venerable elders with long white beards which made them look like Chinese sages, told how they traded with the mainland and with other tribes who lived further north on their own island – for an island it was, with a navigable strait into the Sea of Okhotsk. This was an important point: some maintained that the strait was more a long inlet, closed off in the north by a tongue of land that provided access from Siberia to Sakhalin.

> One of the old men rose and, with the tip of his pike [a copyist's error in the Milet-Mureau edition of the voyage has 'the tip of his pipe'], he drew the coast of Tartary, to the west, trending approximately north and south, on the east, facing it and in approximately the same direction, he drew his island ... he left a strait between Tartary and his island and turning towards our ships, which could be seen from the shore, he showed by a line that it was passable.

Navigability was all-important, because shallow straits would endanger the frigates. As it eventually turned out, the old man had underestimated the draught of the heavy French ships. Fortunately, La Pérouse decided to proceed with caution. It was the anniversary, to the very day, of the Lituya Bay tragedy and no one on board could have failed to remember the dreadful events of 13 July 1786 when twenty-one of their number had perished.

The two frigates sailed north, slowly because of frequent fog and changeable depths, until 19 July, when they dropped anchor in a bay close to modern Uglegorsk. La Pérouse called it D'Estaing Bay. Once again, the natives confirmed that Sakhalin was an island. They themselves were from the mainland, having crossed over to get a supply of fish. Sakhalin appeared to be less and less populated as the French sailed north, but fish were astonishingly plentiful. Clonard, sent to survey a small rivermouth, came back with 1,200 salmon 'although his men had neither nets nor lines' – they had simply killed them with sticks.

On the 23rd, another bay appeared, and now La Jonquière could be given his memorial on the charts. There were a few huts scattered along the shore of Jonquière Bay – the site of modern Aleksandrovsk – but no inhabitants. The coast was becoming more sandy, the depth was gradually diminishing with each sounding, and La Pérouse began to worry that the so-called strait might end in a jumble of sandbanks and shallows. For every five kilometres that he sailed north, the depth dropped by almost a metre. Three more days went by. The shores on both sides, when not obscured by fog, looked barren and uninhabited. There was no current to indicate the existence of a central channel. La Pérouse lowered two boats, with Boutin and Vaujuas, and sent them to sound not only ahead of the ships but to the side as well: a sudden gust of wind could drive either frigate onto a sandbank. The crew had fallen silent. There was only the low whistle of the wind, now rising through the rigging, and the screams of unfamiliar seabirds.

Vaujuas pulled ahead into the growing gloom. By eight o'clock, those on board could no longer distinguish his boat, though the regular calls of the sailor shouting the depths were faintly audible. Darkness fell. Vaujuas returned at midnight. He had gone five kilometres ahead, into the strait, and had not found more than 11 metres anywhere. There is in fact a navigable channel, as the Russian Gennadi Nevelskoi was to discover in 1849, but Vaujuas missed it.

The weather was worsening. 'We spent four hours raising anchor; the capstan had broken and this accident seriously wounded three men.' The frigate turned back south, towards the Tartary coast. When the fog cleared, they discovered a bay 'which seemed very deep and offered a commodious and safe anchorage'. It was the evening of 28 July 1787. La Pérouse named the bay after the Marquis de Castries; it is still known as De-Kastri today. These waters were too dangerous to risk his two frigates much further. Time was pressing, making the detailed and careful survey that was obviously needed increasingly risky. La Pérouse, anxious to reach Kamchatka before the end of the short summer, decided to cut his stay in Castries Bay to five days.

The anchorage was safe, the inhabitants courteous and generous, the surroundings attractive, at least to the scientists. Lamanon, even though he had been in poor health for some time, could not be kept on board. He joined Monges and Receveur on their walks along the shore and inland. La Martinière marched indefatigably along the river shore and into deep gullies in search of plants. The officers went hunting. But, midsummer or not, this was no primitive paradise:

The cormorant, the sea gull that gather in flocks under happier skies live like hermits on top of rocks. A sorrowful and dark sense of mourning seems to reign along the shore and in the forests where only the cawing of a few crows can be heard and where white-crested eagles and other birds of prey seek their retreat ... Although I did not have the soil dug, I believe it to stay frozen below a very slight depth, because the water at our watering place was only a degree and a half above freezing point, and the temperature of all the running water we tested with a thermometer never exceeded four degrees even though the mercury remained at 15 degrees in the open air, but this temporary heat does not penetrate; it merely hastens the growth of vegetation which must emerge and die in less than three months, and brings life to a multitude of flies, mosquitoes and sandflies who balance by their importunities the benefits brought about by the sun coming closer.

Collignon, the gardener, went around untiringly sowing seeds, as his instructions required him to do. Caught in a sudden freezing shower, he tried to light a fire by using some gunpowder. It blew up in his hands, breaking his thumb, and 'only the skill of Mr Rollin, our chief surgeon, enabled him to save his arm'. But Rollin had other worries: several of the men reported swellings of the gums and legs. Scurvy was making its appearance. It was really time to leave.

The expedition sailed back the way it had come, hugging the coast of Sakhalin this time to find the southern straits that would lead into the open sea. Strong gales blowing up from the south did nothing to help. It took a week to reach Langle Bay, which they had left on 14 July. Two days later, a gap appeared, but it was merely a channel between the coast and an uncharted island. It was Monneron's turn to gain immortality: La Pérouse named the discovery Monneron Island and it appears as Ostrov Moneron on present-day charts. Soon came better news: the appearance of a cape that marked the southern extremity of Sakhalin.

Cape Crillon, like the other geographical features named by La Pérouse, has retained its name, somewhat Russianised as Mys Kriljon. The strait that now opened before him led into the Sea of Okhotsk and enabled him to make for Kamchatka without delay. To this day it bears La Pérouse's name.

Entering the strait marked the end of weeks of slow and dangerous navigation, but also of an invaluable survey of unknown waters. It was one of the most rewarding parts of the entire voyage. The east coast of Sakhalin and the chain of the Kurile Islands they had reached were better known. The Dutchman Martin de Vries in the *Kastricum* had sailed in this area in 1643, as had James King in the *Discovery* in 1779. There was still much that was uncertain, points that should be clarified, positions to be calculated with greater precision, observations to be made, but the tension and excitement of sailing into the unknown had gone. The Kuriles stretch away like a set of links binding Japan to the Kamchatka peninsula. La Pérouse passed through it between the central islands of Urup and Simusir – through what is known as Boussole Strait – back into the Pacific and along the eastern coast. 'I believe this channel to be the finest of all those that can be found among the Kuriles,' he wrote, with a sailor's relief at nearing a long-hoped-for haven. The date was 30 August 1787. On 6 September, the expedition anchored at Petropavlovsk (St Peter and St Paul's) in Avacha Bay, the main – indeed, the only – town of Kamchatka.

Kamchatka was the edge of Asia and had only recently become the furthest possession of the Russian Empire. The empty wastes of Siberia had grown to include the Kamchatka peninsula when in 1760 it had been placed under the control of the military governor of Okhotsk, 1125 kilometres to the west across the sea. Not that there was a great deal to govern: there were no roads, few tracks, and only scattered groups of inhabitants surviving on fishing and hunting. Only Petropavlovsk, with 100 or so people, was of any value – it was strategically situated in the northern Pacific and although icebound for several months of the year it was at the time the only port Russia could use in the east. The Russian view of Kamchatka, at least from the impression their hosts were anxious to give him, was rosier than La Pérouse's own:

> Since the winter is generally milder in Kamchatka than at St Petersburg and in several provinces of the Russian empire, the Russians speak of it as we do of the winter in Provence; but the snow that surrounded us as early as the twentieth of September, the white frost covering the ground every morning and the greenery that was as faded as it is around Paris in the month of January, all this told us us that the winter here was of a harshness the people of southern Europe could not endure.

This was the impression the French had gained as soon as they sighted the coast: 'The whole of this coast appeared frighhtful. It was painful and almost frightening to behold these enormous rock formations covered with snow in early September and on which no vegetation had ever grown.'

The people, however, were extremely hospitable, even overwhelming, in their welcome. They saw few visitors, they knew La Pérouse was due to call and they granted him every facility. There were hunting and fishing expeditions and even what passed for a grand ball in this lost outpost where Russian formality merged oddly with local customs:

> The assembly might not have been large, but at least it was unusual: 13 women, including 10 Kamchatkans with round faces, small eyes and flat

noses, were seated on benches around the room, dressed in local silks which were wrapped around their heads rather like the mulatto women of our colonies ... We began with Russian dances with very pleasant tunes very similar to the *Cosaque* that was being danced in Paris not long ago; Kamchatkal dances followed – they can only be compared with those of the convulsionaries of the famous tomb of St Médard, only arms and shoulders and almost no legs are needed ... They become so exhausted during these exercises that they drip with perspiration and lie prone on the ground without the strength to get up. The powerful effluvia they give out perfume the room with a smell of oil and fish to which European noses are insufficiently accustomed to appreciate.

The local garrison consisted of forty soldiers under a lieutenant. The rest of the population was made up of a few sailors and traders, some local Kamchatkans, and a handful of Russians serving out a term of exile. Siberia was used as a depository for the unwanted or the unlucky. In 1760 landowners had been granted the right to exile to Siberia lazy or rebellious serfs; it is estimated that by the 1780s there were over 20,000 peasants in eastern Siberia who had been sent there by their masters. Only a few, however, would have been desperate enough to make for this desolate land's end. One famous exile, mentioned also in the accounts of James Cook's third voyage, was Pieter Matteios Ivashkin, exiled to Kamchatka, after being flogged and having his nostrils split, for having made some careless comments about the Empress Elizabeth. He was twenty at the time. Elizabeth had now been dead for twenty-five years, but he was still living in eastern Siberia, working for Kassloff Ougrenin, the Governor of Okhotsk.

Ivashkin showed La Pérouse the tomb of Louis de La Croyère, who had died in 1741. He described the funeral he had witnessed almost 50 years earlier, and La Pérouse affixed a copper commemorative plaque to the austere monument. La Croyère belonged to a famous family, the De l'Isle or Delisle. His father was the author of numerous learned works, including a history of Siam and a *Summary of Universal History* in seven volumes. His brother was Guillaume, the first Royal Geographer. Another brother had been commissioned to set up a school of astronomy in St Petersburg and he himself had travelled across Siberia to Kamchatka, had joined Vitus Bering's expedition of 1741 and, worn out by his travels, died in Avatcha.

There was another tomb to be visited. Charles Clerke, the commander of the *Resolution* on Cook's last voyage, had died just before the expedition dropped anchor in Avatcha on 22 August 1779. Once again, a copper plaque was engraved and Kassloff promised that a monument to both men would be erected before long.

One great disappointment on arrival in Petropavlosk had been the absence of mail from France. How could they have been forgotten? The Minister of Marine knew that the *Astrolabe* and the *Boussole* were bound for Kamchatka, so mail should have been sent there to await their arrival. They had in fact reached it a little later than planned, so it should already have been there. This was the same blow they had suffered on reaching Macao. It was now more than two years since their departure from Brest, and being forgotten and cut off from all news added greatly to all the hardships they had to endure.

Luckily, their bitterness was short-lived. A courier rode in from Okhotsk with the missing mail packets. With an unbeatable sense of drama, he burst in during the ball, just as the Kamchatkan ladies, in a sweaty swoon, had concluded their dances. The ball ended immediately, the dancers sent on their way with large glasses of brandy. Let the mail be opened now, urged Kassloff. There were letters from families, dispatches from Versailles. There was no bad news for anyone, but several were to receive promotions. La Pérouse was promoted to the rank of *chef d'escadre* – commodore – and Clonard to post-captain. Kassloff brought out more vodka and ordered all the guns of the port to fire a salute. It was a long and memorable night.

Among the dispatches was an important letter from the Minister of Marine. The British were apparently planning a settlement in New South Wales in eastern Australia: La Pérouse was asked to sail there and discover the extent of these plans. There was no better way for France to obtain a tactful first-hand report.

On 21 September, La Pérouse had written to Castries that he intended to continue his voyage by sailing to Guam, then to go down to the Solomons and across to New Zealand. This was consistent with the original plan which, though it had expected La Pérouse to be sailing west from Tahiti, laid down a route that would have taken him to the Solomons, the New Hebrides, New Caledonia and eventually to Queen Charlotte Sound in New Zealand.

A change of route was now forced on him. He advised Castries on the 28th that he would make for Botany Bay without delay. He would avoid the dangerous waters around the Solomons and New Hebrides – there was no point in running risks since he would not have time for any useful survey work there. Instead he would sail almost due south to the Samoa group and sweep back west to Botany Bay. All being well, he should be there within three months.

The French got ready for a prompt departure. They had never intended to spend more than a few weeks in Petropavlovsk. It was time to go anyhow: the brief summer was ending, and early snow flurries warned them not to put too

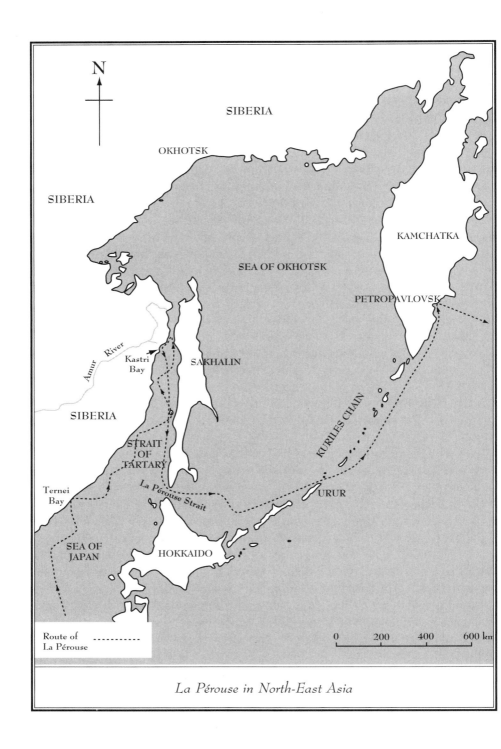

La Pérouse in North-East Asia

much faith in the Russians' boast that a Kamchatkan winter was often no worse than one in southern France.

There was one important matter to be arranged: the dispatch of reports and journals to Paris. La Pérouse had been cautious in what he had sent home from Monterey since the Spanish were not always dependable and communication with the rest of the Spanish world was slow and irregular. It had been a little easier in Manila and Macao where they had met French officers who could be entrusted with letters for home. However, full reports needed to be sent. Petropavlovsk was not an ideal place. It was a lonely port, soon to be further isolated by snow and ice. No ship would be able to call here for months. It was obvious that the only route for the expedition's mail was overland to Moscow – and for this La Pérouse had the services of young Lesseps, who spoke Russian, knew the people and held the rank of vice-consul.

Lesseps' voyage across Asia and Europe is an epic in itself. Eastern Siberia was little known, even to the Russians; there were few roads, few river crossings and a mere sprinkling of inhabitants. Distances were immense. And he was expected to travel during the winter months when snow obliterated the tracks and made rivers hazardous to cross, and the bitter cold killed off both men and animals. The spring would not make matters any easier, since the thaw rendered roads impassable and the break-up of the ice swept away bridges.

The two frigates sailed from Avatcha Bay on 30 September 1787. Lesseps left with Kassloff a week later. His plan was to cross the peninsula to the west shore and either sail to Okhotsk or follow the coast that ran north and south in a 1600-kilometre arc. Merely crossing the peninsula to Bolsheretsk, some 160 kilomteres as the crow flies, took a fortnight and involved building a raft to cross the Bolchaiareka River. Bolsheretsk was a dismal place, with fewer than 300 inhabitants. Lesseps stayed there until late January while a caravan of thirty-five sleighs was assembled. It snowed most days. The tracks to the next village were obscured by snow or blocked entirely by drifts. Not only the weather but Kassloff's official duties slowed the travellers down. Eventually Lesseps chose to separate from the official party. It was now February and he was still travelling north. In March he was following the shores of the northernmost bays of the Sea of Okhotsk. The grey skies merged with the grey horizon, hiding the coastal ranges. It was an alien, silent world, save when a sudden blizzard screamed down from the unseen mountains. At the end of April he reached Yamsk, a desolate outpost in a frozen inlet, but at least there was a road of sorts to speed him down to Okhotsk itself, which he reached on 8 May.

Eager to leave, he made his way inland along the route to Yakutsk, more than 1200 kilometres away, but his six sleighs, essential in winter, were useless in the thaw. Spring had come, turning the tracks into quagmires in which the sleighs bogged down. He dragged them back to Okhotsk, bought what horses the township could spare him, 'frightful, half-starved beasts', and on 6 June left again for Yakutsk. After that, it was a matter of sailing up the Lena River. Downstream would have been easier, but the Lena flows north towards the mysterious frozen expanse of the Laptev Sea. He sailed upstream in a primitive river boat on 5 July towards Lensk and Kirensk, mere huddles of log houses, tiny lonely military posts scattered in the empty wilderness of central Siberia. Who but an exile or a discarded serf would settle in such a hostile environment?

At Kirensk, his boats broke up among the rapids. It was midsummer and the water was no longer freezing, but great clouds of black midges danced a welcome on the banks. He completed the journey to Irkutsk on horseback. In spite of all his misfortunes, he could not fail to be moved by the silent beauty of Lake Baikal brooding in the August sun. But 160 kilometres to the south lay the secret world of Mongolia, ruled by no one, the home of roaming tribesmen who had once terrorised Asia and even central Europe.

Lesseps had to turn north-west, in a carriage this time, bumping over the ridges and ruts of the road to Krasnoyarsk, and then west, clear of the great marshlands, towards the north-to-south wall of the Urals, through dreary staging posts and settlements that have now grown into cities or whose names have been swept away by the storms of history – Achinsk, Tomsk, Tobolsk, Tumen, Katerinburg – over the ranges to Kongur, and on to Kazan and Nijni Novgorod.

The young man was hurt in an accident after leaving Kazan but he pressed on, driven by the need to avoid the early onset of a second winter. It was September by the time he crossed the Volga, with the first warnings of the coming cold sweeping over the plains, but he was now travelling north towards Novgorod and St Petersburg where he arrived on 22 September 1788, over a year after he had set out.

He handed all his dispatches to the French Ambassador, the Comte de Ségur 'as instructed to do by the Count de La Pérouse', but he was wanted in Paris. He pressed on by way of Riga, Konigsberg and Berlin to Paris, which he reached on 17 October. The new Secretary of State for the Navy, the Comte de Luzerne, was waiting for him at Versailles. As soon as Lesseps' carriage rumbled over the cobblestones of the great courtyard, Luzerne stepped forward and took him to Louis XVI. He was the hero of the moment. The king ordered that the account of his travel should be printed as soon as he had finished writing it. Then he was appointed consul at Cronstad, thus missing the storm of the French Revolution. Lesseps still had his share of adventures ahead of him: imprisonment in Turkey when he was serving there as First Secretary, and the retreat from Moscow in 1812 with Napoleon's defeated army. Kind fate allowed him to spend the last twenty years of his life as chargé d'affaires in the warm, mild backwater of Lisbon.[3]

21. Kamchatka to Australia

October 1787–March 1788

A VAST EXPANSE of empty ocean spread out before them as the French sailed from Kamchatka on that cool September morning. But there were, inevitably, islands on some of the charts, which might or might not exist. They had to be checked and either properly surveyed or eliminated.

The names were irresistible. Isla Grande, a large island, was nothing special: without further details it could be an illusion, a bank of fog in the distance, a mirage. But Rica de Oro and Rica de Plata, 'rich in gold and rich in silver', were something else. Though La Pérouse had his doubts, considering the evidence too skimpy, the Spanish and even the Russians thought he should look for these places. 'Somewhere in the northern Pacific', they had told La Pérouse. The Dutch, too, had thought these destinations worth a special effort. French geographers, though not altogether convinced, mostly shared their views. Louis Milet-Mureau, who wrote the first substantial account of La Pérouse's voyage in 1790, included a lengthy marginal note regretting that the explorer had not spent longer on the search.

He did slow down and tack about when he reached the area where the islands – or island – were supposed to be, and he promised a golden *louis* to the first sailor who saw either of them, and said he would name the land after him. There were possible indications of nearby land on 14 October: a few flights of cormorants, probably on a migration flight. They rested for a while on the yards, bringing a touch of activity to what was turning out to be a futile search. More of these 'birds that do not stray far from land' were seen several times during these October days, but the land they were believed to announce never appeared. The sailors did their best to scan the horizon, climbing up the masts when they were off duty, but with no success. In fact, the search cost a young sailor's life: he fell from the yards and disappeared into the waves, drowned or killed by the fall.

The winds were strong and favourable, the seas heavy. Creaking, straining, lumbering, the two frigates ploughed their way south, and the cold of the northern autumn gave way to the heat of the tropics – so speedily in fact that the abrupt change affected the health of crew and particularly of the scientists, but no one could find any comfort in the damp cramped cabins or the rope hammocks. La Pérouse ordered frequent rations of coffee to restore waning energy. It was better than nothing. Kamchatka had provided almost no fresh food, and what little he had been able to buy had quickly gone, so everyone, the officers included, was living on tough dried meat and ship's biscuits. On 6 November, eight bonitos were caught, providing a welcome feast for all on board. The fact that this was mentioned in La Pérouse's journal shows the dire straits to which they were reduced – for the fish had to be carefully shared between 200 people.

On 21 November, the expedition crossed the equator for the third time since sailing from Brest. Two days later, there was something of a celebration on board the frigates: a couple of sharks were hauled aboard and cut up to make a meal for the crew. The officers shared 'one curlew, very thin, served in a salmi, and it was hardly any better tasting than the sharks'. The weeks were passing. 'Nothing happened to interrupt the monotony of this crossing.'[1] Once more, the empty seas and the dreary routine frayed people's tempers. La Pérouse and Fleuriot de Langle did their best to avoid clashes, pointing to the warmer weather and the bluer skies of the tropics. But a clammy heat filled the 'tween decks, and dawn offered only a brief respite before the sun began to beat down implacably on the decks and make walking around them intolerable. And what was there to see, anyhow, but the endless horizon and the seabirds whirling and shrieking around the vessels? The sails, rotted, split with sudden shifts of wind; the ropes, perished by the long months of use in damp and sun, snapped as the men hauled on them to adjust the canvas.

The route was almost due south. There were islands to be visited somewhere to the south-west. The instructions had mentioned New Caledonia, whose western shore was still unknown, Santa Cruz and Jean de Surville's Arsacides – which Fleurieu was convinced, rightly as it turned out, were the lost Solomon Islands, the Louisiades discovered by Bougainville a few years earlier and the many offshore islands of eastern New Guinea, still imperfectly known. But all these plans had been set aside when the new instructions had arrived in Petropavlovsk. It was now a matter of making for Australia, as quickly and directly as possible, to report on the activities of the British. Australia was a prize that could not be lost by default. It was the continent the Spanish, the Dutch, the French and the British had sought for so long. Admittedly, it was not the southern Eldorado that people's imagination had built up over the centuries, but at least it existed, enormous, inhospitable but promising, a gigantic enigma in a Pacific that everywhere else was so empty. Every one of the leaders of French expeditions, indeed every one of their officers, had fought against Britain at some time to hold back her tide of conquests. But everywhere, be it India, Canada or the West Indies, the British had made advances. The British might well sing 'Rule Britannia' at their gatherings but the French had no desire to see them rule the world, and French naval officers especially had no wish to see them rule even the waves.

As far as the French could make out, however, it was no conquering fleet that had sailed from Portsmouth in May 1787 for Botany Bay, but a fleet of convict transports. A convict settlement was a logical move for the British, following the loss of their American colonies. Versailles understood that perfectly well, even if it did not quite trust its counterpart in London. The pressures put on the British authorities to get rid of their convicts had grown and was widely discussed. In March 1786, the Mayor and Corporation of London had petitioned the king to do something about the 'rapid and alarming accumulation of convicts within the kingdom'.[2] Until recently, felons had been transported to America – at the rate of 1000 a year. When this outlet was closed up by the war and then, more finally, by independence, attempts had been made to use Africa, but this proved a poor substitute because the convicts died off so quickly that the public became upset. Disposal, not death, was what English justice intended, and transportation had shown that convicts, if they were not reformed by being sent out of Britain, were at least of use in building up a colonial empire. Clearing British prisons of what was regarded as human refuse could pay dividends. The climate of New South Wales was suitable for Europeans. Men like Sir Joseph Banks and James Matra, who had sailed with Cook, were convinced that a successful colony would develop there in much the same way as colonies had spread along the Atlantic seaboard of America. The French government agreed with this point of view, but worried about the political and imperial consequences.

As it turned out, this Botany Bay plan was very much a make-do affair. The ships were a scratch lot; the fitting out, in spite of all the delays, was rushed; the men chosen to found the settlement, of uneven quality. The primary aim, clearly, was to ease the pressure on British prisons by dumping their surplus population half a world away, out of sight and out of mind, and it was not something a government bent on balancing the budget wanted to spend very much money on.

So, as La Pérouse sailed on towards his first landfall, which was to be Samoa, Captain Arthur Phillip's fleet was struggling towards New South Wales, but being constantly driven off course by storms in empty southern seas where whales blew and albatrosses swooped, in weather that grew more piercingly cold day by day. So, inevitably, scurvy began to appear among his wretched crew and his far more wretched human cargo.

On 6 December 1787 the French sighted the first of the Samoan islands, the easternmost Tau and then Tutuila. At last here, among the islands that Bougainville had called the Navigators, La Pérouse could find the supplies and refreshments his crew so badly needed. He could see numbers of coconut trees, picturesque villages set among the greenery on the hill slopes, and the canoes of the islanders, mediocre craft mostly, but manoeuvred through the waves with the skill that Bougainville had so admired.

Fleuriot de Langle in particular was impressed by the welcome he received. Admittedly, this was not the golden paradise of Tahiti, as Bougainville himself had remarked nearly twenty years before – 'I do not believe these islanders are as gentle as our Cythereans. Their features are more savage and they displayed a great deal of mistrust'[3] – but after over two months at sea any landfall had charms. La Pérouse did not share de Langle's enthusiasm. He stayed on board initially because although there were no incidents, he did not find the Samoans attractive. They were large, heavy men, well suited to cope with their environment, but they did not seem to warm to the white-skinned strangers and were too loud and unruly.

When he did go ashore, he gained more confidence and realised that fruit and poultry could be obtained as long as an orderly market was set up. The soldiers were lined up to protect it and the bartering began. It was brisk and tumultuous. La Pérouse left the market area and hazarded himself 50 or 60 metres into the trees to a village where he was almost effusively greeted. He unbent a little: 'This charming country presented the double advantage of a soil that was fertile without needing cultivation and a climate that required no clothing'. He had been unfair in his first judgement, he realised, and this was truly 'an enchanting site'. The charm of the South Seas was beginning to work its magic on him.

Still, this was not the abode of the happy, relaxed Noble Savage, a concept that he could not easily accept:

their bodies were covered with scars, which was evidence that they were often warring or quarrelling, and their features betrayed a ferocity one did not see in the women's appearance. Nature had no doubt left this mark to warn that, in spite of all the academies that crown the philosophers' paradoxes, Man in an almost savage state and living in anarchy is a more malevolent being than the wolves and tigers of the forests.

These were not the words of a follower of Rousseau. La Pérouse trusted only his own eyes. He wished no one any harm, considered reprisals as nothing more than an act of revenge that brought a man down to the level of the savages, but he had no time for romantic notions. His views were confirmed when he learnt on his return that a Samoan had climbed into the longboat and struck a sailor, that stones had been thrown at Rollin and that Monneron had almost had his sword stolen from its scabbard. These were still only minor incidents.

De Langle brushed La Pérouse's misgivings aside. He had found 'a charming village, close to a waterfall of the most limpid water', and believed that the French should stay longer. La Pérouse felt there was enough drinking water in the barrels and that there was no need to waste time among islands that were by now well known to geographers. The two men held a heated discussion over this. 'I argued,' La Pérouse wrote, 'that we did not need any, but he had adopted Captain Cook's approach and believed that fresh water was preferable to what we had in our holds.'

Fleuriot de Langle's argument, like Cook's, seems perfectly logical. They still had water in the barrels below deck, but after several weeks at sea, it had become corrupted. Rainwater collected on deck during periods of rain was usually preferable. But at the time many scientists held the view that though water kept in casks might look unappealing after a few days, it soon purified itself as the corrupting elements sank to the bottom, after which it was as palatable as fresh water. Their opponents, who urged navigators to get water on land whenever they could, often overlooked the fact that creeks and waterways, meandering attractively through trees towards the sea, could be polluted by the villagers who lived on the banks and threw refuse, including sewage, into the nearest streams. It all depended on the quality of the so-called fresh water obtained from along the shore.

De Langle insisted that water drawn from this particularly idyllic neighbourhood would be better for the men than anything left swilling around in the barrels. He saw no reason why the islanders should object and threaten the sailors who would be merely collecting some of the water that flowed so abundantly. La Pérouse gave way: 'M. de Langle was a man of such excellent judgement and such ability that these considerations more than anything else finally caused my own will to bow to his.'

On the morning of 11 December 1787, de Langle led a group of 60 men to the shore near this 'charming village'. But the tide was out and the shoreline looked less enticing. It was also more difficult to bring up the boats and to roll the barrels ashore. Worse still, the boats were out of sight of the two frigates. By the time the sailors had struggled along the beach to fill and load the barrels back into the boats, a crowd of over 1000 had gathered. The tide had still not fully turned and the heavily laden longboats would not float. Langle was forced to wait. He was vulnerable, stranded on this lonely beach in boats encumbered by heavy barrels. Suddenly, with a great roar, the Samoans attacked.

By the time the boats managed to struggle back to the *Astrolabe* and the *Boussole,* it was past five o'clock. De Langle was dead, as were Lamanon and ten of the men. Many others had been wounded. Boutin had five head wounds, Collinet's arm was broken and Father Receveur had almost lost an eye. Once the wounded were cared for, the crews readied for reprisals, but the atmosphere around the ships had not changed. They were still surrounded by Samoans in canoes happily trading their fruit and their poultry:

> with a sense of security that proved they were not accomplices in this perfidious action – but they were the brothers, the children, and the compatriots of these barbarous murderers, and I must admit that I needed all my powers of reasoning to stop me from giving way to the anger and rage that burned inside me, and prevent our crews from killing them.

Firing on innocent people was not a form of revenge La Pérouse could accept. All he allowed was one blank shot to warn the canoes away. And when the next day they returned, not to trade this time, but to shout challenges and yell their scorn, he ordered once again that only a single shot should be fired, though carefully aimed so that the cannonball curved over the foremost boats and splashed down in the midst of the crowd. The Samoans fled, saved by La Pérouse's sense of justice: 'I could have destroyed or sunk a hundred canoes, with more than five hundred people in them; but I was afraid of striking the wrong victims: the call of my conscience saved their lives'.

The *Astrolabe* and the *Boussole* sailed from what they now named Massacre Bay, on the island of Tutuila, on 14 December. Whatever illusions La Pérouse might have harboured had vanished: 'I am a hundred times more angry against the philosophers who praise them [the Noble Savages] than against the savages themselves. Lamanon whom they murdered was telling me the day before he died that these men were worth more than us'.[4]

As had happened after the Lituya Bay disaster, shipboard life had to be reorganised. The dead men's belongings were sorted through, to be packed and eventually sent out to their families, or auctioned among the crew. It was a sad task. Men had gone out in the morning as part of their work routine, some, like Lamanon, hoping to find a new botanical specimen to take home, and their lives had ended abruptly. They left behind a few pitiful mementoes of the voyage – curios bought in a port, partly completed woodcarvings, pressed leaves, markers in a half-read book.

Monti took over command of the *Astrolabe* by virtue of his position as first officer; Clonard, who was senior to him, would take over when it was convenient to transfer him from the *Boussole*. Young Lauriston, whom De Langle had trained in the mysteries of astronomy and lunar observations, helped out. Others were compelled to do less: Father Receveur had been more seriously wounded than he cared to admit, and scurvy was making itself felt. Already, on 10 December, David, one of the cooks, had died of 'scorbutic dropsy'.

A pall had fallen over the ships. They sailed west to the other islands of the Samoan group – Upolu and Savai'i – but the sailors who had laughed and catcalled at the girls and waved at the men, remained silent. The sky was still the same tropical blue, the coconut trees still arched their slim trunks and heads of greenery over the golden beaches, the sea still foamed white over the reefs, but they knew these paradise islands hid sudden, inexplicable death. The canoes came out to the ships, filled with islanders offering food, shouting and gesticulating to barter pigs and coconuts for glass beads and cloth, but who could tell what plans they might be hatching? La Pérouse reduced canvas so that the ships slowed down and trading could proceed, but he made no attempt to land, and any signs of challenge or warlike attitudes were met by the display of firearms. The country was breathtakingly beautiful; the people, because they were related to those of Tutuila, had to be considered dangerous.

Bernizet and Dagelet worked to fix the position of the islands which the Spanish navigator Francisco Maurelle, sailing in 1781, had not been able to determine with accuracy: 'he showed these islands some six degrees too far west, from which a new archipelago would have been created which would have been copied by geographers from one century and one age to the next, and yet would have had no basis in reality'.

One senses in La Pérouse's journal signs of the weariness and the dejection that were affecting both ships. The dig at the geographers, safe in their study, is another instance, though not an isolated one in his writings. The presence of scurvy among the crew depressed him further. He ordered regular issues of brandy and water for the men, and the killing of the small pigs he had bought in Tutuila. These measures helped, and the swellings in legs and gums that had worried the surgeons disappeared – 'which shows that sailors have a less pressing need of land air than of good food'.

What really mattered now was reaching Botany Bay. The bad weather, the need to sail cautiously through the Tongas, the pitifully small amounts of food they managed to obtain from the few islanders who ventured near the ships, determined the French to get away as soon as they could. On the first day of

1788, La Pérouse ordered the expedition to sail west by south-west direct for Australia. It was a route no one had yet followed. There was little to be found on the way, except Pylstart Island, or Ata, discovered by Abel Tasman nearly 150 years earlier, a lonely island south of the main Tonga group. Even so, La Pérouse would not have gone near it had the winds not driven him in that direction. It gave him the minor satisfaction of correcting the position James Cook had assigned to it – the Englishman had placed it 6.5 kilometres too far south.

But now the winds dropped, the skies cleared and the two frigates found themselves becalmed. They remained for three days in view of this bare rocky island, scarcely 1.6 kilometres across. A welcome gale blew up on 6 January, driving them south-west, through heavy seas admittedly, but this was the kind of progress they had prayed for.

On the 13th they were-in sight of Norfolk Island. There was little hope of getting supplies since the island was believed to be uninhabited, but La Pérouse took pity on the bored naturalists 'who, since our departure from Kamchatka, have had very few occasions to consign any observations to their journals'. It would improve morale generally if they could be given a chance to go ashore and perhaps find a few unknown specimens of plants or rocks. But first he sent Clonard to look for a landing place. It was a wise move: the place looked too dangerous for a boatload of eager scientists rowed around by weary sailors. Everywhere Clonard looked, he found the sea breaking angrily at the foot of steep cliffs. It was not worth risking any lives for. The expedition sailed on and the scientists went back to their books, their grumblings and their endless card games.

A few days later, they could still make their 'little bets', but in a geographical context. There was something to speculate about: a multitude of seabirds surrounded the ships. As ever, the presence of birds was interpreted as a sign of land somewhere in the vicinity. But how close? And was it rocks or some unknown shore? Was it by any chance a northern outcrop of the Australian coastline? There were no answers, and the birds vanished as quickly as they had appeared.

Then, on 23 January 1788, the French gathered on deck. This time, it was really land, a low coastline, some 30 to 50 kilometres away. The next day, they tacked about to round what was Cap Solander – they had reached Sir Joseph Banks's famous Botany Bay. And as they came nearer, they beheld a sight they had not seen since Manila – British ships at anchor.

Phillip had arrived in the *Supply* a mere six days earlier; the rest of the fleet had joined him two days later. La Pérouse therefore arrived while the British were still surveying the shores of Botany Bay. Phillip had been bitterly disappointed on discovering that, attractive though it might be to a botanist like Banks, it was quite inadequate for a permanent settlement:

> I began to examine the bay as we anchored, and found that though extensive, it did not afford shelter to ships from the easterly winds; the greater part of the bay being so shallow that ships of even a moderate draught of water are obliged to anchor with the entrance to the bay open, and are exposed to a heavy sea that rolls in when it blows hard from the eastward ... The small creek that is in the northern part of the bay runs a considerable way into the country, but it has only water for a boat. The sides of this creek are frequently overflowed, and the lowlands a swamp ... Several good situations offered for a small number of people, but none appeared calculated for our numbers, and where the stores and provisions could be landed without a great loss of time.[5]

Shallows, swamps, sandy shores, midsummer heat, a plague of insects,[6] and a land that seemed incapable of producing crops – this was what they had come to after a voyage lasting more than eight months. Still cooped up in the transports were more than 700 convicts, male and female, ill-fed, ill-clothed, guarded by soldiers as surly and as tired of the voyage as the rest. Even the few Aborigines Phillip encountered were unfriendly or, at best, indifferent.

Botany Bay would not do so Phillip set out with a small party to seek a more suitable place to found a new colony. James Cook had sighted an inlet further north, which he had named Port Jackson, but he had not explored it and there was no particular reason to expect that it would prove any more attractive. But it turned out to be 'the finest harbour in the world, in which a thousand vessels of the line may ride in the most perfect security'. Phillip was away three days on this exploration, returning on the 23rd. The next day, the *Boussole* and the *Astrolabe* arrived.

The unexpected arrival of two French frigates caused a stir among the British. Was Britain at war with France, and were these enemy vessels come to destroy the colony before it was established and free the convicts so that they might hold this land against those who had sent them here to rot? Or were they friendly ships bringing supplies? Phillip knew that La Pérouse was in the Pacific with two ships and he quickly realised who the intruders were. But the weather held up contact for two more days. Then Clonard went in the *Boussole*'s boat to speak to the British and explain that La Pérouse had no intention of remaining in the bay for any length of time, but wanted simply to rest his crew, carry out a few repairs and take on water and firewood.

The British made it clear they could do little to help him. Indeed, surveying the fleet, grimy-looking after months at sea, and its cargo of rotting humanity, La Pérouse did not expect anything:

> An English lieutenant and a michikmane [sic] were sent by Captain Honter [sic], commanding the King of England's frigate *Sirius;* they offered on his behalf every assistance he could give, adding however that circumstances allowed him to give us neither food nor ammunition nor sails. And since they were on the point of weighing anchor to go further north, their kind remarks amount merely to good wishes for the ultimate success of our voyage.[7]

There was one crucial service the British could provide and that was to take letters and reports back to Europe. Without this, we would have no record of the voyage from Kamchatka to Australia, no knowledge of the tragedy that had occurred at Tutuila. The man entrusted with this important mission was Lieutenant John Shortland, who had travelled with the fleet as agent for the transports, and was to leave on 14 July in the *Alexander,* taking Phillip's first reports of the New South Wales settlement. He was given the most recent section of La Pérouse's journal, plus his personal letters and those of the officers and scientists. His successful return to Europe not only made sure that people had details of the French frigates' recent voyage, but also knew of La Pérouse's plans for the final stage of his journey.

The French ships spent more than six weeks in Botany Bay, watching the British complete their move to Port Jackson and begin to set up their struggling settlement. La Pérouse must have reflected that its chances of survival were not great and may have shared the thought Captain Phillip had once expressed in a memorandum to the Home Department that 'he would not wish convicts to lay the foundations of an Empire'. Certainly, during those weeks, escaped convicts caused both of them trouble, as they fled from Port Jackson in the hope of finding asylum in the French vessels. Embarrassed and punctilious, La Pérouse returned them to Phillip, who had them flogged.[8]

On 17 February, Father Receveur died. He had made light of the wounds sustained at Tutuila, writing to his brother: 'We shall be back in France in the spring of 1789 or even earlier. So write to me at Brest or at Rochefort.'[9] But he was worn out by the voyage and the privations he had suffered, and he may have strayed too far from the French camp and been further injured or even killed. Ten days after writing that letter he was dead. He was buried ashore, in what is now the La Pérouse district of southern Sydney, and La Pérouse put up a small memorial over his grave, bearing the Latin inscription: '*Hie jacet*

L. Receveur E.F. Minoribus Galliae sacerdos, physicus in circumnavigatione mundi, Duce de Laperouse, obiit 17 februarii Anno 1788'. The Aborigines destroyed it. When Phillip heard of this vandalism he had a new memorial erected. Father Receveur's death is now commemorated each year by a special service and ceremony.

Captain Phillip's despatches tells us a little about the activities of the French in Botany Bay. They built two longboats, 'the frames of which they had brought from Europe'. Conditions in New South Wales were far from pleasant at the time. Heavy rain fell during February, and scurvy was raging among the convicts. Aborigines roamed around the rough encampments the French had erected and 'Mons. La Pérouse … was obliged to fire on them'. Some of his men ate of 'a large fruit, not unlike a pineapple, but which when eaten by the French seamen occasioned violent retchings'.[10] To protect his men from possible attacks, La Pérouse erected a defensive fence around the longboats he was having built on the shore: 'These precautions were necessary against the Indians of New Holland who, although weak and not numerous, are like all primitive people very ill-natured and would set fire to our boats if they had the means of doing so'.[11]

The shock of Tutuila was still affecting him. Any illusions he and his fellow officers may have had about the people of the South Seas had been shattered, replaced by suspicion and antipathy towards native people in general. And the long voyage of exploration had taken its toll. In a letter to a friend, La Pérouse expressed his weariness and some disenchantment:

> Whatever professional advantages this expedition may have brought me, you can be certain that few would want them at such cost, and the fatigues of such a voyage cannot be put into words. When I return you will take me for a centenarian, I have no teeth and no hair left and I think it will not be long before I become senile … Farewell until June 1789. Tell your wife she will mistake me for my own grandfather.[12]

Among the letters handed to Shortland there must have been some for Eléonore, but none seems to have survived the politically troubled times she was to live through. Fortunately for posterity, the letter he wrote to the minister on 7 February outlining his plans reached its destination and has been carefully preserved:

> I shall go up to the Friendly Islands and will do exactly what my instructions require me to do with respect to the southern part of New Caledonia, Mendana's island of Santa Cruz, the south coast of

Surville's Arsacides [the Solomons], and Bougainville's land of Louisiades, endeavouring to assess whether the latter form part of New Guinea or not. I shall pass, towards the end of July, between New Guinea and New Holland, by another channel than the Endeavour's, if such exists. In September and part of October I shall visit the Gulf of Carpentaria and the entire west coast of New Holland as far as Diemen's Land; but in such a way as to enable me to go back north in good time to reach the Isle de France in December [1788].[13]

For someone as weary as he was claiming to be, this was an ambitious programme, but La Pérouse was never a man to shun what he considered to be his duty. On 10 March 1788 the *Boussole* and the *Astrolabe* weighed anchor from Botany Bay. The sailors of Captain Phillip's fleet saw them sail past, going north, not far from the coast. They were the last white people to see the French expedition. La Pérouse, his ships and his men vanished in the Pacific, and almost forty years would pass before the first hints of what happened began to reach Europe.

22. FORTY YEARS OF OBLIVION

1788–1827

'MAY THEY RETURN to our shores, even though they die of joy as they kneel to kiss this free land!' Eloquence was *de rigueur* in the French National Assembly if one wanted to be heard and cheered by the other deputies. This French parliament had not met for 175 years and now that Louis XVI had been forced to call it together, its members, especially those who represented the middle class, were making up for lost time. France was going through a period of drastic changes. The Bastille, that symbol of arbitrary rule, had fallen, the king was reluctantly turning into a constitutional monarch – and even that position was being challenged – the aristocracy with all its privileges was under threat, and almost every decision now had to get parliamentary approval.

This included a search for the missing *Boussole* and *Astrolabe*. By the time that flowery statement was being uttered in the Assembly, they were more than two years overdue. No one knew where they were, and most people by now feared the worst. Although Louis XVI had been closely involved with the planning, this was not the king's expedition, but the nation's, with officers and scientists well known to the *philosophes* and the reformers who were now in power, to say nothing of the sailors, true Frenchmen drawn from the working classes, symbols of the new France that was beginning to rise from the ashes of the old.

La Pérouse's broad itinerary after leaving Botany Bay was known and the time required for the final stage of the voyage was easy to estimate. Allowing for a month or so in New Caledonia and the New Hebrides and a similar period in the Louisiades and the Solomons, La Pérouse could have completed a partial circumnavigation of Australia all the way to the west coast of Tasmania, then turned back and reached Mauritius by the end of 1788 at the latest. During that period no news was expected from him, since he would not have called at any European-held port and the chances of meeting another European vessel were very slight.

But by the middle of 1789 news of his arrival in Port-Louis should have reached Paris. As weeks turned into months, concern grew into anxiety. By mid-1790 men like Fleurieu were drawing up plans for a rescue operation. Eléonore moved from Albi to Paris, to be on the spot should news of the expedition reach the ministry, but also to press for government action. These were troubled times, with growing unrest. Economic problems dominated, aggravated by civil disorders. It was not merely the old social order that was collapsing, but an entire national and regional administrative structure. But this did not cause the problem of La Pérouse's fate to be forgotten.

Claret de Fleurieu had summarised the facts as they were known or could be surmised in a report of 21 April 1790, which he discussed with the king. At the same time, the Academy of Sciences was debating what might be done. Its members were concerned because of their earlier involvement in the planning – this was a scientific voyage in keeping with the mood of the time, staffed by scientists, colleagues of the men who were not only ushering in a new era of knowledge but who had, by their logical reasoning, made an important contribution to the new egalitarian society now dawning. But all the Academy could suggest was that the explorer Louis de Bougainville, who was commanding a squadron at Brest, should sail 'to meet' La Pérouse.

As an alternative, the French government considered asking the Spanish to help. Two ships under Alessandro Malaspina and José Bustamante had sailed from Cadiz for the Pacific in July 1789. But by mid-1790 they had not even reached Guayaquil, in Ecuador, and anyhow they were first bound for the North-West Coast. They would not reach the area where La Pérouse was known to have gone until 1793.[1]

Fleurieu was appointed Minister of Marine in October 1790. In this position, he could do a great deal more to hasten a search. Unhappily, Louis XVI was losing his remaining grasp on power. His popularity was still high, but he was now little more than a traditional and increasingly superfluous figurehead. The real power had moved to the parliament. Fleurieu consequently worked through his scientist friends to have the matter raised in the National Assembly. He could depend on the help of men like the mathematician Condorcet, to whom La Pérouse had written from Botany Bay, and who was now a prominent parliamentarian. On 22 January 1791 the Academy of Sciences joined with the *Société d'Histoire Naturelle* to make a formal appeal to the National Assembly. To formalise matters, Fleurieu declared officially that the expedition had to be considered lost and ordered the navy formally to close their accounts as at 31 December 1788, this being the latest date by which La Pérouse had said he would reach Mauritius.[2]

The deputies met on 9 February 1791, under the chairmanship of the influential

Comte de Mirabeau, to debate the issue with the fervour and eloquence that had become typical of those heady days. It was unanimously agreed that a rescue expedition should be sent to the Pacific. The problem was the cost. Economic troubles had been the immediate cause of the Revolution, and they were increasing daily. As an interim measure, the Assembly voted a decree on 15 February promising 10,000 francs and a life pension to anyone discovering traces of the two frigates. That showed willingness, but a much greater effort was needed. On the 25th, a budget was approved of 400,000 francs for the first year of a rescue expedition and 300,000 francs in subsequent years. Fleurieu could now set the machinery in motion and did so with impressive speed – the expedition would be ready to sail by September. Louis XVI had never lost his concern for the safety of the expedition – indeed, tradition has it that his last words as he walked up the steps to the scaffold were 'Is there any news of La Pérouse?'[3] He had no hesitation in signing the 'Loi relative à la découverte des deux frégates françaises *La Boussole* et *l'Astrolabe*' on 7 April.[4]

Eléonore, in Paris, was also active on her own behalf. She had little money and, like the women who wrote to her, the wives of those who had sailed with her husband, she was faced with the problem that the expedition's accounts had been closed and that the men's pay had stopped at the end of 1788. Fleurieu was successful in getting the Assembly to examine this problem and agree to her receiving the balance of any sums due to La Pérouse. Not surprisingly, this decision, on 22 April, led the other wives to protest about their own penury. Eléonore did not in fact fare all that well: she was promised 40,000 *livres*, but payment was postponed time and time again. The treasury was empty and the ponderous administrative machine was slowing down day-by-day.

The political situation was worsening too. Mirabeau, who might have worked out some form of agreement between the court and the Assembly and held extremists at bay, died on 2 April. Fleurieu was removed from his post as Minister of Marine on 6 May. On 20 June, Louis XVI tried to flee the country to join the growing number of *émigrés* abroad, but he was arrested as he neared the frontier and brought back to Paris. Republican extremists rose in anger at this obvious betrayal by their notional head of state. This particular uprising was nipped in the bud in a bloody clash at the Champs de Mars, but it was obvious that the days of the monarchy were numbered. In Britain, after a wave of enthusiasm – Charles James Fox had hailed the fall of the Bastille as 'the greatest and best event in the history of the world' – people began to agree with Edmund Burke who had predicted in his *Reflections on the Revolution in France* that it would all end in war and bloodshed.

Meanwhile, the National Assembly had been approached by a partnership formed by four merchants from the port of Lorient – Garnier, Torkler, Piron and

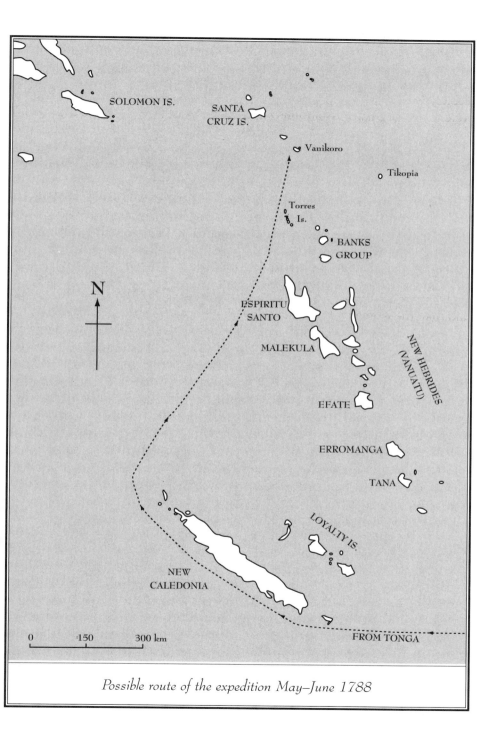

N

SOLOMON IS.

SANTA
CRUZ IS.

Vanikoro

Tikopia

Torres
Is.

BANKS
GROUP

ESPIRITU
SANTO

MALEKULA

NEW HEBRIDES
(VANUATU)

EFATE

ERROMANGA

TANA

LOYALTY IS.

NEW
CALEDONIA

0   150   300 km

FROM TONGA

Possible route of the expedition May–June 1788

Dussault – for a permit to trade in furs in Kamchatka and look for remains of La Pérouse. Their offer had a familiar ring: get government support in cash and passports for an essentially commercial undertaking. They overlooked the fact that La Pérouse had no intention of returning to Kamchatka. They did intend to look elsewhere for his expedition as they made their way home, but that would be many months away. Their proposal was laid aside.[5]

A second proposal came forward soon after from Aristide-Aubert Dupetit-Thouars. It was once more a mixture of commerce and altruism, but it was more worthy of serious consideration since finding La Pérouse was clearly stated to be his primary objective, and his itinerary was much more sensible. He planned to travel to New Holland and New Guinea, through areas where the frigates could be presumed to have been lost, and only then would he go on to Nootka Sound on the North-West Coast of America where he would buy furs to cover a part of his very considerable costs. His main problem was that by now the Assembly had already authorised one major expedition that was getting ready to sail as quickly as possible under the noted navigator Bruny d'Entrecasteaux. Dupetit-Thouars accordingly suggested that he might join the latter with his own ship and abandon any idea of trade. This completely undermined his proposal – it was up to D'Entrecasteaux to choose his own ships and officers without having to deal with volunteer searchers asking the National Assembly to approve their joining in. Not discouraged by this first rejection, Dupetit-Thouars launched an appeal for funds for a separate voyage under his own command. Two expeditions must surely be better than one.

He was a respected and well-connected captain, and his proposal, tinged with chivalry, earned him a good deal of sympathy. Louis XVI headed the subscription list, but money did not come as readily as was hoped. While Dupetit-Thouars waited impatiently for donations to come in, D'Entrecasteaux's expedition sailed from Brest, so he decided to appeal once more to the National Assembly, whose membership had been transformed by recent political upheavals. The previous parliamentarians had declared themselves ineligible for election to the new Assembly, so that when Dupetit-Thouars appealed for funds, he was in fact approaching a new audience. He received a grant of 10,000 *livres* and the legislators' blessing for an expedition which included trade once again among its aims.[6] This was still not enough. He made a second appeal for funds, but it now looked as if D'Entrecasteaux's expedition was on the verge of success.

In April 1792 news came that some wreckage had been seen in the Admiralty Islands, north of New Guinea, which it was believed had come from the frigates. It was certainly along the route La Pérouse had been expected to follow, and D'Entrecasteaux's ships were almost there. The Assembly consequently rejected Dupetit-Thouars' second appeal for funds. A wiser man, a little less of a romantic, would have taken the deputies' advice and given up. Instead, Dupetit-Thouars, who had already mortgaged his property and borrowed from his relatives, now mortgaged his future. On 29 May 1792, the Assembly granted his request for a cash advance equal to two years of pay. He sailed finally on 22 August in the *Diligent*.

He failed, but his downfall came through a gesture of romantic generosity. In Cape Verde he found some forty marooned Portuguese sailors whom he felt he could not ignore. He took them aboard. The ship became hopelessly crowded, and sickness, possibly dysentery, combined with the inevitable scurvy, spread rapidly through the crew and the Portuguese. By the time he reached Fernando de Noronha, off the coast of Brazil, nearly one-third had died and all were in poor shape. Moreover, the French were suspect. The Revolutionary Wars had been raging since April when France declared war on Austria; the French monarchy had been abolished, Louis XVI and Queen Marie-Antoinette were in prison, facing charges of treason and soon to be guillotined. The authorities, wisely, would not allow anyone to land. Soon after, Dupetit-Thouars was arrested as an enemy officer and his ship seized. He was not freed until 1796, when he returned to France to serve under Napoleon and die at the Battle of the Nile.

Thus it fell to D'Entrecasteaux alone to sail in search of La Pérouse with two ships – heavy storeships of 500 tonnes – renamed, appropriately, the *Recherche* and the *Espérance*. Few men had his experience. He had entered the navy in 1754 at the age of seventeen as a *garde de la marine* and had taken part in numerous campaigns. He had commanded the Indian Naval Station and carried out his duties in eastern waters with efficiency, indeed with brilliance. To mark the importance of his new mission he was raised to the rank of rear-admiral, and so became the first French admiral to enter the Pacific.

He carried with him, however, the seeds of the Revolution. The navy was similarly affected. Louis de Bougainville had been struggling to run the Brest naval base in the face of desertions, the emigration of officers to join royalist forces abroad and the setting up of local revolutionary committees. Fleurieu, equally plagued, gladly gave up the marine portfolio. D'Entrecasteaux, although of a noble background, was leading an expedition promoted by the increasingly republican parliament but with Louis XVI's full backing, and he hoped consequently to be free from the sectarian struggle, but he was overoptimistic: leaving the troubled shores of France did not mean escaping the virus of unrest and of challenges to the established order and consequently to naval discipline.

Some of his officers, like Alexandre d'Hesmivy d'Auribeau, Elisabeth Paul

Edouard de Rossel and Armand Louis Bourgeois de Boynes, belonged to the
nobility; others belonged to lesser families, were *volontaires* of middle-class
descent, or endorsed the egalitarian ideals of the Revolution. And among the
scientists, especially the botanist Jacques Julien de La Billardière, there were
open adherents of the republican cause. It was only a matter of time, as the
usual tensions developed between officers and *savants,* and sickness, shortages
and disappointments arose, before the two ships' complements divided into
openly warring camps.

Taking scientists on board, though it added to the basic purpose of the
expedition a secondary scientific research programme, inevitably made matters
worse. Speed was essential if the Frenchmen presumed wrecked somewhere
in the vast ocean were to be rescued. Collecting botanical and zoological
specimens, and carrying out hydrographical surveys, was bound to cause
delays. In times of social unrest, when scientists were particularly conscious of
the role they had played and were continuing to play in transforming French
society, these problems rapidly multiplied to danger point.

Progress was irritatingly slow. It took almost four months to reach the Cape
of Good Hope where D'Entrecasteaux received the reports about wreckage
sighted in the Admiralty Islands. They were third-hand and included the
information that La Pérouse had told a British captain in Botany Bay he would
sail north of New Guinea rather than south of it as he had written to Fleurieu.
Garbled though the information seemed to be, D'Entrecasteaux felt compelled
to sail for the Admiralties. The winds decided otherwise. He was forced to give
up and made for Tasmania instead. His stay there produced important results
from the scientific point of view, but was of little use as far as the lost ships were
concerned. It was the end of May 1792 before the *Recherche* and the *Espérance*
set off for New Caledonia, along the route La Pérouse was believed to have
taken. Most of June was spent around New Caledonia; then D'Entrecasteaux
sailed to the Solomons, to New Ireland and finally to the Admiralty Islands. It
had taken ten months – and the reported wreckage, with its rumoured jumble
of broken masts and spars washed up high on the shore, turned out to be
nothing more than the bleached remains of great trees.

After a stay in the Dutch Indies, D'Entrecasteaux proceeded to sail around
Australia and back to Tasmania. On 21 January 1793 the ships dropped anchor
in Recherche Bay, having completed a full circumnavigation of the continent.
But he had found no trace of La Pérouse. A month later, the two ships sailed for
New Zealand, then veered north towards Tonga. On 23 March they anchored
off Tongatapu. The islanders, friendly and boisterous, had no information to
give him about the *Boussole* or the *Astrolabe.* In May, D'Entrecasteaux was back
in New Caledonia.

The search seemed hopeless: there were so many islands, so many inlets. Communication with the natives who all seemed to speak different languages and dialects was well nigh impossible. The scientific results of the expedition were impressive, but the strains and hardships were becoming unbearable. Huon de Kermadec, the commander of the *Espérance*, died, and D'Entrecasteaux's own health was getting steadily worse. On 9 May the expedition sailed towards the Santa Cruz group in the northern New Hebrides. On the 19th, while off Utupua, the French sighted Santa Cruz itself and another island to the south-east, which was not shown on any chart. They did not sail close to it, merely recording it on their maps and naming it Recherche Island before sailing away for a second exploration of the Solomon Islands.

The island was Vanikoro, the very place where the La Pérouse expedition had met its doom and where, it seems likely, some survivors were still living. 'We saw [the island] at such a great distance that we could not show it with any accuracy on our charts,'[7] reported the searchers. D'Entrecasteaux's failure to locate the remnants of the 1788 expedition, when he was so tantalisingly close, has weighed heavily on his reputation, but with two slow ships and an immense expanse of sea to explore, only extreme good fortune could have brought him success. He had been almost two years on the way, supplies had run low, his officers and men were split into antagonistic camps and he was now seriously ill. He sailed on to the Solomons and the Louisiades. On 20 July 1793 he died and was buried at sea. D'Auribeau took over command and struggled back to Surabaya, in the Dutch Indies, where the expedition, plagued by increasingly bitter squabbles, finally disintegrated.

Meanwhile in Paris the publication of an official account of La Pérouse's voyage was slowly proceeding. This had been decided by the National Assembly on 4 May 1791, just two days before Fleurieu gave up the navy portfolio for the rather less stimulating but potentially dangerous post of tutor to Louis XVI's son. Preparing La Pérouse's journals for the press might have been more suitable for a man like Fleurieu, but he found it too daunting. Eléonore herself asked him to do it, but he still declined, alleging ill-health. She next suggested François Etienne de Rosily, who had sailed with Kerguelen. The government turned instead to an army general, Louis Marie Antoine Destouff, Baron Milet de Mureau, who in accordance with the egalitarian mood of the times, became known as Milet-Mureau. His native town, Toulouse, had sent him to Versailles in 1789 as a member of the States-General. He had worked on numerous committees, displaying a talent for marshalling facts and writing reports. A spell in the artillery with Bonaparte's Army of the Alps sent him to Italy, but his views were suspect, he did not get on with his superiors and he returned to Paris.

Eléonore had still not been paid anything. Indeed at this stage in France's history, when the issue of paper money, the *assignats,* and the cost of the war were causing severe inflation, the navy accounts are far from clear. It had been decided that all the families of the men who had disappeared with La Pérouse were to be paid until the D'Entrecasteaux expedition returned. Any members of the crew still alive would have remained on the navy's books; as for those who had died, the date of death would determine the amount the widows were due. But only a few occasional grants were made. The assembly had decided that it would be fair if Eléonore were paid out of the proceeds of the sale of the 1800 projected copies of the Milet-Mureau narrative. She was owed 40,000 *livres:* she could receive up to 144,000 if each copy was sold at 80 *livres.*

Milet-Mureau found himself entangled in technicalities: how should he refer to the king, how often should he mention him, and how should he deal with the various titles and practices that had vanished when the monarchy was abolished? This was no mere politically correct pedantry: Milet-Mureau was worried about his own head. The period later known as the Terror had begun, the guillotine was daily claiming its quota of aristocrats, moderates and out-of-favour politicians, and he had no wish to join them. He wrote to the Naval Office, which passed the matter on to the Education Committee, which referred it to the Committee for Public Safety, whose most prominent member was Robespierre. The committee praised his punctiliousness and his concern, but it had other things on its mind. The months went by; the task was far more time-consuming than he had imagined. Then Robespierre was overthrown. By 1796, when Milet-Mureau completed his voluminous manuscript, France was being ruled by a Directory of five elected members, and a young general named Napoleon Bonaparte was its rising star. The terms that would have angered the more extreme republicans were now acceptable. Milet-Mureau did some last-minute revisions, was thanked and went back to the army.

The book appeared in 1797 in three volumes with a great deal of introductory material and a number of notes. It sold poorly and was eventually remaindered.[8] The economic situation was still bad and people's attention was concentrated on the war. In 1799 Bonaparte overthrew the Directory. Five years later, as emperor, he signed a decree giving Eléonore a pension of 2400 francs a month. The relative wealth which the publication of the *Voyage* had intended to provide for her never materialised. She was granted a grace-and-favour apartment at the chateau of Vincennes, a bleak place that she disliked, preferring to stay in Paris with a friend, the Comtesse Hocquart. She died in genteel poverty on 4 April 1807, at the age of 52.

Part 7

THE UNENDING SEARCH

AFTER THE D'ENTRECASTEAUX expedition came to an end – or collapsed – in the Dutch East Indies, the mystery of La Pérouse's disappearance became a matter of secondary importance. This is clearly shown by the poor sales of the narrative. But there was so much happening in France and in Europe that the loss of even a major expedition slipped into second or third place.

For centuries, the throne had embodied France and French aspirations, dominating every facet of daily life. But it turned into a weak form of constitutional monarchy, then disappeared altogether. The king and queen tried to flee the country, failed and were guillotined. Thousands, either of noble birth or otherwise associated with the Ancient Regime, escaped to Germany or England. Naval officers disappeared overnight, fleeing across the Channel and causing widespread disruption. Local revolutionary committees were set up in the main ports, and eventually in numerous inland towns. Louis de Bougainville, placed in charge of the port of Brest, gave up in the face of constant indiscipline. Fleurieu had found it impossible to continue as Minister of Marine. The Terror brought about the public execution of notable men and women, not merely from the upper classes, but from the ranks of the *philosophes* and the less extreme politicians. Even Antoine Lavoisier, the founder of modern chemistry, died on the scaffold.

A reaction set in, leading to the gradual rise of Napoleon Bonaparte, firstly as one of a government of three 'Consuls', then as sole ruler and, in 1804, as emperor. By then, France has resisted foreign invasions, eliminated the *émigré* forces and controlled directly or through treaties much of Europe, from the Netherlands to Bavaria, Switzerland, Italy, Malta even, and Spain. Almost every month came news of new victories, setbacks and counter-moves that led to France dominating almost all of continental Europe. In time came the disastrous attempt to capture Moscow itself, and the fall of Napoleon at Waterloo.

His first abdication had led to the restoration of the monarchy, but only for the uneasy Hundred Days. It was only after Waterloo and Napoleon's exile in Saint Helena that a king once again sat on the French throne. But the country he now ruled over, after nearly twenty years of upheaval, had changed beyond recognition. The legal system had been totally restructured, as had taxation and even weights and measures with the introduction of the metric system. The dreams of many of the *philosophes* had been realised, with economic reforms and the rise of new social classes.

It is not surprising, therefore, that La Pérouse's expedition had faded into the background. So much had happened in those exciting and dangerous years, and many of the main backers and scientists had died. Condorcet had not survived the Revolution. Castries had died in 1800, the Comte d'Hector in 1808, Fleurieu in 1810, Bougainville in 1811. Only the influential Sir Joseph Banks lived on until 1820, never forgetting the vanished navigator he had helped. Among others, he ensured that Britain did not forget to urge any ships sailing into the Pacific to bear in mind the lost French vessels. Similar instructions were issued to their own captains by the Spanish and Russian governments, but it was almost a matter of routine – so many ships, mostly Spanish, had disappeared in the great ocean over the centuries, not to mention Polynesian and Melanesian migrating canoes, that few really believed that any traces could be found after so many years.

However, in 1827 when Peter Dillon arrived in Calcutta saying he believed he had found the final resting place of the *Astrolabe* and the *Boussole*, the officials, both British and French, understood his claim and knew what their respective governments expected them to do. They acted promptly to make a return to the Santa Cruz Islands possible. Apart from solving a mystery that had puzzled so many people over the years, there was the faint possibility that some of the participants might still be alive – not La Pérouse himself, who would have been in his mid-eighties by then, but some of the younger members of the crew.

The British authorities supplied Dillon with a suitable ship, appropriately named the *Research*, and loaded it with supplies for the voyage; the French contribution came in the form of an official with the rank of consul, Eugène Chaigneau. For good measure, the world of science joined in with the appointment of one Doctor Tytler, who proved to be a complete nuisance from the moment the ship left Calcutta. Dillon sailed south and west to circle around western Australia before veering east to Tasmania. There, to everyone's relief, he rid himself of Tytler and went on to Port Jackson, crossed to New Zealand and made his way to Tonga and the island of Tikopia in the Santa Cruz group, where he had first heard of the two mysterious ships wrecked on nearby Vanikoro almost forty years earlier. It was now September 1827.

Dillon enquired about other relics from Vanikoro the islanders might have, and he was successful in buying a ship's bell, part of a plank showing a *fleur-de-lys* and guns with the maker's identification mark still visible. An elderly Tikopian named Rathea also came forward and gave him the clearest and most detailed account of what had happened nearly forty years earlier:

I learned that the two ships ... ran aground in the night on reefs a considerable distance from the shore. The one that got on shore near to Whannow was totally lost, and such of the crew as escaped to land were murdered by the islanders. Their skulls were offered to a deity in a temple where they remained for many years and were seen by many Tucopians. The narrator did not see the skulls himself, but believed they were not mouldered away. The ship which had been wrecked at Paiow, after being on the reef, was driven into a good situation. The crew of these ships consisted of several hundred men. The ship stranded at Paiow was broken up to build a two-masted ship. The people, while employed building the two-masted ship, had a fence built round her of wooden palisading, within which they lived. There were several of the islanders friendly disposed towards them: others were very hostile, and kept up a continual war with the shipwrecked people. When the new vessel was built, all but two of the men embarked in her, and sailed away for their native country, after which they never returned.[1]

Allowance must be made for language difficulties and for faults of memory on the part of Rathea, who had not witnessed these events. In time, divers would help to reconstruct what had happened. For the present, Dillon had enough to confirm that the *Boussole* and the *Astrolabe* had been wrecked on this lonely island and that there were no survivors left alive. On 8 October 1827, he sailed for New Zealand and then for Europe.

In Paris the ageing Lesseps tearfully identified the relics. Dillon was the hero of the hour. King Charles X, reminded that his brother Louis XVI had once signed a decree promising 10,000 francs and a pension to whomever discovered the fate of the vanished explorer, gave Peter Dillon the cash grant and an annuity of 4000 francs, and also bestowed on him the rank of *chevalier* of the Legion of Honour.

Meanwhile a French expedition had been making its way to Vanikoro. Though it had not been sent out specifically for that purpose, its leader Jules-Sébastien César Dumont d'Urville had, like all navigators of the time, been instructed to keep the lost La Pérouse expedition in mind. He was in Hobart in December 1827 where he was told of Dillon's voyage and decided to alter his plans and sail without delay for Vanikoro.

D'Urville arrived on 21 February 1828 and remained until 17 March, charting the coastline, questioning the natives as best he could and purchasing more relics. Even more important, he was shown remains of a wreck lying in four metres of water. With great difficulty, since the wreckage was already encrusted in coral growth, the French brought up an anchor weighing more than 800 kilograms, and some guns bearing identification numbers. He also set up a memorial on Vanikoro, the first of many. Using kauri timber from New Zealand, he built a simple monument with a lead plaque bearing the words: 'To the memory of La Pérouse and his companions in the *Astrolabe*. 14 March 1828.'

Shortly after Dumont d'Urville, another French vessel appeared off Vanikoro. She was the *Bayonnaise,* commanded by Legoarant de Tromelin. Arriving in June 1828, she stayed twelve days, but Tromelin was unable to obtain any additional information – the islanders could hardly do more than repeat what they had told D'Urville. A few more items were found – a length of chain, a key, a pulley wheel. But Tromelin added a 'medal' to the monument. It was in fact a bronze 10-centime coin, but not one in current use. Tromelin used a coin that had been issued some time between 1795 and 1800. He may have chosen it because it was the oldest he had, the one nearest to La Pérouse's own day, issued while D'Entrecasteaux's companions were still struggling back to France after the collapse of their ill-fated expedition.

Vanikoro fell back into its age-old isolation. No ship, other than an occasional trading schooner, is reported as calling there until the centennial of the La Pérouse voyage approached. In 1883, the *Bruat* was sent by the Governor of New Caledonia to look for more remains of the wrecked ships. Three anchors and various guns were brought up after explosives freed them from the encroaching coral. They were sent to France and deposited at the foot of the monument that Albi erected to her famous son.

From time to time, a French naval unit on manoeuvres in the Pacific or based in New Caledonia did call at Vanikoro, but there was no attempt to recover further relics until 1938 when a group of Frenchmen from New Caledonia and the New Hebrides spent a month on the island. They found little of interest, but they did erect a metal cross on a part of the fatal reef.

After the Second World War, however, the technology of diving operations made great advances. Divers no longer needed to encase themselves in heavy diving suits linked by an air tube to the mother ship. With the aqualung they could now swim freely among the reefs and along the sea floor. The expedition in 1958 led by Pierre Anthonioz managed to bring up a number of relics, including a large anchor. By now D'Urville's memorial was smothered by mangroves. The discovery of the anchor again focused attention on the Pacific's most discussed mystery. During 1959 the French sent two ships, the *Rossinante* and the *Tiare*, to Vanikoro with a team of researchers led by the vulcanologist Haroun Tazieff.

It was believed for years that only one wreck had been discovered, that of the *Astrolabe*. A resident of Port Vila, in Vanuatu, discovered the site of the second wreck. Reece Discombe, a New Zealander, had made several visits to Vanikoro. In 1962 and 1963 he dived along the reef, exploring the many undersea caverns formed by the coral. More than a kilometre along the south wall of the reef he found a trove of objects ranging from guns to small metal weights. The presence of the weighty guns ruled out the possibility of the current carrying pieces of wreckage from the site where it was believed the *Astrolabe* had foundered.

This opened up new fields of research. France organised three expeditions in 1964 to survey the site identified by Discombe and others. The first of these, under the Port Vila Resident Maurice Delauney, sailed in February in the *Aquitaine*, accompanied by Reece Discombe. In three days, divers brought up a bronze gun and various small items, the most valuable of which was a metal plaque bearing the name Langlois and the date April 1736. Claude Langlois was more than a noted Paris instrument maker; he was the official supplier of *the Académie des Sciences* and it was known that he had provided a quadrant for Lepaute Dagelet, who was the *Boussole's* astronomer. Unless Dagelet's quadrant had been transferred at some time to the *Astrolabe,* this was evidence that the *Boussole* and the *Astrolabe* had been wrecked close to each other.

A later 1964 expedition, under Rear-Admiral Maurice de Brossard of the *Service historique de la Marine*, brought up more evidence that there was a second wreck. A new study of Peter Dillon's reports showed that he had in fact mentioned two sites, but that Dumont d'Urville had overlooked this, with the result that, for nearly 140 years, people had been allowed to wonder whether the *Boussole* might not have floated off, only to be finally wrecked in some other disaster. There are two wrecks and there is no doubt that the entire expedition was wrecked during a tropical cyclone on the coral reef of Vanikoro. As if to assist the 1964 searchers to reconstruct the scene, another cyclone struck the island, whipping up the waves into a foaming frenzy, uprooting trees, destroying buildings and swamping the island with torrential rain.

In 1981 an Association Salomon was set up in New Caledonia to organise further research. The political situation in the region was becoming complicated, with increased decolonisation. Vanikoro was part of the Solomon Islands and officially administered from Honiara. The association, backed by the French government, was able to negotiate with the Solomons authorities and in time acquire a semi-official status. It has carried out a number of searches since then, each one of growing importance. Large numbers of remains have been found, painstakingly identified and carefully catalogued. This has enabled the reconstruction of La Pérouse's itinerary from the time of his departure from Botany Bay, in particular confirming that he sailed along the south coast of New Caledonia.

Then, in 2003, came the most important find – part of a skeleton was brought up from the reef. It was discovered 15 metres down in the part of the reef where it is believed the *Boussole* foundered. Taken to police and other forensic laboratories in Paris, it was analysed and shown to be that of a man in his mid- to late thirties, and unlikely to have been a professional sailor. The facial features were similarly reconstituted, and it appeared that he was one of the scientists or possibly the expedition's artist, Duché de Vancy. However, the 2005 expedition, although operating in appalling weather conditions, was able to explore the reef further and retrieve several scientific instruments, including a valuable sextant. These and a survey of the wrecks suggest that the body may well be that of Lepaute Dagalet, and that La Pérouse is unlikely to have been among those who managed to struggle ashore. It is also possible that DNA analysis, through family descendants, may enable these remains to be finally identified.

Further expeditions to Vanikoro are planned. The search for an answer to the La Pérouse mystery is an unending one.

EPILOGUE

TO A CONSIDERABLE extent, the mystery of the lost expedition overshadowed its achievements. The Romantic age that began with the end of the eighteenth century seized upon the tragedy and wrote plays, poetry and novels about it – and what had been accomplished in the geographic and scientific arenas was eclipsed. It has been said that the death of James Cook was one of the great dramatic points in Pacific history.[1] Another of these great dramas was the disappearance of La Pérouse and his two frigates with their complements of men, prominent officers and leading scientists. Cook's third voyage had been affected in the same way: the events in Hawaii captured the attention of educated Europe and turned people's minds away from what had been achieved during the voyage.

Indeed the parallel between Cook and La Pérouse is worth drawing. France had hoped for someone who could stand close to the man they called 'the incomparable Cook', and in La Pérouse they found their hopes realised, even in the tragic end that befell them both. One can say of La Pérouse, as did Beaglehole of Cook, that:

> he was the genius of the matter of fact. He was profoundly competent in his calling as a seaman. He was absolutely professional in his trade as an explorer. He had, in large part, the sceptical mind: he did not like taking on trust. He was therefore the great dispeller of illusion. He did have imagination, but it was a controlled imagination that could think out a great voyage in terms of what was possible for his own competence. He could think, he could plan, he could reason; he liked to be able to plan clearly for a specific objective. But he liked to be elastic: there was always in his mind, as he planned, the possibility of something more, the parenthesis or addendum, there was also the sense of proportion that made him, more than once, refuse to waste time looking for what he was not sure to find.[2]

There is, of course, the difference of temperament: the man from the warm region of the Languedoc, and the austere Yorkshireman; the Frenchman who served an absolute king, and the Englishman who was guided by the influence wielded by a learned society in a semi-democracy.

Appreciating the achievements of La Pérouse's scientists is similarly hampered by the tragedy of Vanikoro. Their vast collections of plants, animals and mineralogical specimens – with a few exception in the latter group – were destroyed. Many of the charts, of Duché de Vancy's drawings, of the notebooks and diaries, private notes and journals, vanished. The fruit of many long months of painstaking work, the collective experiences of a voyage that lasted almost three years, an entire human dimension – all that has been lost.

But, fortunately, at every port of call where it was possible, the French posted letters, reports and journals. These documents lie today in the National Archives in Paris, housed in the former home of the Rohan-Soubise family, a town residence of elegant classical proportions. The most precious of all is La Pérouse's own journal – not his captain's log, admittedly, which vanished with his ship, but his detailed personal narrative, irrational syntax and erratic spellings included.

The expedition swept from the maps rumoured islands that had troubled geographers and sailors alike. It produced a careful survey of the complex North-West Coast of America and the mysterious coasts of distant Tartary. The frigates criss-crossed the Pacific in a breathtaking pattern, verifying latitudes and longitudes, adding their own discoveries – Necker Island, French Frigates Shoals and, in the Samoan group, Savaii, Manono and Apolima – thereby tidying up the map of this vast ocean which was still only emerging from centuries of conjecture and speculation.

The *mémoires* sent back included lengthy reports on Chile, on the fur trade, on the American Indians, the people of Easter Island and of Tartary, on California, Formosa and Manila, taking up over 200 pages of manuscript. In addition, they posted to France tables of longitudes and latitudes, bearings and hydrographic information, observations on currents, water temperature and climatic conditions. And there were enough charts and drawings to enable Milet-Mureau to add engravings to the account of the voyage. They enshrine, with the journal, the letters, the scraps of notes and jottings, a world of endeavours, hardships and devotion to the cause of knowledge.

There have been plays and poems, speeches and monuments devoted to La Pérouse and his companions; islands, mountains, and straits, streets and buildings bear their names, enshrining their achievements and ensuring that they will not be forgotten. They mark a great undertaking carried out in the face of enormous odds right across the great expanse of the Pacific Ocean where, in utter loneliness and isolation, it ended.

LA PÉROUSE COMMEMORATED

The name of La Pérouse (also spelt Lapérouse) is commemorated in various ways around the world:

Geographical features: La Pérouse Bank, British Columbia; La Pérouse Bay, Easter Island, also Maui, Hawaiian Islands; La Pérouse Bay Research Station, Hudson's Bay; La Pérouse district, Sydney, New South Wales; La Pérouse Peak, Kamchatka; La Pérouse Pinnacles, Emperor Chain, Hawaii; La Pérouse Strait, Kamchatka; Mt La Pérouse in Lituya Bay, in the South Island, New Zealand, and in Tasmania.

There is also a La Pérouse underwater peak off the coast of Madagascar, and a La Pérouse Crater on the moon.

Zoology: Micronesian scrubfowl *Megapodius* lapérouse.

Educational institutes: Lycée La Pérouse in Albi, Los Angeles, Noumea, Périgueux and San Francisco; La Pérouse Library, IFREMER Institute, Brest; La Pérouse Museum, Albi and Sydney; Ecole Primaire, Albi.

Streets and other town features: Allée La Pérouse in Créteil, St Gildas and Sevran; Place La Pérouse, Albi and Gaillac; Port La Pérouse, Algiers; Quai La Pérouse, Port Camargue; Square La Pérouse, Nantes; and Rue La Pérouse in Blois, Bois d'Arcy, Brest, Chatelaillon, Concarneau, Eau Coulée, Mauritius, Fouras, La Barcarès, La Ciotat, Lattes, Le Creusot, Le Havre, Le Pradet, Mantes-la-Jolie, Mazamet, Nantes, Ozoir-la-Ferrière, Pantin, Paris, Perpignan, Rennes, Roche-la-Molière, Saint-Sulpice, Toulouse and Valence.

Commemorative plaques and other memorials: Albi; Botany Bay, Sydney; Carmel Bay Church, Monterey; Maui Island, Hawaii; Mauritius; Petropavlovsk, Kamchatka; Port Prince of Wales, Hudson Bay; Tutuila, Samoa; Vanikoro, Santa Cruz Islands.

Postage stamps: 1928–39, eighteen stamps issued in New Caledonia, with a separate series overprinted 'Îles Wallis et Futuna'; 1941, thirteen of these were overprinted 'France Libre'; 1974, one stamp in honour of La Pérouse, part of a set marking the bicentennial of the discovery of New Caledonia, plus one for Wallis and Futuna; 1988, various issues, including special philatelic souvenirs, marking the disappearance of the expedition, issued by France, French Polynesia, New Caledonia, Norfolk Island, Samoa, Solomon Islands, Wallis and Futuna.

NOTES

Chapter 1

1 Jolibois, Emile, *Le Livre des consuls de la ville d'Albi*, Albi, 1863.
2 For a family tree, see Dunmore, John, *Pacific Explorer: The Life of Jean-François de la Pérouse*, Palmerston North and Annapolis, 1985, p. 13, and for the family background, Vieules, P. M., *Centenaire de La Pérouse: notice sur la famile et la vie privée du célèbre marin*, Albi, 1888.
3 La Joncquière, Henri, 'Les Taffanel de la Joncquière', in Amalric, Pierre (ed.), *Colloque Lapérouse Albi*, pp. 30–40.
4 See Pons, J., and Amalric, Pierre, 'L' ami du Collège des Jésuites: L' Amiral Henri Pascal de Rochegude', in Amalric (ed.), pp. 41–3.
5 Bru, H., 'Lapérouse: un Albigeois du XVIIIe siècle' in *Exposition Lapérouse d'Albi à Vanikoro*, Albi, 1985, p. 11.
6 See the study by Breuil, Michel, *De La Particule dite nobiliaire*, Paris, 1903, p. 86.

Chapter 2

1 Le Gallo, Yves, *Histoire de Brest*, Toulouse, 1976, p. 140
2 Anon, *Histoire de l'Ecole navale*, Paris, 1889, p. 326.
3 Levot, Prosper Jean, *Histoire de la ville et du port de Brest*, Brest, 1864, II, p. 113.
4 Manavit, M., 'Ce que La Pérouse doit à La Joncquière', *Revue du Tarn*, No. 5, 1964, p. 168.

Chapter 3

1 Plank, Geoffrey, *An Unsettled Conquest: The British Campaign Against the People of Acadia*, Philadelphia, 2001. For Lawrence's instructions, see Brebner, John B., *New England's Outpost: Acadia before the Conquest*, Hamden, 1965, p. 221.
2 Brossard, Maurice, *Lapérouse: des combats à la découverte*, Paris, 1978, p. 23.
3 *Ibid.*, pp. 30–1, quoting reports in Archives Nationales, Marine, B4-88, f° 162ff.
4 *Ibid.*, p. 34, footnote.

Chapter 4

1 Quoted in *Bulletin de la Société de Géographie*, *Centenaire de la mort de Lapérouse*, Paris, 1889.
2 Brossard, *Lapérouse*, p. 87.
3 The protracted negotiations are detailed in Rashed, Z. E., *The Peace of Paris 1763*, Liverpool, 1951.

Chapter 5

1 Cameron, Ian, *Lost Paradise: The Exploration of the Pacific*, London, 1987 p. 57.
2 Brossard, *Lapérouse*, pp. 109–11.
3 *Ibid.*, p. 123.
4 *Ibid.*, p. 125, quoting Archives nationales, Marine, B3-569 f° 69.
5 *Ibid.*, p. 126.
6 Levot, *Brest*, pp. 148–9.
7 La Pérouse to Terray, 14 January 1771, in Archives nationales, Marine, C7-165.
8 Dunmore, *Pacific Explorer*, p. 72.
9 Girod, F., *La Vie quotidienne de la société créole à Saint-Domingue au 18e siècle*, p. 82.
10 *Esprit des lois*, part I, xv, 1.
11 Archives nationales, Marine, B4-117:103.

Chapter 6

1 Duyker, (ed.), *An Officer of the Blue*, p. 105.
2 Brossard, *Lapérouse*, p. 213.
3 Dunmore, John, *Monsieur Baret*, p. 173.
4 *Ibid.*, p. 174.
5 Monnier, Jeannine, *et al.*, *Philibert Commerson*, Châtillon, 1993, p. 163.
6 *Ibid.*, p. 179.
7 'Extrait du voyage fait aux terres australes', p. 4, in Bibliothèque nationale de France, MS NAF 9439.29.
8 Dunmore, John, *French Explorers in the Pacific*, Oxford, 1965, Vol. I, pp. 199–202.
9 Dunmore, *Pacific Explorer*, p. 87, quoting letters of 20 and 21 March 1772, in Bibliothèque nationale de France, NAF 9438-78, 9438-91.
10 'Mémoire sur l'établissement d'une colonie dans la France australe', NAF 9438-86, in Dunmore, *French Explorers*, I, p. 215.

Chapter 7

1 Now held in Archives nationales, Marine, C7-165:124-145.
2 Brossard, *Lapérouse*, p. 223.
3 On this episode, see *ibid.*, pp. 224–6.
4 Gaxotte, P., *Le Siècle de Louis XV*, p. 61.
5 Brossard, *Lapérouse*, p. 229, quoting from La Pérouse's 'Journal'.
6 Rochon, A.M., *Voyages aux Indes orientales*, p. 233.
7 Dunmore, *Pacific Explorer*, p. 102, quoting a report from Chevalier to De Boynes of 6 October 1773, Archives nationales, Marine, C7-165.

8   Trobriand's letter of 17 December 1773, Archives nationales, Marine, B4-121:185.

9   Brossard, *Lapérouse*, p. 244.

Chapter 8

1   Certificate of baptism of Louise Éléonore Broudou, Nantes, 15 May 1755, Archives nationales C7-165, f° 121.

2   Quoted in *Bulletin de la Société de Géographie, Centenaire 1889*, pp. 159–60.

3   See Mousnier, R., 'Les Concepts d'ordre, d'états, de fidélité et de monarchie absolue en France de la fin du XVe siècle à la fin du XVIIIe siècle', in *Revue historique*, No. 247, 1997, pp. 289–312.

4   Report in Archives nationales, Marine B4:125, f° 234.

5   *Ibid.*

6   Brossard, *Lapérouse*, p. 261.

7   *Ibid.*

8   See 'Campagne de Lapérouse dans l'Inde', in *Revue de l'histoire des colonies françaises*, No. XXXIII, 1929, pp. 301–6. No author given.

9   Manceron, Claude, *Les Hommes de la liberté, Les vingt ans du roi*, Letter from Louis XVI to Phélipaux de Maurepas, Paris, 1972, p. 78.

10   Dunmore, *Pacific Explorer*, p. 115.

11   See Brossard, *Lapérouse*, pp. 252–8, 283–8.

12   La Pérouse to Ternay, Archives nationales, Colonies C5-A6, No. 13.

13   Bellecombe's report, Archives nationales, Colonies C5-17, No. 8.

14   See on this episode and its sequel, Dunmore, *Pacific Explorer*, pp. 119–20, and Brossard, *Lapérouse*, pp. 284–6.

15   Maillard Dumesle to the Minister, 22 November 1776, Archives nationales, Colonies C5-A6, No. 76.

16   *Ibid.*

Chapter 9

1   Quoted in *Bulletin de la Société de Géographic, Centenaire*, p. 255.

2   Brossard, *Lapérouse*, pp. 449–50.

3   *Ibid.*, p. 325, quoting from La Pérouse's report in Archives nationales, C7-165.

4   On Fleurieu, Sartines and others' views and reports, see Castex, R, *Les Idées militaires de la marine au XVIIIe Siéde*, Paris, 1911, pp. 167ff.

5   Quoted in Brossard, *Lapérouse*, p. 313.

6   Archives nationales, Marine B4:136.

7   This famous incident has been retold a number of times, see Manceron, *Les Hommes de la liberté*, I, p. 614, and Fay, B, *Louis XVI, ou la fin d'un monde*, Paris, 1955, p. 174.

Chapter 10

1 Lacour-Gayet, G., *La Marine militaire en France sous le règne de Louis XV*, Paris, 1910, p. 137.
2 See on this Christian Guigue's website list, *Les Francs-maçons célèbres*, at www.guigue.com.
3 Brossard, *Lapérouse*, p. 341.
4 'Extrait du Journal de Lapérouse commandant la frégate l'*Amazone*', *Société de Géographie, Centenaire*, p. 238.
5 *Ibid.*, p. 239.
6 *Ibid.*, p. 240.
7 Brossard, *Lapérouse*, pp. 356–7.

Chapter 11

1 Letter of 9 April 1780 in Archives nationales, B4-185:6.
2 Dunmore, *Pacific Explorer*, pp. 142–4.
3 Manceron, *Le Vent d'Amérique*, p. 287.
4 Brossard, *Lapérouse*, p. 371, quoting from Rochambeau's Memoirs, published in 1809.
5 Letter to Castries of 7 March 1781, in Archives nationales, B4-191 f° 264.
6 Brossard, *Lapérouse*, p. 380.

Chapter 12

1 Letter to Colonel Davis, 22 June, quoted in Charlemagne Tower, *La Fayette et la Révolution d'Amérique*, Paris, 1902, II, p. 322.
2 Brossard, *Lapérouse*, pp. 395–6.
3 *Ibid.*, p. 396.
4 Correspondence in Archives nationales, B4-191, f° 281, letter of 27 November 1781.
5 *Ibid.*
6 Archives nationales de France, B4-206, f° 63.
7 Brossard, *Lapérouse*, p. 408, quoting from La Pérouse's report to the minister, Archives nationales, B4-206.
8 *Ibid.*, p. 416. The Battle of the Saintes is narrated at length in this work and has been the subject of a number of other studies and reports.
9 La Pérouse provided these extracts from his journal for the court-martial of 1784. Quoted in Brossard, *Lapérouse*, pp. 413–23.
10 Brossard, *Lapérouse*, p. 418.

Chapter 13

1 The correspondence between La Pérouse and Fleurieu is held in the Archives nationales de France, B4-183. Accounts of the expedition have been published in Fleuriot de Langle, Paul, *La Tragique expédition de La*

Pérouse et Langle, Paris, 1954. See also, Bonnichon, Philippe, 'L'Expédition de Lapérouse en 1782 à la Baie d'Hudson' in Association Lapérouse Albi, *Bicentenaire du voyage de Lapérouse: actes du colloque d'Albie*, Albi, 1988, pp. 55–65.

2   La Jaille's papers in Archives nationales de France, 3JJ, 68, 23–3.
3   The French had been particularly interested in the works of Samuel Engel, who published several *Mémoires* between 1765 and 1779, Henry Ellis's voyage to Hudson Bay, published in French in 1750 and John Phipps's voyage of 1773, published in French in 1775.
4   Fleuriot de Langle, *La Tragique expédition*, pp. 56–7.
5   These and the following extracts from La Monneraye's lively journal were published in *Bulletin de la Société de la geographie: Centenaire*, pp. 268ff.
6   Letter of 4 September 1784, quoted in Williams, G., 'Remarks on the French Raids on Churchill and York', *Hudson's Bay Miscellany 1670–1870*, London, 1975, p. 94.
7   Brossard, *Lapérouse*, p. 436.
8   La Monneraye, journal.
9   Fleuriot de Langle, *La Tragique expédition*, p. 56.

Chapter 14

1   Letter of 20 October 1977, quoted in Brossard, *Lapérouse*, p. 450.
2   *Ibid.*, p. 454.
3   Most of their correspondence was reprinted in Barthès de Lapérouse, N., 'La Vie privée de Lapérouse', in 1888. See Dunmore, *Pacific Explorer*, pp. 173 and 181.
4   *Ibid.*, p. 174.
5   See *Bulletin de la Société de Géographie, Centenaire*, 1889, pp. 246–55.
6   Brossard, *Lapérouse*, pp. 457–8.
7   *Ibid.*, p. 459.
8   *Ibid.*, pp. 459–60.
9   Archives nationales, marine C7-197.
10 Brossard, *Lapérouse*, pp. 460–3, quoting from the same document and papers held originally by Barthès de Lapérouse.

Chapter 15

1   Dunmore, John, *Storms and Dreams, Louis de Bougainville: Soldier, Explorer, Statesman*, Auckland, 2005, p. 247.
2   Brossard, *Lapérouse*, p. 473. The various documents are held in the Bibliothèque nationale, NAT 9423 f° 247-301.
3   Brossard, *Lapérouse*, p. 472.
4   *Ibid.*, p. 473.

5 *Bulletin de la Société de Géographie, Centenaire,* 1889, p. 259, quoted in
Brossard, *Lapérouse,* pp. 473–4.
6 Dunmore, *Pacific Explorer,* p. 184.
7 Dunmore, *Storms and Dreams,* p. 248.
8 Brossard, *Lapérouse,* p. 475.

Chapter 16
1 See Hallward, N.L., *William Bolts: A Dutch Adventurer under John Company,*
Cambridge, 1920.
2 I am indebted to Robert J. King of Canberra for these documents currently
in the Swedish Archives, Asien 1786–1790, Vol. 193.
3 *Bulletin de la Société de Géographie, Centenaire* 1889, p. 175.
4 See Gough, B.M., 'William Bolts and the Austrian Attempt to Establish an
Eastern Empire', in Hardy, John P., and Frost, Alan, (eds), *European Voyaging
towards Australia,* Canberra, 1990, pp. 73–80, and Brossard, *Lapérouse,* p.
479. On the secret funds, see Gaziello, Catherine, *L'Expédition de Lapérouse
1785–1788: replique française aux voyages de Cook,* Paris, 1984, p. 50, n. 36.
5 Now in Bibliothèque nationale de France, ref. C4349.
6 Girault de Coursac, Pierrette, *L'Éducation d'un roi: Louis XVI,* Paris, 1972, p.
200.
7 Letter to La Pérouse, 11 April 1785, in Archives nationales de France ANM
102:9.
8 On Montarnal's links with the La Pérouse family, see Fleuriot de Langle, *La
Tragique expédition,* pp. 87–8.
9 Bartel, P., *La Jeunesse inédite de Napoléon,* Paris, 1954, p. 257.
10 Archives nationales, Marine, 4JJ-389 22-12.
11 Gaziello, p. 133.
12 Letter of 7 April 1787 to his friend Prévost, reprinted in the *Bulletin de la
Société de Géographie, Centenaire* 1889, p. 298.
13 Gaziello, p. 147.
14 MS 378-7 held in the Naval Archives.
15 Browning, O., (ed.), *Despatches from Paris 1784–1790,* London, 2 vols,
1909, I, p. 58.

Chapter 17
1 Unless otherwise stated, all quotes and comments referring to the expedition
are taken from Dunmore, John, (ed.), *The Journal of Jean-François de Galaup
de la Pérouse 1785–1788,* 2 vols, London, 1994–5.
2 La Pérouse to Fleurieu, 28 August 1875, Naval Archives 3JJ 386:2-19.
3 McKenna, J.F., 'The Noble Savage in the *Voyage* of La Pérouse', *Kentucky
Foreign Language Quarterly,* XII (1965), No.1, p. 39.

Chapter 18

1   See Barratt, Glynn, *Russia in Pacific Waters 1715–1825*, Vancouver, 1981, p. 92.
2   This and following quotes from Dunmore, *Journal*, I and II.
3   See Emmons, G.T., 'Native Account of the Meeting between La Pérouse and the Tlingit', *American Anthropologist*, 13 (April–June 1911), pp. 294–8.
4   Browning, I, p. 188.
5   This and following quotes from Dunmore, *Journal*, I and II.

Chapter 19

1   Dunmore, *Journal*, I, pp. 204–5.
2   Brossard, *Lapérouse*, p. 534.
3   *Ibid.*, p. 538.
4   See Gaziello, pp. 195–8.
5   Dunmore, *Journal*, I, p. 218.

Chapter 20

1   La Pérouse's *Journal* provided detailed information on this part of the voyage, see Dunmore, *Journal*, II, pp. 250–376. For his reports on the settlement see pp. 345–376.
2   See Dunmore, *Journal*, Introduction, p. clxxix.
3   Lesseps had quickly set to and written an account of his epic journey. This *Journal historique* appeared in 1790 and was promptly translated into English, becoming a bestseller in both languages.

Chapter 21

1   All quotes relating to this part of the voyage are from Dunmore, *Journal*, II, pp. 376–448.
2   City of London Records Office, ref. 186, reprinted in Ingleton, G.C., *True Patriots All: or News from Early Australia*, London, 1952.
3   Journal entry of 4 May 1768 in Dunmore, John, (ed.), *The Pacific Journal of Louis-Antoine de Bougainville*, London, 2002, p. 82.
4   Letter to Fleurieu written from Botany Bay, dated 7 February 1788, in Dunmore, *Journal*, II, p. 540.
5   Phillip's first report to Lord Sydney, 15 May 1788, *Historical Records of Australia,* I, p. 17.
6   In a letter written to the scientist Condorcet from Botany Bay, Dagelet apologised for his bad handwriting, saying, 'I am blinded by the bites of flies that infest my wretched observatory'. Institut de France Library, MS 867-4.
7   Dunmore, *Journal*, II, p. 447.

8   One or two escaped convicts may have been smuggled on board by sympathetic sailors, possibly including Anne Smith, the subject of a semi-fictional work by Guillou, Jean, *L'Odyssée d'Ann Smith: Une femme en révolte*, Beauvoir-sur-mer, 2002, but there is no firm evidence, and the convicts who disappeared at this time may have died trying to escape into the hinterland.

9   Letter dated 7 February 1788, quoted in Gautier, A., 'Le Père Receveur, aumonier de l'expédition La Pérouse', in *Courrier des Messageries maritimes*, 140 (May–June 1974), pp. 24–34.

10 *Historical Records of Australia*, I, p. 28.

11 Letter to Fleurieu of 7 February 1778, in Dunmore, *Journal*, II, p. 539.

12 Letter to Lecoulteux de La Noraye, 7 February 1788, in Bibliothèque nationale, N.A.F., 9424.

13 Letter of 7 February 1778, in Dunmore, *Journal*, II, pp. 541–2.

Chapter 22

1   See Cutter, Donald C., Introduction, *The Malaspina Expedition 1789–1894*, London, 2001, I, pp. xxix, xxxvii.

2   Letter to Comte d'Hector, Archives nationales de France, C6 885.

3   So ingrained is this tradition that the Association Salomon Nouvelle-Calédonie entitled its 1997 account of searches in Vanikoro, *A-t-on des nouvelles de Monsieur de Lapérouse?*.

4   See on these and later debates and the legislation signed by Louis XVI, Delattre, François Pascal, *Rapport sur la recherche à faire de M. de la Pérouse, fait à l'Assemblée nationale,* and *Bulletin de la Société de Géographie*, Centenaire 1889, pp. 305–6.

5   *Bulletin de la Société de Géographie*, Centenaire 1889, pp. 305–6.

6   'Projet de décret', in *Moniteur* newspapers, 24 December 1791.

7   Rossel, Elisabeth Paul Edouard de, *Voyage de Dentrecasteaux envoyé à la recherche de La Pérouse*, 2 vols and atlas, Paris, 1808, p. 368.

8   A note appended to a report for Napoleon states 'The edition was handed over at a knock-down price to a bookseller … .Whether it was because the circumstances were unfavourable, or the *Voyage* itself aroused little interest, or that people were generally dissatisfied with the narrative, the fact is that the work did not sell.' Eléonore herself had 100 unsold copies, which she returned when she was given a pension. Dunmore, *Pacific Explorer*, pp. 297–8, quoting from letters and reports in Archives nationales Marine, C7:165.

Part 7: The Unending Search

1   Dillon, Peter, *Narrative and Successful Result of a Voyage in the South Seas … to*

Ascertain the Actual Fate of the La Pérouse Expedition, 2 vols, London, 1829, II, p. 120.

Epilogue

1   Beaglehole, John Cawte, *The Life of Captain James Cook*, London, 1974, p. 698.
2   *Ibid.*

SELECT BIBLIOGRAPHY

Published Narratives and Journals

Milet-Mureau, Louis Marie Antoine d'Estouff de, *Voyage de la Pérouse autour du monde, publié conformément au decret du 22 avril 1791*, 4 vols and atlas, Paris, 1797. Translations and translated versions: English (London, 1798, 1799; Edinburgh, 1798; Boston, 1801); German (Berlin, 1799; Leipzig, 1799); Danish (Copenhagen, 1799); Swedish (Stockholm, 1799); Russian (St Petersburg, 1800); Dutch (Amsterdam, 1801); Polish (Krakow, 1801–3); Italian (Milan, 1815).

Brossard, Maurice de and Dunmore John (eds), *Le Voyage de Lapérouse 1785–1788*, 2 vols, Paris, 1985.

Dunmore, John, (ed.), *The Journal of Jean-François de Galaup de la Pérouse 1785–1788*, 2 vols, London, 1994–5.

Other Printed Accounts and Narratives

[Anon.] *Sketch of a Voyage of Discovery undertaken by Monsieur de la Pérouse under the Auspices of the French Government*, London, 1798.

— *Fairburn's Edition of the Voyages and Adventures of La Pérouse*, London, 1800.

— [Barbou & Cie] *Voyage de La Pérouse autour du monde 1785–1788*, Limoges, 1885.

Arvengas, Hubert, *L'Exploration et le mystérieux naufrage de Lapérouse*, Albi, 1941.

Bancarel, François, *Voyage de Lapérouse pendant les années 1785–1788*, 2 vols, Paris, 1809.

Bellec, François, *La Généreuse et tragique expédition La Pérouse*, Rennes, 1985.

Benoit-Guyot, Georges, *Au temps de la marine en bois: sur les traces de Lapérouse*, 2 vols, Paris, 1942–4.

Blanchard, Victor, *Voyage de La Pérouse autour du monde,* Limoges, 1848.

Chatenet, E. du, *Voyage de La Pérouse autour du monde 1785 à 1788*, Limoges, n.d.

Fleuriot de Langle, Ivan, *Le Voyage extraordinaire de La Pérouse,* 3 vols, Nice, 1971–2.

Fleuriot de Langle, Paul, *La Tragique expédition de La Pérouse et Langle,* Paris, 1954.

Gassner, Julius S., *Voyages and Adventures of Lapérouse, from the Fourteenth Edition of the F. Valentin Abridgment*, Honolulu, 1969.

Girault de Coursac, Paul and Pierrette, Le *Voyage de Louis XVI autour du monde: l'expédition La Pérouse,* Paris, 1985.

Hyenne, Robert, *La Pérouse: aventures et naufrage,* Paris, 1859.
La Harpe, Jean François de, *Histoire abrégée du voyage de La Pérouse pendant les années 1785, 1786, 1787 et 1788,* Leipzig, 1799.
Lesseps, Jean-Baptiste Barthélémy de. *Journal historique de M. de Lesseps, Consul de France, employé dans l'expédition de M. le Comte de la Pérouse en qualité d'interprète du Roi.* 2 vols, Paris, 1790. English edition: *Travels in Kamchatka during the Years 1787 and 1788, translated from the French of M. de Lesseps, Consul of France and interpreter to the Count de la Pérouse,* 2 vols, London, 1790. [Other translations of Lesseps's narrative appeared in German (1791, Berlin and Leipzig, and 1792,Vienna), Dutch (1791, Utrecht), Swedish (1793, Upsala), Italian (1794, Naples) and in Russian (1801–2, Moscow); there were new editions of the French text in Leipzig in 1799 and in Paris in 1831 and 1880, and of the English translation in London in 1798.]
Locatelli, Amilcare, *La Spedizione di La Pérouse nel Grande Oceano,* Turin, 1929.
Mantoux, Georges, *Voyage de La Pérouse, capitaine de vaisseau, autour du monde (années 1785, 1786, 1787 et 1788), raconté par lui-même,* Paris, 1882.
Marcel, Gabriel, *La Pérouse: récit de son voyage; expédition envoyée à sa recherche,* Paris, 1888.
Móntemont, Albert Etienne de, *Voyage de La Pérouse autour du monde,* 2 vols, Paris, 1885.
Sauvan, Jean Baptiste Balthazar de, *Voyage de Lapérouse rédigé d'après ses manuscrits originaux,* Paris, 1831.
Shelton, Russell C., *From Hudson Bay to Botany Bay: The Lost Frigates of Lapérouse,* Toronto, 1987.
Valentin, Robert François, *Voyages et aventures de La Pérouse,* Tours, 1839.
Vattemare, Hippolyte, *Vie et voyages de La Pérouse,* Paris, 1887.

Studies and Related Works
Allen, Edward Weber, *The Vanishing Frenchman: The Mysterious Disappearance of Lapérouse,* Rutland, 1959.
Anon., *Histoire de l'Ecole navale,* Paris, 1889.
Association Laperouse Albi, *Bicentenaire du voyage de Lapérouse: actes du colloque d'Albi Mars 1985,* Albi, 1988.
Association Salomon, *A-t-on des nouvelles de Monsieur de Lapérouse?,* Noumea,1997.
'—, *Lapérouse à Vanikoro: Résultats des dernières recherches,* Noumea, 2001.
Barratt, Glynn, *Russia in Pacific Waters 1715–1825,* Vancouver, 1981.
Bancroft, Hubert Howe, *Alaska 1730–1885,* San Francisco, 1886.
Bartel, Paul, *La Jeunesse inédite de Napoléon,* Paris, 1954.

Barthès De Laperouse, N. de, 'La Vie privée de Lapérouse', *Société de géographie, Bulletin du centenaire*, Paris, 1888, II, p. 28.

Bayly, G., *Sea-life Sixty Years Ago: A Record of Adventures which led up to the discovery of the Relics of the Long-Missing Expedition commanded by the Comte de la Pérouse*, London, 1885.

Beaglehole, John Cawte, (ed.), *The Journals of Captain James Cook on his Voyages of Discovery*, 3 vols in 4 and portfolio, Cambridge, 1955–69.

— *The Exploration of the Pacific*, 3rd ed., London, 1966.

— *The Life of Captain James Cook*, London, 1974.

Bellesort, André, *La Pérouse*, Paris, 1926.

Bergasse du Petit-Thouars, *Aristide-Aubert du Petit-Thouars, héros d'Aboukir*, Paris, 1937.

Bériot, Agnès. *Grands voiliers autour du monde: les voyages scentifiques 1760–1850*, Paris, 1962.

Brebner, John Bartlet, *New England's Outpost: Acadia Before the Conquest*, Hamden, 1965.

Breuil, Michel, *De la particule dite nobiliare*, Paris, 1903

Broc, Numa, *La Géographie des philosophes, géographes et voyageurs français au XVIIIe siècle*, Lille, 1972.

Brossard, Maurice de, '179 ans après son départ de Brest, la frégate de Lapérouse est retrouvée', *Cahier des explorateurs*, (June 1964), pp. 8–9, 12–13.

—, *Lapérouse: des combats à la découverte*, Paris, 1978.

—, *Rendez-vous avec Lapérouse à Vanikoro*, Paris, 1964.

Browning, Oscar, *Despatches from Paris 1784–1800*, 2 vols, London, 1909.

Buache, Jean Nicolas., 'Mémoire sur les terres découvertes par La Pérouse à la côte de Tartarie et au nord du Japon', *Mémoires de l'Académie des sciences morales*, V:i (1803), pp. 1–42.

Burney, James, *A Memoir on the Voyage of d'Entrecasteaux in search of La Pérouse*, London, 1820.

Cameron, Ian, *Lost Paradise: The Exploration of the Pacific*, London, 1987.

Carleton, Frank R.L., 'Père Receveur Bicentenary Commemoration 1788–1988', in *An Australian Mosaic,* ed. Leo J. Ansell, Toowoomba, N.S.W., 1988, pp. 71–9.

Castex, Raoul, *Les Idées militaires de la Marine au XVIIIe siécle*, Paris, 1911.

Chaplin, S.L., 'Scientific Profit from the Profit Motive: the Case of the La Pérouse Expedition', *Actes du l2e Congrès international d'histoire des sciences, 1968*, XI (1971), pp. 45–9.

Chapman, Charles Edward, A *History of California: the Spanish Period*, New York, 1921.

Chinard, Gilbert, *Le Voyage de Lapérouse sur les côtes de l'Alaska et de la Californie (1786)*, Baltimore, 1937.

Collins, D., *An Account of the English Colony in New South Wales*, London, 1798.

Cook, Warren L., *Flood Tide of Empire: Spain and the Pacific Northwest 1543–1819*, New Haven, 1973.

Cordier, Henri, 'Deux compagnons de Lapérouse [Lamartinière and Clonard]', *Bulletin de la Société de géographie*, XXXI (1916), pp. 54–82.

Coxe, W., *An Account of the Russian Discoveries between Asia and America*, London, 1780.

Davidson, James Wightman, *Peter Dillon of Vanikoro*, Melbourne, 1975.

Delattre, François Pascal, *Rapport sur la recherche à faire de M. de la Pérouse, fait à l'Assemblée nationale*, Paris, 1791.

Delignières, E., 'Note sur Gaspard Duché de Vancy', *Réunion des sociétés des beaux-arts des départements (1910)*, pp.72–90.

D'Estampes, J., *Catalogue de l'exposition du centenaire*, Paris, 1888.

Dillon, Peter, *Narrative and Successful Result of a Voyage in the South Seas, performed by Order of the Government of British India to Ascertain the Actual Fate of La Pérouse's Expedition*, 2 vols, London, 1829.

Dixon, George, *A Voyage Round the World; but more particularly to the North-West Coast of America, Performed in 1785...1788 in the* King George and Queen Charlotte, *Captains Portlock and Dixon*, London, 1789.

Dodge, Ernest Stanley, *Beyond the Capes: Pacific Exploration from Captain Cook to the* Challenger *1776–1877*, Boston, London, 1971.

Dondo, Mathurin Marius, *La Pérouse in Maui*, Hawaii, 1959.

Dumont D'Urville, Jules Sébastien César, *Voyage de découvertes autour du monde et à la recherche de La Pérouse... sur la corvette* l'Astrolabe *pendant les années 1826, 1827, 1828 et 1829*, 5 vols and atlas, Paris, 1832–3.

Dunmore, John, *French Explorers in the Pacific*, 2 vols, Oxford, 1965–9.

— 'Le Vrai Journal de Lapérouse', *Revue du Tarn*, 38 (1980), pp. 175–80.

— *Pacific Explorer: The Life of Jean-François de la Pérouse*, Palmerston North, New Zealand, Annapolis, Maryland, 1985.

— *Monsieur Baret: First Woman around the world 1766–68*, Auckland, 2002.

— *Storms and Dreams, Louis de Bougainville: Soldier, Explorer, Statesman*, Auckland, 2005.

— 'The Louis-Napoleon La Pérouse', *Turnbull Library Record*, 17:2 (1984), pp. 106–7.

— *Who's Who in Pacific Navigation*, Honolulu, Melbourne, 1992.

Dupetit-Thouars, Aubert Aristide, *Prospectus d'un armement particulier pour la recherche de M. de la Pérouse*, Paris, 1790.

Duponchel, A., *Voyage autour du monde 1785–1788 par La Pérouse*. Paris, 1841.

Dupont, Maurice, *D'Entrecasteaux: rien que la mer, un peu de gloire*, Paris, 1983.

Duyker, Edward, *An Officer of the Blue: Marc-Joseph Marion Dufresne, South Sea Explorer, 1724–1772*, Melbourne, 1994.

Emmons, George Thornton, 'Native Account of a Meeting between La Pérouse and the Tlingit', *American Anthropologist*, 13 (April–June 1911), pp. 294–8.

Fay, Bernard, *Louis XVI, ou la fin d'un monde*, Paris, 1955.

Fidlon, Paul G. and R.J. Ryan (eds), *The Journal of Philip Gidley King R.N.*, Sydney, 1980.

Fisher, Raymond Henry, *The Russian Fur Trade 1550–1770*, Los Angeles, 1937.

Fitzhardinge, Laurence Frederick (ed.), *Sydney's First Four Years, being a Reprint of A Narrative of the Expedition to Botany Bay...by Captain Watkin Tench of the Marines*, Sydney, 1961.

Freminville, Christophe Paulin, *Nouvelle Relation du voyage à la recherche de Lapérouse, exécuté par ordre du Roi pendant les années 1790–1794 par M. Dentrecasteaux*. Brest, 1838.

Furneaux, Rupert, *The Seven Years War*, London, 1973.

Garnier, J., 'Traces du passage de La Pérouse à la Nouvelle-Calédonie', *Bulletin de la Société de Géographie* (Nov. 1869), pp. 407–13.

Gautier, A., 'Le Père Receveur, aumonier de l'expédition La Pérouse', *Courrier des Messageries maritimes*, 140 (May–June 1974), pp. 24–34.

Gaxotte, Pierre, *Le Siècle de Louis XV*, Paris, 1974.

Gaziello, Catherine, *L'Expédition de Lapérouse 1785–1788: réplique française aux voyages de Cook,* Paris, 1984.

Girault de Coursac, Pierrette, *L'Education d'un roi: Louis XVI*, Paris, 1972.

Girod, F., *La Vie quotidionne de la société créole à Saint-Domingue au XVIIIe siècle*, Paris, 1972.

Golder, Frank Alfred, *Russian Expansion in the Pacific 1641–1850,* Gloucester, Mass, 1960.

Gordon, Mary, *The Mystery of La Pérouse,* Christchurch, New Zealand, 1961.

Guedan, Bertrand (ed.), *Voyage de La Pérouse autour du monde, publié d'après tous les manuscrits de l'auteur.* Paris, 1930

Gunther, Erna, *Indian Life on the Northwest Coast of North America as seen by the Early Explorers and Fur Traders during the Last Decades of the Eighteenth Century*, Chicago, London, 1972.

Hallward, Norman Leslie, *William Bolts: A Dutch Adventurer under John Company*, Cambridge, 1920.

Hardy, John P. and Frost Alan (eds), *European Voyaging towards Australia*, Canberra, 1990.

Huard, Pierre and Zobel, Maurice., 'La Société royale de médecine et le voyage de La Pérouse', *Actes du 8e congrès national des sociétés savantes,* *1962*, pp. 83–91.

Hunter, John, *An Historical Journal of the Transactions at Port Jackson and* *Norfolk Island, with the Discoveries which have been made in New South Wales* *and in the Southern Ocean since the Publication of Phillip's voyage.* London, 1793.

Ingleton, Geoffrey Chapman, *True Patriots All: or News from Early Australis,* London, 1952.

Inglis, Robin, *The Lost Voyage of Lapérouse,* Vancouver, 1986.

— 'The Effect of Lapérouse on Spanish Thinking about the Northwest Coast', in Cook, W. L. (ed.), *Spain and the North Pacific Coast,* Vancouver, 1992, pp. 46–52.

Jackson, D., 'Ledyard and Lapérouse: A Contrast in North Western Exploration', *Western Historical Quarterly,* 9 (1978), pp. 495–508.

Jolibois, Emile, *Le Livre des consuls de la ville d'Albi,* Albi, 1863.

Kerallain, René de, 'La Pérouse à Botany-Bay', *La Géographie,* 33 (1920), pp. 41–8.

Kerneis, A.A., 'Le Chevalier de Langle, ses compagnons de *l'Astrolabe* et de *la Boussole;* expédition envoyée à la recherche des bâtiments', *Bulletin de la* *Société académique de Brest,* 2-XV (1900), pp. 221–88.

Labillardière, Jacques Julien Houtou de, *Relation du voyage à la recherche de* *La Pérouse fait par ordre de l'Assemblée constituante pendant les années 1791,* *1792 et pendant la 1ère et la 2de années de la République Française,* 2 vols and atlas, Paris, 1800.

Lacour-Gayet, Georges, *La Marine militaire sous le règne de Louis XV,* Paris, 1910.

Lamb, W. Kaye (ed.), *The Voyage of George Vancouver 1791–1795,* 4 vols, London, 1984.

Le Gallo, Yves (ed.), *Histoire de Brest,* Toulouse, 1976.

Lepaute, Gabriel Joseph, 'Notice biographique sur Lepaute-Dagelet', *Bulletin de* *la Société de géographie,* (1888), p. 149.

Levot, Prosper Jean, *Histoire de la ville et du port de Brest,* Brest, 1864.

Linnekin, J., 'Ignoble Savages and Other European Visions: The La Pérouse Affair in Samoan History', *Journal of Pacific History,* XVI: i (1991), pp. 3–26.

Loir, Maurice, *La Marine Royale en 1789,* Paris, 1892.

Mackaness, George, *Admiral Arthur Phillip, Founder of New South Wales,* Sydney, 1937.

McKenna, J.F., 'The Noble Savage in the *Voyage* of La Pérouse', *Kentucky* *Foreign Language Quarterly,* XII (1965), No. 1, pp. 33–48.

McLaren, Ian Francis (compiler), *Lapérouse in the Pacific, including Searches by d'Entrecasteaux, Dillon, Dumont d'Urville: An Annotated Bibliography*, Melbourne, 1993.

Maine, René, *Lapérouse*, Paris, 1946.

Manceron, Claude, *Les Hommes de la liberté, I Les Vingt ans du roi*, Paris, 1972, II *Le Vent d'Amérique*, Paris, 1974.

Marcel, Gabriel Alexandre, *Une Expédition oubliée à la recherche de Lapérouse*, Paris, 1888.

Marchant, Leslie R., *France Australe*, Perth, 1982.

Margolin, Malcolm, *Monterey in 1786: The Journals of Jean François de La Pérouse*. Berkeley, 1989.

Martin-Allanic, Jean Etienne, *Bougainville navigateur et les découvertes de son temps*, 2 vols, Paris, 1964.

Meares, John, *Voyages Made in the Years 1788 and 1789 from China to the North West Coast of America*, London, 1790.

Meissner, Hans Otto, *Die Verschollenen Schiffe des Lapérouse*, Munich, 1984.

Monnier, Jeannine *et al.*, *Philibert Commerson*, Châtillon, 1993.

Nisbet, Anne-Marie and Blackman, Maurice, *French Navigators and the Discovery of Australia*. Sydney, n.d.

Ovigny, Pierre Lionel, 'A la recherche de La Pérouse: relation sur l'expédition de l'amiral d'Entrecasteaux de 1791 à 1795', *Revue économique française*, 101 (1979), pp. 19–25.

Paris, Frédéric Edmond, 'Comment on a retrouvé les restes de l'expédition de Lapérouse à Vanikoro', in *Centenaire de la mort de Lapérouse*, Paris, 1888, pp. 191–207.

Petit, G., 'Le Chevalier Paul de Lamanon 1752–1787', *Actes du 90e congrès des sociétés savantes*, (1965), pp. 47–58.

Phillip, Arthur, *The Voyage of Captain Phillip to Botany Bay, with an Account of the Establishment of the Colonies of Port Jackson and Norfolk Island*, London, 1789.

Pisier, Georges, 'Lapérouse en Australie', *Bulletin de la Société d'études historiques de la Nouvelle-Calédonie*, 23 (April 1975).

Plank, Geoffrey Gilbert, *An Unsettled Conquest: The British Campaign Against the People of Acadia*, Philadelphia, 2001.

Pomeau, René, 'Lapérouse philosophe', in *Approches des Lumières: mélanges offerts à Jean Fabre*, (Paris, 1974), pp. 357–70.

Protos, Alec, *The Road to Botany Bay: The Story of Frenchman's Road*, Randwick, NSW, 1988.

Rashed, Zenat Esmat, *The Peace of Paris 1763*, Liverpool, 1951.

Rich, Edwin Ernest, *The Fur Trade and the Northwest to 1837*, Toronto, 1967.

Richard, Hélène, *Une Grande Expédition scientifique au temps de la Révolution française: Ie voyage de d'Entrecasteaux à la recherche de la Pérouse*, Paris, 1986.

Rochon, A.M., *Voyages aux Indes orientales et en Afrique pour l'observation des longitudes en mer*, Paris, 1807.

Rossel, Elisabeth Paul Edouard de, *Voyage de Dentrecasteaux envoyé à la recherche de La Pérouse*, 2 vols and atlas, Paris, 1807–8.

Roy, Bernard, *Dans Ie sillage de La Pérouse*, Paris, 1946.

Rudkin, Charles N., *The First French Expedition to California: Lapérouse in 1786*, Los Angeles, 1959.

Scott, Ernest, *Lapérouse*, Sydney, 1912.

Sharp, Andrew, *The Discovery of the Pacific Islands*, Oxford, 1960.

Société de Géographie de Paris, *Centenaire de la mort de Lapérouse, Paris, 1888. Bulletin de la Société de Géographie*, (Nov. 1889), reprinted at Fiac, France, 1985.

Spate, Oscar H.K., *The Pacific since Magellan*, 3 vols, Canberra, 1979–88.

Stephan, J.J., *Sakhalin: A History*, Oxford, 1971.

Taillemite, Etienne, *Bougainville et ses compagnons autour du monde 1766–1769*, 2 vols, Paris, 1977.

Tench, Watkin, *A Narrative of the Expedition to Botany Bay, with an Account of New South Wales*, London, 1789.

Thomas, Jacques, 'La Pérouse ou Lapérouse: légitimité d'une orthographe', *Bulletin de la Société d'études historiques de la Nouvelle-Calédonie*, 71 (April 1987).

Tower, Charlemagne, *La Fayette et la Révolution d'Amérique*, 2 vols, Paris, 1902.

Trammond, Joannes Martial, *Manuel d'histoire maritime de France des origines à 1815*, Paris, 1927.

Varshavskii, Anatolii Semenovich, *Laperuz,* Moscow, 1957.

Vinaty, J.A., *Eloge de Lapérouse*, Paris, 1823.

Wagner, Henry Raup, *The Cartography of the Northwest Coast of America to the Year 1800*, 2 vols, Berkeley, 1937.

White, John, *Journal of a Voyage to New South Wales*, London, 1790.

Williams, Glyndwr (ed.), *Hudson's Bay Miscellany 1670–1870*, Hudson's Bay Records Society, London, 1975.

INDEX

Also by John Dunmore

STORMS AND DREAMS

THE LIFE OF LOUIS DE BOUGAINVILLE

Louis-Antoine Comte de Bougainville (1729–1811) is best known for his circumnavigation of the globe from 1766 to 1769. Throughout a long and distinguished life, however, he participated in many of the turning points of world history: the birth of the United States, the fall of French Canada, the opening of the Pacific, the French revolution and the Revolutionary Wars, the crowning of Napoleon and the modernisation of France. Bougainville was also a witty and charming courtier, becoming one of Napoleon's senators. A true Man of the Enlightenment, he was gifted in navigation, seamanship, soldiering, mathematics, longitude and latitude – many of the arts that made his age one of most productive and creative in modern history.

This is the first biography of Bougainville to be published in 25 years. John Dunmore brings the man and his era to life in this vividly written book.

'Dunmore writes with elegance, wit and authority … [he] captures both the ambitious spirit of the golden age of exploration and the courtly yet hard-headed nature of France's greatest 18th-century voyager.' *The Press*

Available from the University of Alaska Press